MASTERPLOTS II

JUVENILE
AND
YOUNG ADULT
LITERATURE
SERIES
SUPPLEMENT

MASTERPLOTS II

JUVENILE AND YOUNG ADULT LITERATURE SERIES SUPPLEMENT

3

Pla–Z
Indexes

Edited by
FRANK N. MAGILL

Project Editor
TRACY IRONS-GEORGES

SALEM PRESS

Pasadena, California   Englewood Cliffs, New Jersey

TMC
011.62
Mast
1991 Suppl.
V.3

Editor in Chief: Dawn P. Dawson
Project Editor: Tracy Irons-Georges
Research Supervisor: Jeffry Jensen
Production Editor: Janet Long
Proofreading Supervisor: Yasmine A. Cordoba
Layout: William Zimmerman

∞ The paper used in these volumes conforms to the American National Standard for Permanence of Paper for Printed Library Materials, Z39.48-1984.

Library of Congress Cataloging-in-Publication Data
Masterplots II. Juvenile and young adult literature series: supplement / edited by Frank N. Magill; project editor, Tracy Irons-Georges.
    p.   cm.
    Supplements the Juvenile and young adult fiction series (1991) and the Juvenile and young adult biography series (1993); includes for the first time poetry collections, plays, short-story collections, and books on art, history, sociology, and science for young readers; the cumulative indexes cover the contents of the earlier series as well as those covered in the Supplement.
    Includes bibliographical references and indexes.
    1. Children's literature—Stories, plots, etc. I. Magill, Frank Northen, 1907-   . II. Irons-Georges, Tracy. III. Masterplots II. Juvenile and young adult fiction series. IV. Masterplots II. Juvenile and young adult biography series.
Z1037.A1M377   1991 Supplement
011.62—dc21   96-39759
ISBN 0-89356-916-X (set)   CIP
ISBN 0-89356-919-4 (volume 3)

First Printing

PRINTED IN THE UNITED STATES OF AMERICA

LIST OF TITLES IN VOLUME 3

LIST OF TITLES IN VOLUME 3

MASTERPLOTS II

PLANET OF THE APES

Author: Pierre Boulle (1912-1994)
First published: La Planète des singes, 1963 (English translation, 1963)
Type of work: Novel
Type of plot: Allegory and science fiction
Time of work: The future
Locale: A planet in the Betelgeuse star system
Subjects: Animals, science, and social issues
Recommended ages: 13-18

A journalist explores a strange planet where apes rule and human beings are savages and learns much about his own society and its attitudes in the process.

> *Principal characters:*
> ULYSSÉ MEROU, a French journalist who travels to the Betelgeuse star system and lands on the "planet of the apes"
> NOVA, a human native of the planet who befriends Ulyssé
> ZAIUS, a male orangutan and the leader of the apes' scientific hierarchy
> ZIRA, a female chimpanzee who uses her skills to aid Ulyssé
> CORNELIUS, Zira's fiancé, a chimpanzee and archeologist whose interest in Ulyssé is both personal and professional

Form and Content

In *Planet of the Apes*, two space travelers, Jinn and Phyllis, discover a manuscript in a bottle. The manuscript's narrator, a journalist named Ulyssé Merou, tells of accompanying Professor Antelle, his disciple Arthur Levain, and a chimpanzee named Hector on a journey to the star Betelgeuse. Discovering a habitable planet, they leave their spaceship in orbit, taking a launch to the planet's surface.

They christen the planet "Soror, because of its resemblance to our Earth." The first human they see, who "possessed the most perfect body that could be conceived on earth," they name Nova. Nova's bodily perfection is matched by her apparent weakness of mind. Human voices frighten her, and she is agitated when the Earthlings don clothes. When Nova kills Hector, the Earthlings begin to suspect that all is not well. These suspicions are exacerbated when they meet more humans: All, like Nova, are naked and nonverbal. Before the Earthlings act, however, the indigenous humans destroy their clothes, take their weapons, and disable their launch. Merou, Antelle, and Levain, therefore are physically indistinguishable from the native humans when they encounter one of the intelligent species on the planet: a band of gorillas on horseback who hunt, shoot, and capture humans. Professor Antelle is lost, Levain is killed, and Merou is captured in a net and taken to the city.

There, Merou is placed in an individual cage, as are several other captives, including Nova. Merou quickly realizes that the apes are conducting psychological experiments on the humans. He speaks French to the two gorilla guards, Zoram and Zanam. Although they do not understand his language, they bring Zira, a chimpanzee, to see him. Merou speaks French to her. Zira summons Dr. Zaius, the orangutan who runs the institute, to see Merou.

Zaius is less impressed, eventually ordering Nova thrown into Merou's cage. The intent—to observe mating rituals—could not be clearer. Merou, "a man created in the image of God," finds himself manipulated into doing a "mating dance" with Nova.

Zaius intends to present Merou at a scientific conference as a curious, but not sentient, human. With coaching from Zira and her fiancé, Cornelius, an anthropologist, Merou learns the language of the apes. He gives a speech to the conference relating his origins and accomplishments, after which he immediately collapses. Merou wakes to find himself installed in an apartment. He joins the chimpanzee research team and teaches some of the humans the rudiments of speech.

While he was less successful linguistically with Nova, she has become pregnant, a matter that Zira goes to great length to keep from becoming generally known. The knowledge that a human can talk and rumors that he is teaching other humans to speak is spreading fear among the general ape population. Meanwhile, Cornelius, conducting an archaeological dig in the southern hemisphere, uncovers relics of an advanced culture, including a talking human doll. The conclusion is inevitable: Human civilization preceded ape civilization on the planet.

This discovery increases the danger to Merou and his newborn son. With assistance from Zira and Cornelius, Merou, Nova, and their child are substituted as "animals" on an experimental spaceflight and rendezvous with the ship that brought Merou to the planet. Merou pilots the original ship back to Earth, while the chimpanzees report their experimental flight destroyed. While Merou expects Earth to have changed since his departure, the magnitude of that change becomes apparent when they arrive—and are greeted by a uniformed gorilla. They hastily return to their ship, destined to wander the galaxy in search of intelligent human life.

In the denouement, Jinn and Phyllis, having read the manuscript, are amused by what they perceive to be a work of fiction. The two chimpanzees continue their pleasure jaunt, content in their superiority.

Analysis

Readers of this novel who have only seen the 1968 film version starring Charlton Heston will be pleasantly surprised by the relative subtlety of the society that Pierre Boulle limns. Even though the metaphors are occasionally strained, obvious, or both—the planet's surface is described as "green grass reminiscent of our own meadows in Normandy," Nova's vocalizations sound like the cry of "young chimpanzees"—Boulle's parallels are rarely unreasonable.

The most problematic aspect of the book is its relationship with science and scientists. While this book is Boulle's major foray into science fiction, little attention is paid to scientific knowledge, even as it was in 1960. The exception—the difference between subjective time on the ship and time passage in the universe, so that while

Merou's experiences only take him about three years, nearly seven hundred years pass on Earth—also serves the narrative purpose of allowing apes to have evolved on Earth.

Boulle disregards science whenever it might conflict with the story. The planet on which Merou's party lands, especially the descriptions of its orbit and its climate, are improbable at best. Even more doubtful is the likelihood that Merou and Nova would be able to procreate. In each case, however, the reader should willfully suspend disbelief; the center of this novel is social conceits, not scientific veracity.

The portrayal of the scientists themselves is the weakest part of the novel. The apes are clichéd: Zira is identified because she wears a white laboratory coat and Dr. Zaius is the stereotypical image of a crotchety old scientist, pontificating when he should be listening. Professor Antelle fares no better. Merou eventually discovers the professor caged in the zoo, apparently uninjured but not speaking and unwilling or unable to show any hint of his legendary intelligence.

Of the apes themselves, it must be noted that the sole description of their hierarchy is provided by the chimpanzees, who accordingly claim the highest value for themselves. While the gorillas provide the strength and the orangutans the administrative skills, the chimpanzees consider themselves to be the most intelligent of the races, even as some white Europeans or Chinese people have at times in their history considered other humans inferior. For adolescent readers especially, the resulting cliques will strike a familiar chord. Indeed, if there is an overwhelming theme to Boulle's novel—one emphasized by Jinn and Phyllis' self-satisfaction—it is that superiority is at best a transient thing.

That "talent will tell" is revealed in the relationship between Zira and Merou. From Zira's initial reaction of researcher to subject until their final moment when she does not kiss him despite her desires because he is "really too unattractive," they develop an intense enough relationship that Cornelius confides that his own relationship with Zira is likely to improve with Merou's departure. Anyone who has ever felt like or been treated as an inferior will be heartened by Merou's transformation in Zira's eyes from beast to beloved, even though their final moment is disheartening. *Planet of the Apes*, for all of its virtues, is ultimately a novel of frustrations and near-misses—but one in which the importance is in having made the effort, not simply in the results alone.

Critical Context

Planet of the Apes continues the tradition of such works as Jonathan Swift's *Gulliver's Travels* (1726) and George Orwell's *Animal Farm* (1946) in its use of the conceits of a society as a foil against which to reveal the foolishness of contemporary practices and mores. Indeed, Pierre Boulle is at his best in describing the psychological testing and its possible misinterpretations. While all three tales are closer to allegories than fantasies, the science-fiction conceits that Boulle employs limit his tale. That Professor Antelle finances the expedition privately is also an acknowledgment of the novel's literary antecedents, especially those of Jules Verne. Verne's tales tend to be more about adventure, however, and are usually without Boulle's poignant examinations of social conventions and conceits.

The underpinning premise of Boulle's novel—that of humans causing their own apocalypse—is less blatant here than in other popular works that dealt with the possibility of self-species destruction, such as Nevil Shute's *On the Beach* (1957). As a cautionary tale, Boulle's work is necessarily muted—and, like a trumpet, enhanced by its subtlety.

Ultimately, Boulle's tale of "man's inhumanity to man" strikes a chord with readers because of its belief that, even in the face of overwhelming prejudice, the values and virtues that make people "human" will prevail. Humanity, like earth, will abide.

Kenneth L. Houghton

PLAYING AMERICA'S GAME
The Story of Negro League Baseball

Author: Michael L. Cooper (1950-   )
First published: 1993; illustrated
Type of work: History
Time of work: The first half of the twentieth century
Locale: The United States
Subjects: Race and ethnicity and sports
Recommended ages: 13-18

Prior to the integration of Major League Baseball in 1947, the Negro Leagues existed as a means by which African American athletes could play professional baseball.

Principal personages:
RUBE FOSTER, a pitcher instrumental in the establishment of the Negro Leagues
LEROY ("SATCHEL") PAIGE, among the most talented and charismatic of pitchers
JOSH GIBSON, a catcher noted for his home run power
TED ("DOUBLE DUTY") RADCLIFFE, a pitcher, catcher, and all-around star athlete for several Negro League teams
JAMES ("COOL PAPA") BELL, an outfielder noted for his outstanding speed
JOHN HENRY LLOYD, one of the greatest infielders playing in the Negro Leagues
JACKIE ROBINSON, the athlete who broke Major League Baseball's wall of segregation when he was signed by the Brooklyn Dodgers

Form and Content

During the decades between 1890 and 1947, African Americans were barred by an unwritten agreement among management from playing professional baseball with white players. Nevertheless, these athletes developed their own brand of professional baseball epitomized by the Negro Leagues. Within this organization was played a quality game often equivalent to that in all-white Major League Baseball. *Playing America's Game* is a story of the Negro Leagues.

In his opening chapter, Michael L. Cooper describes the excitement of "The Dream Game," the annual East-West All-Star Classic played between the stars from the Negro Leagues. It was in this annual event that African American athletes truly were able to demonstrate their talents. Held at Chicago's Comiskey Park, the game regularly was attended by as many as fifty thousand fans, most of them African American.

In both text and pictures, Cooper illustrates the talent that was generally missed by white baseball fans because of the racism inherent in organized baseball. From Rube Foster, the organizer of the Negro Leagues and one of its early stars, to Jackie Robinson, perhaps the most famous of league alumni, the author moves through the events that made up much of the leagues' history.

Cooper begins his history with a summary of professional baseball's early years in the nineteenth century. The belief that Robinson was the first African American Major League ballplayer is common but incorrect. During the 1880's, numerous African Americans played on (primarily) white professional clubs. An increasingly racist climate, however, led to an unwritten agreement that black men would not be hired, and, by the 1890's, African Americans would no longer be found on these or any other clubs within organized baseball.

In succeeding chapters, Cooper describes how Foster and others formed their own leagues. Many of the teams were poorly organized outfits, frequently filing for bankruptcy. Others became very successful, however, allowing fans to see these men display their talents in legitimate competition. The author moves on to a description of "barnstorming," the criss-crossing of the country by many of these teams as they brought baseball to small towns and hamlets. Often, they played local white teams and held their own in such competition.

Cooper finishes his brief saga with the story of Robinson and other African American stars who finally made it to the Major Leagues. With the end of World War II and knowledge of the contribution made by African Americans in that war, it was clear that segregation in baseball would have to end. After Robinson was signed by the Brooklyn Dodgers in 1946 and had a chance to show what he could do on the ballfield in competition with white athletes, other clubs began signing African American players. The Cleveland Indians quickly signed Larry Doby, who became the first African American to play in the American League. The Dodgers themselves signed numerous stars from the Negro Leagues. Ironically, the end of segregation in organized baseball was to be the death knell for the Negro Leagues. When given a choice between playing in the Negro Leagues or in the formerly white Major Leagues, most African American athletes deserted their former clubs. By the 1950's, even the most successful Negro League clubs had gone out of business.

Analysis

Playing America's Game is a history of baseball and a sociological look at a time when American sport, and indeed much of America itself, was segregated. The author conveys both the excitement of professional baseball and the difficulties encountered by African American athletes in their sport and in their everyday lives. Whether the outstanding members of the Negro Leagues—players such as Josh Gibson, "Satchel" Paige, and "Cool Papa" Bell—were as good as their counterparts in all-white Major League Baseball is something that can never be known for certain, but in both words and images, the author makes a strong case.

The excitement of the sport is conveyed in the first chapter, a discussion of the annual Dream Game, the East-West All-Star Classic. Begun in 1933, the event lasted until after World War II. Even more than the Negro League World Series, the all-star game was able to highlight the stars of the leagues. Prominent African Americans, including boxer Joe Louis, track-and-field champion Jesse Owens, and entertainer Cab Calloway, would be found at the game, among a crowd of fifty thousand persons.

Written for a youthful audience, *Playing America's Game* is not a detailed account of the times; the writing is concise. Numerous photographs are included along with the text. These images not only feature the athletes but also illustrate the racism inherent in much of society during this period. The photograph of a sign welcoming "Colored Only" indicates the difficulty that these men had simply in finding a room in which to sleep.

Cooper reveals that Jackie Robinson was not the first African American to play Major League Baseball. During the years after professional baseball's inception, the 1870's and 1880's, there were numerous African American baseball players. The refusal of many white athletes to play on the same fields with these men, however, created pressure to exclude them. By the 1890's, organized baseball had become exclusively white. (Light-skinned Cubans and American Indians, however, were able to play within these leagues.) As a result, African Americans began to form their own teams and leagues. Cooper describes the role played by Rube Foster in this endeavor. Foster, arguably the founder of the Negro Leagues, organized the Negro National League in 1920 and became its first commissioner. During the years of Foster's tenure, the Negro National League, if not always financially sound, was at least able to demonstrate a reasonable level of stability. The presence of this league inspired the establishment of other leagues, culminating in the first official Negro World Series in 1924.

Few of these teams could maintain themselves financially on the sole basis of attendance. Thus, they joined the tradition of barnstorming, in which teams traveled across the country playing one another, or more often playing local or other professional teams. In some cases, they even played white teams. Cooper conveys the excitement, and difficulties, of these trips. Barnstorming generated much-needed cash and brought professional baseball to regions where it had never appeared. Some names became as well known as Babe Ruth's. Satchel Paige, a lanky six-foot, three-inch pitcher, was said to throw a ball so fast that it could not be seen. Equally known for his showmanship, Paige was one of many players who could guarantee a large crowd. He joined the Cleveland Indians in 1948, but, at the age of forty-two, his blinding speed was gone. Nevertheless, he was still able to win six games and play a major factor in a pennant for the Indians.

Perhaps the most important aspect of Cooper's book is its ability to convey to young people both what was lost and what was gained. These men were rarely able to demonstrate their prowess against the stars of the Major Leagues, but the baseball that they played was just as skilled.

Critical Context

Michael L. Cooper's *Playing America's Game* is one of the first major works on

Negro League baseball addressed to a young adult audience. The topic is an important one, given that few readers within this age group are aware of the obstacles that were encountered by African Americans in "playing America's game" during the first half of the twentieth century. Many are aware of the contribution made by Jackie Robinson; few have ever heard of the other athletes who came before Robinson and made his way a little easier. The Negro Leagues did not exist in a void; they filled a real need as an outlet for men unable to compete in their chosen profession of baseball. The leagues provided entertainment for an audience that wished to follow their own sons in that profession.

As the author states, few white-owned newspapers covered these events, and African American-owned papers rarely had the resources for the extensive coverage of sports. Consequently, many of the stories are anecdotal. Most of these athletes were either elderly or dead at the time that the book was written, and with their deaths are lost the history of their times. Detailed stories of the Negro Leagues had been written, but, with the exception of a few biographies, most were addressed to an adult audience. Cooper reversed that trend with this book. It is ironic that an increasing number of young people in the generations that followed that of Robinson are unaware of his contributions. This book is also an attempt to address such a problem.

Richard Adler

POMPEII
Exploring a Roman Ghost Town

Author: Ron Goor (1940-   ) and Nancy Goor (1944-   )
First published: 1986; illustrated
Type of work: History
Time of work: A.D. 79
Locale: Pompeii, located on the coast of the Bay of Naples in southern Italy
Subjects: Nature, politics and law, and religion
Recommended ages: 10-15

Photographs, maps, drawings, and a carefully researched text reveal life in the ancient Roman city named Pompeii, preserved by volcanic ash since A.D. 79.

> *Principal personages:*
> GIUSEPPE FIORELLI, an archaeologist who in 1864 discovered a way of creating plaster casts of the organic objects (humans, animals, and plants) killed in Pompeii when volcanic ash covered them in A.D. 79
> WILHELMINA JASHEMSKI, an archaeologist who has determined the identities of plants growing in Pompeian gardens in August, A.D. 79
> L. CAECILIUS JUCUNDUS, a wealthy Pompeian auctioneer whose belongings were preserved by volcanic ash
> PLINY THE YOUNGER, a natural historian who, in a letter to Tacitus, provides the only eyewitness account of the eruption of Mount Vesuvius and the submersion of Pompeii under lava and ash

Form and Content

In *Pompeii: Exploring a Roman Ghost Town*, Ron and Nancy Goor write in the objective third-person point of view as historians and archaeologists to establish the relationships among centuries of activities at the site of Pompeii—ranging from the earthquake in A.D. 62 to the volcanic eruption in A.D. 79—through the gradual excavation and partial restoration of the town. The Goors divide *Pompeii* into an introduction, five chapters, and an epilogue. The introduction, a letter written by the historian Pliny the Younger, an eyewitness, tells of the eruption of Mount Vesuvius and the burial of Pompeii under lava and ash. The first chapter, "Death and Discovery," describes both the catastrophe and the archaeological attempts to excavate the Roman town centuries later. The first inept archaeological explorations began in 1748. By the 1860's, Giuseppe Fiorelli instituted more careful methods for excavating the buried city.

The second chapter discusses the arrangement of Pompeii, a walled Roman town with eight city gates. Streets intersect to form blocks called *insulae*. Pompeii had three large public areas: a sports area, a theater area, and a political area. Because Roman law forbade burial within the town, tombs lined the roads leading to the gates of the city. The most remarkable element of Pompeii was its water system. An aqueduct brought water to large public baths, swimming pools, private villas, gardens, and fountains.

Chapters 3 and 4 describe the public and private lives of the Pompeians. Public life revolved around government, religion, and entertainment. The principal site of government in Roman cities was the forum; the map of Pompeii also shows seven temples. Two theaters, an immense gymnasium, public baths, and an amphitheater were places for entertainment. Private life centered around the home, a dwelling that had an atrium with *cubiculae* (small rooms) located around it.

Chapter 5, entitled "Work," explains the commercial interests of this city, which had two ports—one on the Mediterranean and one on the Sarno River. Pompeians grew and processed grapes, olives, and flowers for perfume. The wool industry required the growing of sheep and the establishment of fulleries to clean, bleach, and dye wool from which togas were made. Professional work included medicine, architecture, engineering, and teaching. The Goors close *Pompeii* with an epilogue in which they call Pompeii a "living" ghost town because its continued presence re-creates the past. Maps, black-and-white photographs, and drawings illustrate the text.

Analysis

Ron and Nancy Goor write of what remains after the abrupt destruction of Pompeii, a city that serves as an example of ancient Roman civilization, a culture that has contributed so much to later civilizations.

The wall surrounding Pompeii was twenty feet thick and twenty-six feet high. Eight gates and eight roads led out of and into Pompeii. Two-story colonnades enclosed three sides of the forum. On the fourth side stood the imposing Temple of Jupiter. The large theater held five thousand spectators; the amphitheater, twenty thousand. An eighteen-mile-long aqueduct, a vast Castellum Aquae for holding water, plus twenty-foot-high water towers were located throughout Pompeii. All these structures offer, two thousand years later, testimony to the architectural and engineering prowess of the Pompeians. Paintings, mosaics, vases, sculptures, and fluted columns speak of the abilities of artisans in the town. Business records kept on wax tablets tell of loans and rent payments. Graffiti announce that Pompeians idolized gladiators and actors. Love poems, political advertisements, lost-and-found announcements, and insults remain on the walls of tombs, houses, and shops. Bread, hermetically sealed for centuries, shows the name of its baker, Celer, the slave of Quintus Granius Verus. Rules for dining etiquette painted on the wall of one villa, instructions for creating a mosaic, and a recipe testify about life in Pompeii in A.D. 79.

Through text and photographs, the Goors reveal similarities between life in A.D. 79 and life in modern times. In the theater, Pompeian stagehands could change backdrops, create sound effects, or flood the stage to re-create naval battles. In medicine, Pompeians used scissors, forceps, clamps, and scalpels that resemble their present-day counterparts. Lead pipes laid beneath streets paved with stone brought running water to public fountains located at the intersections of city blocks and to the kitchens and baths of private villas. A bone comb made two thousand years ago is a likeness to combs still used. The Goors never intrude in the exploration of Pompeii. Instead, they let the ghost town speak for its late inhabitants and their culture.

This ghost town can speak in part because the archaeologist Giuseppe Fiorelli was innovative and painstaking in his work. Fiorelli divided the walled city into regions. He numbered each block within the city and each doorway within each block. Digging proceeded methodically and by the 1990's had yet to be completed. Each object excavated has been numbered and catalogued. Perhaps the most important contribution made by Fiorelli is his discovery of how to preserve the forms of humans, animals, and plants.

Fiorelli knew that the molten lava and ash flowed over and through the city. The lava hardened around objects, and, within the hardened lava, organic objects decayed and left cavities that could serve as molds into which Fiorelli poured liquid plaster. When the plaster solidified, the lava was chipped away to leave plaster castings that capture the forms and positions of humans, animals, and plants. More than the buildings and streets, more than the graffiti on the walls, these plaster forms speak of the Pompeians and of similarities among humans from ancient to modern times. A muleteer, taking what measures he can against overpowering forces, sits on the floor with his knees drawn up and his hands holding a cloth over his mouth and nose. A compassionate doorkeeper covers his daughter's head with a pillow.

Archaeologist Wilhelmina Jashemski filled the cavities left after plants decayed within the hardened lava. She studied not only her castings but also carbonized seeds and grains of pollen recovered from volcanic debris. From her studies, Jashemski determined the types and locations of plants in Pompeian gardens.

Critical Context

Pompeii: Exploring a Roman Ghost Town unites the study of history with the discoveries of archaeologists. The book shows the many specific parts that make up a civilization and the care necessary in the excavation of such a complex site. Each excavated item gains significance when it is fitted into the whole, and the whole gains actuality from the tangible parts. *Pompeii* can supplement historical studies because it reveals the multiple sources from which historians must draw in order to create a complete and valid assessment of a past civilization. Those interested in the discoveries of other ancient civilizations may want to read Robert Silverberg's *Lost Cities and Vanished Civilizations* (1962) and Malcolm Weiss's *Sky Watchers of Ages Past* (1982).

The Goors' interest in Pompeii may have originated during their travels in Italy. To Ron Goor, Pompeii offered an opportunity to use photography to depict the objects of Pompeii. Through these objects, the life of the people of the city can be reconstructed. Other books by the Goors in which photography plays an integral part include *Shadows: Here, There, and Everywhere* (1981), an American Library Association Notable Book, and *In the Driver's Seat* (1982), a Junior Literary Guild selection.

Insect Metamorphosis: From Egg to Adult (1990) stems from the Goors' earlier work with the Smithsonian Institution's National Museum of Natural History, where they created an insect zoo.

Lana White

PORTRAIT OF JENNIE

Author: Robert Nathan (1894-1985)
First published: 1940
Type of work: Novel
Type of plot: Fantasy
Time of work: 1938
Locale: New York City and Cape Cod, Massachusetts
Subjects: Arts, emotions, and love and romance
Recommended ages: 13-18

Eben Adams recovers his artistic creativity through an attachment to the beautiful Jennie Appleton.

Principal characters:
EBEN ADAMS, a twenty-eight-year-old New York artist who is experiencing a loss of creative inspiration
JENNIE APPLETON, a fantasy child who becomes Adams' model
GUS MEYER, a New York taxi driver and friend of Adams
MRS. JEKES, Adams' New York landlady
MR. MATHEWS, a sympathetic New York art dealer
MISS SPINNEY, the assistant to Mr. Mathews
ARNE KUNSTLER, a Cape Cod artist and friend of Adams
MR. MOORE, the owner of the Alhambra, a Manhattan café

Form and Content

Portrait of Jennie is a fantasy that depicts romantic love as a source of artistic inspiration. Its fifteen chapters are narrated in the first person from the viewpoint of the main character, Eben Adams, a New York artist. In the narrative, Adams takes a retrospective on his experience in 1938 from an indefinite future time. The Manhattan setting, beginning in winter during an economically depressed period, contributes to the optimistic theme that love, even tragic love, can enable one to triumph over adversity.

The book opens with Adams confessing that he is experiencing a "winter of the mind" when none of his paintings seems to be inspired and little hope exists that any will be; he suffers from an artistic loss of confidence. Adams paints mostly landscapes during a time when the market for them is poor. During an aimless walk through Central Park on a winter afternoon, he meets a beautiful young girl playing hopscotch alone. In conversation, she identifies herself as Jennie Appleton but puzzles Eben by explaining that her parents are acrobats at the Hammerstein Music Theater, a building that had burned several years earlier. She sings a childlike song that indicates that her origin and destination are shrouded in mystery, and, when they part, she asks Eben to wait for her to grow up.

Eben later makes a few sketches of Jennie and inadvertently places one in a collection of landscape paintings that he hopes to sell to Mr. Mathews, the owner of a small gallery. Although he has little interest in the landscapes, Mathews is taken by the sketch of Jennie and buys it, along with one other painting. The sale provides rent money for Eben, who had been in arrears. Mathews suggests that Eben paint women instead of landscapes, for he might be able to capture something in the feminine form that transcends time. With help from his friend Gus Meyer, a taxi driver, Eben lands a commission to paint a mural, a picnic scene, over the bar of the Alhambra café owned by Mr. Moore; for this work, he receives free meals at the restaurant.

When Eben later encounters Jennie, she is ice skating in the park. She appears to have grown older, as if entering her teens. After making and selling additional sketches of Jennie, Eben accepts her suggestion that he paint her portrait. Each time that she sits for the painting, Jennie seems to have aged more than is normal, and each time she disappears unexpectedly. Efforts to find out where she lives end in failure. In the portrait, Eben paints Jennie as a teenager, but the work manages to capture her childlike appearance and to reflect the beauty of a woman as well. When Mr. Mathews and his assistant, Miss Spinney, see the portrait, they consider it a masterpiece and accept it on consignment, offering Adams a larger advance than he has ever received before. Only after he has concluded the painting does he realize that he and Jennie belong together.

When she returns to his apartment in the spring, Jennie is enrolled in a boarding school. They arrange to spend a day together on a picnic to New Jersey, but their idyll is ended when the prim, disagreeable landlady Mrs. Jekes orders Jennie away from the house in the evening. Jennie sails for France to continue her schooling abroad, and Eben leaves New York to spend the summer on Cape Cod, where he paints fishermen at their work.

In September, he and his friend Arne Kunstler venture out in a sailboat and are almost lost in an intense hurricane that strikes the area. As he watches from the safety of his house, he senses through intuition that Jennie is caught in the angry waves. He approaches the water's edge and is united with the drowning young woman, but he cannot rescue her. Later in New York, he sees a newspaper account of the loss of a passenger, identified as Jennie, who had been swept from the deck of an ocean liner returning from Europe.

Analysis

The novel's strong fantasy element rests upon Jennie as a character, who in a few months is transformed from a charming, delicate child into a beautiful young woman. She replaces the realism of the other characters with a romantic fantasy that suggests that time can be transcended through an effort of will. Eben comes to believe Jennie when she tells him that she is trying to grow up. He sees her at intervals of weeks or months, but her experiences during the gaps have taken years, and her changed appearance establishes as much. Her poignant loss reminds readers that such an idyllic love cannot last.

Jennie's sylphlike character contrasts with numerous other finely etched realistic characters in the novel. Both Mr. Mathews and Miss Spinney are warmly human and eager to do a good turn to impoverished artists, but both possess crusty exteriors. Gus Meyer, the taxi driver, exudes good will and is streetwise. Arne Kunstler is vehement, contradictory, and energetic, a mad artist who is kept from going over the edge by his links with nature and the sea.

Eben's love of Jennie sheds light on the other important theme of the novel—that of art itself—and the story suggests that even lost love creates a lasting imprint. Unlike his friend Arne, who believes that art is for the masses, Eben has no theory of art except as an external expression of the artist's emotions. While Arne's ideal is a popular appeal, he paints works so far removed from reality that not even an experienced artist such as Eben can understand them. Until he meets Jennie, Eben is isolated, friendless, and filled with self-doubt. After he sketches her, he begins to reach out to others, to form friendships, and to include human figures in his landscape paintings, such as the mural in the Alhambra. Through her influence, he reestablishes a connection with human beings and thus reinvigorates his art.

Eben's portrait of Jennie, entitled "Girl in a Black Dress," is his masterpiece; eventually, it becomes part of a famous museum collection. Its beauty suggests that like Jennie, the artist triumphs over time. She can speed her development through an act of will, but only the artist can preserve her existence. The painting itself connects with reality by portraying the feminine form realistically, but it achieves more than reality by illuminating the subject's past and future appearance. When he goes to Cape Cod, Eben paints human forms with seascapes as background and thus retains his focus on the humanity of art. After returning to New York, he grieves for the loss Jennie, but he retains his ability to relate to people. Despite numerous realistic details, the novel blurs the line between imagination and reality, so that the reader is left wondering whether Jennie belongs only to Eben's imagination.

Narrated in mostly colloquial prose, *Portrait of Jennie* achieves literary effects that enhance its poignant romantic theme. Robert Nathan's narrative style is especially effective in its use of foreshadowing to anticipate the book's tragic conclusion. In one brief scene, Eben glimpses Jennie as she weeps while looking through the studio window at his landscape painting of the Pamet River in Cape Cod, the site where she later drowns. In his picnic scene over the Alhambra bar, one female figure represents Jennie, and, unaccountably, the girl looks as if she has drowned.

Critical Context

A prolific writer in several literary genres, Robert Nathan is known for celebrating the power of love to transcend time and place. *Portrait of Jennie*, his best-known work, is known to many readers through a popular screen adaptation in 1948.

The tragic story of lost young love arose early in literature, and its origins are lost in antiquity, but Nathan's novel bears close resemblance to late nineteenth century and early twentieth century predecessors such as W. H. Hudson's *Green Mansions* (1904), which captured the tragic fate of Rima, a beautiful girl living in a South American forest. In its aesthetic theme, Nathan's novel may owe something to George du Maurier's *Trilby* (1894), a story of an artist who attempts to transform a young girl into a work of art. Nathan enhances the aesthetic theme through an exploration of the artist's role. His heroic artist remains the romantic individual, seeking proper inspiration and discovering it in the beauty of the human form.

Stanley Archer

THE POSTMAN

Author: David Brin (1950-   )
First published: 1985
Type of work: Novel
Type of plot: Adventure tale, science fiction, and social realism
Time of work: Early in the twenty-first century (from approximately 2009 to 2012)
Locale: The Northwestern United States, primarily Oregon
Subjects: Gender roles, social issues, and war
Recommended ages: 15-18

This post-nuclear holocaust novel following the travels of Gordon Krantz through the Northwestern United States in search of a civilized community.

Principal characters:
GORDON KRANTZ, a man in his late thirties who has lived through a nuclear holocaust and the disease and famine that followed
CYCLOPS, a surviving intelligent supercomputer that is supposedly helping the community of Corvallis in the Willamette Valley of Oregon toward restoration
DENA SPURGEN, a feminist of the Corvallis community who becomes Gordon's lover and who leads an attack by forty trained women against the Holnists, a group that believes in a philosophy of "might makes right"
PHILIP BOKUTO, an African American man from the Corvallis community who has military skills and who travels with Gordon and John Stevens in an effort to enlist the help of George Powhatan
JOHN STEVENS, an idealistic but practical young man whom Gordon appoints as a postmaster and who helps Gordon survive when he is captured by the Holnists
GENERAL VOLSCI MACKLIN, an "augmented" high-ranking officer of a Holnist group planning an attack on Corvallis
GEORGE POWHATAN, the leader of a southern Oregon community whom Gordon Krantz approaches for help in defending the Willamette Valley against the Holnists

Form and Content

The Postman, like David Brin's other science-fiction novels, explores the society that is created by the interactions of its characters, rather than merely the effects of technology on those characters. This post-nuclear holocaust novel is told from the perspective of Gordon Krantz, using both the first-person point of view and reprints of documents and letters. The book is arranged in four sections, with a prelude to the first section and an interlude between each of the following sections allowing the author to impart more general background information outside the main character's knowledge. Each of the four sections has its own set of chapters, independently numbered from the other sections. The final section, although following the preceding section in chronology by only a few weeks, can be considered an afterword.

As *The Postman* opens, Gordon Krantz has lived through the nuclear war that took place during his college years, three years of nuclear winter, and the destruction, through disease and attack, of his militia unit, which protected grain supplies in the Minneapolis-St. Paul area of Minnesota.

Sixteen years after the war, Gordon is just leaving Idaho and entering Oregon when his camp site is attacked by bandits. He escapes with only the few supplies and equipment that he manages to grab; the rest is stolen or destroyed, along with his journal. Gordon attempts to track the bandits because he needs more supplies in order to survive. He becomes lost and finds a crashed postal truck still containing the skeleton of the driver. Gordon uses the mail sacks and vehicle to survive the night cold and buries the driver in the morning. He acquires the uniform, shoes, and some survival equipment from the vehicle. He also takes some of the letters to read and to use as paper so that he can resume his journal.

In a few days, Gordon reaches the village of Cottage Grove, where, because of the uniform, he is accepted as a postman. Later, circumstances at other Oregon communities cause Gordon to play on his mistaken identity for his own safety and the betterment of the communities that he visits. Because of this mistaken identity, however, Gordon is denied the opportunity to settle in Cottage Grove, the one community that he has found with a semblance of civilization.

During Gordon's travels, he rescues a boy whose mother has been killed by a raiding party of Holnists, men who have formed barbaric communities based on the teachings of Nathan Holn. The Holnists raid other communities for slaves, women, and supplies. The boy and his mother were from the Corvallis community governed by Cyclops, the remaining intelligent supercomputer. Gordon returns the boy to Corvallis and, as a "postal inspector," has an interview with Cyclops.

After pushing on to contact more communities in order to bring them into Gordon's invented "Restored United States" postal system, Gordon realizes that Cyclops is a sham—a hoax being perpetrated on the people of Corvallis to encourage cooperation and technological acceptance. In the closing chapters of the novel, Gordon realizes that he has learned an important lesson: that someone has to start by taking responsibility in order to create the civilization that he has spent his traveling years trying to find.

Gordon tries to organize the Willamette Valley farming communities into an army when he discovers the planned takeover of the area by the Northern California Holnists. He contacts George Powhatan, a famed leader from southern Oregon, at Sugar Loaf Mountain, but is turned down for help. A letter addressed to Powhatan that Gordon and appointed "postmaster" John Stevens carry explains that feminist leader Dena Spurgen and her female military "Scouts" have a plan to stop the

Holnists. Leaving Sugar Loaf Mountain, Gordon and John are captured by the Holnists.

John is killed in an escape attempt, trying to rescue a sack of mail. Their companion Philip Bokuto is killed trying to rescue Gordon from the Holnists. Dena Spurgen is tortured to death by the Holnists after her raid fails. George Powhatan comes to Gordon's defense in a final showdown with the Holnist "augment," General Volsci Macklin, a prewar scientifically enhanced soldier.

After the final fight scene between Powhatan and Macklin, when Gordon asks Powhatan why he decided to rescue Gordon and join the fight, Powhatan explains that Dena's letter caused the women of his community to put pressure on him to change his mind.

Analysis

David Brin presents several messages in this novel, not all of them in the form of clear opinions or stances. The most obvious message is that social identity is a product of one's interactions with society. The main character, Gordon Krantz, becomes "the Postman" when he dons the uniform and enters the town of Cottage Grove. Although Gordon worries throughout the novel about the false image that he is presenting, he continues to play the role, past the end of the novel, and people continue to treat him as a representative of past and future organized societies.

Gordon's emotions toward Dena Spurgen are mixed, even though he admires her intelligence and they become lovers. The primary messages that the character Dena Spurgen embodies as a feminist are twofold. Her letter calls for women to judge men and eliminate the bad ones, giving women an air of higher moral authority. Her efforts in the war with the Holnists also emphasize the theme throughout the novel that with freedom comes duty. Dena is not a strongly developed character, and, except for Gordon Krantz, neither are any of the others. It is not unusual for authors to use poorly developed characters in science fiction as props for the true goals of the novel: an extrapolation of what human society might be like if a particular technology is developed and used.

John Stevens' noble sacrifice of his life for an ideal is handled as a mixed message as well. Gordon, having recruited John as a postmaster and being aware that the "Restored United States" is a sham, feels guilt that John has lost his life attempting to rescue the mail. Yet, several times in the novel, Gordon puts his own life in danger in order to protect letters.

Brin also points out the value of knowing history, of understanding what has gone before; this important lesson is often taught in post-nuclear holocaust novels. The author also espouses the opinions that science benefits everyone ("especially the weak") and that soldier-citizens who long to return to their civilian lives form the best type of military force for a nation.

The Postman is suitable for high school students. The vocabulary is challenging at times, and the fact that no clear resolution to the problems is presented invites discussion of the novel's themes.

Critical Context

The Postman won the John W. Campbell, Jr., Memorial Award for best science-fiction novel of 1985. Other novels by David Brin that would appeal to this age group and that end with more satisfying resolutions for the main character are *The Practice Effect* (1984), the story of an alternate universe where the more something is used, the newer and more modern it becomes; and *Glory Season* (1993), an exciting, adventurous, coming-of-age story set on a feminist colony planet.

Brin won Hugo Awards (science fiction achievement awards) for *Startide Rising* (1983) and its sequel, *The Uplift War* (1987), novels in which intelligent dolphins and chimpanzees cooperate with humans in space exploration and colonization.

Two other post-nuclear holocaust novels that would also be suitable for this age group are *False Dawn* (1978), by Chelsea Quinn Yarbro, and *Warday and the Journey Onward* (1984), by Whitley Streiber and James W. Kunetka.

B. Diane Miller

PRIDE AND PREJUDICE

Author: Jane Austen (1775-1817)
First published: 1813
Type of work: Novel
Type of plot: Domestic realism
Time of work: The late eighteenth century
Locale: Longbourn, a village in Herfordshire, England
Subjects: Emotions and love and romance
Recommended ages: 13-18

*In this comedy of manners, Elizabeth Bennet grows and changes so that ultimately
she integrates feeling with custom and necessity through her marriage with Darcy.*

> *Principal characters:*
> ELIZABETH BENNET, a young woman of lively intelligence and
>   considered behavior, who wishes to marry a compatible husband
> FITZWILLIAM DARCY, the hero, who seeks to win Elizabeth's love
> JANE BENNET, Elizabeth's kind, sweet older sister, who also seeks a
>   husband
> CHARLES BINGLEY, a man in love with Jane

Form and Content

Pride and Prejudice revolves around love and marriage in an acquisitive society.
While the Bennets are members of the leisure class, the family fortune is entailed upon
a male heir. This difficulty causes Mrs. Bennet to act frantically to find husbands for
her five daughters. Elizabeth, the heroine, looks toward marriage with her clear sense
of self and her ability to judge others accurately. To unite with a worthy husband,
however, she must change her perceptions and grow in understanding. The novel is
presented in three volumes, the sections mirroring Elizabeth Bennet's emotional
growth through her response to the hero, Fitzwilliam Darcy.

The story begins with Elizabeth, like the other young women in Meryton community, looking forward to a party that introduces two eligible bachelors with fortunes.
She sees with pleasure that Charles Bingley is attracted to her older sister Jane. She
dismisses the other bachelor, the aristocrat Darcy, as a proud man who considers
himself their social superior. Elizabeth painfully recognizes the truth of his assessment
as she observes her mother and sister Lydia in unseemly attempts to ensnare any
possible suitor. Elizabeth's sentiments and values are further revealed when she
rejects the offer of Mr. Collins, the pompous, condescending gentleman on whom
their fortune is entailed and is instead attracted to the handsome Wickham, who
beguiles her with his charm and his story of ill-treatment by Darcy. His story evokes
her sensitive feelings and increases her resentment toward Darcy.

Elizabeth is reconnected with Darcy when she visits her friend Charlotte, who, in a spirit of expediency, accepts Mr. Collins. Their home is the parsonage on the estate of Lady Catherine de Bough, Darcy's aunt. After several visits from Darcy, Elizabeth is shocked and angered when he proposes to her, despite what he calls her low family connections. Elizabeth not only refuses but also rebukes him for the part that she suspects he has played in separating Jane and Bingley and for his reprehensible treatment of Wickham. She is later astonished by the long letter from Darcy explaining how he misjudged Jane's affection and how he and his sister were, in fact, misused by the profligate Wickham. Elizabeth recognizes the error of her judgment.

In the third section, she develops admiration for Darcy, and indeed he too changes. Believing him to be away, she accidentally encounters him at Pemberly, his beautiful and tasteful estate that she tours while traveling with her aunt and uncle, the Gardiners. Here, she observes his gracious manners with her relatives and learns of the esteem that his servants and tenants have for him. As her regard for Darcy grows, Elizabeth is once again embarrassed by her family when Wickham and Lydia run off together. Darcy makes use of this incident to exhibit his care for Elizabeth by quietly paying off Wickham. He further promotes himself in Elizabeth's eyes by influencing the renewed connection between Bingley and Jane. With her feelings for Darcy transformed, Elizabeth now hopes that he will repeat his request, which he does, and both couples are united. Elizabeth and Darcy, however, have undergone the trials of love and learned to value each other.

Analysis

Pride and Prejudice was written for a literate public familiar with comedy and contemporary didactic and romantic fiction. Today, the novel is read as a classic work of fiction and an ageless tale of the evolution and growth of personal attachment and personality. The plot, the theme, the artistic execution, the humor, and the underlying moral comment continue to appeal to young people and adults.

In assessing this novel, critics have persisted in noting the artistic achievement of the work despite its limited scope. This scope—the trials associated with marriage, the social initiation into adulthood in this acquisitive culture—Jane Austen herself recognized as her "two inches of ivory." Within that scope, the work describes the uniting of both the fortunes and the feelings of two passionate people within such a tightly constructed comic plot that virtually every detail focuses on the artistic conclusion.

The novel has a plot and subplot, both of which end in marriage. The progression of these two plots—one complicated, the other simple—presents an assessment of moral character while it moves toward resolution. Elizabeth and Darcy are strong individuals whose paths present opportunities to grow emotionally. They contrast with an instructive array of characters and behaviors: the good but modest Jane and Bingley, who do not change; the more complex Charlotte Lucas and Mr. Bennet, who choose the simple life by giving in or giving up; and the simple fools Mrs. Bennet, Lady Catherine, Mr. Collins, Wickham, and Lydia, who have only superficial understanding and strive to manipulate others to their own ends.

Austen's careful selection of events, economic descriptions, and use of irony fortify each detail with artistic purpose. The title suggests the complicated, ironic reversals that will take place. Elizabeth's prejudice is based on pride in herself and her judgment; Darcy's pride is based on social prejudice. Events serve several purposes simultaneously. The arrival of Mr. Collins explains the extreme need of the Bennet sisters to marry well. It also presents a pompous fool against whom readers can measure other characters' behaviors and shows Elizabeth's integrity of feeling in her refusal to succumb to external pressures. On the other hand, the description of Pemberly is austere and vague, employing general adjectives such as "vast," "grand," and "natural." What is important about Darcy's estate is that it reflects positively his taste and style, gives him an opportunity to change his impression of Elizabeth's family connections, and gives Elizabeth an opportunity to change her impression of him. The two appearances of Lady Catherine are functional. First, she presents a portrait of an ill-mannered and pompous aristocrat, provides for the renewed acquaintance of Darcy and Elizabeth, and facilitates Elizabeth's new insights into Darcy's character; then, she inadvertently reveals to Darcy Elizabeth's changed feelings. Ironic statement and observation contribute to meaning by allowing for both what is said and what is implied. For example, the opening assertion, "that a single man in possession of a good fortune, must be in want of a wife," implies the obverse as well: that a single woman lacking a fortune is in need of a husband.

While the behaviors of all the characters contribute to the moral comment of the novel and the culmination of the plot, they also present a source of comedy. The work satirizes human behavior, especially that of the pompous and self-important. The final marriages are both artistically and morally satisfying. The right people get together and, most important, Elizabeth and Darcy have grown. By recognizing and altering their own pride and prejudices, they have earned mutual respect and love.

Critical Context

Jane Austen's early work began as satire, parodying the excessive sensibility of contemporary fiction. Her work continued in this vein in the tradition of the domestic comedy of Samuel Richardson, Henry Fielding, and Fanny Burney. With an appreciation of the ridiculous in human behavior, she developed skill in presenting the pompous and socially imprudent character. Her more mature work, like the domestic comedy of Burney, takes on moral undertones as her protagonists are challenged to grow and change within the confines of social custom. *Pride and Prejudice*, acclaimed as Austen's best novel, combines these elements.

Begun in the 1790's and offered for publication under the title "First Impressions," the novel was initially rejected by publishers. Austen then reworked and resubmitted the piece under the new title, and it was published in 1813. While initially Austen's works were not as popular as were the works of Richardson and Burney, they have endured and developed a wide readership among general readers as well as scholars. *Pride and Prejudice* has been adapted to film and television, making Austen's works ever more accessible to the general public. The popularity of her fiction can be attributed to its themes of love and marriage, growth and self-discovery, as well as to their comic presentation of domestic life. Its tightly structured, focused plot, moving so purposefully and subtly toward its conclusion, distinguishes *Pride and Prejudice* as a classic work of literature.

Bernadette Flynn Low

THE PRINCE OF TIDES

Author: Pat Conroy (1945-   )
First published: 1986
Type of work: Novel
Type of plot: Domestic realism
Time of work: The 1950's to the 1980's
Locale: South Carolina and New York City
Subjects: Coming-of-age, family, friendship, gender roles, and suicide
Recommended ages: 15-18

Tom Wingo, while trying to help a psychiatrist save his suicidal twin sister, reconstructs his family history, in which he finds his identity and the tools for rebuilding his damaged family.

Principal characters:
> TOM WINGO, a high school English teacher and football coach who is struggling to understand his chaotic, violent family history
> LUKE WINGO, Tom's older brother, a loyal, simple victim of parental abuse, combat in the Vietnam War, and social upheaval
> SAVANNAH WINGO, Tom's twin sister, a suicidal, gifted poet tormented by the pain and shame of family secrets
> DR. SUSAN LOWENSTEIN, Savannah's psychiatrist, who helps Tom find himself and come to terms with his family history

Form and Content

The Prince of Tides begins with a prologue and ends with an epilogue that frame this three-generational family saga. The story's opening setting is located in the deceptively placid marshland and coastal islands near the fictional town of Colleton, South Carolina. The pace of this long, complex novel at times moves as slowly as the gradual ebb of the tides in the sleepy, rural South. At other times, especially when the setting shifts to New York City, the story's pace is punctuated with the frantic and relentless recollections of the violence and calamities that have tainted and tortured the Wingo family.

Tom Wingo, the first-person narrator of the Wingo family history, is the family's voice. In contrast to his older brother, Luke, and his twin sister, Savannah, Tom has survived childhood and adolescence traumas of emotional and physical parental abuse. A college graduate and churchgoing citizen, he appears to be the sole member to escape the inherent madness of his family lineage.

Tom introduces his parents, whose lives have been interrupted and scarred by poverty, family separations during World War II, and cycles of family dysfunction. His father, a shrimp boat operator whom Tom maintains would have been a splendid father had it not been for his violent treatment of his wife and children, was himself abused as a child. Tom describes his mother as a beautiful woman, talented at weaving words descriptive of natural beauty, but mum about a host of horrific family secrets.

The first chapter of this pain-filled family memoir begins like a Greek epic, in the middle of things, with a phone call to Tom from his mother. Savannah, who fled the family chaos and sought refuge and family anonymity in New York City immediately after her high school graduation, has attempted suicide and is hospitalized in Manhattan. Lila, Tom's mother, prevails upon her son to go to the rescue of his troubled sister. The subsequent chapters of the book leapfrog back and forth from this present summer in New York and the past of the Wingo siblings' tormented childhood as Tom, with the assistance of his sister's psychiatrist, begins to reconstruct the family history in search of the demons that have twisted Savannah's mind.

In one of the novel's early flashbacks, Tom and his older brother visit their sister in her new home of New York City, where they are introduced to Savannah's childhood demons, which she has failed to leave in her birthplace. This encounter further defines the characters in their young adult period. In a social Darwinian fashion, Savannah is selected as the family's psychotic scapegoat, burdened with the emotional pain and paralysis of the family secrets. Luke, their older brother, is selected to play the role of the lost child, a courageous and simple person destined to bear the brunt of the family damage. The role that Tom was destined to assume was the family hero, the consummate people pleaser, who as a teacher and coach in his own high school salvaged his family's respectability while unknowingly preserving the family secrets.

Like layers peeled from an onion, the family secrets are painfully revealed in each of the following chapters as Tom begins to reconstruct the Wingo family history. With a relentless and irresistible momentum, the saga of brutal secrets is examined and one after another of the demons that have tormented the family psyche are revealed, named, and discarded. Each new revelation provides another puzzle part that explains the complex passions, motivations, and calamities of the Wingo family.

Intervening subplots collectively demonstrate the impact of these discovered secrets on Tom's self-understanding. When Luke's political protest over the construction of a nuclear materials plant on the local river boils over into violence, Tom tries to intervene and end his brother's insane self-destructive behavior. He is unsuccessful; Luke is killed. Savannah expresses her grief in a memorial poem for her brother that she entitles "The Prince of Tides."

When Tom's wife leaves him for another man, Tom realizes that he has been the real source of his wife's alienation. He becomes involved in a tempestuous liaison with his sister's psychiatrist but later ends this affair and returns home to seek true family healing.

Analysis

Although this book was not intended exclusively for a young adult readership, it certainly addresses social issues, life themes, and personal struggles of compelling interest to this audience. *The Prince of Tides* joins a body of literature that young adult readers have found appealing which uses sea images and voyage metaphors to navigate the protagonist in the search for meaning to life's chaotic episodes and painful challenges. Pat Conroy, the author, is certainly conscious of this literary device. "Writing," he maintains, "is a journey for me, it builds like a coral reef."

Another appealing dimension of this book can be found in the way in which Conroy uses family history as a therapeutic tool for uncovering the devastating secrets that warp and paralyze the lives of children and adolescents who grow up amid familial dysfunction. Living in such "crazy-making" families forces young people to learn and live a fabricated family history built on lies, denial, and shame. These fictitious family stories burden young people with the baggage of guilt that they will carry into their adult years. If left secret and unpacked, this baggage can destroy lives, as it did for Luke Wingo, or marginalize lives, as it did for Lila and Savannah Wingo.

The Prince of Tides is a story in the tradition of the sweeping Southern saga. It provides another important lens for contrasting the South that was—tradition-filled and rooted—with the South that now is—fundamentally altered and ever-changing. It is a narrative of the Southern tradition with a vast sweep of melodramatic events intermingling despair and hope, damnation and redemption.

One final theme makes *The Prince of Tides* a compelling book for young adult readers: In the final analysis, it is a book about survival. Faced with a devastating childhood and adolescence, burdened with a cycle of dysfunctional living that pollutes and victimizes his early adult life, Tom Wingo survives to rewrite an alternative story for his future and the future of his family.

Critical Context

The Prince of Tides is seldom seen on a required reading list for young adult literature courses. It is not likely that this novel will replace classics such as J. D. Salinger's *The Catcher in the Rye* (1951), nor can one expect that Tom Wingo will become as recognizable a protagonist as Holden Caulfield in the young adult canon. This novel's potential to offend because of its blunt language, situations of violence, and sexual explicitness may limit the general appeal of *The Prince of Tides*.

Nevertheless, this book is and should be found on supplemental or optional reading lists from which young adults can make their own individual choices. *The Prince of Tides*, like its predecessors, *The Great Santini* (1976) and *The Lords of Discipline* (1980), has an impressive following among young readers. They overlook the epithets of "sloppy emotionalism," "saccharine sentimentalism," and "historical carpetbagging" leveled by less enthusiastic critics of Pat Conroy's autobiographical novels. Instead, many of the young readers who await each new Conroy novel are drawn by the themes of survival and self-discovery. They are attracted by the multilayered, baroque imagery that the author uses to capture the rapture of a moonrise and the haunting memory of a family tragedy. Conroy is a gifted storyteller who knows how to chronicle the wayward, ephemeral human passions. His manifold narrative gifts easily permit the reader to forgive occasional lapses into pedantic clichés and tear-jerking episodes. His novels of human survival are affirmations of life. When stories affirm life, young readers will seek them out.

Stanley J. Zehm

THE PRINCESS BRIDE

Author: William Goldman (1931-　　)
First published: 1973
Type of work: Novel
Type of plot: Fantasy
Time of work: An imaginary medieval time
Locale: Florin, a fictional kingdom
Subjects: Death, friendship, and love and romance
Recommended ages: 13-18

Buttercup and Westley, a couple united by true love, undergo many hardships and discover in fighting evil that life is not fair and that happiness is not guaranteed.

Principal characters:
　　BUTTERCUP, a beautiful milkmaid
　　WESTLEY, a farm boy
　　HUMPERDINCK, the prince of Florin
　　COUNT RUGEN, Humperdinck's evil henchman
　　INIGO MONTOYA, a Spanish swordsman
　　FEZZIK, a Turkish giant
　　VIZZINI, a Sicilian assassin

Form and Content

Buttercup, a beautiful milkmaid, falls in love with Westley, a farm boy, who sails away to seek his fortune. She sinks into grief when she hears that he has been captured by the Dread Pirate Roberts, who never leaves survivors. When Humperdinck, the prince of Florin—who cares only for hunting but demands a good-looking bride to bear his children—orders Buttercup to marry him, she refuses, claiming that she will never love again. Because Humperdinck does not seek love and the alternative is death, however, they become engaged.

Before the wedding, Buttercup is kidnapped by Vizzini, Inigo Montoya, and Fezzik, whom Humperdinck has paid to kill her and leave evidence that will incriminate the country of Guilder, Florin's enemy, so that Humperdinck can declare war. Fezzik is a powerful giant, and Inigo is the best swordsman in the world, having spent twenty years becoming a master fencer in order to find and kill the six-fingered nobleman who murdered his father. They are pursued, however, by a man in black, who follows them up the Cliffs of Insanity and then bests Inigo in a swordfight, Fezzik in a wrestling match, and Vizzini in a battle of wits.

Buttercup is now in the power of the man in black, who insults her faithlessness and greed. When she pushes him down a ravine, she discovers that it is Westley, who was merely testing her love for him.

Humperdinck and the evil Count Rugen are hunting them, so Buttercup and

Westley flee down the ravine into the Fire Swamp, where they are nearly killed by various dangers. Westley explains that he has actually been operating as the Dread Pirate Roberts for some time and that they will be safe when they reach his ship. When they escape the swamp, however, Humperdinck is waiting for them. Buttercup surrenders on the condition that the prince not harm Westley, who is promptly imprisoned in Humperdinck's Zoo of Death once her back is turned.

Plagued by guilt and nightmares, Buttercup realizes that she can marry only Westley. Humperdinck promises to send a message to learn whether Westley will return to her, but he secretly joins Count Rugen to torture Westley each night. He also plots to strangle Buttercup on their wedding night, again to frame Guilder for the murder.

Fezzik finds Inigo and reveals that the six-fingered man is Count Rugen. Inigo decides to find the man in black in order to devise a way into the castle so that they can rescue Buttercup and kill the count. That night, Buttercup realizes that Humperdinck never sent the message. When she mocks him as a coward, the enraged Humperdinck storms to the torture pit and kills Westley. Inigo and Fezzik sneak into the Zoo and find Westley's corpse, which they carry to Miracle Max, who resurrects him with a magic pill. During the wedding ceremony, Westley, Inigo, and Fezzik storm the castle and rout the guards. Inigo finds Rugen and kills him, Westley ties up the prince, and the protagonists escape on four white horses.

Analysis

William Goldman subtitles his novel *S. Morgenstern's Classic Tale of True Love and High Adventure: The "Good Parts" Version*, claiming himself merely the abridger of an earlier, lengthier satire by Simon Morgenstern. The first thirty pages explain that Goldman chose to abridge the story so that his ten-year-old son would enjoy it. Yet, this "introduction" merely disguises, and does not apologize for, Goldman's desire to spin a fun, fast-paced adventure. As the characters' names alone indicate, the work is also a parody of conventional European fairy tales.

What makes the novel unusually amusing is Goldman's constant interruption and annotation of the tale. The "introduction" portrays Goldman's (fictional) unpleasant wife and son, his beloved father, and his editors, and, throughout the novel, he inserts parenthetical remarks about them and their reactions to the story. "Morgenstern" includes his own parenthetical remarks, which are hilariously self-contradictory—for example, that the story occurs before Europe but after Paris, before the concept of glamour but after the invention of blue jeans. Goldman's comments occur in italic type and accompany typographical jokes such as a "SPLAT" that takes up half a page.

The result may leave unsophisticated readers confused about how much is serious "editorial commentary" and how much merely pranksterism. Goldman's most notable gag, which fooled many readers, consists of a complaint that Morgenstern does not depict the romantic reunion between Westley and Buttercup in the ravine and an explanation that Goldman has written his own. Goldman gives the address of Ballantine Books and encourages readers to write in and request the scene, adding that his publishers deserve the distribution expense because they have not spent much money promoting his books. *The Princess Bride*, then, is as much a satire on storytelling, the book industry, and the roles of author and audience as it is an adventure story. Young teenagers may not understand these jokes, while older readers may at least suspect that the joke is on them.

The adventures of Buttercup, Westley, and Inigo are told not in the high, romantic language that teenagers might expect from a tale of medieval times, but in a contemporary, New York-ish tone reminiscent of the wit of Woody Allen and the *Harvard Lampoon*. For example, at one point Buttercup thinks, "I'm a dead cookie." Miracle Max, likewise, seems totally out of place. Fairy tales frequently feature wizards, but they do not bicker with their wives and haggle over prices, as Max does. Young readers who enjoy sword-and-sorcery tales will find these anachronisms amusing, although they may not realize Goldman's cynical purpose is to sabotage fairy-tale conventions.

Goldman anticipates that a young audience may be confused by his unconventional treatment of the damsel-in-distress and revenge themes so common in fairy tales. He frequently interrupts moments of high drama and suspense to "remember" his own reaction when his father allegedly read the book to him. These interruptions take the form of an assurance that Buttercup will be rescued or a warning that Westley is about to die. He also reports that his father concealed the story's conclusion from the ten-year-old Goldman, because "Morgenstern's" ending implies that Humperdinck will recapture the protagonists and that Westley and Inigo will die of their wounds. Young readers who fear that the evil prince will prevail and that the heroes may die might wonder why Goldman speculates that even if Buttercup and Westley live, they may not live happily ever after: Fairy tales show that order and good are always restored, while Goldman's book teaches that real life is not fair, that friendship and love are the only comforts in a cruel, meaningless universe. These are important lessons for young people, since much juvenile fiction depicts an unrealistically happy ending.

Critical Context

The Princess Bride assumes a familiarity with fairy tales and folktales, which commonly depict sorcerers, beautiful princesses, evil noblemen, and young heroes on quests. In this tradition, evil is thwarted, rightful kings are restored to their thrones, and the hero marries the beautiful girl. William Goldman's book argues that things rarely work out so neatly in real life. He shows too that heroes do not possess endless strength or always make the right decisions. The admirable Inigo, for example, turns to drinking when he feels depressed, and Buttercup suffers terrible guilt over choosing to live without love rather than to die with Westley in the Fire Swamp. The book shows, however, that friendship can strengthen weakening resolve and rouse the courage to survive hard times. Inigo's dedication of his life to avenging his father's death is problematical, but his kindness and loyalty to the dim-witted Fezzik are poignantly portrayed and contribute to a depth in his character that the more conventionally heroic Westley lacks. Young readers will feel that these characters are more realistic than the one-dimensional figures of folktales, and they may take the next step of understanding that Goldman is contrasting fiction with real life.

Young people may not comprehend fully the parody of the novel, but they can enjoy the rapidly paced adventures and appreciate the "life is not fair" moral. The lasting appeal of Goldman's novels and screenplays arises from his consistent emphasis on the importance of friendship and loyalty. *The Princess Bride* has retained its popularity, especially after its 1987 adaptation as a successful film directed by Rob Reiner.

Fiona Kelleghan

THE PYRAMIDS OF EGYPT

Author: I. E. S. Edwards (1909-1996)
First published: 1947; illustrated
Type of work: History
Time of work: From approximately 2686 B.C. to A.D. 350
Locale: Upper and Lower Egypt
Subjects: Arts, death, religion, science, and the supernatural
Recommended ages: 13-18

This peerless classic on the Egyptian pyramids has gone through several revised editions to incorporate new archaeological findings and photographs that will fascinate young readers.

> *Principal personages:*
> ZOSER, the king of the Third Dynasty who built the first stone step
> pyramid at Saqqara near Cairo
> CHEOPS (KHUFU), the king who founded the Fourth Dynasty and built
> the Great Pyramid of Giza, marking the apogee of these monuments
> TUTANKHAMEN, the king of the Eighteenth Dynasty whose highly
> valued tomb was discovered by British Egyptologist Howard Carter
> in 1922 under a natural pyramid at Luxor, Upper Egypt
> NAPOLEON BONAPARTE, the French general and later emperor whose
> scholars surveyed the pyramids of Giza during his Egyptian
> campaign
> AUGUSTE MARIETTE, an important French Egyptologist who studied
> the pyramid of Chephren at Giza in 1853
> GASTON-CAMILLE-CHARLES MASPERO, an important French
> Egyptologist who, like Mariette, discovered structures in pyramid
> complexes

Form and Content

Against an outline of Egyptian dynastic history and an analysis of ancient Egyptian religion, I. E. S. Edwards, who once served as the keeper of Egyptian antiquities at the British Museum in London, traces the evolution of the royal tomb from the simple burial mound through the subsequent *mastaba* (bench), the step pyramid, and the familiar true pyramid, only found in Egypt. All of these are funerary monuments with wider religious and spiritual significance.

For those not conversant with pyramid complexes, Edwards describes the solid pile of stones, square in plan and with triangular sides, directly facing the points of the compass, sloping at varying angles of about fifty degrees, and meeting at the apex. By far the longest chapter of the eight in the book is devoted to the Giza group of pyramids, the largest and finest of their kind. A general description, often with illustrations, is offered of the buildings adjacent to the pyramid, which frequently include a chapel for the performance of religious rites as well as the smaller pyramids of the most important wives, lesser kin, and notables.

Historic, artistic, and religious presentations of pyramids defined by date, sites, size, and other details follow. The final chapter of *The Pyramids of Egypt* speculates on the probable methods of construction and on the purpose of the pyramids. The author covers the problems connected with the exact orientation of a pyramid on the four cardinal points, ensuring that its base forms a perfect square as nearly as possible, as well as several other difficulties associated with this type of construction. For the purpose underlying these monuments, Edwards suggests a material representation of the sun's rays and hence a means whereby dead kings (in the case of true pyramids) could ascend to heaven.

The book contains color plates, a larger set of black-and-white plates, and figures of various kinds, such as maps, plans, and sketches. The inclusion of representative artwork such as a color photograph of the ivory figure of King Cheops (or Khufu) displays ancient Egyptian art at its finest. A table of major Egyptian pyramids listing approximate date, location, dimensions, and name is especially helpful. An excellent bibliography with sources in English, French, and German—including works by scholars from what at the time were communist countries—follows. The book tantalizes young readers, inspiring them to probe further the mysteries inherent in things and individuals from long ago.

Analysis

Even though the author discusses entire pyramid complexes, there is never any question that the familiar triangular stone structure is the focus of his book. The everlasting human quest for immortality becomes evident from the ancient Egyptians' concern with the afterlife. Monarchs built pyramids in which their mummified bodies might be protected for eternity from human view and sacrilege. Unfortunately, the plunder of these burial sites over the centuries has removed much of their contents, and deterioration from the weather has added to the damage. Enough has been preserved, however, to make the pyramids an archaeological and artistic treasure trove.

A great amount of time, materials, and labor went into producing the pyramids and thus into preparations for the afterlife of the high and mighty. Pyramid complexes have also been found to contain the furniture, clothing, jewelry, boats, and other accessories—as well as the human and horse skeletons—of those destined to continue serving their royal masters after the kings' final exits.

Edwards points out the intricacies of the pyramid structures themselves by describing their entrances, passages, and chambers, including the sepulchral chambers. Among other things, he mentions the difficulty in balancing masses of stone on top of these excavated hollow places. The author manages to present a considerable amount of scholarly material over which he has complete mastery in simple, lay language. Furthermore, he adds some interesting details about individual monuments throughout the text, such as how huge blocks of rock were moved from the various quarries to the construction site. Some of these megaliths weighed as much as two hundred tons. The approximately two million smaller stones—for example, the two-and-a-half-ton stones used in the Great Pyramid of Cheops—involved the mobilization of at least a hundred thousand workers over many years working on a structure nearly five hundred feet high (more than one-third the height of the Empire State Building in New York). Water transport in a tricky, fast-flowing river with sand-bank obstructions was difficult enough. Moving such huge rocks on land without the use of wheeled vehicles—for reasons unknown, they were shunned by the Egyptians, who opted for sledges and ramps—was even more challenging.

By presenting such details, Edwards refrains from editorializing about the magnitude of the accomplishment. Neither does he feel the need to rhapsodize about why the most familiar of all Egyptian pyramids—the threesome at Giza—are among the world's ancient wonders. Nevertheless, there is a romantic quality to his observation that on a late winter afternoon, the sun at Giza (near Cairo) strikes down through a gap in the clouds at about the same angle as the slope of the Great Pyramid and that there is therefore a proximity between the immaterial prototype and its material replica. Seemingly, Edwards was not simply well-informed: His book was a labor of love.

The author cites the role of a substantial number of other Egyptologists and documents his information in footnotes and a bibliography. For example, he mentions the American James H. Breasted, whom Edwards quotes regarding the importance of pyramids to the ancient Egyptians. Edwards often notes the contributions of these other scholars in the discovery and explanation of the monuments. These individuals dedicated their lifetimes to these archaeological treasures. Thus, the reader comes to realize that the pyramids of Egypt have changed the lives of many people. These people are not only those involved in the complexes in some way—for example, it often was customary to bury a departed king's servants, whose lives were terminated by execution or suicide, beneath their master so that they could continue to serve him in the next life—but also those individuals who were captivated by the thought of rediscovering objects that had lain undisturbed for thousands of years.

This book, which was first published in 1947, may kindle the imagination of young readers about how, in the prehistoric past, people were so different but also so similar.

Critical Context

The body of Iorwerth Eiddon Stephen Edwards' publications covering the years 1939 to 1991, when the fourth revised edition of *The Pyramids of Egypt* appeared in paperback in Britain, has set standards in the field. The other works of this Cambridge-trained author and renowned Egyptologist—such as three publications on King Tutankhamen—have much to do with his seminal effort. While competing books in this relatively crowded field—for example, John D. Clare's *Pyramids of Ancient Egypt* (1992) or James Putnam's *Pyramid* (1994)—may dwell more on the details of daily life in ancient Egypt or other aspects, Edwards' book does not run the risk of being dethroned any more than the Egyptian pharaohs whose burial cenotaphs are discussed so absorbingly.

Young readers are interested in learning about piles of stone and their ancillary complexes because they are the relics of an ancient and fascinating era and as such have historical value. Studying the pyramids also opens doors to the understanding of the skill and dedication of ancient people working with primitive tools and ingredients and yet managing to build these structures of size and beauty, often containing the well-preserved remains of royalty who died ages ago. To the extent that humans are the sum total of everything that has gone before, getting into the minds of these creative ancient people through their monuments, artifacts, customs, beliefs, and rituals may help modern people understand themselves better.

Peter B. Heller

QUEENIE PEAVY

Author: Robert Burch (1925-   )
First published: 1966; illustrated
Type of work: Novel
Type of plot: Domestic realism and social realism
Time of work: The 1930's
Locale: Cotton Junction, a small town in Georgia
Subjects: Coming-of-age, education, emotions, family, and social issues
Recommended ages: 10-13

Queenie Peavy finally faces the truth about her father, a convict, as well as about her own delinquent behavior, and realizes that life can be more rewarding when one accepts it as it really is, not as one wishes that it could be.

> *Principal characters:*
> QUEENIE PEAVY, an intelligent and talented thirteen-year-old whose loyalty to her incarcerated father is interfering with her ability to choose right from wrong in her own life
> MR. PEAVY, Queenie's father, a cold, vindictive, and selfish man who is not the father that Queenie imagines him to be
> MR. HANLEY, the school principal with fatherly traits deserving of Queenie's attention
> CRAVEY MASON, the school bully and Queenie's primary tormentor
> AVIS CORRY, a five-year-old African American girl who lives near Queenie and who adores her
> DOVER CORRY, Avis' eight-year-old brother, who, along with Avis, encourages Queenie to be herself
> MARTHA MULLINS, known as "Little Mother," Queenie's best friend

Form and Content

Robert Burch creates a portrait of a young girl in a small rural town in Georgia during the Great Depression. *Queenie Peavy* is the story of an adolescent who loves her father, who is an inmate at the penitentiary in Atlanta, Georgia. Cravey Mason, the school bully, leads the other children as they tease and torment Queenie about her father being on the chain gang. Queenie cannot bear for the children to make fun of her father's situation, and she retaliates by throwing rocks at the children or by playing tricks on them. She goes to great extremes to defend her father's honor whenever Cravey Mason taunts her. On one occasion, Queenie causes him to break his leg. She is constantly at odds with the people who love her and who want to see her change her delinquent behavior. It takes the threat of a possible term at a reformatory school and the realization that her view of her father is not entirely accurate for Queenie to confront the internal and external conflicts occurring in her life.

Written in third-person narration, the story introduces Queenie in the first sentence; Burch describes her as "the only girl in Cotton Junction who could chew tobacco." As the story progresses, Queenie and the other characters are quickly and clearly developed through their actions and dialogue. The setting is described by the narrator, but from Queenie's point of view. It is through these descriptions of her thoughts that readers begin to suspect that Queenie's perception of her father is a contradiction to the selfish, impulsive, and uncaring Mr. Peavy. Queenie's home is a two-room house with an outdoor toilet. She sleeps in the kitchen on a cot. The yard is grown up in weeds and the front porch is in need of repair. Queenie tells herself that if her father were there, the porch would be fixed and they could enter the house by the front door. The narrator continues where Queenie stops, however, by informing readers that Mr. Peavy could have prevented the decay of the porch, as it was in need of repair before he left.

When Queenie finally faces the truth about her father, she realizes that he is a different man from the one she wants him to be. Her loyalty to her father has caused unnecessary grief for her. All along, she knew the truth, but she refused to accept it. Facing the truth about her father, herself, and life, Queenie begins a new adventure as a young adult who thinks before acting—and, even then, acting only wisely.

Jerry Lazare provides a few pen-and-ink illustrations throughout the original text, as well as for the cover. In the paperback versions, however, only the cover offers an illustration, one created by another artist.

Analysis

Growing from adolescence into adulthood involves many hard lessons. *Queenie Peavy*, although considered an example of regional fiction, is an excellent novel for young people reaching adolescence. Through Queenie's actions, readers are introduced to conflicts, both internal and external, often encountered in life: person against person, person against society, and person against self.

Queenie's internal conflict involving person against person develops as she struggles with her beliefs about her father. She imagines him to be a loving, caring, and warm human being. It is this imagined father to whom she pledges her fierce loyalty, no matter what personal price she has to pay. When her father comes home, Queenie treats him as if he were a king. She chops firewood, rushes home after school, and tip-toes quietly through the house as she does the chores that she has assumed for her father while he was away in prison. The irony of this relationship is that while Mr. Peavy is the one person who hurts Queenie the most, he is also the person who helps her the most. It is when she realizes that he is not the father she wanted him to be, nor the imagined father that she created in her mind, that Queenie begins to change. Had he not come home, Queenie may never have realized how much she was hurting only herself, or at least not in time to prevent her life from being one of delinquency and reform schools, always "in the shadow of the jail."

Burch's inclusion of the African American Corry family as the Peavys' closest neighbors serves a dual purpose. Queenie's relationship with them provides readers with a true picture of Queenie's personality. She is kind, loving, and creative, and she is a hard worker. It also portrays the relationships developed over time between white and black people in the South. In the 1930's, they sometimes worked together and were neighborly, but they did not attend school together. Burch does not mention segregation, instead allowing readers to come to that realization themselves: Dover Corry is old enough to go to school but is never mentioned when the setting is the school or its playground.

Burch, through *Queenie Peavy*, allows adolescent readers to realize that growing up means learning about many things: respecting authority, handling problems, using morality as a guide, and accepting one's self even when rejection by others hurts so much. Perhaps the most difficult of these themes is the acceptance of one's self. Queenie, after resisting the advice of Mr. Hanley, her school principal, the judge, her teachers, and her best friend, Little Mother, finally realizes that she is not the person she tried to be as she defended her father's honor. She begins to listen to her own inner voice, and she vows to do better. She almost regresses when her mother tells her that her father has been sent back to prison. Picking up a handful of stones, she is tempted to renew her old habits. She even throws some at a fence post and minor targets. When she reaches the church and looks at the remaining unbroken window, she throws back her arm, ready to fire the last stone.

It is at this point that Queenie listens to all the advice from the past. She returns the stone to its "friends," the other stones on the ground. Burch makes an important, although implied, statement to young readers. He writes that Queenie notices that the stone looked just like the others, except that its "jagged edges reflected more sunlight." Young readers know that even when people do things that are wrong, they can change and be stronger for it. The best part is that they will still be loved by their friends and their family. Unconditional love, which is so important for young people to have in their lives, exists—even for the ones who have "jagged edges."

Critical Context

Queenie is a girl ahead of her time. *Queenie Peavy*, written during a time when juvenile delinquency was of minor concern to society, offered adolescent readers the opportunity to realize what might happen if one continued to be a juvenile delinquent. By the late twentieth century, the increase in juvenile delinquency had become a major concern in American society, especially for educators. Juvenile delinquents were being sentenced as adult offenders because of the serious nature of their crimes, and educators were being asked to teach in classrooms where these criminals were students. As a result, there was an increase in the number of books written about juvenile delinquents.

Published in 1966, *Queenie Peavy* was immediately recognized as a book of literary merit by a number of critics. In 1966, it received the Child Study Association of America Children's Book Award as the best book that dealt realistically with a problem of the contemporary world. In 1967, the Jane Addams Book Award, given for books exploring the theme of brotherhood and displaying literary merit, was given to

Queenie Peavy. The children of Georgia chose the book as their favorite with the Georgia's Children's Book Award in 1971. In 1974, it won the George G. Stone Center for Children's Books Award. Virginia Haviland included the novel in *The Best of Children's Books* (1981). Finally, in 1986, the novel earned the Phoenix Award from the Children's Literature Association; this award recognized books of literary merit published for children twenty years before that had not received a major award. As with all classics, *Queenie Peavy*, a beautifully written book, has stood the test of time.

Frances Agnes Johnson

THE RAILWAY CHILDREN

Author: E. Nesbit (1858-1924)
First published: 1906 (serialized 1905-1906)
Type of work: Novel
Type of plot: Domestic realism
Time of work: The early 1900's
Locale: A country house, village, and railway station in England
Subjects: Coming-of-age, family, and social issues
Recommended ages: 10-13

After their father is sent away, Roberta, Peter, and Phyllis move to the country, where they have a series of adventures at the railroad tracks and station and begin to grow up.

>*Principal characters:*
>ROBERTA (BOBBIE), a twelve-year-old who tries to help out her mother and take care of her younger siblings
>PETER, Bobbie's ten-year-old brother
>PHYLLIS, the youngest child
>MOTHER, who supports the children by writing
>ALBERT PERKS, the porter at the railway station
>THE OLD GENTLEMAN, a man who travels on the railway and befriends the children
>DR. FORREST, the village physician

Form and Content

The first chapter of *The Railway Children* begins by establishing Bobbie, Peter, and Phyllis as ordinary middle-class children in Edwardian England, but such normalcy quickly vanishes when Father mysteriously leaves home. Father's disappearance is the key problem of the novel and the force behind Bobbie's growing up, and the book concludes with his return to the family. The primary events, however, are the adventures that the children have after moving with their mother to a country house near the railroad tracks.

Besides having their father absent and moving to a new place, the children must also cope with changing economic conditions; Mother must conserve both food and coal. The children's scrapes and misadventures in the first part of the book are a result of their recent poverty. One time, Peter steals coal from the railway station and is caught; the station master forgives him, but Peter learns both shame and responsibility. When Mother falls ill and the children worry that they cannot afford the food that the doctor says she needs, they ask for help from the old gentleman whom they wave to every morning when his train goes by. When Mother recovers and learns what they have done, she is angry and tells them never to ask strangers for assistance.

Their later adventures, however, revolve around helping others. Their mother takes in a Russian political prisoner and writer who has escaped to England in order to look for his family, and Bobbie, trusting in the old gentleman (now revealed as a railway director) to help once more, asks him to find the man's family. The old gentleman succeeds and shows great admiration and respect for the children's mother. The children also manage to avert a train accident after a landslide has covered the tracks; provide a birthday party for the railway porter, Albert Perks; rescue a baby and dog from a burning barge on the canal; and help a boy named Jim who has broken his leg in the railway tunnel.

Eventually, Bobbie stumbles on an old newspaper article about her father and learns that he has been sentenced to hard labor for treason. Distraught, she speaks to her mother and learns that her father has been framed but that nothing can be done. They keep his true situation a secret from Peter and Phyllis, but Bobbie writes once more to the old gentleman, asking him to help clear her father. He turns out to be Jim's grandfather, and he not only restores the family's economic standing but also assures Bobbie that he has always had doubts about her father's case and will do what he can. Several weeks later, their father is freed and returns to the family.

Analysis

The Railway Children is a straightforward narrative of what happens when a family is disrupted by the absence of one of its members, and E. Nesbit uses the disruption to examine the responsibilities that people have to one another and themselves within the English class structure. The book conveys the basic sense that people and the world are largely good; although the children's father has been wrongfully imprisoned, justice does prevail in the end. Dr. Forrest appears to treat family members for a minimal fee, if any, although he is poor himself. The children avert tragedy several times and are rewarded for it with the friendship of the rich old gentleman and a poor barge worker, among others. When they do wrong, they are forgiven—and learn from their mistakes.

This theme of goodness, however, is closely tied to self-sufficiency. While Nesbit makes it clear that the children can and should help others, they are not expected to receive charity themselves. Bobbie's entrance into the adult world is marked by a transition from asking for help to learning to help herself and others. At the beginning of the novel, she joins in asking the old gentleman for food and pleads with Dr. Forrest about his fees. By the end of the novel, she is capable not only of keeping her father's condition a secret from the other two children but also of sitting in a dark railway tunnel and comforting the injured Jim. The need for self-sufficiency rather than charity becomes clear when Mother is upset about the children asking the old gentleman for food, and Nesbit reinforces the theme when Perks is greatly offended at his birthday party because he thinks that he is receiving charity that he does not need. He comes to understand, however, that people gave gifts out of genuine friendship for him, what the village clergyman calls "loving-kindness" and what Nesbit seems to value most highly.

The kind of assistance that the adults provide to the children and one another is based on such loving-kindness, rather than the charity of an upper class to a lower class; in the case of the Russian prisoner, for example, Mother takes care of him partly because she respects his writing and partly because she compares him to her own wrongfully imprisoned husband. The old gentleman provides financial assistance in return for Mother nursing his grandson. The release of the children's father comes about through the efforts of the old gentleman, but such efforts have been spurred on by Bobbie's friendship with him. Nesbit suggests that loving-kindness and friendship cross economic lines.

The great accomplishment of the novel, however, is to present these themes of loving-kindness and self-sufficiency without preaching. Bobbie, who is taking on more responsibility and beginning to understand that the adult world is difficult and painful, can still quarrel with Peter only a few days after Mother has praised them for not quarreling. The children grumble and struggle with their schoolwork when lessons resume. The girls say nasty things about boys, and Peter disdains the girls. While the children are essentially good and their mother seems almost unbelievably perfect, the characters are still capable of sharp words and mistakes.

Nesbit also briefly raises the issue of gender roles. Before Father is taken away, he declares that girls can do anything that boys can, and Mother supports herself and the children through writing. Although the children have stereotyped views of marriage and Dr. Forrest at one point tells Peter that girls need to be protected so that they can have babies, both Bobbie and Mother are strong, capable, and intelligent. When the old gentleman provides money for Mother to nurse his grandson and hints that, because he is trying to free Father, she may not have to write anymore, Mother quickly responds that she loves writing, an unusual attitude for women of that era. Nesbit's theme of self-sufficiency in place of dependency is essentially a humanist one, applying to both men and women.

Critical Context

Edith Nesbit was recognized as an excellent writer for children during her lifetime and remains an important figure in children's literature. While her adult characters are generally offstage or not well developed, her children are realistic and believable. They argue with one another, make mistakes, and struggle to be good without being priggish or too virtuous; Nesbit's moral lessons are always accompanied by humor.

The Railway Children is typical of her work in its episodic structure, occasional sibling rivalry, and happy ending. Many of her other books, however, are more fantastical than *The Railway Children*. In *Five Children and It* (1902) and its sequels, *The Phoenix and the Carpet* (1904) and *The Secret of the Amulet* (1906), the children's adventures occur through magic, such as the wishes that almost never turn out the way the children want them to in *Five Children and It*. Magic provides an opportunity for the children to learn about the world and themselves. Nesbit also uses it occasionally to make points about the English social order; in *The Secret of the Amulet*, the Queen of Babylon declares that her slaves are better off than the English working class.

Nesbit's work has endured not only because of its humor and realistic representations of children but also because of its way of engaging the reader with complex questions about human relationships and responsibilities.

Elisabeth Anne Leonard

A RAISIN IN THE SUN

Author: Lorraine Hansberry (1930-1965)
First presented: 1959
First published: 1959
Type of work: Drama
Type of plot: Social realism
Time of work: The 1950's
Locale: Chicago
Subjects: Family, gender roles, race and ethnicity, and social issues
Recommended ages: 15-18

> *As the members of the Younger family debate the best way in which to invest the proceeds from a $10,000 life insurance policy, the audience gains an insight into the tensions in the African American community at the start of the Civil Rights movement.*

>   *Principal characters:*
>   LENA YOUNGER, a retired domestic and the matriarch of an extended
>   African American family
>   WALTER, her son
>   RUTH, Walter's wife
>   BENEATHA, Walter's sister
>   TRAVIS, Walter and Ruth's son
>   JOSEPH ASAGAI, a Nigerian student, Beneatha's suitor
>   GEORGE MURCHISON, a student, Beneatha's suitor
>   BOBO, Walter's friend
>   MR. LINDER, a representative from a suburban homeowners' association

Form and Content

A Raisin in the Sun is a three-act play set entirely in the Younger family's Chicago tenement apartment. As the play opens, Walter Younger, Sr., referred to as "Big Walter," has recently died, leaving his widow, Lena, a life insurance policy worth $10,000. Lena wants to use the money as a down payment on a house in the suburbs so that her family can leave its crowded, shabby apartment. Lena's son, Walter, wants to invest the money in a liquor store so that he can quit his job as a rich white man's chauffeur and become his own boss. Beneatha, Walter's younger sister, a college student, wants to use part of the money to pay for her medical school tuition. Ruth, Walter's pregnant wife, sides with Lena.

The debate over how to spend the insurance money threatens to destroy the Younger family. Walter insults his sister by telling her to forget about medical school and become a nurse or get married like other women. Lena expresses misgivings about Walter's plan to invest in the liquor business, and he, in turn, accuses his mother of destroying his dream of becoming a successful businessman and providing for his family. When Lena refuses to give Walter the $10,000 that he needs for his investment, he stops working and starts drinking heavily. Ruth considers having an abortion because she does not want to add another family member to the Youngers' crowded apartment.

Watching her family unravel, Lena attempts a compromise that she hopes will satisfy everyone. She puts $3,500 down on a single-family home in Clybourne Park, an all-white suburban neighborhood, and hands Walter the rest of the money, ordering him to deposit $3,000 in a bank account earmarked for Beneatha's medical school tuition and allowing him to invest the remaining $3,500 as he sees fit.

Initially, Lena's compromise appeases all parties, but disaster strikes the Youngers a few weeks later, as the family is packing for its move to Clybourne Park. Walter's friend, Bobo, arrives and informs Walter that their partner in the liquor store business has taken Walter's money—including Beneatha's tuition money—and skipped town. Humiliated, Walter announces that the family will recoup some of its lost money by selling its house to the Clybourne Park Improvement Association, whose representative, Mr. Linder, has made an offer to buy the Youngers' property at a profit in an effort to keep a black family from integrating an all-white neighborhood.

At the end of act 2, as the Youngers glumly await Mr. Linder's arrival to close the deal, the family is once again at the point of disintegration. Beneatha calls Walter a "toothless rat" for losing the family's money and capitulating to Mr. Linder. Lena chastises Beneatha and offers sympathetic words for her son, but Walter seems a defeated man. When Linder arrives, however, Walter undergoes a dramatic change. Standing behind his son, Travis, whom Lena has ordered to be present when the sale of the home is made, Walter calmly explains to Linder that his family has decided to occupy its new home. Walter speaks eloquently of his father's hard work and his family's pride. He introduces Beneatha as a future doctor and proudly introduces Travis as the sixth generation of Youngers in the United States.

In the short final act, the moving men have arrived, and the Youngers are proudly departing for Clybourne Park, optimistically looking forward to living in their new home.

Analysis

Lorraine Hansberry's play introduces young readers to crucial issues in the African American community: the fragmentation of the family, the black male's quest for manhood, and the problems associated with integration. Lena is the prototypical African American matriarch who struggles to hold her family together in the face of poverty and discrimination. Although Walter's eloquent speech to Mr. Linder at the end of act 2 saves the Youngers from disgrace, Lena is the play's moral center, urging the members of her extended family to end their quarreling, accept their responsibilities, and love one another.

Walter's quest for manhood is another key theme in Hansberry's drama. Walter wants to replace Big Walter as the head of the Younger family, but he is barely able to support the Youngers on his chauffeur's wages. He also shows himself to be irresponsible with money, and he has a tendency to walk away or turn to drink when family problems arise. Although he frequently falters along the way, Walter demonstrates by the end of the play that he can replace his deceased father as the head of the family. In the play's final scene, Lena tells Ruth that Walter "finally come into his manhood today . . . like a rainbow after the rain." Hansberry wants the audience to believe that Walter's change is both significant and permanent: He has become a man.

Equally absorbing is Hansberry's dramatization of Beneatha's quest for womanhood. She is a young woman attempting to break away from the pattern set by the other Younger women, Lena and Ruth. They are wives, mothers, and maids; Beneatha is in college and aspires to become a physician, a virtually unattainable occupation for African American women of the 1950's. During the play, she is pursued by two suitors who try to steer her in their own directions: George Murchison, the son of a wealthy African American businessman, and Joseph Asagai, a Nigerian student studying in the United States. Beneatha rejects the option of becoming the well-to-do wife of George, and, although she is fascinated by the lost African culture that Asagai represents, she will probably remain independent and go in her own direction.

Hansberry's play gives young adult readers insights into the African American community at the beginning of the Civil Rights movement. At the time of the play, the doors of opportunity, if not open, are at least unlocked for African Americans. Walter can dream of becoming an entrepreneur. Beneatha can hope to become a doctor. Lena can purchase a house in the suburbs. Nevertheless, as the bitter arguments among Lena, Walter, and Beneatha suggest, the age of new opportunities creates problems in the Younger family, problems that reflect the tensions in the African American community at the commencement of the Civil Rights movement. Moreover, Hansberry suggests that many of the old prejudices persist, as evidenced by Mr. Linder's attempt to keep an African American family out of his neighborhood.

The play's title comes from a poem by Langston Hughes entitled "Harlem": "What happens to a dream deferred?/ Does it dry up/ Like a raisin in the sun?/ Maybe it just sags/ Like a heavy load./ *Or does it explode?*" The Younger family's dream of breaking out of poverty and enjoying the fruits of American society has been deferred for many years. Big Walter's insurance policy presents an opportunity for the Youngers' dream to become a reality. Through the Youngers, Hansberry asks how African Americans will deal with the opportunities confronting them in the post-World War II years. Will those deferred dreams dry up? Will they explode in frustration and anger? In *A Raisin in the Sun*, the playwright seems to suggest that those deferred dreams at last can be fulfilled, although the struggle to fulfill them will be difficult.

Critical Context

A Raisin in the Sun holds an important place in the history of African American drama. It was the first play by an African American woman to be produced on Broadway. It enjoyed a successful run, won the prestigious Drama Critics' Circle Award, and is still frequently performed in regional and university theaters. Two quality film versions of the play have been produced, the first in 1961 with Sidney

Poitier (who starred in the original Broadway production) as Walter and a second in 1989 (an American Playhouse production filmed for television) with Danny Glover in that role. The play has been enjoyed by audiences of all races and age groups. It is frequently included in literature anthologies used in high school and college courses.

Unfortunately, Lorraine Hansberry never duplicated the success that she achieved with *A Raisin in the Sun*. A handful of subsequent plays received mixed reviews and are rarely performed, and Hansberry died of cancer before her thirty-fifth birthday. Nevertheless, the success of *A Raisin in the Sun* opened theater doors to other African American playwrights such as James Baldwin, LeRoi Jones, Ed Bullins, and Ntozake Shange.

James Tackach

RAMS, ROMS, AND ROBOTS
The Inside Story of Computers

Authors: James Jespersen (1934-   ) and Jane Fitz-Randolph (1915-   )
First published: 1984; illustrated
Type of work: Science
Subjects: Education, jobs and work, and science
Recommended ages: 10-15

The authors discuss the history of computers, those individuals who contributed to their evolution, and possible developments in this field in the future.

Form and Content

The first half of *RAMs, ROMs, and Robots: The Inside Story of Computers* is a discussion of the historical development of computers and the people who aided in that development. James Jespersen and Jane Fitz-Randolph begin their story of computers by explaining how and why people count items in order to reveal the reasons for building calculating machines. They start with simple stories of counting farm animals, bushels of food, warriors, and seasons. The authors then describe one of the earliest computing devices—the arrangement of massive stones known as Stonehenge. The overview in chapter 1 ends with an explanation of how analog devices influenced computer development and of the need for new ideas.

Chapters 2 through 5 continue the history of computers. Young readers are introduced to some of the major figures who directly influenced the construction of modern computers. For example, the authors present a brief biographical sketch of Charles Babbage, who invented the "Analytical Engine." Included in the sketch is an anecdote about Babbage correcting two lines written by the poet Alfred, Lord Tennyson, because they were not mathematically sound. The authors provide information about the Analytical Engine and how its four parts—the store, mill, bus, and the input/output—are related to modern computers. Other contributors to computer development are discussed in these chapters: Ada Lovelace, who wrote a detailed account of the Analytical Engine and for whom the programming language ADA is named; Herman Hollerith, who conceived of the idea to use punch cards to aid in calculations and who was one of the founders of International Business Machines (IBM) Corporation; Alan Turing, who created the Universal Turing Machine, which was a forerunner to intelligent computers; John von Neumann, who was the first to propose storing programs as digital instructions in the computer's memory; and J. Presper Eckert and John W. Mauchly, who built the Electronic Numerical Integrator and Calculator (ENIAC), the predecessor to the all-electronic digital computer.

Chapters 6 and 7 lead the reader through a discussion of how computers work and how they interpret data. An example of a simple program is used, along with tables to help the reader visualize the process. Chapter 8 explains the applications of computers and the way in which they can help assimilate information. In chapter 9, the limitations and problems associated with computer use are evaluated. Chapter 10 discusses how computers talk through the examples of instructional toys (such as spelling programs) and games (such as electronic football). The authors discuss how computers can have "voices" and the problems that are encountered in trying to make these computer voices more realistic.

Chapter 11 offers a short discussion about robots and their uses. Chapter 12 reviews the limitations of modern computers, and chapters 13 and 14 examine the possibilities for future computers. A glossary of key terms and an index help the reader understand and find information in the book.

Analysis

RAMs, ROMs, and Robots can be read easily by young people. Jespersen and Fitz-Randolph use many analogies to help readers understand complex concepts involving computer language, processes, and uses. For example, the authors explain how a computer stores and controls information by using the analogy of a library. The analogy begins simply by comparing a computer to the card catalog in the library in the way that it keeps track of information. The analogy becomes more complex as the computer is also likened not only to the books in the library but also to an index containing all the words in all the books in the library.

The information that the book provides about the early contributors to computer development is both enlightening and entertaining. Charles Baggage becomes more than a name to remember; the authors portray him as a real person who had both a genius for understanding mathematics and the inability to appreciate the meaning behind Tennyson's poem because he could see only the inaccuracy of the computation. In the same way, the authors paint a vivid picture of Alan Turing as a small boy, uniquely solving a problem that caused his bicycle chain to slip. These anecdotes help young readers identify with these important people.

In their discussion about the inner workings of the computer and how it interprets data, the authors use uncomplicated language and illustrations to help young people comprehend a sample program. Readers come away with an appreciation for the difficulty in formulating commands for programs without having to be expert in computer languages. The authors give a clear explanation of the problems that can occur in writing a computer program and how complex the solutions can become.

The authors' discussion of robots, however, is not as clear and complete as other parts of the book. Although the information is not erroneous, several important details about robots and robotics are missing: Much of the history of robots is not given, the simplistic overview of how a robot interprets data may lead readers to believe that all robots work in the same way, and uses for robots are not detailed. The chapter does indicate some of the problems in designing and using robots, especially in industry.

The last part of the book attempts to bring together the information already presented and new concepts. Again, the authors use illustrations and analogies to help make their information clear. Younger readers may have difficulty in understanding some of the concepts in the last section. The discussion on networking is not as clear as an earlier discussion about the processing of information. Readers may become confused by the large numbers, such as "100 trillion-trillion-trillion-trillion years"; they may understand that the number is large, but they may not comprehend how much time the number represents.

The next chapter suggests what may be in the future for computers. Using Albert Einstein's equation "$E = mc^2$," the authors lead young readers through a discussion on the ways in which nature and natural laws affect and limit a computer's ability to process information. Examples of the Cray-1 and the Cray-2 are used to explain how computers can process information quickly and the necessity of operating computers at low temperatures. The authors then jump to how information is stored both on a disk and using holographic images. These chapters give a simplistic overview of a complex problem, and readers may have to investigate other sources for clarification.

The last chapter considers artificial intelligence. Once again, the authors use analogies to help the reader understand the difference between intelligence and artificial intelligence. Examples of the ways in which computers work and how they could work are discussed, but the authors refrain from offering specific suggestions. Instead, readers are encouraged to use their imaginations and to discover their own possibilities for computers.

The glossary is useful in helping readers define difficult or puzzling terms, and the index is easy to use for readers in this age group. *RAMs, ROMs, and Robots* is a good source for young people who are interested in how and why computers work.

Critical Context

RAMs, ROMs, and Robots, although somewhat dated in its information on the future of computers, is an important book for young readers. Too often, books about computers deal with one specific aspect, launch into details about applications, or use language that the young reader has difficulty understanding. In addition, many computer books omit information concerning the history of computer development.

Young people will have an interest in this book for three main reasons. First, while many of them are familiar with or even expert in using computers to help them calculate difficult problems or write papers and reports, most lack an appreciation for the history behind the development of modern computers, a basic understanding of how a computer processes information or carries out commands, and knowledge about solving simple command errors; James Jespersen and Jane Fitz-Randolph provide overviews of these areas. Second, after reading the book, young readers will be more familiar with why a computer does what it does and how better to utilize it as a tool.

A third reason that young people will want to read *RAMs, ROMs, and Robots* is that it will encourage them to discover future ways to use computers and robots. The authors give examples of ways in which technology is changing and how that change could affect computers in the future. Some of their examples from the mid-1980's were already being applied a decade later.

Linda Runyon

RATS, LICE, AND HISTORY

Author: Hans Zinsser (1878-1940)
First published: 1935
Type of work: History
Time of work: From antiquity to the 1930's
Locale: Worldwide
Subjects: Health and illness, nature, and science
Recommended ages: 15-18

Occurring in epidemic and endemic forms transmitted in two different ways, typhus fever resisted the efforts of scientists to map its life cycle fully until the early twentieth century.

> *Principal personages:*
> TYPHUS FEVER, a disease second only to bubonic plague in the deadliness of its epidemics, referred to variously as tabardillo, febris petechialis, jayl fever, ship fever, and famine fever, among other names
> THE COMMON LOUSE (*Pediculus humanus*), a parasite of human beings and a known host of the virus that causes typhus
> THE BLACK RAT (*Rattus rattus*), a known host of both bubonic plague and typhus

Form and Content

The chief protagonist of this pseudo-biography—subtitled *Being a Study in Biography, Which, After Twelve Preliminary Chapters Indispensable for the Preparation of the Lay Reader, Deals with the Life History of Typhus Fever*—is a deadly disease against which humans have struggled helplessly for centuries. Supporting roles are played by familiar enemies such as smallpox, bubonic plague, tuberculosis, and influenza, as well as by historical curiosities such as the mysterious English sweating fever. Several classes of people are pitted against these inhuman foes: early medical historians who observed the ravages of diseases at first hand and recorded descriptions of what they could not understand or control; scientific researchers who gradually tracked diseases to their hiding places in insects and rodents, accumulating knowledge sometimes at the cost of their own lives; and untold millions of victims.

Hans Zinsser begins *Rats, Lice, and History* by exploring such issues as the theory and practice of biographical writing in his day and the relationship between art and science in order to prepare the way for his own biography of the life cycle of a disease organism and the history of its impact on human affairs. He views typhus fever as a "protoplasmic continuity" and generally avoids anthropomorphism except for the sake of dry, tongue-in-cheek humor. After a short, digressive chapter critical of modernist poetry, he reviews the necessary background information on parasitism, disease-causing bacteria and viruses, and evolutionary adaptation in two further chapters, generally displaying a broad erudition that extends far beyond the medical field. He digresses again with a lengthy history of infectious disease, devoting two chapters to the ancient world and one to more recent military history, concluding that infectious diseases are more important than generals in determining the victor in wars. The common louse requires two chapters, since it is an alternative host of the virus that causes typhus and a vector for transmitting the disease to humans. Rats, mice, and fleas share a single chapter; they are important because they harbor the epidemic form of typhus that is capable of routing armies and toppling empires.

After Zinsser has explained the role played by rats and lice in shaping the course of human history, he introduces the actual subject of his biography, typhus fever, in chapter 12 and describes every aspect of its existence in the last five chapters of the book. The thorough background provided by the earlier chapters makes this examination highly accessible: The reader is by now familiar with the key episodes in the history of epidemics, with the importance of insect and rodent population demographics, and with the subtle transformations of which disease organisms are capable through evolutionary adaptation. The significance of Zinsser's own research to distinguish the endemic strain of typhus (passed from human to human by lice) from the epidemic strain (passed from rats to humans by fleas) becomes apparent: Thanks to this knowledge of its complete life cycle, the disease can be controlled and humans are no longer at its mercy.

Analysis

Zinsser was a working scientist and a distinguished professor of bacteriology at the time that he wrote *Rats, Lice, and History*; within a year of publishing this book, he was the first researcher to isolate the typhus germ, and in the year before his death he produced a vaccine against the disease for humans. The book, however, is not so much his own personal story as it is the story of the larger human struggle against infectious diseases.

Although the title page, chapter headings, and repeated authorial comments refer to *Rats, Lice, and History* as a biography, it is an unusual book. The author is decidedly opinionated; however, his wit generally blunts the edge of his criticisms. His interests are highly diversified, and, in the relaxed environment of a book for general readers, he takes up several topics that are tangential to his subject or even completely unrelated to it. Zinsser is aware that he is breaking the unwritten rules of academic writing and perhaps even risking his own reputation as a bacteriologist by crossing into the territory of literature, history, biography, and criticism. He defends his unorthodox approach by claiming that "this book is a protest against the American attitude which tends to insist that a specialist should have no interests beyond his chosen field" and that "art and sciences have much in common and both may profit by mutual appraisal."

In spite of what may seem to be a whimsical approach to disease and to medical history, Zinsser's explicit goal is to write a genuinely scientific book about infectious disease that addresses generally well-educated readers rather than specialists. Since he also wishes to avoid popularizing his subject by oversimplifying or sensationalizing it, he provides detailed explanations, quotations from established authorities, and careful reasoning where the facts are uncertain. He assumes a high level of sophistication in his readers and frequently does not provide translations of short passages in Latin, German, and French, although he does translate classical Greek phrases and Spanish passages. Readers not conversant with medical terminology may want to keep a specialized dictionary at hand in order to appreciate sentences such as this one, from a discussion of literature: "There is no arsphenamin for the psychic treponema."

Since Zinsser allows himself to comment on every aspect of life that intersects the existence of typhus fever, *Rats, Lice, and History* becomes an indirect history of his own lifetime and a commentary on the follies that continue to threaten human well-being. World War I figures prominently in his criticisms, as does the increasing nationalism occurring in Europe at the time that he was writing, as Adolf Hitler and other dictators rose to power. Zinsser saw the devastation of World War I in person, since he served in the Red Cross and in the U.S. Army as a specialist in modern sanitation. His references to recent and contemporary events, however, are frequently highly allusive rather than expository. Anyone not familiar with the politics and the poetics of the early twentieth century will find his references to events in his own lifetime to be obscure.

Rats, Lice, and History would be of great value to a young adult who has ambitions of attending medical school or doing research in microbiology. It would also be relevant to anyone interested in scientific history and historiography. Much of the science has been superseded by more recent work, but the idiosyncrasies of how Zinsser goes about telling the story of typhus as it was known up to 1934 make the book appealing for more than simply factual reasons. It is a thorough-going intellectual reading experience.

Critical Context

At the midpoint of chapter 13, more than two hundred pages into the book, Hans Zinsser admits that he has been following the model provided by Laurence Sterne's rambling eighteenth century novel *The Life and Opinions of Tristram Shandy* (1759-1767). Only at that late point does he bring his main subject into sharp focus. His biography of typhus, like the novel that inspired him, is filled with digressions, examinations and reexaminations of evidence, blind alleys, witty asides, and a small amount of slightly cranky literary criticism that finds fault with modernist writers such as T. S. Eliot, Gertrude Stein, and James Joyce.

Rats, Lice, and History is admired by scientists who are concerned about overspecialization and the public's misperception of them as number-crunching drudges. Zinsser shows that scientists are intellectuals. He himself was nearing the end of a distinguished career as a scientist: He had held teaching posts at Columbia, Stanford, and Harvard universities; had conducted research on allergies and rheumatic fever in addition to his work on typhus; and had published two textbooks that became classics in their field, *Textbook of Bacteriology* (1911) and *Infection and Resistance* (1915). In *Rats, Lice, and History*, Zinsser shows his readers a different side of science by interlacing his review of medical history with erudite comments on politics, literature, and economics. He speaks from the point of view of a well-rounded humanist rather than that of a scientific specialist.

Victoria Gaydosik

THE RELUCTANT DRAGON

Author: Kenneth Grahame (1859-1932)
First published: 1938, excerpted from *Dream Days* (1898); illustrated
Type of work: Novel
Type of plot: Fantasy
Time of work: Long ago
Locale: The countryside near the Downs, in southeast England
Subjects: Animals, arts, friendship, and social issues
Recommended ages: 10-15

A boy helps to arrange a mock fight between a peaceable dragon and St. George the Dragonslayer that ultimately mocks prejudice and ignorance.

> *Principal characters:*
> THE BOY, a bookish, intelligent child
> THE DRAGON, a poetic, peace-loving creature
> ST. GEORGE, a sensible if duty-bound public figure

Form and Content

Initially appearing as one of several stories and sketches in Kenneth Grahame's *Dream Days* (1898), *The Reluctant Dragon* was published in a self-contained volume several decades later, with illustrations by Ernest H. Shepard. Grahame wrote *Dream Days* as a sequel to *The Golden Age* (1895), the work that established him as a major literary figure. *Dream Days* features the same characters as in the earlier book, grown somewhat older: five orphaned siblings and the unsympathetic adults, known as "Olympians," in charge of them. Both books are narrated in the first person by an unnamed sibling.

In its original context, Grahame's dragon tale unfolds as a story within a story. The framing story finds the narrator and his younger sister Charlotte "tracking" mysterious prints, which they believe belong to a dragon, to the doorstep of a neighbor whom the siblings have dubbed "the funny man." This character, first encountered in the previous story "The Magic Ring," is "funny" because, unlike most adults in their experience, he is responsive to children. Brother and sister enjoy a pleasant visit with "the funny man," who, as he walks the two home, succumbs to Charlotte's entreaties for a story. The tale that he tells is *The Reluctant Dragon*.

The story approximates a fairy-tale beginning as it is placed indeterminately in time and space: "long ago" and "in a cottage half-way between an English village and the shoulder of the Downs." In this cottage live the Boy and his parents, who are in awe of his "book-learning." Drawing on this learning, the Boy confirms that the creature that his father has spied while herding sheep is a dragon. To help reassure his parents, he determines to "have a talk" with the beast regarding its intentions.

The Dragon is revealed to be a sensitive, artistic sort who composes poetry and tells exciting tales about earlier times. He and the Boy become friends. Much to the Boy's exasperation, the Dragon shrugs off warnings that the villagers will seek his bloody end once they know that he is nearby, as dragons are popularly believed to be monsters and scourges.

The Boy's suspicions are confirmed when he discovers that the townsfolk have summoned the famed dragonslayer St. George to rid them of the beast. The Dragon refuses to be roused by the news and suggests that the Boy "arrange" something. St. George echoes this suggestion when the Boy, gaining an audience with him, attests the Dragon's peaceable character.

What the Boy arranges is a meeting between the two. Insisting on upholding tradition, St. George proposes a mock fight, during which he will appear to vanquish the Dragon and "convert" him to civil behavior. The Dragon, happily anticipating the ensuing feast—during which he expects to endear himself to the populace—agrees. All goes according to plan, and the story concludes as it began, with a nod to fairy-tale convention. Closing the tale is a "happily ever after" tableau: the Boy, Dragon, and St. George arm-in-arm.

Analysis

Critics describe *The Reluctant Dragon* as a gentle satire in which structure and content conspire to mock, rather than openly defy, convention and prejudice. The centerpiece of the story—the "pretend" fight between the Dragon and St. George— epitomizes the theme that nothing is as seems. The Dragon prefers daydreaming and versifying to rampaging, St. George proposes a sham (if a humane one), and adults readily delegate responsibility to a child. Grahame playfully confounds fairy-tale convention to affirm a fairy-tale theme: that appearances can be deceiving, that a deeper reality lies beneath the surface.

This theme pays tribute to the imagination. In the story, it is imagination that bonds child and beast and that overcomes prejudice. A shared love of imagined adventure leads to friendship for the Boy and Dragon. The Dragon's ability to amuse and entertain endears him to others; the imaginative playacting of Dragon and Dragon-slayer serves to sublimate the townsfolk's bloodlust.

The triumph of imagination is a theme that children readily embrace. Almost powerless in the real world, children rehearse ambitions and confront fears in the sphere of their imaginations. As theorized by psychologist Bruno Bettelheim, children make sense out of their emotions imaginatively, gaining access to meaning from the experience of literature. Fairy tales in particular take the predicament of children seriously, offering models for achieving self-determination.

Bettelheim's theories are based on Freudian psychology, which analyzes the personality into conflicting modes: the ego, which is rational and enterprising; the superego, which is rigid and convention-bound; and the id, which is sensual and unbridled. At least one critic, Peter Greene, interprets *The Reluctant Dragon* as a reconciliation of Grahame's conflicting selves: the Boy as ego, balancing fantasy and disillusionment; St. George as superego, upholding a Victorian sense of duty; and the

Dragon as id, anarchistic and pleasure-loving—described in the story as a "happy Bohemian."

It is significant for the young reader that the Boy represents the ego, arguably the "hero" in Freudian psychology. The ego has the task of integrating the personality, of bringing the self into alignment and negotiating among competing realities. In the story, the Boy is enlisted to resolve conflict: between the Dragon's reluctance and the dragonslayer's reputation, between the responsibilities of friendship and the demands of convention, between knowledge and ignorance. He, more than the Dragon or St. George—who at least publicly must adhere to their expected roles—is able to "arrange" things. That he does so successfully engenders confidence in readers who are themselves young.

A major conflict that the Boy faces in the tale involves his friendship with the Dragon, which brings him comfort and happiness but anxiety as well. As he invests in the Dragon's safety and well-being and acts on behalf of their friendship, he is drawn into further conflict: with the narrow-mindedness and inflexibility of others and also with his own resistance to shouldering the burden of "arranging" things. The need to resolve the escalating conflict challenges the Boy to be ever more resourceful and, ultimately, to grow. The friendship also contributes to the Boy's range of experience, and thus his growth, when he must rely on the Dragon to keep his word about restricting his deadly powers during the fight.

Grahame builds the tension in his story by raising the formidable obstacles of custom and prejudice, as well as the natural urges toward preservation and the avoidance of pain. Moreover, he has created appealing characters in the Boy, the Dragon, and St. George, their vulnerability effectively increasing readers' affection for and sense of identification with them. Consequently, their victory is all the more satisfying.

Critical Context

The Reluctant Dragon introduces what writer and critic Margaret Blount describes as the "prototype" of dragons in modern juvenile fiction whose "sting has been removed." Grahame's Dragon can be convincingly fearsome, and his contemporary E. Nesbit's dragons are formidable, if redeemable, beasts. The trend in twentieth century fiction for children, however, was toward domesticating the dragon, such as in C. S. Forester's *Poo Poo and the Dragons* (1942), Rosemary Manning's *Green Smoke* (1957), and Margaret Mahy's *The Dragon of an Ordinary Family* (1969).

The Reluctant Dragon also has the distinction of remaining popular while *Dream Days*, from which is excerpted, has not. Educator and critic Elizabeth A. Cripps traces this divergence to a difference in "implied readership." Writing in the 1890's, when a romantically tinged cult of childhood was at its peak in English literature, Grahame created a narrator in *Dream Days* whose dual perspective is that of a child and the adult he becomes. Such a state of mind is naturally foreign to children. In fact, adults were the most eager readers of *Dream Days* when it first appeared.

Contributing to the sense of nostalgia that infuses *Dream Days*, its narrator expresses himself with a languid, self-conscious lyricism that fails to engage most young readers. By contrast, the narrator of *The Reluctant Dragon* launches immediately into his tale. It is related with minimal reflection in a direct, conversational style that relies on simple, fluid syntax and vivid pictorial detail. Such a narrative approach is accessible to the young reader—as it most likely was, in the story's initial context, to the two youngsters who heard it from "the funny man."

Lois Kuznets credits the popularity of *The Reluctant Dragon* with children, relative to *Dream Days*, to the fantasy situation that it presents. Moving into the realm of fantasy not only lightens the story's tone but also gives the Boy gratifying control over an adult situation, something that the orphans in the framing text sorely lack.

Amy Allison

THE RESCUERS

Author: Margery Sharp (1905-1991)
First published: 1959; illustrated
Type of work: Novel
Type of plot: Adventure tale and fantasy
Time of work: The present
Locale: England
Subjects: Animals and friendship
Recommended ages: 10-13

Three adventurous mice journey to Denmark, where they rescue a poet held prisoner in the fearsome Black Castle.

> *Principal characters:*
> MISS BIANCA, a vain but plucky mouse with absurdly aristocratic manners
> BERNARD, an unassuming but brave mouse of humble station
> NILS, a Norwegian seafaring mouse
> MADAM CHAIRWOMAN, the leader of the mice's Prisoner's Aid Society
> THE PRISONER, a Norwegian poet
> THE HEAD JAILER, a brutish man in charge of the Black Castle
> MAMELOUK, the head jailer's fierce cat

Form and Content

Margery Sharp's *The Rescuers* is the story of three mice who daringly save a prisoner from the dreaded Black Castle. The heroes are representatives of the Prisoners' Aid Society, a community of mice whose mission is to console and rescue prisoners. Bernard, a humble mouse who lives in the pantry of a diplomatic embassy, is dispatched by the society to recruit the beautiful and aristocratic mouse Miss Bianca for the mission to the Black Castle. As a pet of the ambassador's son, Miss Bianca frequently travels in the official diplomatic bag and can therefore journey to Norway to find a mouse who can communicate with the imprisoned poet, who is also Norwegian. Although reluctant to forsake her pampered life in a gilded cage, called the Porcelain Pagoda, Miss Bianca is flattered by Bernard's admiration and agrees to help.

In Norway, Miss Bianca encounters a friendly crowd of sailor mice in the local embassy's pantry. One of them, Nils, agrees to join the mission, and Miss Bianca offers personally to show him the way back by boat to the Prisoners' Aid Society, where he is to join Bernard. Unwilling to admit that she has no idea how to get back there herself, Miss Bianca draws a picture of a garden party hat, which Nils interprets as a map. Through sheer good luck, they eventually find their way back to the society's Moot-House and from there embark on the trip to the Black Castle.

A jolly journey in a provision wagon brings them to their destination, where they establish themselves in a mouse hole in the room of the head jailer. While Nils and Bernard explore the castle, Miss Bianca learns from Mamelouk, the head jailer's fierce cat, that the jailers indulge in a huge feast on New Year's Eve, after which they all sleep in very late. Even the cat intends to let down his guard, as he takes pride in gorging himself on this occasion.

Nils discovers that the river rushing by the base of the castle has dislodged some stones that had been used to block off an old water gate. Exploring further, he and Bernard find that the water gate leads to a secret passageway to the prison cells. Before they can communicate this discovery to Miss Bianca, however, Mamelouk succeeds in trapping them under his paw. Miss Bianca's snobbish teasing distracts the cat and enables the two mice to escape. The following night is New Year's Eve, and the three intrepid mice steal the head jailer's key while he is asleep after the feast. A raft, fortuitously tied up just outside the old water gate, enables them to return to the Prisoners' Aid Society with the prisoner.

On their return, the mice are decorated with medals, and the poet, after an affecting leave-taking from his rescuers, departs for his home. Although tempted to accept Bernard's offer of marriage, Miss Bianca resumes her life of companionship with the ambassador's son in the comfortable surroundings of the Porcelain Pagoda.

Analysis

The Rescuers is a delectable story, full of humor and linguistic wit. The story's purpose is neither to provide moral instruction nor to explore serious philosophical themes, but instead to delight readers with the comical notion of a heroic quest carried out by mice. This situation, along with a melodramatic plot, Byronic settings, and bursts of purple prose, parodies the conventions of popular romantic literature.

The variety and descriptions of the settings suggest romantic parody: The rescuers travel from the Moot-House of the Prisoners' Aid Society to Norway, where Miss Bianca's task is to "simply seek out the bravest mouse in Norway"; back across the stormy North Sea and the English Channel to the Moot-House; and finally to the "country of great gloomy mountains, enormous deserts, [and] rivers like strangled seas" where the Black Castle stands. In contrast to the sweeping drama of these scenes, the cage in which Miss Bianca lives as a pet of the ambassador's son strikes a note of overdecorated whimsy, with its golden wires, painted flowers, Venetian glass fountain, and flowery name, the Porcelain Pagoda.

Parody is also evident in the characterization of Miss Bianca, with her "small . . . perfect figure" that suggests "a powdered beauty of the court of Louis the Fifteenth"; her "low, sweet voice"; and her affected upper-class mannerisms and diction. She is given to such pseudo-poetic exclamations as "My poor playfellow! Ah me!" and writes terrible poetry: "Though timid beats the female heart,/ Tempered by only Cupid's fires,/ The touch of an heroic hand/ With unaccustomed bravery inspires." Snobbery adds another dimension of comedy to Miss Bianca's character. When the intrepid Nils happily talks of his large seafaring family, Miss Bianca cries, "How the poor live! It's quite dreadful to think of!" Ironically contrasting Miss Bianca's preciousness with her companion's common sense, the author has Nils reply, "Is it? Myself, I don't know any poor. . . . Except, maybe . . . for one poor little female that hadn't any galoshes . . ." (It was Miss Bianca who lacked proper footwear for the long sea voyage with Nils.) Miss Bianca's aristocratic affectations are turned to good use, however, when her teasing saves Nils and Bernard from Mamelouk's paws. Thus, Miss Bianca plays the dual role of trickster and fool: The reader laughs at her absurd posturing, yet savors her ability to outwit a powerful foe.

Along with Nils, Bernard provides an effective foil for the poetical Miss Bianca. His humble nature is exemplified in his agreement that the medal struck in honor of the successful rescue be named "The Nils and Miss Bianca Medal," since " 'and Bernard' would have made it sound awkward." The reader is not surprised when Miss Bianca declines Bernard's proposal of marriage at the story's conclusion. The humble pantry mouse's faithful but unrequited love for the aristocratic Miss Bianca is yet another comical twist on the popular romantic tropes that give this story its distinctive character.

A richly described world envelopes the comic-romantic characters of *The Rescuers*. Such concrete details as Nils's boots that smell of tar, Miss Bianca's signature silver chain, and the piles of cigar butts and chewing gum wrappers that litter the head jailer's room create an involving, multisensory experience for the reader. Garth Williams' black-and-white illustrations ingeniously chronicle the small details of this physical world from a mouse's-eye perspective. Open spaces are awe-inspiring, small spaces are intimate, and enemies are grotesque. The personal foibles of the mice are humorously shown in the illustrations through posture and facial expressions.

This sensory immediacy combines with the fast-paced plot, striking characters, and clever dialogue to produce a memorable, readable, and inventive story. In its dexterous use of language and concepts to suggest romantic parody and comic contrast, *The Rescuers* is a unique work of humorous fantasy.

Critical Context

The Rescuers is part of a strong tradition of miniaturism in children's literature. Like other classics of this subgenre, such as Jonathan Swift's *Gulliver's Travels* (1726), E. B. White's *Stuart Little* (1945), and Mary Norton's *The Borrowers* (1952), *The Rescuers* sympathetically reflects children's physically and psychologically weaker position in relationship to adults. Like Norton's stories of elflike people who live in the hidden crannies of a human's mansion, it expresses a purely concrete fascination with the material aspects of a small creature's life: the lovingly decorated mouse holes and large objects ingeniously converted for small folks' use. Unlike the great classics of miniaturism, however, *The Rescuers* eschews biting social satire and philosophical reflections on issues such as the nature of existence and the meaning of life, remaining primarily a comedy of manners and a literary parody.

Initially published as an adult title, *The Rescuers* quickly came to be regarded as a family classic, winning a commendation from the British Library Association in 1959.

Margery Sharp continued the adventures of the Prisoners' Aid Society in equally imaginative and witty sequels. Miss Bianca and Bernard remain the protagonists throughout the series, and various other characters are introduced as assistants on each new rescue mission. The Walt Disney films *The Rescuers* (1977) and *The Rescuers Down Under* (1991) are based on the characters and ideas found in the series, but they do not replicate Sharp's stories.

Constance Vidor

RICH IN LOVE

Author: Josephine Humphreys (1945-   )
First published: 1987
Type of work: Novel
Type of plot: Domestic realism
Time of work: The 1980's
Locale: Mount Pleasant, South Carolina, outside Charleston
Subjects: Coming-of-age, family, gender roles, and love and romance
Recommended ages: 15-18

Surviving her mother's departure from home and her parents' subsequent divorce, seventeen-year-old Lucille gains a stronger sense of self and a more flexible concept of family.

> *Principal characters:*
> LUCILLE ODOM, a seventeen-year-old high school senior who must cope with her mother's departure from home and other changes in her family
> WARREN ODOM, Lucille's father, who grieves over his lost wife before finally remarrying
> HELEN ODOM, Lucille's mother, who leaves home to rediscover a larger world and a more independent self beyond her traditional family
> RAE ODOM MCQUEEN, Lucille's independent older sister, who has difficulty adjusting to her new roles as wife and mother
> BILLY MCQUEEN, Rae's husband, a historian who searches for ways to love Rae without hurting her
> WAYNE FROBINESS, Lucille's boyfriend, who gives her love, companionship, and advice on life
> VERA OXENDINE, a hair stylist who marries Warren Odom and renews his sense of life
> RHODY POOLE, a black woman who is Rae's best friend, Helen's surrogate daughter, and another important female mentor for Lucille

Form and Content

Rich in Love is Lucille Odom's first-person account two years later of events that occurred over a six-month period when she was seventeen years old. Her story begins on a bright May day when her mother disappears from home and ends with Lucille looking forward to beginning a new life in college in January.

After Helen Odom abandons her family out of a need for independence and self-discovery, Lucille's father, Warren, becomes paralyzed with grief and regret.

Soon, Lucille's older sister, Rae, arrives with Billy McQueen, who has sabotaged their contraception to cause Rae to become pregnant so that he might persuade her to marry him. Meanwhile, Vera Oxendine, a hair stylist, resolves to bring Warren back to the world of the living. Lucille's confusion about her changing family situation and Billy's rejection by the restless Rae bring them closer together, and one night they make love although they know that their relationship will be a platonic one.

By the conclusion of the novel, Lucille's parents have divorced; her father has remarried and moved into the bungalow of his new bride, Vera; Rae has come back to Billy, given birth to a girl, and settled into a new home; the family homestead has been sold; and Lucille has moved into her mother's newly built house, works at the local library, and is preparing to leave for college.

Everything that Lucille has valued seems to have changed or vanished. Her family has scattered; the shelter of her past lies in ruins. Yet, *Rich in Love* is an optimistic work that reveals human adaptability and resiliency. Even the extremely traditional Lucille, with her love of home and past—that of her family, the South, the United States, and the world—finds that she has been strengthened by the changes she has experienced. Her love of life has grown. Even while putting her future on hold, having missed her final exams and high school graduation in her attempt to take charge of her shattered family and patch things back together, Lucille moves forward into a new life of her own. In failing to bring her mother back, restore their family life, prevent her father from becoming entangled in a new relationship, or keep her sister Rae unchanged, Lucille discovers her own identity.

Life, Lucille finds, is richly complex and love too multifaceted to be controlled. Billy has "loved" Rae so much that he has trapped her into marriage through a pregnancy that makes her temporarily insane. Warren has "loved" Helen so much that he has removed and protected her from the very world that she needed. Her mother loves Lucille but recognizes her independence and encourages her development by refusing to come home; Helen believes that she and Lucille's father have used up their love for each other and are ready for new lives. To complicate matters further, Lucille finds herself attracted to her brother-in-law and resistant to the attentions of her boyfriend, Wayne Frobiness. She begins to recognize the variety of love's forms, their inexplicable and often-contradictory demands. She learns from her mother that love of others must be balanced by love of self. The adventures of her own family and its new intricate and expansive design help prepare her to meet life's challenges and appreciate its richness. Lucille has become an adult.

Analysis

While the novel was not intended for young adult readers, it relates to their lives and can provide insight into their problems. The protagonist, Lucille Odom, is a well-adjusted, intelligent high school senior who has thought about the greenhouse effect, the psychology of shopping, the relationship between Charleston's past and that of the ancient town of Herculaneum, how Charleston's new developments have laid waste the tranquil countryside around her, and the troubled history of white and black people in the United States. Nevertheless, Lucille believes that she is not "ready" to deal with the world. She is, she finds, too threatened by change and unable to accept its inevitability.

Whereas in the past she has discouraged her mother from remodeling the house or throwing away bric-a-brac stored in family cupboards, Lucille learns to become more flexible, adventurous, and open to change in the course of the novel. Her mother's new life, Rhody Poole's advice, and her sister Rae's changing roles all help Lucille reformulate her concept of adult femininity. There is no secure past, no traditional role, that guarantees human happiness; identity must be sought from within. Lucille is ready for change, ready to meet life's challenges. She is eager to help the next generation of women (through her niece, Phoebe) develop an inner strength and meet life's trials.

Because of her mother's sudden departure from home, Lucille has learned that life is not arranged in neat packages; appearances can be deceptive. She finds that traditional roles do not sustain everyone, that families must be adaptable and their love inclusive, that an outmoded past cannot sustain the future, and that self-knowledge and self-fulfillment are essential for all members of a successful family or community. At the outset of the novel, Lucille believes that she could not live anywhere but in her special, seaside, rambling house, in the old-fashioned town of Mount Pleasant, surrounded by an accumulation of everyday objects and comforted by the familiar presence of her parents. By the end of the work, she has learned not only to live without these "essentials" but also to see them as limiting her adult growth. Now that the old homestead has been sold and her family lives in three separate houses, she finds that she does not miss the old house and does not need Mount Pleasant any longer. She has gained confidence in herself, recognizing that her strength comes from within. She is ready to go off on her own to a new life in college.

Lucille's newfound love of self has also enriched her love for others. As her family has multiplied, Lucille's love has grown to include each new addition: first Billy, then Vera, and now Phoebe. She has discovered through the events of recent months that there is no one way, no clear path, and no set answers in life (or houses or families). She has so much to give, so much to look forward to, and so much to accomplish. Uncertain of the future, of what she will do—whether she will marry or live alone— Lucille nevertheless feels strong and unafraid. She is ready for the challenge of the future.

Critical Context

Rich in Love, Josephine Humphreys' second novel, was made into a film starring Albert Finney as Warren Odom in 1992. The novel is one of many by American women writers of late twentieth century South focusing on the confusions of growing into female adulthood, including Anne Tyler's *The Clock Winder* (1972), Lee Smith's *Black Mountain Breakdown* (1980), Gail Godwin's *The Finishing School* (1984), Bobbie Ann Mason's *In Country* (1985), Fannie Flagg's *Daisy Fay and the Miracle Man* (1981), and Kaye Gibbons' *Ellen Foster* (1987).

Increasingly, young heroines such as Humphreys' Lucille Odom learn that they must turn away from the past in order to face the future. To their surprise, they find their inner resources sufficient to stand on their own and meet life's challenges. Like Mark Twain's Huckleberry Finn, they seek out adventure and relish the quest of their lives; however, they are more likely than their male counterparts to find their initial struggles are not with the world but with themselves, not outside but inside their homes. They must struggle to keep the weight of tradition, family, and love of others from holding them down, blocking their growth and self-knowledge. If they cling to the past, they may find themselves buried in it (as in Smith's *Black Mountain Breakdown*). Heroines such as Lucille begin to search within to develop important self-knowledge before going forth to seek their fortunes in the world. While these young female protagonists discover no perfect answers and many loose ends, the tone of these novels is usually upbeat, as the heroines discover their inner resiliency and strength. They find themselves capable of meeting life's challenges and facing an uncertain world.

Susan S. Kissel

THE RIGHT STUFF

Author: Tom Wolfe (1931-   )
First published: 1979
Type of work: History
Time of work: 1947-1963
Locale: Edwards Air Force Base, California; Langley Air Force Base, Virginia; Cape
    Canaveral, Florida; Manned Spacecraft Center, Houston; and outer space
Subjects: Politics and law and science
Recommended ages: 15-18

*Wolfe describes the drama, adventure, and cultural context behind the development
of Project Mercury, the United States' first astronaut program.*

> *Principal personages:*
> CHUCK YEAGER, a heroic pilot who was the first to break the sound
>   barrier
> JOHN GLENN, the most famous of the Mercury astronauts and the first
>   American to orbit the earth
> ALAN SHEPARD, the first American into space, who is alternately tough
>   and friendly
> GUS GRISSOM, the second American into space, whose mistake cost the
>   program a capsule
> GORDON COOPER, the youngest astronaut, who made the last and
>   longest Mercury flight
> WALLY SCHIRRA, the competent pilot whose code word was
>   "operational"
> SCOTT CARPENTER, an astronaut who nearly lost his life when he
>   carelessly let his fuel get low
> DEKE SLAYTON, an astronaut who was bitterly disappointed when heart
>   problems prevented his flight
> JOHN F. KENNEDY, the thirty-fifth president of the United States, who
>   used the Mercury program to maintain his political agenda

Form and Content

Tom Wolfe's *The Right Stuff* is about understanding the people and the times
surrounding the United States' entrance into the space race. At the heart of the story
is the "right stuff" itself, the unique quality that test pilots and astronauts possessed
that enabled them to brave danger not only willingly but eagerly as well.

Wolfe begins his story of the Mercury program at Edwards Air Force Base on the
high desert of Southern California. Edwards becomes the mecca of the prime test
pilots after Chuck Yeager reaches Mach 1 and breaks the sound barrier there in 1947.
In addition to his speed record, Yeager's coolness in a crisis, instinctual flying skills,
and combat success during World War II place him at the top of the flying brotherhood

and make him the standard against which all test pilots will measure themselves. Yeager and others of his elite status face death every dawn by testing new jets and arrive promptly for "beer call" at 4:00 P.M., performing flawlessly with a hangover and on little sleep. Even such recklessness was part of the mythical right stuff.

Meanwhile, the gauntlet of space travel is thrown down by the Soviet Union when it launches the first satellite, Sputnik, in 1957. Since many Americans fear that the Soviet Union will soon be dropping bombs from space, the United States turns in a Cold War frenzy to Wernher von Braun and the newly created National Aeronautics and Space Administration (NASA) to play "catch up" in the space race. President Dwight Eisenhower mandates the selection of seven astronauts for the Mercury program. Following stiff and rigorous competition among the best test pilots in the country (excluding non-college-educated pilots such as Yeager), the seven are chosen and burst onto the American scene as virtual "single combat warriors," prepared to go head-to-head with the Soviets in a life-or-death struggle for the domination of space.

Suddenly, for the public, the right stuff is Cold War heroism, inspiring tears and awe and catapulting the seven men to the top of the "true brotherhood" of test pilots. They are given exclusive contracts with *Life* magazine, free cars and houses, and "a free lunch from one end of America to the other." The reaction of other test pilots, however, presents another drama played out at beer call and at flying conferences. The great test pilots, including Yeager and Scott Crossfield (the first pilot to reach Mach 2), are less enthusiastic than the public about the space program because riding a "capsule" does not require piloting skills—or the right stuff—at all. In fact, America's first astronaut into space is a chimpanzee. Yet, despite the howls of laughter from Edwards, the old guard must accept the new reality: Most of the funding and prestige will now go to the astronaut program, piloting skills notwithstanding.

In addition to the squabble for status between astronauts and test pilots, there is also a competition among the astronauts themselves that defines the right stuff in new terms: Who will be the first human into space? Although John Glenn, the Marine pilot holding the cross-country supersonic speed record, is the apparent front-runner in the public eye, Alan Shepard is chosen to be first, leaving the proud and ambitious Glenn to swallow his pride. In one sense, he experiences what had always been a sign that one did not have the right stuff—he is "left behind" on the metaphorical pyramid of pilot greatness. Shepard's flight makes him a hero, and he receives a Distinguished Service Medal at the White House from President John F. Kennedy. For the president, the Mercury program must become a symbol of the success of his administration, particularly important in the restarting of his "New Frontier" program following the Bay of Pigs fiasco in Cuba.

Following Shepard's flight, all of the astronauts except Deke Slayton, who is grounded for a heart condition, make their space flights, with varying degrees of success and fame. While Gus Grissom accidently causes his capsule to sink after splashdown and Scott Carpenter's preoccupation with scientific observations nearly costs him his life, Wally Schirra and Gordon Cooper make "textbook" flights that cement public trust and help prepare the way for extended orbital flights. Glenn becomes the real hero; his first orbital flight becomes the most famous of the program, leaving Shepard's first suborbital flight all but forgotten. Glenn becomes the most sought-after of the seven and, in the eyes of the world, is the greatest pilot of all. With the success and prestige of the Mercury program, NASA begins the Gemini and Apollo programs, leaving no more funding for the Air Force's X-series rocket-jet programs that Yeager and Crossfield pioneered.

Analysis

The major theme of the Mercury astronaut story is the "right stuff" itself. While the pilots and astronauts who have the right stuff avoid directly defining the concept themselves, it suggests putting one's life on the line on a regular basis and having the coolness and the nearly superhuman reflexes to survive. The book's fifteen chapters recount how the right stuff is crucial for understanding the first astronauts who went into space and how that special quality was perceived by the public during this Cold War drama.

While in the news the successive Mercury flights are the pride of the United States' Cold War feud with the Soviet Union, among the astronauts it becomes an internal jockeying for position, as well as a struggle between them and the engineers, doctors, and administrators who "run the program." Within the ranks, the astronauts have occasional "seances" to discuss problems such as the possible bad publicity that could result from their adulterous intrigues. Glenn, Carpenter, and Grissom argue for self-control, while the others, led by Shepard, claim the right to a private life when they are off-duty. While such issues sometimes divide them, they stand united in their insistence on making both linguistic and engineering changes in the program. They want to be called "astronaut-pilots" (not "passengers") and insist on calling the capsule their "spacecraft." They successfully fight for a window on the capsule and for more manual control of flights.

The Right Stuff is slang history, often told in the language in which it was lived. The pilots and their wives are fascinating people whom Wolfe is able to capture in great detail, using the words and concepts, the slang and nuances of pilot lore to usher readers into their world. For example, since the pilots' code prevents them from mentioning the right stuff directly, Wolfe discovers the indirect language by which they allude to it during informal gab sessions. Instead of claiming their own bravery during a flying crisis, they will describe how the radar man is in shock, looking just like a "zombie." That description announces both the danger of the situation and the pilot's right stuff for surviving it unscathed.

Critical Context

The Right Stuff is a contemporary masterpiece, by far the best book ever written on the early period of space travel. Tom Wolfe is a formidable observer of American culture, and although *The Right Stuff* is not specifically targeted for young adult readers (it contains a moderate amount of profanity), the amount of detail concerning the period and the pilots should make enjoyable reading for most high school students.

The Right Stuff solidified Wolfe's position as one of the United States' best contemporary observers and among its very best stylists. While one might call the book a history, it is actually more of a personal essay writ large, a crackling exposé of real people behind the public masks that they wear.

Dennis R. Perry

ROMEO AND JULIET

Author: William Shakespeare (1564-1616)
First presented: c. 1595-1596
First published: 1597
Type of work: Drama
Type of plot: Tragedy
Time of work: The sixteenth century
Locale: Verona and Mantua, Italy
Subjects: Coming-of-age, death, gender roles, love and romance, and suicide
Recommended ages: 13-18

Through an unfortunate series of misunderstandings, two young lovers from rival families kill themselves rather than live without each other.

> *Principal characters:*
> ROMEO, a Montague, in love with Juliet
> JULIET, a Capulet, in love with Romeo
> MERCUTIO, a friend of Romeo
> BENVOLIO, a friend of Romeo
> PARIS, a nobleman in love with Juliet
> TYBALT, Juliet's hot-tempered cousin
> NURSE, Juliet's foster mother
> ESCALUS, the Prince of Verona
> FRIAR LAURENCE, a Franciscan monk

Form and Content

Romeo and Juliet is a five-act tragedy about the protagonists' ill-fated love. By chance, Romeo, the son of Montague, learns of the annual Capulet party, and he allows his kinsman Benvolio to persuade him to attend, even though the Capulets are mortal enemies of the Montagues. Romeo hopes to see his disdainful love, Rosaline, while Benvolio hopes that Romeo will find another woman there.

At the party, Romeo indeed falls in love with another, Juliet, the only daughter of old Capulet. She also falls in love with him. After the ball, Romeo enters the Capulet garden, where he and Juliet converse in the famous balcony scene. She proposes to marry him, and, before they part, she tells him that in the morning she will send her nurse to learn his answer.

That morning, Romeo tells the nurse to instruct Juliet to meet him at Friar Laurence's monastery in the afternoon, and there they secretly marry. Before the lovers can consummate their marriage that night, however, Juliet's cousin Tybalt meets Romeo and challenges him to a duel. Romeo, now related to Tybalt by marriage, refuses the challenge, but Romeo's friend Mercutio accepts. As Romeo tries to separate the two combatants, Mercutio is slain. Romeo must now choose between the masculine code of revenge and the feminine code of love. He chooses the former and kills Tybalt in a fair fight. The Prince of Verona, who has ordered the Montagues and Capulets to avoid fighting on pain of death, banishes Romeo. After a night with Juliet, Romeo flees to Mantua.

Thinking that Juliet grieves for Tybalt's death rather than Romeo's banishment, old Capulet quickly arranges a marriage for his daughter with Paris, a nobleman. Desperate, Juliet consults Friar Laurence, who gives her a sleeping potion that will make her appear dead; she will then be placed in the Capulet vault. Meanwhile, Friar Laurence will send a message to Mantua to tell Romeo about the plot. Romeo will come to the vault, meet the reawakened Juliet, and together the couple will flee Verona.

The friar's potion works, but the plague prevents his messenger from reaching Romeo. Instead, Romeo hears that Juliet has died. Buying a dose of poison, he hastens to Verona and Juliet's tomb. When Paris confronts him there, Romeo kills him in a duel. He then drinks the poison just before Juliet awakens. Friar Laurence has come to the crypt too late to save Romeo, but he tries to convince Juliet to leave. Instead, she takes Romeo's dagger and stabs herself. At last, the feuding families abandon their quarrel and agree to build a statue to the two lovers above their single grave.

Analysis

One key to William Shakespeare's play lies in its poetry. The play begins with a sonnet as prologue, a clue that the work to follow will trace the moods of a sonnet sequence. Thomas Nashe described Sir Philip Sidney's *Astrophel and Stella* (1591), the best and most popular of the sonnet sequences of the 1590's, as "the tragicomedy of love . . . performed by starlight," an apt synopsis of *Romeo and Juliet*. Specific episodes in the play, such as the lovers' nighttime meeting while the household sleeps (act 2, scene 2), seem copied from Sidney's work. Like Astrophel, Romeo develops a more mature and tragic sense of love in the course of the play. In truncated sonnets of a quatrain and couplet, Benvolio urges Romeo to find another love to replace Rosaline, and Romeo swears eternal loyalty to her (act 1, scene 2). In act 1, scene 5, after seeing Juliet, Romeo and his new love compose a sonnet together, revealing their mutual love. When they begin a second sonnet, the nurse interrupts, foreshadowing how their love and their lives will be cut short.

Romeo's language is derived from the sonnet, especially the Petrarchan conceits that Shakespeare parodied in sonnet 130, written about the same time as this play. In act 1, scene 5, Juliet accuses Romeo of kissing "by the book"; he certainly speaks by the book, like Astrophel studying "inventions fine, her wits to entertain" (Sidney's sonnet 1). Later in the sequence, Astrophel recognizes, "My Muse may well grudge at my heav'nly joy,/ If still I force her in sad rhymes to creep," and so too Romeo's speeches shift from quatrains and couplets to the more dignified and mature blank verse.

Yet, Romeo is still given to conventional expressions of love in act 2, scenes 2 and 6. Juliet, although younger, is the more mature in love; she must recall him from his flights of fancy, reminding him, for example, that "Conceit more rich in matter than in words/ Brags of his substance, not of ornament./ They are but beggars that can count their worth." By the end of the play, Romeo has developed his own idiom, at once beautiful and powerful, indicating how much he has grown during his five days of love.

Shakespeare presents the ideal love of Romeo and Juliet against a background of violence, hate, and sexual innuendo. This most romantic of Shakespeare's tragedies contains six deaths and much bawdry to show the odds against which the lovers must struggle. Moreover, the lovers are never alone for an entire scene; some representative of the work-a-day world invariably intrudes upon them. Only in death can they remain together undisturbed.

Time, too, conspires against the lovers. Their alienation from the world of Verona is nowhere more evident than in their treatment of time. For Juliet "'tis twenty years" between dawn and nine o'clock; she would have the nurse travel at ten times the speed of light. For Romeo, a minute with Juliet equals a lifetime. The lovers are hasty, but they must be so because their world gives them no time. Shakespeare condensed the action of his main source, Arthur Brooke's *The Tragical History of Romeus and Juliet* (1562), from nine months to five days. Only at the end of the play, too late, does time stop for the lovers: In act 5, scene 3, the sun refuses to rise.

Critical Context

Romeo and Juliet is a perennial high school text, popular because of its young lovers—Juliet at fourteen is the age of a high school freshman, and Romeo is only slightly older—and its themes of love and youthful rebellion against parents. Critics, on the other hand, have never placed this work among William Shakespeare's great tragedies. One reason is the apparently deterministic nature of the action, a factor that may appeal to young readers who feel overwhelmed by a world not of their making. Yet, the lovers make decisions that determine their fate. Romeo chooses to avenge the death of Mercutio and later poisons himself because he thinks that Juliet has died. Similarly, Juliet chooses death over life without Romeo.

Another objection is the apparent shift in tone between the first two acts, which seem comic, and the tragic three acts that follow. As critic Frank Kermode has noted, however, the comic tone of the early scenes is more apparent than real. The opening scene establishes a mood of violence and bawdry that threatens the love of the protagonists. Such comedy as exists in these first two acts suggests that the lovers have a chance to succeed even in strife-torn Verona. The darker aspects of these scenes indicate how difficult their struggle will be.

Critics also have objected that the play is more poetic than dramatic. Thus, Mercutio's Queen Mab speech in act 1, scene 4, is beautiful but seems to retard the action as Romeo is about to meet Juliet for the first time. In fact, these lines reveal Mercutio's character; he is a man of excellent fancy, but he cannot understand Romeo's love because Mercutio is a materialist. His Queen Mab brings lawyers dreams of fees, parsons dreams of benefices, and maids dreams of sex. Shakespeare was a dramatist before he was a poet, and any good production of this play will demonstrate its stageworthiness. In *Romeo and Juliet*, as in his other works for the stage, language always serves Shakespeare's purpose. Students may find that language strange and dense, but the words will reward their study.

Joseph Rosenblum

ROOTABAGA STORIES

Author: Carl Sandburg (1878-1967)
First published: 1922; illustrated
Type of work: Short fiction
Subjects: Emotions, family, friendship, jobs and work, and nature
Recommended ages: 10-13

> *In a series of whimsical stories set in the Rootabaga Country, Sandburg presents*
> *the natural world and human actions in amusing contexts designed to delight children.*

Form and Content

Rootabaga Stories is a collection of fanciful tales that Carl Sandburg originally told as bedtime stories for his three daughters. Some of his interests as a poet, folksinger, and social activist find their way into the stories, but in lighthearted ways. The stories are primarily intended as whimsical entertainment, not as social commentary or moral inspiration.

The opening story sets the tone for the book. In "How They Broke Away to Go to the Rootabaga Country," Gimme the Ax and his two children, Please Gimme and Ax Me No Questions, sell almost everything, "pigs, pastures, pepper pickers, pitchforks," and buy a "long slick yellow leather slab ticket with a blue spanch across it" to take them to the Village of Liver-and-Onions, the biggest city in the Rootabaga Country. The characters' comic names and imaginative adventure told in humorous and repetitive language are typical of *Rootabaga Stories*.

The stories are grouped in clusters in which a single character or plot thread connects the stories. In the first of "Three Stories about the Gold Buckskin Whincher," for example, Blixie Bimber finds luck in the form of a gold buckskin whincher, which brings her romance. (A whincher is an imaginary object whose name is more important for its sound that for its meaning.) In the other stories in the cluster, the whincher changes the luck of two other characters: Jason Squiff, who wears a popcorn hat, mittens, and shoes; and Rags Habakuk, who gains the company of a pair of magical blue rats.

Although the stories are all based in the Rootabaga Country, and all use the same humorous style, they show considerable variety. Some stories create new American legends, such as "Two Skyscrapers Who Decided to Have a Child," "The Wooden Indian and the Shaghorn Buffalo," or "The White Horse Girl and the Blue Wind Boy," who find love and fulfillment in the west Rootabaga Country. Other stories, such as "Two Stories About Corn Fairies," "How to Tell Corn Fairies If You See 'Em," and "How the Animals Lost Their Tails and Got Them Back Traveling from Philadelphia to Medicine Hat," are quasi folktales with the flavor of agrarian America.

In the stories, children come from and travel to imaginary places, such as the Village of Liver-and-Onions, and actual places, such as Medicine Hat, that are enhanced by imagination. The illustrators, Maud and Miska Petersham, picture a world very much in the spirit of European folktales, but with an art deco style that situates the stories in the 1920's.

"Two Skyscrapers Who Decided to Have a Child" is one of several stories without children, or even humans, as protagonists. This distinctly American, distinctly twentieth century tale describes how two skyscrapers in the Village of Liver-and-Onions fell in love and had a child. One skyscraper is identified by a "tin brass goat," and the other by a "tin brass goose." As time passed and the Northwest Wind blew news to the buildings, they learned of the mountains and the sea, which they could not visit because they were rooted in the city: "And they decided when their child came it should be a *free* child." When their child arrived, "It was a railroad train, the Golden Spike Limited, the fastest long-distance train in the Rootabaga Country. It ran across the prairie, to the mountains, to the sea." Although the buildings were at first happy about their child's freedom, the story's poignant ending tells of how the train crashed, a disaster that brought the buildings grief. After the Northwest Wind howled the sad news of the train wreck to the skyscrapers, the emblematic goat and goose appeared next to each other in the middle of the street.

Analysis

Although in his other work, Sandburg was a passionate social activist, in *Rootabaga Stories* he relaxes and has fun. In a different context, for example, Sandburg might have treated the Potato Face Blind Man as an object of pity or as a victim of the social system. A street person, he "used to play an accordion on the Main Street corner nearest the postoffice in the Village of Liver-and-Onions." Instead, he tells delightful stories and dreams that amuse the children of the village.

Nevertheless, the words of the Potato Face Blind Man are as close to morality or social commentary as the stories come. Whitson Whimble, "the patent clothes wringer manufacturer," reads the blind man's sign, which says "You look at 'em and see 'em; I look at 'em and I don't. You watch what their eyes say; I can only feel their hair." He then tells his chauffeur to "go on." In this brief exchange, Sandburg's sympathies are with the working poor, represented by the Potato Face Blind Man, rather than with capitalists such as Whimble. Earlier, the Potato Face Blind Man has explained another of his signs to Pick Ups:

> "Some of the people who pass by here going into the postoffice and coming out, they have eyes—but they see nothing with their eyes. They look where they are going and they get where they wish to get, but they forget why they came and they do not know how to come away. They are my blind brothers. It is for them I have the sign that reads 'I am Blind *Too*.'"

This gentle admonition to look around is as much of a moral as appears in *Rootabaga Stories*. If the stories have a message at all, it is to enjoy language and imagination. Sandburg's fun with words—for example, coinages such as "spanch" and "whincher," "snizzling and sniffering"—is intended to delight more than to instruct. The stories are full of lively repetitions and poetic moments that encourage joy in imagination and language.

The Rootabaga Country, which includes the Village of Liver-and-Onions and the Village of Cream Puffs, as well as the Potato Bug Country and the Thimble Country, also encompasses prairies, mountains, and seas and is within traveling distance of places "far up in North America," such as Medicine Hat and Moose Jaw. Sandburg appropriates the names of actual places when they have the right sound, as when the Gimmes sell everything to travel to the Rootabaga Country and their neighbors think, "They are going to Kansas, to Kokomo, to Kankakee, to Kalamazoo, to Kamchatka, to the Chattahoochee."

Having fun with names, Sandburg invents creatures such as "flongboos" and "flummywisters," as well as mentioning actual animals, especially rats and mice. When Sandburg uses names such as Wingtip the Spick and the gringo, he is using them for their comic sounds, not because they have meaning as slang. When names are intended to be insulting, he makes that clear, as in the "wars" in "How Two Sweetheart Dippies Sat in the Moonlight" in the sequel *Rootabaga Pigeons* (1923), in which the boomers and the sooners call one another names.

In another story, an "old woman whose husband had been killed in a sewer explosion when he was digging sewer ditches" appears. She is "carrying a bundle of picked-up kindling wood in a bag on her back because she did not have enough money to buy coal." Bevo the Hike tells her, "You have troubles. So have I. You are carrying a load on your back people can see. I am carrying a load and nobody sees it." Like the Potato Face Blind Man, rather than becoming a figure of pathos, the old woman helps Bevo solve his problem.

Critical Context

Rootabaga Stories and *Rootabaga Pigeons* were the only two books that Sandburg wrote specifically for children. His other books for children were by-products of his larger projects: *Early Moon* (1930), a collection of poems for children, was gleaned from Sandburg's poetry; *Abe Lincoln Grows Up* (1928) came from *Abraham Lincoln: The Prairie Years* (1926); and *Prairie-Town Boy* (1955) was excerpted from *Always the Young Strangers* (1953).

In *Rootabaga Stories* and *Rootabaga Pigeons*, Sandburg responded to a particular moment by turning his daughters' bedtime stories into books that other children might enjoy. Afterward, his monumental six-volume biography of Lincoln took his attention, his daughters grew up, and he never again returned to writing whimsical children's stories.

Rootabaga Stories and *Rootabaga Pigeons* have attracted new audiences since their first publication, and they will no doubt endure to amuse future generations. They came from such diverse antecedents as the nonsense verse of Edward Lear and American folktales, as well as from the more nonchalant tradition of parental story-telling. Both books have affinities with subsequent children's works such as those by Dr. Seuss (Theodore Geisel), which began to appear in the 1930's. *Rootabaga Stories* and *Rootabaga Pigeons*, by-ways in Sandburg's literary career, are also by-ways in the course of children's literature. They remain a unique amalgam of whimsy, poetry, myth, and magic, with a leavening of sympathy for the working class.

Thomas Lisk

ROOTS
The Saga of an American Family

Author: Alex Haley (1921-1992)
First published: 1976
Type of work: Novel
Type of plot: Historical fiction
Time of work: From 1750 to the 1960's
Locale: Gambia, Africa; Virginia; and Tennessee
Subjects: Coming-of-age, family, race and ethnicity, and social issues
Recommended ages: 13-18

> *In tracing his family history, Haley discovers that the story of Kunta Kinte and his descendants parallels the story of racial distancing in America from the slave trade until the twentieth century and discloses the hardships that African Americans had to endure to maintain individual and family identity.*

Principal characters:
KUNTA KINTE, a young West African sold into slavery and brought to America who is the founder Haley's African American family
BELL, the plantation cook whom Kunta marries
KIZZY, the daughter of Kunta and Bell
CHICKEN GEORGE, the son of Kizzy and her master
MATHILDA, George's wife and the mother of his eight children
TOM, George and Mathilda's fourth son, who becomes a blacksmith and is sold to a North Carolina tobacco plantation owner
IRENE, a half Indian who marries Tom
CYNTHIA, Tom and Irene's daughter and the grandmother of Alex Haley
WILL PALMER, Cynthia's husband
BERTHA, Cynthia and Will's daughter, who marries Simon Haley and gives birth to Alex
ALEX HALEY, the author, who makes himself a character in the novel

Form and Content

The first portion of *Roots: The Saga of an American Family* deals with Kunta Kinte's capture, enslavement, and struggle to maintain his identity. From the time that he is dragged from his Gambian home in 1750, Kunta fights to retain his memories and his family identity. Throughout his passage to America in the hold of a slave ship, Kunta attempts to understand what has happened to him, why he was taken from his home.

The narrative intensity grows after Kunta arrives in America and is bought by a plantation owner. The first thing that an owner does is to remove any sense of identity from his slaves—in Kunta's case, by making him accept a slave name, Toby. Kunta refuses and endures severe physical punishment to force him to say his slave name.

When the pain becomes too great, he repeats the name Toby in order to stop the torture, but Kunta keeps his identity inwardly and remembers his heritage.

Kunta's desire to maintain his identity is matched by his constant attempts to regain his freedom. Finally, after Kunta's fourth attempt at escaping, his owner cuts off one of his feet. Kunta is hobbled and unable to make any further serious attempts to escape, but his spirit is not broken. He continues to tell stories of his family's background so that his descendants will not forget who they are. Because of the stories that he tells and the stories that are told about him, Kunta Kinte will remain an inspiration for succeeding generations.

The second major portion of *Roots* centers on Kunta's grandson, Chicken George, who is reared by his white owner and father. After George shows a strong talent for working with animals, his owner turns him into an master trainer of gamecocks. Although his abilities create an identity for George, it is an identity tied to his role as a slave, as trainer of his master's fighting chickens. His life is less traumatic than that of his grandfather, but George never maintains an identity of his own as Kunta had done. He eventually marries Mathilda and fathers eight children. Because of his services to his master, George and his family are not separated. During his successes as a chicken trainer, family stories are still being handed down through oral tradition in the practice begun by Kunta. The family's history continues to be told.

George and Mathilda's fourth son, Tom, represents the next generation to be profiled in *Roots*. Like all slaves, he is taught the trade that will serve his master best. In Tom's case, he is trained to become a blacksmith. When he reaches adulthood, Tom is sold to a tobacco grower from Alamance County, North Carolina. There, Tom meets a young half-Indian woman, Irene, whom he marries and with whom he has eight children. Tom continues the oral history tradition by telling stories of his grandfather's bravery and his father's slyness.

Tom's daughter Cynthia is taken to Henning, Tennessee, when she is only a child as part of a wagon train of freed slaves. Cynthia meets and marries Will Palmer and gives birth to Bertha, who eventually marries Simon Haley and becomes the mother of the novel's author, Alex Haley.

Throughout his formative years, Alex Haley sits and listens as his elders tell stories of their family's experiences, especially of the mysterious figure of Kunta Kinte. As he grows older, Haley wants to know more about this interesting individual, but it is not until he retires from the U.S. Coast Guard that Haley is able to investigate his family fully. The result is the narrative presented in *Roots*.

Analysis

Roots is the result of Haley's extensive research into the history of his own family. He chose the novel form as the means of presenting his findings because the combination of historical research and fictionalization permitted him to do more than merely present facts about his family's past. He was able to tell the story of the lives that they lived. The foundation of *Roots* is the oral tradition through which family stories are passed from one generation to the next, the same process that first caught Haley's imagination as a youngster hearing tales of long-dead ancestors.

Oral tradition has long been an important means of transmitting family and social histories. This method has been most often used by rural and less-educated societies. Haley chose to present *Roots* as if it were the result of generations of oral tellings of the events in his family's history. The significance of the oral tradition lends the novel credibility, as the story of Kunta Kinte, Chicken George, Tom, and Alex Haley would not be as believable if it were told as simply another work of fiction. The fact that the characters were also real people causes the reader to approach the book as if it were a historical work or a biography. Readers often find it easy to forget that *Roots* is generally a fictional work, which is what Haley intended.

Although the popularity of *Roots* cannot be denied, its publication did not go uncriticized. Some reviewers attacked it for oversimplifying the period of slavery in American history, while others took Haley to task for his misuse of historical facts. In two cases, he was sued for plagiarizing passages from other writers' works.

Critical Context

Despite the negative reactions of some critics, *Roots* became one of the most-read modern American novels. In addition, for many people, both black and white, it initiated an intense interest in family histories and genealogies. The 1977 ABC miniseries version of *Roots* brought the novel and its creator to the attention to an even wider audience than the novel itself.

The novel *Roots* and its television offspring created an mini-industry that gave birth to such television projects as *Roots: The Next Generation* (1979), which also aired on ABC, and *Palmerstown, U.S.A.* (1980-1981), a CBS series coproduced by Haley that told the story of another family and community not greatly different from Haley's own family and the community of Henning, Tennessee. This proliferation made Alex Haley a household name and a much-demanded speaker.

Although he is best known for *Roots*, Haley's writing career was not limited to that novel. Haley spent his years in the Coast Guard as a journalist and, after leaving the military, built a career around writing. Haley's interview with jazz great Miles Davis for *Playboy* magazine became the prototype of the formal interviews presented in each issue. In 1965, shortly before the assassination of Malcolm X, Haley completed an extensive interview with the African American leader that covered all of his life. This interview was later published intact as *The Autobiography of Malcolm X* (1965).

By the time of his death, Haley had completed extensive sections of two proposed works: the story of his hometown of Henning, Tennessee, and the story of his paternal grandmother, Queen Haley. The unfinished *Queen* was made into a miniseries in 1993 and published posthumously in book form that same year. Haley's other writings can be found in various journals and magazines. The one theme that tied together all of his works, from *Roots* to his unfinished manuscripts, was Haley's deep interest in and his desire to tell about the history of his family and his race.

Thomas B. Frazier

ROSA PARKS
My Story

Author: Rosa Parks (1913-   ), with Jim Haskins (1941-   )
First published: 1992; illustrated
Type of work: Autobiography
Time of work: 1913-1991
Locale: Tuskegee, Pine Level, and Montgomery, Alabama; Hampton, Virginia; and Detroit, Michigan
Subjects: Activists, education, politics and law, race and ethnicity, and social issues
Recommended ages: 13-15

Born in turbulent Alabama to working-class parents, Parks describes how segregated politics and laws in the Deep South shaped the lives of both black and white citizens.

Principal personages:
> ROSA MCCAULEY PARKS, an impetuous black girl in the South who as an adult refused to give up her seat on a segregated bus to a white patron
> RAYMOND PARKS, Rosa's activist husband and supporter
> JAMES MCCAULEY, Rosa's father, a carpenter and stonemason
> LEONA EDWARDS MCCAULEY, Rosa's mother, a schoolteacher
> SYLVESTER MCCAULEY, Rosa's young brother
> SYLVESTER EDWARDS, Rosa's maternal grandfather
> ROSE EDWARDS, Rosa's maternal grandmother
> JAMES PERCIVAL, the Scotch-Irish father of Sylvester Edwards, Rosa's maternal great-grandfather
> MARY JANE NOBLES, the slave wife of James Percival, Rosa's maternal great-grandmother
> EDGAR DANIEL NIXON, a Montgomery porter and activist
> MARTIN LUTHER KING, JR., a Montgomery pastor and the president of the Montgomery Improvement Association
> RALPH DAVID ABERNATHY, a Montgomery pastor and activist

Form and Content

Rosa Parks: My Story traces the experiences of the author from her reminiscences of both childhood marvels and assaults in segregated Tuskegee and Pine Level, Alabama, to her position as a lauded activist in the office of Congressman John Conyers of Detroit, Michigan, and her subsequent retirement. The book is largely episodic, and each of the twelve chapters explores an aspect of Rosa Parks's sense of cultural isolation and disparagement in a emotional topography in which terror was the norm among African Americans. The first-person narration relates Parks's view of a "separate and unequal" South disinclined to treat black people with respect. The story gains its expansiveness from the author's lively recollection of happenstances and individuals whose lives intersected with hers. The book's most moving episodes are Parks's bus stand, described in "You're Under Arrest" and "They've Messed with the Wrong One Now," and the Montgomery Bus Boycott, in the chapter "Stride Toward Freedom," in which the relentless Old Guard citizenry sparred with the Montgomery Improvement Association. Parks's straightforward, emphatic narration is not only a recollection of one woman's odyssey through Alabama's legalized segregation but also a demonstration of success achieved through nonviolent action.

In *Rosa Parks*, the author provides photographs of herself and her family, as well as scenes of the seven handcuffed Scottsboro Boys, a black classroom, the "colored" section of a segregated bus, a "colored" water fountain in a local city park, a Ku Klux Klan rally, Edgar Daniel Nixon, president of the Montgomery chapter of the National Association for the Advancement of Colored People (NAACP), Martin Luther King, Jr., and Montgomery bus boycotters—all of which illustrate the existence of black people in mid-twentieth century Alabama. The photographs and scenes reinforce Parks's crucial presence in the Civil Rights movement of the 1950's.

Opening with the historic "tired of being pushed around" dialogue on December 1, 1955, between the author and the white male bus driver who made an attempt to execute a local law, Parks positions herself centerfront in a movement that led to the desegregation of public facilities in Alabama—and the entire United States. After frequent setbacks in the movement, such as telephone insults and harassment, firings, jailings, firebombings of homes and churches, unfair and hostile treatment by insurance agencies, and local court injunctions to quell civic activism, on November 13, 1956, the U.S. Supreme Court ruled that segregation on Montgomery buses was unconstitutional.

In the initial chapter, "How It All Started," Parks prefaces her book with an early memory of a "time that a white man treated me like a regular little girl, not a little black girl." As she relates, "A Yankee soldier patted me on the head and said I was a cute little girl." The gesture and remark were atypical. Parks then lists the nurturing people in her family and the community who played some small part in her resolute goal "not to take no stuff off white people." Reared in her maternal grandparents' home, Parks informs readers that Sylvester Edwards instilled in his daughters (Leona and Fannie) and their children "a don't put up with bad treatment from anybody" credo. Parks maintains that this tenet "was passed down almost in our genes."

Out of fear of reprisals, most black people in Alabama did "not stand up to white people," but Gus Vaughn, Parks's childhood neighbor and the father of several little children who often did work in the cotton fields of Pine Level, refused to work for white people or, for whatever reason, anybody else. He was one of a few black men in the town who had "the courage to stand up to whites." Vaughn's lack of deference to them was a source of pride to the young Rosa. Many decades later, one of his descendants almost became a test case for examining Montgomery's discriminatory bus laws. In the spring of 1955, before Parks's historic "I'm tired" defiance to segregation laws, Claudette Colvin, Vaughn's great-granddaughter, refused to give up her seat in the middle section of a bus to a white person. Unlike Parks, who would repeat the young woman's defiance months later, Colvin was dragged from the bus and arrested. Parks admired her courage.

If the Old Guard citizenry in Montgomery had known of the activist role of Raymond Parks, the author's husband, in attempting to dismantle unfair public policies and laws, he would have been beaten or killed. Much like Vaughn, Rosa's grandfather, and her young brother, Sylvester, Raymond refused to kowtow to white supremacy. When Rosa married him in 1932, he was already a long-time member of the NAACP and was working secretly with people outside Montgomery on behalf of the Scottsboro Boys, a group of African American men accused of raping two white women. Raymond Parks supported his wife's volunteerism and encouraged her to complete her education and to register to vote when she turned twenty-one, even though, because of limited schooling, he was unable to pass the literacy test. After the couple moved to Detroit in 1957, he voted for the first time.

Analysis

In its episodic structure, *Rosa Parks* invites an examination of social issues that readers may find riveting. The book is a gold mine of African American history. Cities such as Montgomery, Birmingham, Tuskegee, Mobile, Nashville, Memphis, Charleston, New York City, and Washington, D.C., summon further study on black-white relations before the Great Depression and after World War II. Proscribed issues at the forefront of America's conscience, such as literacy testing, poll taxes, miscegenation, the Ku Klux Klan, the White Citizens' Council, and Black Muslims, are treated with sensitive objectivity. *Rosa Parks* offers readers a glimpse of Julius Rosenwald and his one-room rural schools, the Hampton Institute, Booker T. Washington, and the Tuskegee Institute, as well as celebrated freedom fighters for justice and fairness. Such notable figures as Mahatma Gandhi, Martin Luther King, Jr., Thurgood Marshall, Asa Philip Randolph, Malcolm X, Jesse Jackson, Ralph David Abernathy, Douglass L. Wilder, Tom Bradley, Roy Wilkins, John Conyers, Harry Belafonte, Dick Gregory, Josephine Baker, and Ralph Bunche are documented as crusaders for equality and fairness. In significant ways, the book offers an insider's view of such topics as the marketplace and labor policies, parenthood, absent spouses, segregated neighborhoods, voter registration, racial tensions in the South and North, the rights of women, and World War II, including the war itself, its aftermath, and the role of black soldiers.

Rosa Parks is a compendium of the rituals that white people demanded and to which black people adapted or acquiesced. Parks's narrative voice acquaints readers with an era in which many white people were often mute on civil rights matters, did not shake the hands of black people, refused to address black people by titles or surnames, and became angry when black adults seemed unhappy. For survival and out of their own fears, many African Americans reproved their children soundly in order to protect them from reprisals and often did not seek even "reasonable demands."

Critical Context

Rosa Parks is more than the autobiography of a great freedom fighter. The book unearths myriad civil rights precursors in Rosa Parks's family and community who survived indignities with their pride and courage intact. Besides *Rosa Parks*, young readers may want to peruse Anne Moody's *Coming of Age in Mississippi* (1968) and Maya Angelou's *I Know Why the Caged Bird Sings* (1970) for more glimpses of the challenges that black girls and women faced in the South. Much like *Rosa Parks*, James Baldwin's *Go Tell It on the Mountain* (1953), Malcolm X's *The Autobiography of Malcolm X* (1965), Alex Haley's *Roots* (1976), and Gordon Parks's *The Learning Tree* (1963) and *Voices in the Mirror* (1990) are wonderful melanges on African American cultural history and social critique. Providing a searing glance of what it was like to be black in America before the Civil Rights movement—and especially the South—*Rosa Parks* is a primer on the contradictions of the American Dream.

Bettye J. Williams

RUMBLE FISH

Author: S. E. Hinton (1950-   )
First published: 1975
Type of work: Novel
Type of plot: Psychological realism
Time of work: The mid-1960's
Locale: California and in a rough neighborhood, probably in Tulsa, Oklahoma
Subject: Coming-of-age, drugs and addiction, education, friendship, and poverty
Recommended ages: 13-18

Rusty-James learns through a series of tragic losses that even his street-tough reputation and his idolized older brother, the Motorcycle Boy, cannot counter the violence and poverty of his oppressive environment.

> *Principal characters:*
> RUSTY-JAMES, a fourteen-year-old, abandoned by his mother and
>   neglected by his alcoholic father, who tries to fight his way to
>   survival
> THE MOTORCYCLE BOY, Rusty-James' mysterious older brother, whose
>   tortured intellect isolates him and intimidates most of the local toughs
> STEVE HAYS, Rusty-James' passive, intelligent best friend, who is
>   beaten by his abusive father
> PATTY, Rusty-James' girlfriend, who attends a private school
> SMOKEY, a street kid who eventually challenges Rusty-James
> PATTERSON, a cop who persecutes Rusty-James and the Motorcycle Boy

Form and Content

Rumble Fish opens and closes in California, at least five years after the main action of the story has transpired. Rusty-James, who narrates the story in the first person, describes a chance encounter with his former best friend, Steve Hays, who is now studying to be a teacher. The dialogue, which propels the novel, reveals that Rusty-James has been in a reformatory and creates the framework for the flashback that becomes the novel's vehicle.

Much of the story's action originates in Benny's, a pool hall and bar that serves as a hangout for junior and senior high school students who are disillusioned by the poverty of their neighborhood and the callous indifference of adults to their frustration. They are frequently truant from school, unsuccessful in the classroom, and usually in trouble. School officials are depicted as corrupt; one coach even offers Rusty-James a five-dollar bribe to beat up another student. Police officials add to the conflict and tension of the neighborhood with their abuse of power and prejudiced treatment of Rusty-James and the Motorcycle Boy.

Parental figures, too, are destroyed by their own weaknesses; Rusty-James' father was once a successful attorney, but, as an alcoholic, he now offers no security or role model for Rusty-James or his brother. Their mother, whom the Motorcycle Boy eventually locates in California, has abandoned all responsibility for her sons, and the story of being left alone by her when he was a toddler haunts Rusty-James. He has developed a fear of loneliness as a result of this early loss, but the eventual loss of his girlfriend, his best friend, his street reputation, and his brother leaves Rusty-James dazed; at the novel's close, he is wandering California and still trying to forget the pain of his past.

Although the story's language is somewhat dated—using terms such as "rumble," for example, to refer the frequent street fights—the conflicts are real and transcend time and place. The ready availability of alcohol and other drugs, the pervasive threat of concealed weapons, the alienation and disdain felt by street kids with no power in mainstream society, the constant jockeying for position within the framework of the street—all these issues remain pertinent and challenging for young adults.

The bravado of the young toughs masks the insecurities and vulnerability just beneath the surface, and, as Rusty-James attempts to hold on more tightly to the Motorcycle Boy, his mask falls. Rusty-James suffers a serious stab wound in his fight with Biff, his girlfriend Patty breaks up with him, he gets transferred to a rival school where he knows he will be beaten by his enemies, and he and Steve are jumped after getting drunk in an adult theater with the Motorcycle Boy. Little by little, the thin fabric of their existence tears, and eventually even Steve tells Rusty-James that he is like the ball in a pinball machine, hopelessly buffeted by external forces. Steve recognizes that the randomness of this existence will destroy him, and he, too, abandons Rusty-James. Patty becomes Smokey's girlfriend, and Rusty-James learns that the group leadership has shifted to Smokey as well. The final conflict in a pet store involving the Motorcycle Boy and the fighting "rumble" fish of the title, more than any scene in the story, symbolizes the persecution, the misunderstanding, and the wasted potential of these young lives.

Analysis

In *Rumble Fish*, S. E. Hinton offers even her youngest readers an insightful study of the dynamics of social conflict. In the novel, the institutions traditionally entrusted with the maintenance of order, such as the family, schools, and law enforcement, fail to counteract the poverty, ignorance, violence, and despair that threaten Rusty-James, the Motorcycle Boy, and the other teens in the neighborhood. Sympathy for the boys and their situation develops through the hero/sidekick relationship that exists between Rusty-James and Steve, and their dialogue reveals the submerged emotions of loneliness and dependency that haunt most young people as they attempt to define their place in society. The novel affirms that disappointment, failure, and loss are constants in human existence; that an inability to adapt to expected norms will ultimately lead to conflict; and that order within a disordered society must originate within the self.

The title symbol, that of the freed fighting "rumble" fish, accurately represents the cruel paradox of youthful existence. Like the fighting fish, teenagers exist in a sort of isolated captivity, since interaction often results in conflict. Like the fish, too, teenagers frequently lack the vision to recognize deceptive mirrors (as seen in Rusty-James' vision of the Motorcycle Boy) and occasionally destroy themselves in confusion. The river where the Motorcycle Boy releases the fish marks the line of demarcation between the haves and the have-nots in their community, and when the Motorcycle Boy leads Rusty-James and Steve on an excursion across the river, Hinton contrasts the bright lights to the menacing world of their neighborhood. Boundaries exist that Rusty-James cannot cross, and his increasing alienation from his environment leads to a greater loss of hope.

Although the helplessness, disenchantment, and confusion of Rusty-James and the Motorcycle Boy are decidedly depressing, and Hinton holds out the promise of a brighter future. Her powerful characterizations alert young readers to the hazards of letting limited experience shape one's entire perspective on life. The contrast between Steve and Rusty-James, for example, demonstrates that each individual must find a direction independent of the negative influences that seek to isolate and alienate. Steve's optimistic future is ensured by his decision to remove himself from the chaos of the streets, even though his own family life is fraught with violence and suffering. Steve finds within himself a direction; Rusty-James, on the other hand, continues to seek external definition, particularly via his emulation of the Motorcycle Boy, which leads only to chaos and frustration. Ironically, when Steve sees Rusty-James in California, he continually refers to the similarity between Rusty-James and the Motorcycle Boy, but, even though Rusty-James has always wanted to be just like the Motorcycle Boy, the similarity does not represent any achievement; on the contrary, it seems to suggest certain doom.

Rusty-James' inability to overcome his family's legacy echoes Greek tragedy's message that humanity is motivated by biological necessity and destiny. Those who dare to resist this determinism, like the Motorcycle Boy, are eventually destroyed. Even in the conclusion's very different setting, at the beach where the sun shines and the waves keep coming in, Rusty-James can only hope that he will eventually separate himself from his tragic past.

Critical Context

The publication of S. E. Hinton's *The Outsiders* in 1967 introduced a new form of realism to adolescent literature. Her frank depiction of poverty, family conflicts, addiction, and violence shocked some readers and caused some critics to accuse her of romanticizing the street-tough teenagers and their lives. Young adult readers, however, responded overwhelmingly to *The Outsiders*, as well as to Hinton's subsequent works. *Rumble Fish* has been praised for its memorable dialogue and fast-paced narrative, although some critics believe that it lacks the innovation of her earlier novels.

Most readers agree that Hinton's power lies in her development of sympathetic characters whose stories reveal an unnerving slice of teenage America. Hinton examines the divisive nature of adolescent experience, the complicated relationships between individuals and groups, and, in the case of *Rumble Fish*, the tragic conse-quences of the ways in which some teenagers approach life. The timeless truth of this revelation appeals to young readers, and film versions of *Rumble Fish, The Outsiders, That Was Then, This Is Now* (1971), and *Tex* (1979) have been popular. Hinton's message about the cruelty of the streets goes beyond the familiar stereotypes to illuminate the real problems and, unfortunately, the lack of many real solutions to these common social crises.

Kathleen M. Bartlett

SAILING TO CYTHERA AND OTHER ANATOLE STORIES

Author: Nancy Willard (1936-   )
First published: 1974; illustrated
Type of work: Short fiction
Subjects: Animals, coming-of-age, the supernatural, and travel
Recommended ages: 10-13

In the course of three related short stories, five-year-old Anatole embarks on a series of fantastic, mythic journey-quests, encountering high adventure and gaining wisdom along the way.

Form and Content

The three narratives that make up *Sailing to Cythera and Other Anatole Stories* are unified by their mystical tone and content, by the recurring motif of the heroic quest, and by a common protagonist—five-year-old Anatole, who resides in rural Michigan. The slim volume is evocatively illustrated by David McPhail.

In the first of these stories, "Gospel Train," Plumpet, Anatole's cat, presides at the funeral of her Aunt Pitterpat, who, having exhausted her nine earthly lives, "has gone to get a new skin" in the mysterious and eternal land of the afterlife. Anatole and Plumpet set out to visit her there, boarding a train occupied by anthropomorphized animals, including owls with bonnets, a raccoon reading a newspaper, and singing rabbits. Aunt Pitterpat is duly found in "Morgentown," a place from which "nobody . . . sends postcards" and which can be reached only after a hazardous train ride through a dark forest and across a river (perhaps symbolic of the Styx or the Jordan). The journey home becomes a daunting challenge: Anatole himself, aided by various animals, must navigate the train back across the river, lest they all be stranded forever in the abode of the blessed dead.

Anatole's quest in "The Wise Soldier of Selleback" is to recapture soldier Erik Hanson's thirty lost (or perhaps stolen) years of memory. The recitation of a magical chant transports Anatole first to Norway, where an old man informs him that he must travel to the sun, the delineator of time, in order to regain Hanson's fugitive years. "It's the journeys we make for others," he counsels, "that give us the power to change ourselves." Anatole's journey ultimately involves his climbing a tree that leads, past formidable obstacles (hissing snakes, hideous dogs), to the house of the sun, personified here as a being who is alternately a wizened old man and a mewling infant. The sun's helpers—two ravens, Thought and Memory—are engaged both to restore Hanson's thirty lost years and to return Anatole safely home.

Finally, the collection's title piece, "Sailing to Cythera," finds Anatole visiting the home of Grandma and genially senile Grandpa. Assigned to spend the night in his mother's old room, Anatole is terrified by "the dark space under the bed" and is unable to sleep. This time, his questing journey begins when he is translated into the pattern on the wallpaper, which depicts an idyllic pastoral landscape peopled by idealized shepherds and shepherdesses. Adopting the pseudonym "Frère Jacques," Anatole ignores the warnings of others and accompanies pretty Thérèse aboard the ship of the Emperor of the Moon on a voyage to the mystical island of Cythera, reputed home of "the garden of the golden bough." On the island, Anatole encounters the much-feared Blimlin, a monster who, despite his intimidating appearance, turns out to be helpful, trustworthy, and decidedly lonely. It is he, in fact, who leads Anatole to the lavish garden of the golden bough. When the Blimlin confesses his longing for a "nice dark space" in which to live, a bargain is quickly struck: The friendly monster will guide Anatole home and in turn will inhabit the space under the boy's bed, thereby (in an ironic reversal of a common theme) dispelling Anatole's nighttime fears.

Analysis

Grandma's wallpaper in "Sailing to Cythera" is no doubt patterned after *The Embarkation for Cythera* (1717), a famous painting by Jean-Antoine Watteau that depicts the elegant antics of players from the *commedia dell'arte*. In any event, actual or imagined voyages to mystical Cythera—geographically, the southernmost of the Greek Ionian Islands—have abounded for centuries in Western (especially French) art, literature, and mythology. For that reason, it is fitting that the island's name is incorporated into the title of Nancy Willard's fanciful collection of stories about Anatole's quests for adventure and mythic transformation.

Indeed, familiar mythic archetypes and paradigms show up conspicuously in these pages: wise old men, nurturing earth mothers, dark woods of adventure, frightening obstacles, talking beasts, hard-won treasures, and the eternal return of the questing hero. While Willard's intended juvenile audience may not recognize these literary models as the conscious and premeditated products of Willard's craft, her young readers will already be acquainted with her essential themes, character types, and plots from the folktales and fairy tales that they have known since earliest childhood. In "Gospel Train," for example, Anatole nearly misses the "midnight special" train departing from the afterworld, a potentially fatal misstep redolent of the familiar Cinderella story. All this is well-plowed ground for Willard: In her graduate studies at Stanford University, the author studied medieval folk songs, and she routinely taught fairy tales in her own creative writing classes at Vassar College. Clearly, fantasy for Willard is no vehicle for mere escapism and sentiment. On the contrary, the mythically rich fantasies of dream and story are promoted here as metaphorically powerful tools for the expression of abiding human truths; they provide a new perspective from which readers can evaluate the "real" world that they actually inhabit.

In fact, Willard—in this book and in her other works, both poetry and prose—places emphatic value on the actual, the tangible, even the mundane. *Sailing to Cythera and Other Anatole Stories* is littered with hard-edged, everyday objects: cocoa boxes, pocket watches, sneakers, dusty French dictionaries. Although surrounded by talking, personified animals, Plumpet has no qualms about picnicking voluptuously on roasted mice ("Lovely plump little things"), and, once he arrives at the fabled garden of the golden bough, Anatole discovers that he actually prefers the palpable reality and earthy physicality of Grandma's less high-flown (but eminently more edible) vegetable garden back home. Grandma herself has said, "I can't really enjoy a thing unless I can touch it."

At the thematic core of the collection seems to be the mythically sound idea, variously voiced, that any journey is itself ultimately more important than its intended purpose or destination. In the course of his voyage to see Aunt Pitterpat, for example, Anatole learns much about his own nascent competence and the nature of time and timelessness; the departed cat, finally located perched atop a merry-go-round horse, confidently announces, "This ride never stops, and the music goes on forever." In his quest for Erik Hanson's memory, the boy achieves his real boon in overcoming his childish nighttime fears. One wise old man counsels Anatole that, at journey's end, "The hardest part is getting home again." Yet, Anatole is always able to return, and he always brings back much new knowledge.

Critical Context

Nancy Willard's highly literate books of poetry and prose for young audiences have garnered her an unbroken string of awards and honors, including a 1974 Lewis Carroll Shelf Award for *Sailing to Cythera and Other Anatole Stories*; in 1973, the collection was also named one of the fifty best books of the year by the American Institute of Graphic Arts. The critical and popular success of this volume has spawned such sequels as *The Island of the Grass King: The Further Adventures of Anatole* (1979), another Lewis Carroll Award winner, and *Uncle Terrible: More Adventures of Anatole* (1982). Further, Willard won the prestigious Newbery Medal in 1982 and a Special Honor Book Plaque from the Society of Children's Book Writers in 1981 for *A Visit to William Blake's Inn: Poems for Innocent and Experienced Travelers* (1981), a book of poems for children.

These awards (and the many others that her books have attracted) attest the high regard in which Willard is held by both her audience and critics. In noting Willard's accomplishments and contributions to her art, such critics most often cite the sensitive manner in which her works, at their best, create an imaginative world where a pervading sense of magic blends effortlessly with a reverence for concrete, even homely detail. This unlikely fusion of fantasy and reality poses no real dichotomy for the author herself: Willard has asserted that "there are two kinds of truth—the scientific answer and the imaginative answer. And we need both of them."

William Ryland Drennan

SARA WILL

Author: Sue Ellen Bridgers (1942-   )
First published: 1985
Type of work: Novel
Type of plot: Domestic realism and psychological realism
Time of work: 1981-1982
Locale: Sparrow Creek and Tyler Mills, North Carolina
Subjects: Coming-of-age, death, emotions, family, and love and romance
Recommended ages: 15-18

Sara Will, who initially resists change and the presence of other people in her life, gradually learns tenderness and love, as does teenage Eva, who comes to love Michael.

> *Principal characters:*
> SARA WILL BURNEY, a middle-aged isolated woman who learns to love others
> SWANEE HOPE CALHOUN, Sara Will's kind, more sociable sister who lives with her
> SERENA BURNEY JESSOP, Sara Will's deceased sister, buried in an almost-inaccessible cemetery
> EVA JESSOP, a teenage single mother
> LAFAYETTE "FATE" JESSOP, Eva's caring uncle
> RACHEL, Eva's baby
> MICHAEL LOGAN, Eva's friend who wants to marry her
> CHET ARMSTRONG, the uncaring biological father of Rachel
> CLEMENT and HARRIET JESSOP, Eva's parents

Form and Content

Sue Ellen Bridgers' *Sara Will* is about the changes that love can bring to empty lives. Written in the third person, the novel explores how Sara Will, Fate, and Eva find meaning as they learn to care for one another. Sara Will Burney lives with her sister Swanee Hope Calhoun in an isolated mountain home on Sparrow Creek. Across the flooded valley is the grave of their sister Serena Burney Jessop. A middle-aged woman, Sara Will lives a self-contained, routine existence until Fate Jessop arrives with Eva, his sixteen-year-old niece, and her baby, Rachel.

Just as Fate, Eva, and her baby come unbidden into the Burney sisters' lives, Eva had arrived a year earlier into her Uncle Fate's life. Seven-months pregnant, she had fled her parents to an uncle she barely knew because her parents thought that she should give up her baby for adoption. Eva and the baby give Fate's life purpose and love. When Eva's friend Michael tracks down Eva because he wants to marry her, even though he is not the baby's father, Fate flees with Eva and Rachel into Sara Will's and Swanee's hitherto uneventful lives.

Swanee welcomes the three strangers, but Sara Will only reluctantly permits them to stay. When Michael finds them, Eva rejects him. In spite of this dismissal, however, he stays with Sara Will, helping Fate make needed repairs to the neglected house. The presence of all these people in Sara Will's home confuses her almost to a state of panic. Yet, she begins to be touched by them, feeling tenderness for the first time in years. On Thanksgiving Day, she recognizes the "possibility of loving them," but loving makes her feel vulnerable.

Eva begins to treat Michael in a civil manner after he saves the baby from eating poisonous berries. Because Eva does not love Michael as he loves her, however, he decides to return home to college. His return address on the letter to the registrar reveals where he and Eva are. Eva's worried parents, who previously had not known Eva's location, arrive at Sara's house on Christmas Day, only reluctantly to accept Eva's decision not to return home with them.

Early on Christmas morning, Fate expresses his feelings for Sara Will, by whom he had been moved years ago when she cried out at Serena's funeral. Christmas evening concludes with their aching first kiss. The next day, when Fate wrecks Sara Will's beloved Mustang, Sara Will feels that he has betrayed her trust, so she moves to Mrs. Bloxton's boarding house in Tyler Mills while the car is being repaired. Her agonizing loneliness there is broken when Fate sends her a note declaring that he does not want to lose her. After a brief, gentle courtship, they marry.

Although afraid of the water, Sara Will, along with her extended family, crosses the lake in the spring to the island where Serena is buried. There, Eva tells Michael that she loves him. As Sara Will restores her sister's grave, she realizes that she has learned to live and to love.

Analysis

Sara Will focuses on an adult protagonist, but she, like many teenagers, must learn to cope with turbulent emotions as she experiences love for the first time—insecurity, confusion, and the sweetness of being loved. The juxtaposed character of the teenage unwed mother, Eva, also learns to love. Both women come of age, and although each initially resists change, both eventually do change. Sara is frequently confused by her own emotions, but she recognizes Eva's developing maturity. Therefore, *Sara Will* is a novel of initiation in which adult and teenage characters discover themselves and love.

The major subject of this novel is emotions and the tensions in human relationships. Treasuring her grief and almost never leaving her home, Sara Will is afraid of relationships and has a lifelong history of not taking risks. As she learns to care for Eva, Rachel, and Fate, however, she experiences the pain and the joy that risk-taking and love entail. Eva, too, must free herself from the past, especially her parents' control, and learn to trust and love her Uncle Fate and Michael. Each woman eventually makes commitments to others, as does Fate, who rejects his empty life to help Eva and to love Sara Will.

Sara Will is also about family. Sara Will's grief is crippling, and she will not let her living sister into her emotional life. Yet, as her family expands to include four strangers, she learns to appreciate her unconventional family and to welcome them into her heart. Eva also understands the importance of family. She is a loving mother, and she gradually comes to love Michael, who wants them to be a family.

Sara Will emphasizes setting because isolation is one of its major subjects. The physical isolation of Sara Will's home and of Serena's grave provides the context for emotional isolation. As Sara Will's emotional isolation decreases, so does her physical isolation. She ventures from her home into Tyler Mills. The trip across the lake to Serena's grave shows that she is no longer isolated because she loves Fate enough to risk the journey. In the cemetery, she brings her past and present together so that she can live life more fully.

Critical Context

Originally published as an adult novel, *Sara Will* was later accepted as a young adult novel and was recognized as an American Library Association (ALA) Best Book. *Sara Will*, like Sue Ellen Bridgers' other young adult novels, stresses the importance of family. Critics, such as Joseph O. Milner in "The Emergence of Awe in Recent Children's Literature," see this emphasis on family as setting Bridgers apart from other young adult authors. Her novels examine relationships among the generations, often with teenagers connecting with their grandparents or people who represent tradition. Bridgers states that family life is "the core of my writing" in "Stories My Grandmother Told Me" in the *ALAN Review*. *Permanent Connections* (1987) expresses the importance of family connections in its title and in its story of Rob Dickson, who learns to accept his connections to his senile grandfather, his agoraphobic aunt, his injured uncle, and his father. *Home Before Dark* (1985) explores the changes that occur when Stella's mother dies and her father remarries, causing Stella first to make their cabin a home and eventually to move to her new home. In both *All Together Now* (1979), the winner of the Boston Globe/*Horn Book* Award and the Christopher Award, and *Notes for Another Life* (1981), teenagers live with grandparents who nurture them.

Bridgers is a Southern writer whom critics praise for vivid evocations of the small-town North Carolina setting with which she is familiar, for rich characterization, and for the authentic voices of her characters. According to Bridgers, Sara Will came to her suddenly and fully developed, a compelling character. Bridgers captures Sara Will's repression, emotional turmoil, and growing self-awareness in concrete, vivid details. Pamela Sissi Carroll, the author of the first doctoral dissertation on Bridgers, ranks her with writers of the Southern Renaissance. Both *All Together Now* and *Notes for Another Life* were nominated for the American Book Award and were named ALA Best Books. In 1985, the Assembly on Literature for Adolescents honored Bridgers with the ALAN Award for her outstanding contributions to young adult literature.

Eleanor Parks Gaunder

SARAH BISHOP

Author: Scott O'Dell (1898-1989)
First published: 1980
Type of work: Novel
Type of plot: Historical fiction
Time of work: The 1770's
Locale: Long Island, New York City, Wallabout Bay, northern Westchester County at Long Pond, and Ridgeford
Subjects: Death, family, friendship, gender roles, and war
Recommended ages: 13-18

An adolescent in mourning, Sarah Bishop must fight herself, the British troops, and nature in order to survive after her father is killed by Patriots and her brother dies on a British prison boat during the revolutionary war.

Principal characters:
SARAH BISHOP, a fifteen-year-old who is trying to cope with the loss of her family
JAMES BISHOP, Sarah's father, a Tory who is faithful to King George
CHAD BISHOP, Sarah's brother, a Patriot who enlists in the rebellion
DAVID WHITLOCK, a friend of Sarah's brother and a fellow Patriot
MRS. JESSOP, a neutral, Christian neighbor who cares for Sarah
MR. and MRS. PENNYWELL, owners of the Lion and Lamb tavern, where Sarah works
CAPTAIN CUNNINGHAM, a British officer who tries to hold Sarah responsible for a fire that she did not start
SAM GOSHEN, a trapper and trader who tries to befriend Sarah
ISAAC MORTON, a Quaker storekeeper who becomes a friend to Sarah

Form and Content

Scott O'Dell's *Sarah Bishop* is a straightforward narrative of a young woman's fight to survive the personal consequences of the American Revolution. The early conflict in the book centers on Sarah's father and brother, who have chosen different sides in the rebellion. Sarah's father, James, has remained loyal to the "homeland," while her brother, Chad, enlists with the Patriots. At first, the Patriots merely warn James that his views are unpopular, but one night they burn his barn and house while tarring and feathering him. He dies the next day. After her father's death, Sarah leaves her neighbor, Mrs. Jessop, and sets out to find her brother, having had no word from him since his enlistment.

While negotiating the various levels of the military, Sarah finds a place to stay for the night but is caught in a fire, one that a British officer accuses her of starting. While held by the British troops, a kind lieutenant allows her to go to the prison ship where Chad was sent. When she arrives, she talks with her brother's friend, David, who tells her that Chad died that morning. Escaping from her captors, Sarah returns to Mrs. Jessop, acquires a gun, and "disappears" into the wilderness for solace. Relying on her own survival skills, she creates a home for herself in a cave on Long Pond, sharing it with a white bat that becomes her pet.

Sarah's peaceful life is upset when she rescues Sam Goshen, a trapper and trader whose leg is caught in his own bear trap, and brings him back to her cave to recover from the accident. Sarah knows that Sam Goshen as a womanizer because he gave her a ride when she was running from the British and made advances. Consequently, she is uncomfortable in his presence and uneasy having him in her cave.

Sarah makes periodic visits from Long Pond to Ridgeford, a nearby town, to get the essentials that she cannot create from the wilderness. There, she meets Isaac Morton, a Quaker who realizes who Sarah is by the posters that the British troops have posted asking for her capture. He does not turn her in, however, and tries to befriend her, asking her to attend a Quaker meeting. Because of what are perceived as antisocial ways, including her attachment to her musket, Sarah is accused by Isaac's father of performing witchcraft and causing an extensive drought and rampant illness in the town. "Rescued" by the town constable and jailed for her own protection, Sarah is eventually allowed to testify in her own defense, as does Isaac. Deciding that he does not have enough support to prosecute her, Isaac's father dismisses the charges and a more sociable Sarah leaves town to return to her cave home, promising Isaac that she will return for the next meeting.

Analysis

Based on the experiences of a real young woman named Sarah Bishop, O'Dell's novel is engaging because of its heroine. While Sarah is not a heroine in the classic sense of accomplishing a single spectacular deed, she is a heroine because she survives and does so through the strength of her own character, an important message for female readers and male readers alike.

As the novel opens, Sarah has already lost her mother, but the specific circumstances are not revealed. Almost immediately, Sarah's father is killed and her brother enlists, leaving Sarah on her own. As one could imagine, Sarah has a difficult time accepting her father's death, especially such a preventable and excruciatingly painful one as being tarred and feathered, and so tries to maintain her family by searching for her brother. When she finally earns enough money by working at the Lion and Lamb tavern, she goes in search of him, only to discover that she is hours too late to see him and that he has already been buried at sea. Lost and now truly alone, she is used as a Patriot pawn of the British troops and is held responsible for starting a fire. She escapes to the wilderness, where she uses the solitude and abundance of nature to nurture her spiritual well-being.

An interesting aspect of her personality is her abrupt departure from her earlier reliance on the church and the teachings of the Bible as these life-altering events occur in her life. Before Sarah leaves town to find her brother, Mrs. Jessop gives her a Bible. As Sarah settles into her new home, she admits that she has "no desire to read the

Bible," and she realizes as she reads aloud to Sam Goshen that she has only read from the Bible twice since her father's death. It is clear that Sarah feels abandoned by everyone, including God, and for a time does not find solace in the religion that had once comforted her. Such questioning of values is appropriate for an adolescent, however, even one whose experiences have not been so trying.

The serenity and life-renewing forces of nature do mend Sarah's heart. She hunts only to eat and is quite comfortable with all of nature, especially those creatures that could be considered outcasts—perhaps because of the way she is feeling about herself. Sarah seems to develop a kinship with the white bat, a rare variety, who shares the cave with her. In fact, Sarah even invents and plays a game with her small friend, perhaps the only lighthearted event in the novel. She also has tenderhearted feelings toward a muskrat that she rescues from a trap, an animal that chewed off its own foot in an effort to free itself. Sarah takes the muskrat to her cave and nurses it back to health, releasing it only when she knows that it can survive on its own.

The cave becomes a symbolic womb from which Sarah is reborn. She will live there long enough for her heart to heal from the effects of the war on her life, and, while she still lives in the cave at the end of the novel, she has noted that she is beginning to feel "spells of loneliness" and has promised Isaac that she will return to town for the next Quaker meeting. Sarah is beginning to become part of the real world again. She has marshalled her inner strength to survive physically, which in turn has enabled her to survive emotionally—a lesson for all.

Critical Context

Like *Sarah Bishop*, most of Scott O'Dell's work is historical fiction, so it comes as no surprise that an award for a work of this genre set in the New World is given in his honor: the Scott O'Dell Award for Historical Fiction. O'Dell wrote other novels with strong, female characters such as Sarah. Karana, the central character of *Island of the Blue Dolphins* (1960), which won the Newbery Medal, lives alone on an island off the coast of California. She is finally rescued by Spanish priests after eighteen years, but one wonders whether Karana will find as much peace and happiness at the mission—and within civilization—as she did on her island home, a question that could be asked of Sarah as well. The question for Karana is answered in the sequel, *Zia* (1977), which reveals her last days as witnessed through the eyes of her niece.

Bright Morning is a similarly strong female character in O'Dell's Newbery Honor Book *Sing Down the Moon* (1970). In a memorable story that reflects the dignity of the Navajo people, Bright Morning convinces her wounded fiancé to escape from a U.S. fort after their imprisonment there along the "Long Walk," the horrific three hundred-mile forced march of the Navajo from their canyon homes to Fort Sumner. Like Sarah, they find refuge in a cave in their familiar homeland and, once there, begin a new life with their newborn son, their spirits healed. Other Newbery Honor Books by O'Dell are *The King's Fifth* (1966) and *The Black Pearl* (1987).

Alexa L. Sandmann

THE SATURDAYS

Author: Elizabeth Enright (1909-1968)
First published: 1941; illustrated
Type of work: Novel
Type of plot: Domestic realism
Time of work: The early 1940's
Locale: New York City
Subjects: Coming-of-age, family, and friendship
Recommended ages: 10-13

> *The four precocious Melendy siblings, weary of facing boring Saturdays at home in Manhattan, conceive an innovative plan in the form of I.S.A.A.C.—the Independent Saturday Afternoon Adventure Club.*

Principal characters:
MONA MELENDY, the eldest of the Melendy children, thirteen years old and an aspiring actress
RUSH MELENDY, twelve, a pragmatic musician
MIRANDA "RANDY" MELENDY, ten, the artistic creator of I.S.A.A.C.
OLIVER MELENDY, the youngest of the four siblings, an amiable and thoughtful six-year-old
MRS. EVANGELINE "CUFFY" CUTHBERT-STANLEY, the long-suffering housekeeper and surrogate parent to the motherless Melendy children
MR. MELENDY, the weary father of the four siblings
WILLY SLOPER, the Melendy family caretaker and furnaceman
MRS. OLIPHANT, an elderly family friend who becomes the children's generous benefactor

Form and Content

The Saturdays is an optimistic account of the creativity of four almost impossibly precocious yet somehow believable children. Elizabeth Enright's Melendy siblings exude talent and good-natured enthusiasm, presenting an idealized family in which all members work together in respectful harmony.

The novel opens as Mona, Rush, Randy, and Oliver Melendy, assembled in their beloved "office" (actually a large playroom on the uppermost floor of their New York City home), complain about the prospect of spending another dreary and boring Saturday with nothing to do. The children, who live with their father and their adored nurse, Cuffy, are all inordinately talented and sophisticated for their ages: Mona is an aspiring actress who quotes William Shakespeare prolifically; Rush is an expert pianist and a lover of classical music and opera; Randy harbors both an appreciation for art and a talent for painting; and even contented young Oliver seems driven by an intellectual curiosity that exceeds his years. Randy offers a proposition: The Melendys will pool their weekly allowances and give the resulting sum to one child each week, in turn; the recipient of the money will then select a particular adventure on which to embark alone on Saturday afternoon. The club is christened I.S.A.A.C., or the Independent Saturday Afternoon Adventure Club.

Because I.S.A.A.C. was Randy's idea, it is agreed that the first Saturday will be hers. She chooses to walk the length of Fifth Avenue to the art gallery where a collection of "French pictures" is being shown. Randy immerses herself in the paintings, finally choosing as her favorite a work called *The Princess*. As she admires the painting, she is greeted by Mrs. Oliphant, an elderly family acquaintance who informs Randy that she herself was the young subject of *The Princess* when she was about Randy's age and a resident of Paris. Mrs. Oliphant invites Randy to a grand afternoon tea and enthralls her young guest with tales of her own girlhood adventures.

The novel proceeds in much the same manner, with each chapter dealing with a single Saturday and its events. Rush attends the German opera *Siegfried*. Mona, lured by the fancy script on a Broadway window, submits herself to the talents of Mr. Edward and Miss Pearl; she emerges from the beauty parlor several hours later, having been transformed from a girl with long pigtails to a sophisticated young lady with a bob and manicure. Oliver goes to the circus in Madison Square Garden, where he enjoys both the spectacle of the performance and a vast array of foodstuffs; sick and lost at the end of the afternoon, he must be escorted home by a police officer astride a grand horse.

All the Melendy family's experiences, however, are not fun and games. Randy carelessly leaves a dress hanging over a heated lightbulb in the family storeroom and causes a small fire. Similarly, Rush's attempts to care for the household's aging furnace in Willy Sloper's absence result in a near-tragic encounter with coal gas. Father's decision to replace the decrepit furnace with a more efficient model warrants financial cutbacks and a decision to eliminate the rent payments on the family's usual vacation spot away from the city. Stoically, the four young Melendys try not to complain, but they inadvertently let slip news of their situation during an outing with Mrs. Oliphant. The old lady offers her family lighthouse at the seashore as an alternative, and the family eagerly accepts her offer. The lighthouse proves to be idyllic, and the Melendy children prepare for a summer in which every day will be a "Saturday."

Analysis

The Saturdays is a cheerful and upbeat novel that provides happy endings and positive solutions while resorting to neither a condescending tone nor unrealistic plot contrivances to manipulate its action. Enright offers incredible optimism in the face of troubled times, and the financial and emotional uncertainty of the war years depicted in the novel can transfer to a multitude of other eras and situations to which young readers will be able to relate. The author depicts the angst, crises, and issues appropriate to her story, but she provides resolution time and time again. Her message is straightforward and undeviating: Bad things happen, but there is always a certain stability upon which one may rely.

In Enright's world, stability is largely found in the family. The Melendys are loving and devoted to one another. The vacant spot in the familial structure is rapidly filled by the remaining members; the Melendys have no mother, so Cuffy has assumed the role of family matriarch, and all the older siblings act as mother to the young Oliver. Cuffy's and Father's reactions to any given situation are totally and refreshingly predictable. Furnaceman Willy Sloper will have a position in the family's household even after they acquire a maintenance-free furnace. Similarly, new extensions of the family are readily absorbed into the current structure, as is the case with Isaac, the lost dog that Rush adopts, and with Mrs. Oliphant, who proves her loyalty to the Melendys once and is never questioned afterward.

Another way in which Enright creates the positive atmosphere that informs her tale is by structuring her story in a predictable, comforting manner. Each chapter of the novel is itself a Saturday, allowing the reader to be lulled and reassured by the cyclical nature of the work. The author also provides a number of examples of the story-within-a-story, that is, an independent tale placed within the framework of the main story of the Melendys and their adventures. On several occasions, a Melendy child encounters an adult who has a fascinating real-life success story to offer; Mrs. Oliphant, who was captured by gypsies as a young girl in Paris, and Miss Pearl, the beautician who escaped from a wicked stepmother, are examples. Enright always returns to the comfort and confines of New York City and her frame story, however, indicating that one need not travel the world for adventure; in Enright's world, excitement lurks, safely, around every familiar corner.

The strength of *The Saturdays*, however, lies in Enright's exceptional protagonists: four exceedingly artistic and literate children who make one believe in the possibility of a thirteen-year-old who quotes Shakespeare's tragedies at will or a twelve-year-old who would choose as his ideal Saturday activity an afternoon at the opera. Yet, at the same time, Enright allows the Melendys to remain real children who love to swim, get dirty, and frolic with their pets; they are likable characters, and their personalities make their exceptional talents and gifts qualities for which young readers can strive rather than oddities. Enright's novel encourages creativity, adventure, and an open-minded acceptance of others, while it also stresses the reality of a safe and stable place for everyone.

Critical Context

Elizabeth Enright, originally trained as an illustrator, won a Newbery Medal for her novel *Thimble Summer* (1938), the story of nine-year-old tomboy Garnet Linden and her experiences growing up on a Wisconsin farm during a hot, Depression-era summer. The title of this work refers to the main character's discovery of a thimble in a stream; Garnet views her find as a good omen, and this attitude contributes the same optimism to *Thimble Summer* that is found in Enright's later works. Garnet's story also features the stable, single-parent family found in Enright's other novels and that is, in fact, a part of the author's own biography.

The Saturdays is the first novel in a series of four about the Melendy family. In *The Four-Story Mistake* (1942), the family moves from their Manhattan home to the country, an experience that also mirrors the author's own childhood. *Then There Were Five* (1944) tells of the addition of a new Melendy family member, and *Spiderweb for Two: A Melendy Maze* (1951) finds Randy and Oliver pursuing a mysterious scavenger hunt after the older children leave for boarding school. Later, Enright introduced another family, the Blakes, in her novels *Gone-Away Lake* (1957) and *Return to Gone-Away* (1961).

Ellen Puccinelli

SCOTTISH FOLK-TALES AND LEGENDS

Author: Barbara Ker Wilson (1929-   )
First published: 1954; illustrated
Type of work: Short fiction
Subjects: Love and romance, race and ethnicity, the supernatural, and war
Recommended ages: 10-15

This collection of traditional tales and fables delineates the character traits that make the Scots a unique people.

Form and Content

In a collection of twenty-five short stories as well as seven tales selected from the adventures of the Fians, Barbara Ker Wilson explores the character traits that set the Scots apart from their neighbors as well as their Celtic kinsfolk. Written in the third person, each story is illustrated with a line drawing that refers in a general way to an event occurring in the narrative. A map following the table of contents identifies the geographic areas associated with the tales, and seven full-page drawings in muted colors are spaced throughout the work.

While each story in *Scottish Folk-Tales and Legends* may be treated as a separate entity, common themes unite the narratives. Love is often a component of Scottish legends, but there is usually an element of sacrifice or danger linked to the winning of the affection of another. Tam Lin is released from service to the Elf Queen because Fair Janet is willing to endure physical pain to rescue him. Like Ulysses, Black Colin of Loch Awe must assume a beggar's rags in order to save his wife from a forced marriage to one of his enemies. Not all the romances related in this work end happily; some are fraught with tragedy and loss. Roderic MacCodrum's wife abandons her family to resume her shape as a seal and return to the ocean, while the fairy bride of Malcolm MacLeod leaves only an enchanted banner as a reminder of her marriage when she forsakes her husband and son.

These stories offer a portrait of the Scottish people as brave, loyal, fearless, self-sacrificing, and reckless. One particular characteristic that is introduced repeatedly in these stories is the awe with which the Scots regard the supernatural. Most of the narratives in this collection contain an element of enchantment, which usually involves the fairy folk who live in two worlds. Some such as Morag MacGregor live to tell of their encounters with that other dominion, while others such as Alasdair, the Piper of Keil, vanish into the realm of the fairies and are lost forever. In every unexplained phenomenon, the average Scot seems to detect the handiwork of mystic beings, and this wonder is an important element in the myths of the Scottish people.

War has been the undoing of the Scots. Their bravery is extraordinary but often foolhardy. Nowhere is this duality better illustrated than in the seven tales of the Fians that form the concluding section of this work. Blessed with almost superhuman strength, these nine thousand warriors seem capable of any quest, but they are destroyed because their weaknesses, like their virtues, are magnified.

Analysis

Like the myths of all peoples, the stories included in *Scottish Folk-Tales and Legends* are intended to instruct readers, especially the young. The strengths and weaknesses that characterize the Scots are plainly set forth in language that cannot be misunderstood. Wilson avoids the use of Gaelic terms or words in the Scottish dialect that might confuse readers who are not familiar with these languages.

While the Scots value warriors, they do not stint their appreciation of women who prevail despite hardship. The wife of Roderic MacCodrum is able to assume the guise of a seal or a woman at will, but, when Roderic hides her seal skin, she is forced to live among humans. Her discovery of his deceit permits her to return to the sea, but in her joy is also pain because she knows that his real weakness is his deep love for her. In Scottish folklore, love that brings both exhilaration and despair or that requires sacrifice is also a favorite topic. The son and daughter of the Ailp king accept a mutual enchantment and the years of anguish that it will bring because they realize that only in sharing the pain can they ever win release. Survival in an harsh environment demands cooperation and oblation, attributes that are prominently featured in these narratives.

Scottish Folk-Tales and Legends also contains stories of fairies and other supernatural beings that teach lessons about morality. Those who suffer the wrath of "the little people" often do so because they ignore or knowingly break the basic rules of courtesy, or needlessly put themselves in jeopardy. Those persons who take unnecessary risks or commit thoughtless acts often pay a bitter price for their folly. When the good wife of Tiree seeks the help of the fairies of Burg Hill, she does not stop to consider the possible adverse consequences until is almost too late. Careful preparation and common sense can often permit one to avoid a potential disaster. On the other hand, by relying on the good advice of "Whippety Stourie," one of the fairy folk, the wife in the story by that name is delivered from a burdensome task that threatens her marriage and her life.

The stability of Scottish society is based on the clan system, in which the members of related families swear loyalty to a common leader as well as to one another. When mutual respect and traditional values are threatened, the very existence of the clan is imperiled. Without loyalty and trust, even bravery is void. The tragic history of Fionn MacChumail and the Fians ably illustrates the fate of those who allow weaknesses such as jealousy to cloud their vision. The story of the nine thousand warriors who composed the Fians, trapped by their own words and their blind loyalties, is like a mirror that reflects the tragic history of the Scottish people.

The educational value of folktales is most easily discernable in fables, and several of them are included in this collection. Short and succinct, their lessons are easily comprehended, and they are not subject to the dual interpretation encountered with allegory. The instructive elements of *Scottish Folk-Tales and Legends* range from the simple to the complex—from the guileless tale of "The Cock and the Fox," in which greed costs the fox a dinner, to the subtle treatment of "The Adventures of Iain Direach," in which love and hate are juxtaposed in a potentially tragic situation.

Critical Context

Several anthologies of traditional Scottish stories have been published, but many of them, such as Sorche Nic Leodhas' *Thistle and Thyme* (1965), demand a knowledge of the clan system and comprehension of several Gaelic words and expressions. Happily, Barbara Ker Wilson's *Scottish Folk-Tales and Legends* avoids this potential problem by retelling many of the cherished legends of the Scottish people without relying on the Gaelic language to create the proper atmosphere. Younger readers in particular will find the stories entertaining, and they serve as an excellent introduction to Scottish literature.

Clifton W. Potter, Jr.

THE SEA AROUND US

Author: Rachel Carson (1907-1964)
First published: 1951, rev. ed. 1961; illustrated
Type of work: Science
Locale: The ocean
Subjects: Nature and science
Recommended ages: 10-18

This absorbing and informative introduction to oceanography was written with a vast understanding of the history and life of the oceans, scientific accuracy, clear and poetic descriptions, and a strong sense of ecological balance.

Form and Content

In *The Sea Around Us*, Rachel Carson lovingly leads her readers through a clear and scientifically careful history of the sea, from the first formation of oceans on the planet to the middle of the twentieth century when the book was written. The text is divided into three main sections: "Mother Sea," "The Restless Sea," and "Man and the Sea About Him."

In part 1, "Mother Sea," provides in eight titled chapters a history and description of the life found in the sea. In "Gray Beginnings," Carson gives a scientific history of the origin of the earth's oceans. In "The Pattern of the Surface," the complexity of life in the surface waters is described: "Unmarked and trackless though it may seem to us, the surface of the ocean is divided into definite zones, and the pattern of the surface water controls the distribution of its life." The chapter entitled "The Changing Year" describes the ways in which the surface waters are affected by seasonal changes, and "The Sunless Sea" describes life in the depths of the ocean and discusses advances in deep-water oceanography. Other chapters in this section provide a history of the scientific efforts to sound the bottom of the ocean and what was learned of its topography; describe the significance of sediment; chronicle the birth and life of oceanic islands; and, in "The Shape of Ancient Seas," assess the evidence of former seas on dry land.

Part 2 of *The Sea Around Us*, entitled "The Restless Sea," describes in three chapters the motion and turbulence of the sea in the form of waves, currents, and tides. "Wind and Water" provides a clear and fascinating description of the scientific study of ocean waves, as well as historical information, such as stories recorded by lighthouse keepers, and explanations of the difference between seismic sea waves and "rollers." The chapter "Wind, Sun, and the Spinning of the Earth" discusses oceanic currents. "The Moving Tides" explains how the force of the tides is even stronger than waves and currents, explaining theories of "tidal oscillation," "bores," and the influence of tides on life in the sea.

Part 3, "Man and the Sea About Him," presents and discusses in three chapters the relationship between humans and the sea. In "The Global Thermostat," Carson notes that, "For the globe as a whole, the ocean is the great regulator, the great stabilizer of temperatures. It has been described as a 'savings bank' for polar energy, receiving deposits in seasons of excessive insolation and paying them back in seasons of want. Without the ocean, our world would be visited by unthinkably harsh extremes of temperature." In this chapter, Carson describes early research on the phenomenon now familiar to the public as "global warming." The next chapter in the book, "Wealth from the Salt Sea," discusses the ocean as "the earth's greatest storehouse of minerals" and includes a discussion of oil and offshore drilling. The final chapter, "The Encircling Sea," considers the history of navigation, the first voyages of marine exploration, and the development of navigational instruments and charts. It also profiles Lieutenant Matthew F. Maury, of the U.S. Navy, whose book *The Physical Geography of the Sea* (1855) "is now considered the foundation of the science of oceanography." *The Sea Around Us* concludes with a hopeful look forward to further advances in oceanography—although "no one now can say that we shall ever resolve the last, the ultimate mysteries of the sea"—and with a final philosophical view of the sea as encompassing all of life.

The book has numerous black-and-white, mostly photographic, illustrations.

Analysis

The Sea Around Us, written by one of America's greatest science writers, was intended for a general audience, but it is accessible to children as well as adults. Carson earned a master's degree in marine zoology from The Johns Hopkins University and worked for many years for the U.S. Fish and Wildlife Service. She also loved poetry and writing, and this love shows up in her science books in her clear language and a style that makes the reader understand easily and want to learn more. Carson's writing conveys a respect for the reader as well as an affection for the subject matter. Young readers will not feel as if she is talking down to them and instead will find Carson's historical and scientific explanations easy to follow.

The Sea Around Us not only informs the reader about the history of the ocean and the variety and complexity of life within it but also makes the reader aware of connections between human beings and the ocean and especially of the dangers of upsetting the ecological balance of oceanic life. In the chapter on islands, for example, Carson explains how human interference with the unique flora and fauna of oceanic islands, such as the Hawaiian Islands, has resulted in the extinction of many species, whose loss she laments.

In her introduction to the revised edition of *The Sea Around Us* in 1961, Carson also discusses advances in oceanography in the intervening ten years and expresses her growing concern over human threats to the balance of life in the sea, particularly the dangers of nuclear testing in the ocean. This awareness of an endangered ecological balance became the theme of Carson's most influential work, *Silent Spring* (1962).

Critical Context

The Sea Around Us was Rachel Carson's second book, after *Under the Sea Wind*

(1941), which was neglected in its first edition because it came out just before the Japanese attack on Pearl Harbor that began the United States' involvement in World War II. *The Sea Around Us* quickly became a best-seller and was followed by *The Edge of the Sea* in 1955. Carson's greatest book, *Silent Spring*, was written to inform and warn the world about the dangers of DDT and other pesticides. It was published to great controversy, as pesticide companies tried to suppress the information. Carson, who was conducting her own private fight against cancer, had to endure many harsh attacks, many of which questioned the validity of her scientific findings simply because she was a woman. Nevertheless, *Silent Spring* proved itself to be accurate and had much to do with the passing of legislation to protect the environment from dangerous pesticides. Moreover, its author received many awards for her service to nature and society.

Carson's last book, *The Sense of Wonder* (1965), was the first written specifically as a children's book. She began it for her grandnephew Roger, whom she had adopted after his mother died, but the book was not published until after Carson's own death in 1964. All of her books, however, can be recommended for young people as models of good writing, good science, and a responsible and caring attitude toward the environment. Rachel Carson was one of America's greatest science and nature writers and is also an inspiring figure in the history of women in science.

Charlotte Zoë Walker

THE SEA-WOLF

Author: Jack London (1876-1916)
First published: 1904
Type of work: Novel
Type of plot: Adventure tale and moral tale
Time of work: Around 1900
Locale: San Francisco Bay and a remote island in the Pacific Ocean
Subjects: Death, friendship, and love and romance
Recommended ages: 13-18

Humphrey Van Weyden is shipwrecked and rescued by a seal-hunting ship, made a prisoner by the captain, escapes with a female friend, survives on a remote island, repairs the ship, and gets them back to civilization.

Principal characters:
  HUMPHREY VAN WEYDEN, a literary critic and man of leisure
  WOLF LARSEN, the captain of the *Ghost*
  THOMAS MUGRIDGE, the ship's cook
  JOHNSON, a rebellious sailor
  MAUD BREWSTER, a poet and essayist
  DEATH LARSEN, Wolf Larsen's brother, the captain of the *Macedonia*

Form and Content

Jack London's *The Sea-Wolf* is primarily an adventure and a journalistic narrative, but it is also a philosophical discussion, the tale of a man coming to terms with what it is to be a man, and a love story. Literary critic Humphrey Van Weyden is thrown off a sinking ferry in San Francisco Bay and is rescued by the *Ghost*, a seal-hunting schooner bound for Japan. The captain, Wolf Larsen, disgusted that Ven Weyden does not really work for a living, offers him the job of cabin boy, through which he will learn to stand on his own legs, for the good of his soul. Thus, Van Weyden becomes a prisoner on the *Ghost*. He discovers that the captain reads literature and studies astronomy and physics, and the two enter into philosophical discussion. Larsen believes that people do not have souls, that the world is a terrible and selfish place, and that humans are all part of a great yeast in which the parts that are the strongest eat the weakest and stay alive.

Morale is not good on the ship, and, as a result of a series of attempted mutinies, Van Weyden is promoted to cook and finally to first mate. At the seal-hunting grounds, Van Weyden is given the job of tallying the skins and overseeing their cleaning, and he observes that he is toughened or hardened by the work. The *Ghost* comes upon a stranded mail steamer from San Francisco bound for Yokohama. Larsen takes the stranded passengers on board and passes by Yokohama, keeping the new passengers. One of them is Maud Brewster, a poet, and she and Van Weyden discover that they know each other, Van Weyden having written about her work. Van Weyden warns Maud about Larsen, and when Larsen looks passionately at Maud, Van Weyden realizes that he himself has fallen in love with her. When Larsen tries to rape Maud, Van Weyden saves her, and they escape together. They set off toward Japan, but winds blow them in the wrong direction, and they land on a remote island, where they learn to survive.

One morning, they awake to see the *Ghost* ashore. Van Weyden goes on board to find Larsen and levels a gun at him, but Larsen tells Van Weyden that his conventional morality will not let him kill an unarmed man. Larsen explains that his brother caught up with them and, in revenge for an earlier attack, persuaded all of Larsen's men to desert and destroyed his rigging. The illness that is destroying Larsen worsens, and he goes blind. When Van Weyden creates shears to help in repairing the masts, Larsen tears down the shears and casts the masts adrift. Van Weyden and Maud start again, handcuffing Larsen to his bunk. Larsen goes deaf in one ear, but his mind is still intact. Van Weyden and Maud continue the work on the ship, and Larsen tries to stop them once more by setting a fire. Larsen finally loses his speech. Van Weyden and Maud finish repairing the ship, and they all leave the island in the *Ghost*, but Larsen dies in the first storm. As Van Weyden and Maud see a ship and know that they will be rescued, they kiss.

Analysis

The Sea-Wolf works on several levels: as an adventure, a survival story, a philosophical discussion, an examination of manhood, and a love story.

As an adventure story, it is fast-paced and exciting. Most of the men hate Larsen and are waiting for an opportunity to kill him. There are chases at sea, dangerous storms, plots, and escapes. In terms of survival, this novel has much in common with London's *The Call of the Wild* (1903). Like the dog Buck, Van Weyden is civilized, protected, and spoiled. He, like Buck, is thrown into unfamiliar surroundings that test his fitness, patience, strength, and ability to stand up for himself. Ultimately, both are tested in terms of their ability to fit in, to work hard without weakness or complaining, to become leaders, and finally to achieve heroic acts that save the ones whom they love in the face of great danger.

The novel is also an interesting combination of philosophy and adventure; in this, it is not unlike Herman Melville's *Moby-Dick* (1851). In that novel, chapters of action are interspersed with chapters of philosophy. In *The Sea-Wolf*, events often prompt philosophical discussions between Larsen and Van Weyden concerning morality, mortality, the value of life, and the existence of the soul. As these discussions evolve through the novel, readers get a fuller sense of how Larsen thinks, and his cynical views of life and the soul are an interesting contrast to Van Weyden's intellectual idealism and to Larsen's own struggle with the illness that is destroying him. Van Weyden learns from his experiences that Larsen is right in his claim that it takes some hardness or toughness to survive in this environment. Larsen never seems to accept the idea of the soul. When his ability to communicate is sinking away in blindness, deafness, dumbness, and paralysis, but his mind is still fully functioning, Maud asks if he is pondering immortality, and Larsen scribbles back "Bosh."

It is clear that Van Weyden learns about manhood from his experiences and from his relationship with Larsen, and Larsen was correct in his belief that Van Weyden's ordeal would make a man of him. Van Weyden is courageous because he quickly accepts his fate and, in spite of his previous experience to the contrary, throws himself into his duties. He not only survives but also excels.

The love story is interesting because it does not begin until more than halfway through the novel. It is as if Van Weyden needs the time before Maud Brewster appears in order to learn what it is to stand on his own. By the time that she comes on board, he can offer her protection and inspire confidence in their ability to survive Larsen's attacks. It is interesting to watch Van Weyden and Maud fall in love in such unusual surroundings. On the ship, she is the only woman, and he almost immediately becomes her protector, which he is now ready to do after his trial by sea. They become closer without any customary courting rituals. In addition to the intellectual stimulation coming from their common ground in literature, it is the constant danger and uncertainty about Larsen that draws them together. When they are alone on the island, they live as polite neighbors. They eat, work, and relax together, but still without anything that resembles a customary courtship. Nevertheless, the romance grows strong. It is only when they are about to be rescued that they give in to any kind of physical expression or admit their feelings, and they kiss. Until then, they had barely even spoken of their feelings. Yet, somehow that restraint—physically, verbally, and even socially—makes their intense love seem great.

Critical Context

When Jack London first got the idea for this book, he was planning to write a narrative based on his travels as a sailor on the *Sophia Sutherland* called "The Mercy of the Sea." As he was writing *The Call of the Wild*, however, he was so inspired by the idea of mastery in that book that he decided to take, as he said in a letter to his publisher, a "cultured, refined, super-civilized man and woman, . . . throw them into a primitive sea-environment, . . . and make this man & woman rise to the situation and come out of it with flying colors." As *The Call of the Wild* was published in 1903, *The Sea-Wolf* completed in 1904, and *White Fang* completed in 1905, it is clear that the theme of survival of the civilized in an uncivilized environment, and then of the opposite situation, was a driving force in London's work during that period.

The Sea-Wolf had a sensational reception, with an advance sale of twenty thousand copies, and there was even some interest in dramatizing it. The story, although not written for young audiences, was not unlike adventure stories for children during this period, which were strongly influenced by the work of Robert Louis Stevenson in that they involved escape, treasure, smuggling, and far-off romantic places.

Luther Hanson

SEASONS OF SPLENDOUR
Tales, Myths, and Legends of India

Author: Madhur Jaffrey (1933-   )
First published: 1985; illustrated
Type of work: Short Fiction
Subjects: Race and ethnicity, religion, and the supernatural
Recommended ages: 10-13

Eighteen stories from the mythology and folklore of India introduce readers to a representative selection of the major stories of the Hindu religion and culture.

Form and Content

Seasons of Splendour retells some of the most characteristic and important myths, fables, and epic stories of India. The collection includes the core stories of the ancient Hindu religious epics, Valmiki's *Ramayana* (c. 500 B.C.) and Vyasa's *Mahabharata* (c. 350 B.C.), as well as a variety of tales about gods, goddesses, demons, magic, and humble men and women.

Seasons of Splendour retells these tales in a clear and accessible format within a series of frame stories that recount the storyteller's childhood experiences of religious festivals in India. The stories are arranged in the order of the festivals of the Hindu year, beginning with the spring equinox in April, and are illustrated by Michael Foreman.

Analysis

The first two stories feature the healing powers of the banyan tree, a cool refuge from the summer heat. In "Savitri and Satyavan," the princess Savitri marries the poor woodcutter Satyavan, who is actually a prince robbed of his kingdom. When Satyavan dies suddenly, Savitri asks the banyan tree to guard him. She then persistently follows the King of the Underworld until he grants her three wishes, which she uses to regain her husband and his kingdom. "Sharavan Kumar and His Wife" tells how a wife who is mean to her husband's parents redeems herself after their deaths. She asks the banyan tree to cure her wounded husband, and the tree is moved by her caring and remorse.

Four stories from the *Mahabharata* tell about the god Krishna, whose birth is celebrated in August. In "The Birth of Krishna, the Blue God," evil King Kans hears a prophecy that his sister's child will kill him. He imprisons his sister and her husband, killing each of their newborn children. Heaven helps the couple switch Krishna with a cousin in the next kingdom just as Kans orders all male newborns in his realm slaughtered. "Krishna and the Demon Nurse" relates how Kans discovers Krishna's rescue and sends the demon Pootana, disguised as a nurse, to poison the child. The infant's powers, however, enable him to destroy the nurse. In "The Serpent King," Krishna, at the age of twelve, destroys the five-headed snake Kaliya, rescuing his friends from its realm beneath the river. "How Krishna Killed the Wicked King Kans" tells how the adult Krishna is tricked into a wrestling match, but his strength allows him to kill a wild elephant, two giants, and King Kans. He then frees his parents and the people from tyranny.

In early September, after the full moon, Hindus remember their dead relatives at the Moon Day festivities. "Doda and Dodi" tells of a brother and sister, one very rich and the other very poor. When Doda's wife mistreats his sister, their father's ghost intervenes. The wife's continued tricks are turned against her by her husband, and she finally learns her lesson.

In late September, Hindus celebrate Dussehra, the Festival of Victory. The five-part "How Ram Defeated the Demon King Ravan" tells the story of the triumph of good over evil in the great epic *Ramayana*. First, "King Dashrat's Special Heir" relates how the gods regretted granting the evil Ravan immortality and arranged for the god Vishnu to be born into the body of Ram in order to undo the mistake. In "Ram Is Banished," King Dashrat decides to abdicate in favor of his son Ram. The mother of Ram's half brother, Bharat, however, uses the two wishes that Dashrat granted her years ago to make her son king and to banish Ram to the forest for fourteen years. Ram honors his father's promise, but Bharat honors his brother's right to the throne by reigning as caretaker, with Ram's sandals occupying the throne until his return. In the third part of the tale, "The Kidnapping of Sita," the evil Ravan's demon sister falls in love with Ram but is spurned by him. In retaliation, she persuades Ravan to steal Ram's wife, Sita. "The Search for Sita" relates how Ram is helped by monkeys, bears, and vultures to discover that Sita is hidden in Lanka, Ravan's kingdom. In "The Siege of Lanka," the final part of the saga, an army of animals assists Ram in battling Ravan. In the end, Ram kills Ravan with a single arrow to the heart.

The Festival of the Wintry Full Moon comes in October. The fable "The Moon and the Heavenly Nectar" tells why there is an eclipse of the moon every year. When Vishnu passed out immortality, he mistakenly gave it to Rahu. Realizing the error, he cuts off Rahu's head, which shines in the sky but which must disappear every year to show its mortality. In the autumn, Hindu women fast and pray for the health of their husbands at the Karvachuath Festival. In "The Girl Who Had Seven Brothers," a girl is tricked into breaking her fast and loses her husband. To restore his life, she watches over his body for a year and then begs each of the nine earth goddesses to restore him until her persistence is finally rewarded. Divali, the Festival of Lights, is celebrated in November. In "Lakshmi and the Clever Washerwoman," a poor washerwoman finds the queen's pearl necklace, returns it, and becomes the only person whom the goddess of wealth and good fortune visits that year.

In late February or early March, Holi, the Indian Spring Festival, is celebrated with the throwing of colored dyes as a social leveler. "The Wicked King and His Good Son" tells of a king who thinks he is God and tries to have his son killed because he does not need an heir. Aunt Holika protects the boy, and God kills the father for his insolence.

In March, sisters pray for their brothers in India. In "The Mango Tree," a man, his wife, and his sister live together until the sister finally marries. The sister asks the wife to take care of her mango tree, but the wife neglects it. As the tree languishes, so does the man. Finally, the sister rescues them, explaining to the wife that it was her duty to watch over both the tree and the man because they share one soul. "The Faithful Sister" tells how a sister endures many sacrifices to ensure her brother's safety, pretending madness and saving him from a streak of bad fate.

In late March or early April, the Nine Days' Festival is celebrated with the telling of a story on each day. In "The Old Man and the Magic Bowl," the goddess Parvati takes pity and gives a poor old man a bowl that fills itself with food. He invites the king and his court to dinner but loses the bowl when the king takes it and forgets to return it. Parvati then gives the old man a wooden rod that reminds the king of his lack of courtesy and restores order and happiness. "The King Without an Heir" tells how a childless king marries seven wives in order to produce an heir. When none of them conceives, he locks them in the attic. They pretend that one wife is pregnant and then pray for the goddess Parvati to save them. The goddess produces an heir while teaching them a lesson. "The Girl in the Forest" tells how a king finds an orphan girl in the forest and marries her, assuming that she is a princess. The goddess Parvati magically provides her with parents and a palace for the husband to visit, but, when he sends servants back for a forgotten item, they find only a pool and a bush. The wife reveals the truth and is forgiven by her husband.

Gunguar is the festival for celebrating the virtues of the goddess Parvati. In "How Ganesh Got His Elephant Head," Parvati grows lonely and makes herself a baby for a companion. She decides to bathe and asks the baby, Ganesh, to prevent anyone from watching her. Shiva, Parvati's husband, comes along and cuts off the boy's head when he is prevented from looking at his wife. Parvati demands that Shiva cut the head off the first creature that he sees in order to restore the child to life. The first animal that he sees is an elephant, and the three live happily ever after.

Critical Context

Seasons of Splendour provides an accessible introduction to Hindu mythology and epic, an important area of world literature that has received little attention from the English-language publishing and academic worlds. Madhur Jaffrey makes a significant contribution to literature for young adults by providing access to some of the classic stories of India. In the last quarter of the twentieth century, many critics and scholars called for a rethinking of the narrow scope of the traditional Western canon of literature. *Seasons of Splendour* makes a strong case for considering Hindu mythology as equal in importance to the Greek, Roman, Norse, and Judeo-Christian traditions.

John D. Beach

THE SECRET DIARY OF ADRIAN MOLE AGED 13¾

Author: Sue Townsend (1946-   )
First published: 1982
Type of work: Novel
Type of plot: Domestic realism and social realism
Time of work: 1981-1982
Locale: The English Midlands
Subjects: Coming-of-age, family, and social issues
Recommended ages: 13-15

Adrian Mole, a boy approaching fourteen in Midlands England, records his life and thoughts in a diary, revealing his secret ambition to become an intellectual as well as his adolescent concerns with family, school, identity, love and sex, and social issues.

> *Principal characters:*
> ADRIAN MOLE, a sensitive and naïve teenager who records the trials of adolescence in his diary
> GEORGE and PAULINE MOLE, his parents
> PANDORA, his girlfriend
> BERT BAXTER, an old-age pensioner
> NIGEL, Adrian's friend
> BARRY KENT, a bully
> GRANDMA MOLE, Adrian's grandmother
> MR. LUCAS, a neighbor

Form and Content

Sue Townsend's *The Secret Diary of Adrian Mole Aged 13¾* is a first-person account of the day-to-day events in the life of a young boy in Midlands England in the early 1980's. Because of the diary style of narration, all the characters and events are presented through the eyes of Adrian Mole. Nevertheless, the reader comes to know intimately not only Adrian but also the other characters in his family and his school. Adrian's diary is understated, ironic, and humorous in tone. He is a naïve, even a comic, character, yet his dilemmas are so human and universal that the reader sympathizes with him and grows to love him.

Adrian's diary opens on New Year's Day of his thirteenth year. From the opening lines, it is clear that he is a naïve and self-involved young adolescent. He has spots on his chin, and this adolescent preoccupation is of more importance to him than his mother's affair with their neighbor, Mr. Lucas. Adrian blindly accepts Mr. Lucas' interest in his mother as neighborly kindness and concern, and he reports the fights between his mother and father with little understanding.

Adrian decides to become an intellectual, and he submits some poems to the British Broadcasting Corporation (BBC). At school, he becomes interested in a new girl,

Pandora. He joins the Good Samaritans, a school community service group, and is assigned to help Bert Baxter, an old-age pensioner.

Adrian's world grows more miserable, in his view, when his mother gets a job. This change in his family makes him worry: Who will prepare his meals and do the housework? Meanwhile, Pandora is dating Adrian's friend Nigel, and Adrian is being bullied by Barry Kent, who demands protection money from Adrian. When his parents announce their intention to divorce, Adrian at last grows suspicious of his mother's feelings toward Mr. Lucas.

As the changes in his life continue, Adrian's problems and responsibilities take on more adult dimensions. When his mother leaves home to live with Mr. Lucas, Adrian and his father become a single-parent family. Adrian's father begins to date a woman, and this time Adrian has no illusions about the nature of their relationship. Adrian also takes on more responsibility for Bert Baxter. His father is short of money, and their electricity is shut off. The situation grows even worse when Adrian's father loses his job.

Adrian begins to look to the outside world as he discovers himself. At school, he rebels by wearing forbidden red socks and admiring a liberal teacher. Pandora and he become involved in a protest at school, and Adrian goes to her home and meets her parents, whom he admires. He becomes critical of his parents' narrow, working-class life.

As the diary continues, Pandora and Adrian begin to date. Bert Baxter has a stroke and moves to an old age home. Adrian reports on school trips and his sexual explorations with Pandora. Life becomes a bit more stable. His mother returns, and his parents reconcile. Bert becomes engaged to Queenie, another resident of the home. Adrian's father finds a job.

Much has happened in one year. Adrian has fallen in love, lived with only one parent, gone "intellectual," and grown in confidence and maturity. The volume ends with Adrian celebrating his fifteenth birthday, on the verge of new possibilities.

Analysis

A key word in the title *The Secret Diary of Adrian Mole Aged 13¾* is "secret." Adrian Mole reveals his secret thoughts and desires in his diary. In this way, major themes of adolescence unfold, observed not objectively by a third-person narrator but subjectively through the eyes and words of one of literature's teenagers, in the tradition of Tom Sawyer, Huck Finn, and Holden Caulfield. Adrian's struggles, while occurring in a specific time, place, and culture, have universal appeal for adolescent readers and a humorous treatment of sometimes bleak themes that will be appreciated more fully as the reader grows older. This is a book that can be read again with pleasure at different stages of life.

A major coming-of-age theme is searching for, and finding, an identity of one's own, separate from parents and family. Adrian's decision to become an intellectual is the beginning of that search for identity. His criticism of his parents' lifestyle and values is a universal symptom of adolescence. The class difference between Adrian's family and Pandora's family is well illustrated, not only by the fact that Pandora owns a pony while Adrian reports on unpaid utility bills and his father's unemployment but also by the choice of summer vacation each family makes: Adrian's family goes off to Scotland or Skegness, while Pandora vacations in Tunisia.

Separation and divorce, and the stress and pain that they cause to family life, are issues that, while no longer unusual among teenagers, are experienced by each individual for the first time with pain and anger that are not lessened by being common. The theme of the separation and reconciliation of Adrian's parents runs throughout the diary and is treated with both understatement and irony, inviting healing laughter.

Adrian's Grandma Mole is a strong female character in the diary. She illustrates changing values as well as a fiercely determined outlook on life. It is Grandma Mole who cooks Adrian homemade dinners when he has had too many "boil in the bag" dinners at home, who is never too busy to make custard from scratch, and who pays the bill when the electricity is shut off. It is also Grandma Mole who intimidates the bully Barry Kent into returning all the money that he has extorted from Adrian.

Love and sex are adolescent themes that are explored in the diary. From his earliest realization that he is attracted to Pandora, Adrian confides in the diary all of his secret longings and worries. Like most teenage boys, he moves from worrying about the size of his "thing" to his first passionate kiss to light to moderate petting to the time when the sensible Pandora tells him that she is not willing to risk pregnancy for him. His own sexuality develops while he observes adult sexuality—first, reluctantly, his mother's affair with Mr. Lucas, and then his father's relationship with Doreen Slater, about which Adrian has no illusions.

When Adrian turns outward to the world around him, social and community themes are explored. The realities of economics in 1980's England under Prime Minister Margaret Thatcher are illustrated through his father's experience with unemployment and the examples of a young, liberal teacher whom Adrian admires. Adrian's relationship with old-age pensioner Bert Baxter enriches his understanding of aging, human dignity, and social services. Adrian comments on socialized medicine when he has a tonsillectomy.

Through Adrian's diary Townsend comments on the major themes of adolescence, school and family relationships, and social conditions in early 1980's England, always with an undercurrent of irony and subtle wit. She succeeds in creating a teenage character who is humorous, sympathetic, and universal.

Critical Context

While *The Secret Diary of Adrian Mole Aged 13¾* falls within the genre of young adult coming-of-age novels, its specific setting in Thatcher's England and the working-class status of Adrian's family place it within the political context of Sue Townsend's adult fiction. She has written a number of plays and novels that are humorous social commentaries focusing on England's lower classes. It was the enormous success of her Adrian Mole diaries, however, that brought her to the attention of the public. By the mid-1990's, the novel had sold more than five million copies in England and had been translated into twenty-two languages.

Some critics in the United States have complained that the distinctly British flavor of Townsend's humor, as well as some specifics of vocabulary and political context, limit the universality of her themes when translated to an American audience. Others have countered that Adrian's Britishisms, rooted in his place and his class, are grasped and appreciated even by young adults and that they add to the humor of the situations.

The diary format of the novel emphasizes the individuality of Adrian Mole's singular point of view. The social realism of the setting and the author's subtle wit contribute to the work's literary merit. The universality of the adolescent themes is the basis for the enormous popularity of the novel.

Susan Butterworth

SHABANU
Daughter of the Wind

Author: Suzanne Fisher Staples (1945-   )
First published: 1989
Type of work: Novel
Type of plot: Domestic realism and social realism
Time of work: The twentieth century
Locale: The Cholistan desert in Pakistan
Subjects: Coming-of-age, family, and gender roles
Recommended ages: 10-15

Eleven-year-old Shabanu comes to terms with the enormous struggle between her independent, adventurous spirit and the constrictions of her culture's expectations for her in this last year of her childhood.

Principal characters:
SHABANU, the adventurous eleven-year-old narrator
PHULAN, Shabanu's docile older sister
MAMA, their mother
DADI, their father
SHARMA, a female cousin of Shabanu's parents
HAMIR, the cousin to whom Phulan has been promised in marriage
MURAD, the cousin to whom Shabanu has been promised in marriage
NAZIR MOHAMMAD, a nefarious landowner in the village of Mehrabpur
RAHIM-*SAHIB*, Nazir Mohammad's older brother, an influential politician

Form and Content

In this coming-of-age novel, Suzanne Fisher Staples uses language rich in imagery to create a memorable world far removed from the average Western youngster's experience. Through the clear narrative voice of Shabanu, an eleven-year-old girl in a nomadic culture, the reader comes to understand the joys and sufferings of life for this extended family—a life so different from, yet hauntingly familiar to, the universal struggles and yearnings of the human heart. The setting of *Shabanu: Daughter of the Wind* is the Cholistan desert between northwest India and southeast Pakistan. The reader learns much about the care of camels, the avoidance of scorpions, the dangers of desert storms, and the priceless value of water. Along with Shabanu, the reader experiences the wonders of birth, the onset of menarche, the wildness of desert carnivals, and the Muslim rituals of weddings and funerals.

Through chapters averaging eight pages, the author moves the reader along quickly. Each of the twenty-three chapter headings is a name or an important event, many in the language of the people of Cholistan. Context usually unlocks the meaning of the words, or the reader may refer to the glossary for a definition and a pronunciation guide. Since many of the words are nearly onomatopoeic, this feature adds to the novel's authentic sound and thus the reader's enjoyment of the words. Furthermore, a map locates the action in the Cholistan desert. The routes and campsites of the protagonist and her family are clearly indicated, helping the reader follow the action of the story.

Shabanu is an adventurous, high-spirited young girl, very unlike her more docile older sister, Phulan, who is soon to marry Cousin Hamir. When Shabanu reaches puberty, she too will marry a cousin, in this case Hamir's brother, Murad. Both marriages have been arranged for years, and the benefits of the sisters marrying cousins who are themselves brothers is a cause of joy for the family. Although somewhat apprehensive about the coming events, Shabanu looks forward with confidence to her fate as Murad's wife, as she knows him and enjoyed playing with him when they were young children.

Events take a catastrophic turn as preparations for the wedding of Phulan and Hamir near completion. Nazir Mohammad, a nefarious landowner, accosts the two sisters with the intent of kidnapping and raping them. Shabanu foils the evil Nazir, but the results are horrific. In an act of desert vengeance, Hamir, Phulan's betrothed, is killed, and the resulting peace negotiations result in upheaval for the two daughters. Now Phulan, who is ready to marry, will have Murad as a husband and Shabanu will be given to Rahim-*sahib*, the powerful politician and older brother of the despicable Nazir, as his fourth wife. This arrangement will save the family's honor as well as the land and will ensure a future for both daughters.

Shabanu resists and attempts to run away to her aunt Sharma. When her beloved camel, Mithoo, falls and breaks a leg, however, Shabanu chooses to stay with him, knowing that her father will find her and beat her and that her fate with Rahim-*sahib* will be sealed. She painfully chooses the path of compassion to stay with Mithoo and ultimately to save the family's lives and fortune. Her only hope is in the remembered words of advice from the wise and revered Aunt Sharma. She resolves to keep her innermost beauty, the secrets of her soul, locked in her heart.

Analysis

Male prerogative in matters, sexual, political, and domestic is a pillar of the culture of the Cholistan people. From the first pages of *Shabanu* when readers, along with the heroine, watch the dominant camel Tipu mate three or four times a day before challenging a younger male, the reader is made aware of the importance of the male in the culture. "May you have many sons," is a common saying, and Shabanu's parents are pitied and somewhat disdained for having only daughters. Although her parents assure her that she and her sister are worth "seven sons," the preference in this culture is definitely for male children. Once they reach puberty, young women are veiled with the *chadr* (veil), restricted to the home, and expected to be obedient to their husbands as they were to their fathers.

In spite of the culture's many overt and covert messages regarding the inferior position of women, Shabanu resists efforts to teach her submission, rejecting her aunt's gift of the *chadr* for the trip to Sibi and later showing anger at her father for selling her beloved camel Gulaband, a foreshadowing event.

Shabanu's parents are devoted to each other and their daughters. They reassure them and love them sincerely, although a harsh element can be found in their love as well: Obedience is expected, and defiance is met with slaps and beatings. The singular voice for self-reliance for women is that of an aunt, Sharma, who left her abusive husband, became financially independent with her own camel herd, and roams the desert with her sixteen-year-old daughter, whom Sharma does not force into a marriage.

It is Sharma who gives Shabanu courage and advice, telling her that the love of a good man is a priceless treasure and that she is a beautiful, alluring woman who can attract and keep a man. At the same time, Sharma counsels Shabanu to keep a part of herself for herself, to fold moments of beauty into her heart and to always keep her innermost beauty, the secret of her soul locked in her heart. Sharma also offers her niece refuge if the conditions of her arranged marriage become unbearable. Wisely, Sharma refuses to make the decision for Shabanu, but rather offers her assurances, love, and support.

Although some may focus on the gender issues in this novel, the larger theme of the individual in relation to society is also at stake. Must Shabanu forfeit her desire to live a free, nomadic life with her beloved camels to become the fourth wife of a man old enough to be her grandfather? In the world of desert justice, she has little choice. Yet, she knows, deep within herself, that she has a right to happiness and self-determination. Shabanu's father too is constrained by the expectations of the culture. The last poignant, climactic scene depicts his dilemma. Finding his defiant, runaway daughter collapsed on the desert sand next to her injured camel, Mithoo, he pulls her up and begins to beat her with his stick. Shabanu refuses to cry out, refuses to bend to the blows of his fury. Finally, she hears sobbing as if from a distance, and, as she crumples into his arms, she realizes that it is her father who is sobbing, not she. Shabanu resolves to keep a part of her individuality even as she capitulates to the demands of her society.

Critical context

Although many coming-of-age novels have been written about the struggle between the individual and society from the perspective of Western society, *Shabanu* is unique in its location and vivid descriptions of the nomadic life in the Pakistani desert.

This novel, the first for Suzanne Fisher Staples, was named a Newbery Honor Book. Staples once lived in Pakistan and became involved with the nomads of the Cholistan desert during her years as a United Press International (UPI) correspondent. Deeply impressed and inspired by the courage and generosity of these desert nomads, she resolved to dispel some of the misconceptions Westerners have about Islamic societies. Thus, Staples' motivation in writing this novel was to reveal the common life and thus the universal humanness of these desert-dwelling Muslims. Through the intelligent and poetic voice of Shabanu, who describes her life and austere desert existence, she succeeds in doing so. The story of this resilient, independent, free-spirited young woman will stay with the reader for a long time. After the novel's publication, Staples promised a sequel, and all who read this book will be eager to hear what happens next to this plucky heroine so different in geographical setting but so like Western teenagers in her heart.

Mary M. Navarre

SHARDIK

Author: Richard Adams (1920-   )
First published: 1974
Type of work: Novel
Type of plot: Fantasy
Time of work: The second rise of the Beklan Empire
Locale: Ortelga, a northern island, and Bekla, a preindustrial fantasy world
Subjects: Animals, religion, and social issues
Recommended ages: 15-18

The hunter Kelderek becomes high priest to the bear-god Shardik and assumes control of the Beklan Empire and its trade in child slavery, but, after many hardships, he realizes that children represent the future and must be treated well.

Principal characters:
    KELDEREK, a hunter
    BEL-KA-TRAZET, the High Baron of Ortelga
    THE TUGINDA, the high priestess of Quiso
    MELATHYS, a priestess of Quiso
    TA-KOMINION, a baron of Ortelga
    ELLEROTH, a nobleman of Sarkid
    SANTIL-KÈ-ERKETLIS, the defeated leader of Bekla and the military
        enemy of the Ortelgans
    GENSHED, a slave trader

Form and Content

Shardik dramatizes complex problems concerning religion and family values. On a hunting trip, Kelderek of Ortelga encounters an immense bear. He realizes that it is the god Shardik, who has not been seen for many generations. Returning to Ortelga, Kelderek refuses to tell even High Baron Bel-ka-Trazet what he saw, claiming that he can inform only the Tuginda, the high priestess of Shardik's cult. The furious baron nearly kills him but is interrupted by the startling request for a meeting with the Tuginda. They journey to the mysterious island of Quiso, where the Tuginda forms a party that includes the priestess Melathys in order to find the bear.

The Tuginda tells Kelderek the history of the Ortelgans, who once ruled the Beklan Empire and served Shardik. A corrupt priestess and her slave trader lover finally slew Shardik, and the empire fell. Centuries later, the priestesses wait for Shardik's return. Another prophecy tells that God will reveal a great truth through Shardik and through two chosen "vessels," who will be "shattered" and refashioned to fit his purpose. The Tuginda believes that she and Kelderek are these vessels.

Kelderek finds Shardik, but Melathys is so frightened by the bear that she flees down the river. Under a young baron, Ta-Kominion, however, the Ortelgans rise and overthrow Bel-ka-Trazet, then follow the bear as it wanders to Bekla. Ta-Kominion tells Kelderek that they can reconquer Bekla if their attack is swift and if Shardik is with them—so Shardik must be drugged and brought there in a cage. The Tuginda protests that the Power of God must not be manipulated for greed and secular force, but Ta-Kominion shames Kelderek into helping him. When the Ortelgans encounter Beklan soldiers, Shardik awakens from his stupor, smashes out of the cage, and destroys the army. Within days, Kelderek becomes the priest-king of Bekla.

Five years later, the Ortelgans are at war with rebellious provinces led by General Erketlis; the Tuginda is imprisoned on Quiso; Shardik is behind bars in Bekla; and Kelderek unhappily prays to learn the mystery that Shardik is meant to reveal. Elleroth, a southern nobleman, visits Bekla. Disliking the Ortelgans for their barbarous ways and their revival of the slave trade—and disbelieving in the godhood of Shardik—he sets fire to the royal house. Shardik gets free and escapes Bekla, and Kelderek follows to recapture him. After a horrific journey, he physically and mentally deteriorates, then falls into the hands of Elleroth's army, where he learns how much he is hated for condoning the slave trade. Elleroth, however, allows Kelderek to go free—to Zeray, the lawless outland. There, he finds both the Tuginda and Melathys, and he learns that Bel-ka-Trazet, recently dead, had also come there and tried to create order. Kelderek realizes that he loves Melathys and decides to abandon his search for Shardik. They then learn that the bear-god is nearby.

Kelderek sets out again to find Shardik, this time to kill him, but he is captured by the evil slave trader Genshed. With the slave children, who include Elleroth's son, he suffers horrendous tortures. Just as Genshed begins to murder the slaves in order to escape Elleroth's approaching army, Shardik appears. Genshed shoots Shardik fatally with his bow, but the bear's final blow likewise kills Genshed. Peace is restored, and Kelderek and Melathys, revealed as God's vessels, civilize Zeray and adopt the slave children.

Analysis

Young adults will find much to enjoy in this story, although it is bleaker than Richard Adams' first novel, *Watership Down* (1972). It will be of particular interest to teenagers who have felt neglected or secondary in their parents' eyes, because even though the book deals with adult concerns such as war, commerce, politics, and slavery, the welfare of children is of primary importance.

Kelderek is nicknamed "Play-with-the-Children" by the Ortelgans, and his simple love for children makes him a holy man. When he seeks secular power, he forgets their special vulnerability and allows them to become sacrifices to slavery and the tactics of war. Kelderek even authorizes the hanging of two children every day in sight of the besieged fortress of General Erketlis, who abandons his stronghold in order to stop the murders. While Kelderek is being "shattered" and "refashioned" through his dreadful journeys following Shardik out of Bekla, he suffers terrible guilt over permitting such cruelties.

The truth that Shardik imparts—the moral of the story—is that there should not be a single neglected child anywhere. Children are the future and their happiness is the world's only security, yet they are the primary victims of adult evils, whether domestic or political. The narrative is a mystery; readers must try to discover the truth that Shardik will reveal. Although the clues are everywhere, the solution comes as a profound revelation.

The story dramatizes other complex issues, including the difficulties of maintaining courage during hardship and the nature of religious faith and doubt. Young people will admire Kelderek for his loyalty and his special relationship with the bear, although they will also realize the necessity for Elleroth's condemnation of slavery. Readers must weigh Elleroth's treachery, which is based on justice and love for children, against Kelderek's errors. The Christian viewpoint underlying the narrative is not deeply buried; Shardik is said to have given his life for the children, as Jesus Christ gave his for humanity, and the Tuginda's strength lies in her unwavering faith, which is shown as more admirable than the skepticism of those who disregard Shardik worship as a mere barbarian cult. In this sense, *Shardik* is connected to C. S. Lewis' *Chronicles of Narnia* (1950-1956) and J. R. R. Tolkien's *Lord of the Rings* (1954-1955), as it shares their interest in Christian morality.

The most difficult section of the book, one that will require young adult readers to search their own feelings and beliefs, involves Kelderek's apostasy. After nearly four hundred pages of suffering for Shardik's sake, then finding Melathys and discovering their mutual love, Kelderek feels that enough is enough. He would rather abandon Shardik and try to live a simple, although dangerous, life with Melathys in criminal-infested Zeray than follow the miserable bear any further. He has reached spiritual bottom, and teenage readers may appreciate his desire for human love over love for a bear, even though it is a god. At the same time, readers know that Kelderek is wrong and that his adventures are not over. Young readers must compare the actions and motives of adults and consider that their decisions may not always be easy.

One of the pleasures of *Shardik* lies in the fact that Adams does not anthropomorphize the bear and instead brings to it the detailed observation of an animal's natural behaviors displayed so successfully in *Watership Down*. Shardik, like Kelderek, undergoes hardships and ill-treatment; in the climactic confrontation with Genshed, the bear is already dying of starvation and illness. Adams portrays the creature's sufferings so movingly that the reader understands that kindness to animals is as essential as kindness to children.

Critical Context

Fantasy tales traditionally dramatize a conflict between good and evil, whose partisans are easy to distinguish. *Shardik* falls into the subcategory of Christian fantasy, whose most famous predecessors for young readers are the *Chronicles of Narnia*. Where Lewis portrayed simplistic moral lessons, however, Richard Adams depicts the difficulties of faith and steadfastness; many characters argue that Shardik is not divine and that they have seen nothing miraculous in the story's events. Also contributing to the characters' believability is the fact that none, except Genshed, is entirely good or evil. Genshed represents Satan and is so evil that he enjoys converting others to evil for the demonic joy of it, but the rest display a mixture of good qualities and bad, giving the novel a deeper psychological realism than much Christian fantasy offers.

Shardik never received the popular adulation of *Watership Down*, being grimmer and far longer, at more than five hundred pages. Where the earlier work was more fantastic and accessible to a younger audience, however, *Shardik* takes a serious look at humanity's greatest cruelties. Much post-World War II fantasy borrows directly from Tolkien's Middle-Earth and is therefore predictable and unable to frighten or involve the reader in any serious way; the happy ending is assured. *Shardik* leaves the reader in serious doubt that Kelderek will understand his mistakes or will deserve to escape his final crisis, the torments meted by Genshed. In this way, the book is truly suspenseful and will grip young adults, so that they care about its ultimate meaning.

Fiona Kelleghan

SHILOH

Author: Phyllis Reynolds Naylor (1933-   )
First published: 1991
Type of work: Novel
Type of plot: Domestic realism
Time of work: The 1990's
Locale: The rural mountain town of Friendly, West Virginia
Subjects: Animals, emotions, and family
Recommended ages: 10-13

Marty Preston finds a stray, abused dog and vows to give him a good home, in the process learning much about personal values and integrity.

> *Principal characters:*
> SHILOH, a brown-and-white beagle that belongs to Judd Travers but runs away because of abusive treatment
> MARTY PRESTON, an eleven-year-old who loves animals, wants a pet of his own, and abhors animal abuse
> MA PRESTON, his compassionate mother
> RAY PRESTON, his father, a mail carrier
> DARA LYNN PRESTON, Marty's seven-year-old sister
> BECKY PRESTON, Marty's three-year-old sister
> JUDD TRAVERS, a mean, cheating, tobacco-spitting animal abuser
> DAVID HOWARD, Marty's best friend

Form and Content

Shiloh is a poignant, realistic story of a boy and a dog and the circumstances that bring them together. Yet, there is more to the story of Marty Preston, an eleven-year-old who befriends a stray, abused dog. This protagonist is faced with a moral decision when he does not want to return the abused beagle to its rightful but mean owner, Judd Travers. He wants to fulfill the hill country code of honor of not lying, not cheating, and showing respect for others' rights. The novel is set in the mountains of West Virginia. Although the events could happen in almost any rural area, Phyllis Reynolds Naylor captures the flavor of the area through the rich West Virginia dialect of Marty, the narrator of the story. The tale covers a brief time span and is written in short, fast-paced chapters.

Marty Preston wants a pet, preferably a dog, but his poverty-stricken parents cannot afford another mouth to feed. One Sunday afternoon, Marty is thrilled when a beagle follows him home from the Old Shiloh schoolhouse. His father, aware that Judd Travers, a mean, bewhiskered, tobacco-chewing neighbor recently acquired a new hunting dog, insists that the beagle be returned. Together, Marty and his father take the dog to its owner, who, after kicking it, promises to "whup the daylights out of him" if he wanders off again. As Marty accompanies his father on his mail route, he gathers aluminum cans for recycling money in hopes of offering to buy Shiloh, the name that he has given the beagle.

Another unpleasant encounter with Judd further instills in Marty the desire to have Shiloh for himself. When the dog again finds his way to the Preston house, Marty decides to hide Shiloh on the hillside, vowing that "Judd Travers is never going to kick you again." Marty builds a pen from some old chicken wire, sneaks food to the dog twice a day, and runs in the fields with him, all the time keeping the truth of Shiloh's whereabouts from his parents, sisters, and Judd.

One evening, his mother discovers Marty with Shiloh. They agree not to tell his father until morning, but that evening a German Shepherd attacks Shiloh, hurting him badly. Ray Preston and Marty take Shiloh to Doc Murphy, the local practitioner, who tends to the dog's wounded leg and ear. Before Marty can return Shiloh to Judd, as his father demands he must do, Judd discovers that the Prestons have the dog. He agrees to let Marty keep the dog until the weekend, when the wound will have healed.

Early Sunday morning, Marty decides to tell Judd Travers that he is not giving Shiloh back. Crossing the field that separates their houses, he spots Judd shooting a deer out of season. Marty uses this event as bargaining leverage—he will not report the killing to the game warden in return for custody of Shiloh. Judd does not accept this reasoning but agrees to allow Marty to work twenty hours to earn Shiloh. When the hours are almost completed, Judd claims that the paper on which the deal is written is worthless because there was no witness. While Marty continues to fulfill his end of the bargain, Judd reveals information about his difficult childhood. Learning that Judd was abused as a child, Marty begins to understand and see Judd in a different light. Upon completion of the twenty hours, Judd hands Marty a dog collar, thus relinquishing ownership of Shiloh. Readers are left to draw their own conclusions as to why Judd has had a change of heart.

Analysis

Marty Preston wants a pet of his own. So great is this desire that when Shiloh appears for the second time, Marty hides him on the hill, despite the fact that he has promised Judd Travers to return him if he ever appears on the Preston property again. Once he hides Shiloh and keeps that fact from his family and Travers, he discovers that one lie leads to another. He lies to his mother as to why he does not eat his entire supper but saves some for later, in order to give food to Shiloh, and to his sister about snakes on the hill, in order to keep her from following him and discovering Shiloh. When Judd comes looking for his missing dog, Marty says, "Haven't seen any dog of any kind in our yard all day." Marty worries about the fact that you can lie not only by what you say but also by what you do not say. He whispers a prayer: "Jesus, which you want me to do? Be one hundred percent honest and carry that dog back to Judd so that one of your creatures can be kicked and starved all over again, or keep him here and fatten him up to glorify your creation?" Marty has been reared in a

God-honoring home, and he has been taught honesty and respect for other people and their possessions. He is confused and concerned, however, about justice. Marty looks for ways to rationalize his decisions—"A lie don't seem a lie anymore when it's meant to save a dog."

Marty Preston confronts real-life questions and issues. What action should be taken by someone who suspects a person of animal abuse? Is it ever right to lie in order to protect someone or something? How should children deal with dishonest adults who takes advantage of their innocence? When Marty catches Judd shooting the deer out of season and wants to trade Shiloh for not reporting him to the game warden, Marty begins to see "I am no better than Judd Travers—willing to look the other way to get something I want." Marty discovers that sometimes there are no black-and-white answers, that shades of gray often color the world. Eventually, Marty does get Shiloh, but not before having both an emotional and a physical workout and maturing in the process.

The characters in *Shiloh* are believable and well developed. Marty is a growing, curious, sensitive boy. Marty's mother is compassionate and understanding, particularly when she discovers Shiloh. Ma has been suspicious because of Marty's eating behavior and the disinterest that he has shown in spending time with his best friend, David Howard. Ray Preston is strict, yet supportive of his son. Open communication and a trusting relationship exists between all family members. Judd Travers is despicable but not beyond redemption, as is evident when he hands over the dog collar to Marty after the boy completes his twenty hours of work.

Critical Context

A prolific and versatile writer, Phyllis Reynolds Naylor has written more than seventy books, both fiction and nonfiction, for children, young adults, and adults. Her list of awards is outstanding, and her titles are consistently listed on American Library Association Notable Book Lists. *Shiloh* is a Newbery Medal winner.

Many of Naylor's works have an autobiographical basis, such as *To Make a Wee Moon* (1969), *Revelations* (1979), *A String of Chances* (1982), *Unexpected Pleasures* (1986), *Beetles, Lightly Toasted* (1987), and *Maudie in the Middle* (1988), the last one written with Lura S. Reynolds. *Shiloh* is based on an experience that Naylor had when visiting friends in West Virginia. While on a walk with her husband in the community of Shiloh, they found a hungry, frightened dog that followed them to their friend's house. She could not get the dog out of her mind, even though her friends explained that abandoned dogs were a common occurrence in those hills. As she stated in her Newbery acceptance speech, "I wanted to write about how, once you become emotionally involved in a problem, all bets are off. Your perspective changes."

Some students may know Naylor best for her Alice series—including *The Agony of Alice* (1985), *Alice in Rapture, Sort Of* (1989), and *Reluctantly Alice* (1991)—which are humorous stories of a motherless preadolescent girl who faces the typical anxieties of growing up. Others may know her Witch series—including *Witch's Sister* (1975), *Witch Water* (1977), and *The Witch Herself* (1978)—or her York trilogy—*Shadows on the Wall* (1980), *Faces in the Water* (1981), and *Footprints at the Window* (1981)—novels in which teenager Dan Roberts travels back in time to fourth century England.

Naylor's versatility, creation of believable characters and empathy for them, and ability to delve into contemporary problem areas for adolescents are hallmarks of her writing, which appeals to a wide variety of readers, both young and old.

Carol Ann Gearhart

SHOELESS JOE

Author: W. P. Kinsella (1935-   )
First published: 1982
Type of work: Novel
Type of plot: Fantasy and historical fiction
Time of work: The late 1970's
Locale: Iowa
Subjects: Death, family, and sports
Recommended ages: 13-18

When Ray Kinsella follows a voice telling him to build a baseball field on his farm, long-dead baseball players come to play there, including his own father and Shoeless Joe Jackson.

> *Principal characters:*
> RAY KINSELLA, an Iowa farmer who builds a baseball field in his cornfield
> ANNIE KINSELLA, his wife, who supports him in his apparently mad project
> KARIN KINSELLA, their young daughter, whose life is saved by Doc Graham
> RICHARD KINSELLA, Ray's twin brother, who comes to Ray's farm just before their father's appearance on the baseball field
> JOHN KINSELLA, the father of Ray and Richard
> J. D. SALINGER, a famous writer who accompanies Ray Kinsella from New England to Iowa
> MOONLIGHT GRAHAM, a baseball player who later became a doctor
> SHOELESS JOE JACKSON, a famous baseball player banned for life from baseball, along with seven teammates, after being accused of throwing the 1919 World Series
> EDDIE SCISSONS, an aged friend of Ray Kinsella who shares his love of baseball

Form and Content

W. P. Kinsella's *Shoeless Joe* is a lyrical fantasy that makes creative use of the importance of baseball in the collective memory of Americans in order to explore attempts to recapture the past and to come to terms with the death of parents. The novel seems to be a curious mixture of autobiography, fiction, and historical reality: It includes several characters whose last name is the same as the author's; real people, such as writer J. D. Salinger and the eight Chicago White Sox players who were banned from baseball for their participation in the so-called Black Sox Scandal of 1919; and clearly fantastic elements, such as the return of dead people to life.

Shoeless Joe is a first-person narrative told by Ray Kinsella. Ray has a loving wife and a beautiful daughter, but something is missing in his life. He still regrets that he never made peace with his father, a hardworking laborer who died shortly before Ray married Annie. John Kinsella spoke repeatedly to his son both of his love for baseball and of his belief that Shoeless Joe Jackson did not participate in the conspiracy to throw the 1919 World Series. Like any adolescent, Ray liked to argue with his parents, but his criticism of Shoeless Joe hurt his father's feelings. Ray wishes that he could change the past and express his appreciation and love to his late father.

A series of almost incomprehensible events enables Ray to accomplish this dream. Twice, a voice from his cornfield speaks to him and tells him first "If you build it, he will come" and then "Ease his pain." Although he neither recognizes this voice nor understands the full meaning of these statements, Ray senses intuitively that he should build a baseball field on his farm so that "he will come," whoever "he" may be. His very sensible in-laws tell Annie that she should leave her strange husband, who is risking their economic future by building a baseball field on his farm instead of planting corn there, but she gives him moral support and allows him to pursue his dream. Their love for each other is absolute, and they share with their young daughter, Karin, both a respect for the past and a love of the values represented by baseball. Annie, Ray, and Karin believe that something miraculous has happened on their farm, and eventually Ray "eases" both his own pain and that of his brother, Richard, and his dead father. All three men in the Kinsella family finally obtain inner peace.

Analysis

The meaning of *Shoeless Joe* may not be immediately clear to readers: Why should they care if Shoeless Joe Jackson and seven other dead members of the 1919 White Sox get the opportunity to play baseball once again, or if Ray Kinsella succeeds in persuading J. D. Salinger that he should resume writing fiction? Readers gradually come to the realization, however, that the main themes of *Shoeless Joe* are not associated with baseball but rather with death and individuals' attempts to deal with the past. Like all people, Ray Kinsella wishes that he could change his past and have a final conversation with his late father. Readers know that this is impossible; nevertheless, they wish that reality could correspond to one's dreams.

When he first hears the voice telling him "If you build it, he will come" and "Ease his pain," Ray Kinsella assumes that the voice is referring only to Shoeless Joe Jackson, and he builds only a left field because Shoeless Joe was a left fielder. He believes that this will "ease the pain" of Shoeless Joe, who was banned for life by Commissioner Kenesaw Mountain Landis from the sport that had brought him so much happiness. Although quite beautiful and green, Ray's left field is not a complete baseball field, and, when Shoeless Joe arrives, he persuades Ray that there are other players who would like to play; Ray then builds a complete baseball field. He also discovers that only those who believe in the miraculous happenings on his baseball diamond see the ghostly players and learn anything from them. Ray's brother-in-law, Mark, who thinks only of all the money that could be made by planting corn in this field, sees no one there and tries unsuccessfully to force Ray to sell his farm.

Then, another idea occurs to Ray: He believes that "he" may refer to J. D. Salinger, the author of *The Catcher in the Rye* (1951) who stopped writing and became a recluse in New England. Ray recalled that there is a character named Ray Kinsella in a 1941 short story by Salinger and a minor character named Richard Kinsella in Salinger's famous novel. He also read in a 1965 interview that Salinger's wish as a child was to play baseball for the New York Giants in the Polo Grounds. Salinger noted that this dream had become impossible because he was too old and because the Polo Grounds were torn down in 1964.

For reasons that neither man can understand, Ray and J. D. Salinger go to a ball game in Boston's Fenway Park, where they alone see on the scoreboard the records of an outfielder named Moonlight Graham, who played one game for the Giants in 1905, and hear a voice telling them "Go the distance." Both characters travel to Chisholm, Minnesota, where Doc Graham practiced medicine from the 1910's until his death in 1965. One evening, Ray speaks with the dead doctor, with the calendar in the doctor's office telling Ray that their conversation is taking place in 1955. As Ray and Salinger leave Minnesota to drive to Iowa, yet another miracle happens. The hitchhiker whom they pick up is the nineteen-year-old Moonlight Graham.

Once they are back in Iowa, Moonlight begins playing with the other dead baseball players. After Ray's brother, Richard, comes to Ray and Annie's farm, the final two miracles occur. First, Ray and Richard talk with their father, a young catcher on this team of ghosts. Second, when Moonlight sees that a piece of hot dog is caught in Karin's throat and recognizes that she is in danger of choking to death, he crosses the foul line, becomes the aged Doc Graham, and saves Karin's life by tapping her on her back, thus dislodging the hot dog from her throat. Near the end of the novel, Shoeless Joe invites J. D. Salinger to talk with the dead players in the cornfield. Readers are left with the definite impression this conversation will inspire Salinger to resume writing.

Critical Context

At first, readers may associate W. P. Kinsella's *Shoeless Joe* with such books as Roger Angell's *The Summer Game* (1972) or Roger Kahn's *The Boys of Summer* (1971), books that take a nostalgic view of famous baseball players and teams of the past. Another possible comparison might be with Eliot Asinof's history of the Black Sox Scandal entitled *Eight Men Out* (1963), which presents a sympathetic view of Shoeless Joe Jackson. Although perfectly appropriate, such comparisons downplay the fact that *Shoeless Joe* treats topics much broader than baseball.

When director Phil Alden Robinson adapted this book as the 1989 film *Field of Dreams*, he made significant modifications beyond simply changing the title. The J. D. Salinger character was renamed "Terence Mann," and this role was played by the famous African American actor James Earl Jones. Like Salinger, Terence Mann is portrayed as a famous writer who became a recluse, but the motivation for Mann's retirement from writing is clearer: The assassinations of President John F. Kennedy,

Bobby Kennedy, and Martin Luther King, Jr., made Mann so depressed that he stopped writing. The idealism of Ray Kinsella and Doc Graham and the inspiration that he discovers in his conversations with these dead baseball players persuade him to resume writing fiction.

Edmund J. Campion

THE SIGN OF THE BEAVER

Author: Elizabeth George Speare (1908-   )
First Published: 1983
Type of work: Novel
Type of plot: Adventure tale
Time of work: The eighteenth century
Locale: The Maine wilderness
Subjects: Coming-of-age and friendship
Recommended ages: 10-13

A thirteen-year-old boy, left alone on the family homestead, tries to earn the respect of the American Indian boy who helped to save his life.

Principal characters:
    MATT HALLOWELL, a white boy who must learn to survive in the wilderness and who becomes a friend of the Beaver clan
    ATTEAN, an American Indian boy who harbors a deep hatred of white people
    SAKNIS, an American Indian chief who forces Matt and Attean to teach each other

Form and Content

In *The Sign of the Beaver*, Elizabeth George Speare creates a wilderness tale with two adolescent boys as principal characters. The adventure elements of the novel provide a setting for the struggles of a white boy and an American Indian boy to prove themselves to be men. Each boy struggles to gain the respect of his elders, and, as their lives become intertwined, a mutual respect becomes part of the goal.

Matt Hallowell, almost thirteen, and Attean, already fourteen, are forced together against their wills. Pa trusts Matt to care for the homestead while he is away, but Matt does not possess the necessary survival skills for the challenges awaiting him in the wilderness. His rifle is stolen, a bear eats much of his food supply, and he is attacked by bees. Attean and his grandfather, Saknis, save Matt's life. Saknis makes a treaty with Matt: He will bring food to the boy in exchange for reading lessons for Attean. Attean proves to be a hostile pupil, while Matt is a reluctant teacher. The reading lessons proceed miserably for both boys until Matt reads aloud from Daniel Defoe's *Robinson Crusoe* (1719). Attean shows interest in the story in spite of his obvious disdain for all white people.

Day after day, the boys read and take walks in the woods, where their roles are reversed as Attean becomes the teacher. Yet, most of Matt's efforts fail to change the coldness in Attean's eyes.

Readers follow Matt and Attean through twenty-five short chapters hoping for friendship to develop. In many chapters, a cultural conflict is revealed through an event in *Robinson Crusoe* or an opposition of perspectives. For example, Attean is offended by the term "slave" in *Robinson Crusoe*, and Matt cannot agree with leaving a wounded fox in a trap because it was not on the Beaver clan's hunting ground.

Speare's use of foreshadowing encourages readers to predict events. Early in the novel, Matt is visited by a man who notices Pa's rifle hanging above the cabin door. Readers can sense Matt's discomfort and are not surprised when the rifle is stolen as Matt sleeps. The mention of animal traps may cause readers to predict fearfully that Matt may be in danger. Neither Matt nor Attean is harmed, but Attean's dog is caught, which becomes a significant event in the forging of the fragile relationship between the boys.

Speare offers the critical reader an opportunity to observe subtle changes in the boys and in their relationship, permitting readers to identify changes before the boys themselves become aware of them. Attean teaches Matt to make and use a snare, a fishhook, and a bow before the boys realize that they are no longer enemies. Attean's speech becomes much improved by the end of *Robinson Crusoe*, as Matt eventually notices.

Many differences in the two cultures are illustrated as Matt and Attean struggle to understand each other. After Attean kills a bear, Matt is confused when the rest of the work is left for the women of the tribe. Attean is scornful when Matt tends crops, which he also views as "squaw work." Each boy struggles with his own culture's standards for becoming a man worthy of the respect of other men. Matt must face the oncoming of winter and the fact that his family is long overdue. Attean must prove himself worthy to go on a long hunt with the tribe's warriors. Together, through being both teacher and pupil, Matt and Attean reach their goals.

Analysis

Speare is a master storyteller with an impressive collection of literary awards. *The Sign of the Beaver* is a work of historical fiction as well as a sensitive portrayal of a clash of cultures and of wills. Attean's face expresses spite at the boys' first meeting, and his scowl deepens when Matt begins the reading lessons. Even as Attean teaches Matt to snare and to fish, his attitude does not change. Matt feels no hope of developing a friendship with Attean, but he does wish to earn his respect. He is painfully aware that Attean only tolerates his presence out of obedience to Saknis. Matt, on the other hand, hates Attean for the look of disdain that is ever present in his eyes. Yet, Matt also trusts Attean. In chapter 11, Matt realizes that their relationship has changed—they are no longer enemies. Speare's skillful writing allows readers to observe that both boys were profiting from their time together: Matt was learning to find his own food and to mark his way through the forest, and Attean was improving in his ability to speak English.

Attean admits telling the story of *Robinson Crusoe* to his brothers in the village. Both boys regret coming to the final page of the novel, until Matt remembers his Bible, which provides a new supply of stories. A turning point in their relationship comes through the Bible story of Noah and the Flood. After Matt tells this story, Attean responds by telling the Beaver people's story of Gluskabe and a flood. Matt wonders how different peoples can have such similar stories. Another major turning point occurs when the boys face an angry bear. Matt distracts the bear long enough for Attean to shoot an arrow between its eyes. They work as a team. When Attean smiles and says, "You move quick, like Indian," Matt knows that he has finally earned Attean's respect.

The two cultures clash because of a lack of the communication necessary to promote understanding. When Attean reveals that white people killed his mother, Matt is speechless. He tells Attean that war causes losses on all sides. Attean responds with a question: "Why white men make cabin on Indian hunting grounds?" Even though the war is over, Matt wonders if the hatred will ever cease. He has gained a clearer understanding of the wall between himself and Attean, a wall that stood between many white people and American Indians.

The answer to the question of whether Matt and Attean can forge a friendship comes with the approach of winter, when Matt must make a man's decision. Ever hopeful of his family's return, he decides to stay at the cabin, even though it could mean facing winter alone. Saknis understands and gives Matt a pair of snowshoes. Attean, at last, offers Matt a gift of friendship—his beloved dog. In return, Matt gives Attean his only possession of value—his grandfather's watch.

With these expressions of friendship exchanged between Matt and Attean, readers can turn their attention to concern for Matt and his family. Matt has grown into a strong young man, capable of survival in the wilderness. He stockpiles firewood and food, and he makes household necessities and gifts to welcome his family. Matt's courage, strength, and unfailing hope are rewarded when his family arrives just before Christmas.

Critical Context

Historical fiction provides an exciting reading experience from which to view historical information, and Elizabeth George Speare is a master of the genre. In 1989, she won the Laura Ingalls Wilder Award for her body of work, which has made a lasting contribution to children's literature. Through her books, children in the United States often connect with the strongly developed characters and gain a sense of time and place as Americans. Readers are drawn past the differences in people and are challenged to look to the common bonds that bring people together. As two cultures collide in *The Sign of the Beaver*, readers learn that through respect, acceptance, and friendship, different cultures can survive and thrive; neither must be sacrificed for the other. Each culture is strengthened by the challenge to grow and to change as a result of this contact.

Both boys in this novel battle with achieving the status of manhood. Matt must prove himself able to accept a man's responsibility. Attean must find his manitou, or spirit, before he is considered worthy to hunt with the braves. Each boy is tested in mind, body, and spirit, yet both desire the same goal of acceptance into an adult world. Their relationship with each other matures as each boy grows into manhood. Speare develops these characters so carefully that the reader is able to identify the changes and maturity in each boy through his actions, without the assistance of a narrator.

The Sign of the Beaver is a highly recommended novel for literature-based instruction in reading and language arts classes in the upper elementary grades. Teachers can challenge students to predict events, record character traits, and suggest ideas for a sequel: For example, will Matt and Attean meet again? Language arts methods books for teachers frequently illustrate instructional techniques from Speare's books.

Barbara Hershberger

SILENT SPRING

Author: Rachel Carson (1907-1964)
First published: 1962; illustrated
Type of work: Science
Subjects: Animals, death, health and illness, and nature
Recommended ages: 15-18

With the skill of a master storyteller and the insight of a poet, a scientist tells how some technological attempts to control the natural world—specifically by the imprudent use of pesticides—imperil all life.

Form and Content

Silent Spring begins with a fable: "There was once a town in the heart of America," Rachel Carson writes, "where all life seemed to live in harmony with its surroundings," a place teeming with wildlife and natural beauty. Then, a "strange blight crept over the area and everything began to change." The town became lifeless, the ultimate effect of "a white granular powder" that had fallen on the community weeks before. "No witchcraft," Carson continues, "no enemy action had silenced the rebirth of new life in this stricken world. The people had done it themselves." Carson explains that although this town is fictitious, "it might easily have a thousand counterparts," for each of the effects described "has actually happened somewhere." *Silent Spring*, she concludes in this initial chapter, is an attempt to illustrate the forces that have "already silenced the voices of spring in countless towns in America."

In the sixteen chapters that follow, Carson describes both in general and in great detail the methods and effects of the carbon-based synthetic pesticides, which, she says, should be called "biocides." In the second chapter, "The Obligation to Endure," Carson expresses the book's central thesis that human intervention into natural processes can undo "the built-in checks and balances by which nature holds the species within bounds." While conceding that she is not calling for an outright ban on the use of pesticides, she states here the book's chief claims: that pesticides have not been thoroughly investigated and thus are used by persons "ignorant of their potentials for harm"; that chemicals are too often applied to the landscape indiscriminately and with an inadequate regard to consequences; and that not only wildlife but also "enormous numbers of people" are being unknowingly exposed, often repeatedly, to these poisons. In this key chapter, she poses the haunting question driving the book: "How could intelligent beings seek to control a few unwanted species by a method that contaminated the entire environment and brought the threat of disease and death even to their own kind?"

In the remainder of the book, Carson fully substantiates her claims, marshalling evidence from scores of documented incidents and scientific findings. In chapter 3, she distinguishes between and describes the pre-World-War-II inorganic insecticides, represented primarily by arsenic compounds, and the post-World-War-II organic insecticides, represented by the chlorinated hydrocarbons (such as DDT, chlordane, dieldrin, aldrin, and endrin) and the alkyl phosphates (parathion and malathion). Carson calls these chemicals and the herbicides (such as dinitrophenol and pentachlorophenol) "elixirs of death," not only because they succeed at killing their target but also because they often damage all life that comes into contact with them, directly or indirectly. One of Carson's main points here and throughout the book is that although pesticides when applied "correctly" may seem inconsequential to the life around the target, the chemicals can move through time and space and sometimes combine—even transforming into more lethal poisons—to cause damage both locally and afar.

Carson then discusses in separate but interrelated chapters the water, the soil, plant life, animal life, cumulative poisoning, and "the human price." Remaining chapters focus on a body's cellular and molecular responses to pesticides, some of which Carson identifies as cancer-producing agents; on the ways in which insects fight back, such as developing genetic resistance to specific chemicals; and finally on alternative methods of insect control, such as ensuring that menacing insects are kept in check by competing or predatory species. Carson closes the book by reminding the reader that "the chemical barrage" that has been "hurled against the fabric of life" is driven by and reveals humankind's "arrogant" relationship to the natural world, an attitude "born of the Neanderthal age of biology and philosophy, when it was supposed that nature exists for the convenience of man."

Analysis

Young adult readers will find in Carson a writer who not only makes science accessible but also reveals some of the crucial lessons of humanity. Her motive in writing *Silent Spring* was not merely to report and examine case after case of environmental poisonings, which she does with amazing breadth, depth, and clarity and with great compassion for the earth and all its creatures. Perhaps more important, especially for young adults, she was attempting to reveal some of the dire consequences of human arrogance—or, as she says in the book's final paragraph, the consequences of humans' attempting "control of nature" with "no humility before the vast forces with which they tamper."

Viewed in this context, the synthetic pesticides (which readers come to know as they do principal characters in fiction) become monsters: Portrayed as both blessing and curse—Carson indeed calls them "sinister" and "evil"—the chemicals run amok, imperiling the life of the natural world and ultimately threatening to destroy their creators. By the end of Carson's book, however, what emerges as the true antagonist in the world she describes is not the chemicals but rather their makers. Carson's central message, as in Mary Shelley's horror novel *Frankenstein* (1818), is a plea for prudence and responsibility in the application of knowledge and power—especially in the manipulation of life-and-death forces.

Much of the scientific knowledge that made the organic pesticides possible sprang from wartime experiments. In chapter 3, Carson explains the baleful genesis of some of these chemicals: "This industry is a child of the Second World War. In the course of developing agents of chemical warfare, some of the chemicals created in the laboratory were found to be lethal to insects. The discovery did not come by chance: insects were widely used to test chemicals as agents of death for man." Images of war pervade *Silent Spring*: Carson speaks of DDT, for example, as a perceived hero "hailed" to win the "war against crop destroyers." She uses such terms as "weapons," "allies," "enemies," and "crusade." Her descriptions of lethal chemicals sprayed "indiscriminately from the skies" recalls nuclear fallout, an "amazing rain of death."

Whether killed or maimed, on contact or by slow accretion, the casualties of this war against insects and "weeds" comprise Carson's focal subject: the western swan grebes in Clear Lake, California; moose, beaver, and fish in some of the sagelands in Wyoming; songbirds, rabbits, and cats in southeastern Michigan; meadowlarks, muskrats, squirrels, sheep, and cattle in Sheldon, Illinois; salmon in the Miramichi River; two children in a playground in Florida; a one-year-old baby in Venezuela; two cousins in Wisconsin. These are only a few of the victims Carson cites throughout the book to indicate the price paid and to show that "the chemical war is never won, and all life is caught in its violent crossfire."

Critical Context

Appearing eight years before the formation of the Environmental Protection Agency in 1970, *Silent Spring* helped awaken many of its readers to a new realm of ecological awareness. Carson's book helped define "ecology" and gave impetus to the "environmental movement." For young adults, it has served to illustrate vital lessons about responsibility, consequences, and humility, and it has also served as a practical introduction to some of the fundamental concepts in biology and organic chemistry.

The book was initially attacked, as Carson had expected, by special-interest groups—among them, some chemical companies and agricultural trade journals. Yet, most of her opponents did not substantiate their claims and refused to cite specific instances of inaccuracy. The soundness of her arguments and her popularity as a world-renowned author combined to give *Silent Spring* a wide and attentive audience. Carson died of cancer only two years after the book's publication, but she lived to see her findings supported by President John F. Kennedy's Science Advisory Committee and saw the beginnings of legislation to protect the earth against chemical assaults.

Although different in tone and purpose from her previous four books, *Silent Spring* is a culmination of Carson's lifelong themes and passions. *Under the Sea Wind* (1941), *The Sea Around Us* (1951), and *The Edge of the Sea* (1955) illustrate in fascinating detail the mysteries and manners of the oceanic world. *A Sense of Wonder* (1965), based on her 1956 article "Help Your Child to Wonder," promotes an abiding reverence for the natural world and humankind's place in it. The themes of interconnectedness and cycles of life are at the heart of all these works. As Carson says in *Silent Spring*, "in nature nothing exists alone"; everything is connected to everything else in an intricate and reverberant web. Informed by the celebration of life so pervasive in her earlier books, *Silent Spring* shows how the magnificent web of life, when altered, can become a web of death.

Morris Allen Grubbs

SING DOWN THE MOON

Author: Scott O'Dell (1898-1989)
First published: 1970
Type of work: Novel
Type of plot: Historical fiction
Time of work: 1863-1865
Locale: Arizona and New Mexico
Subjects: Coming-of-age and race and ethnicity
Recommended ages: 10-15

Bright Morning becomes an adult as she suffers with her people when the Navaho land, way of life, and dignity are taken from them.

> *Principal characters:*
> BRIGHT MORNING, a fourteen-year-old Navaho girl who is looking
>   forward to womanhood and marriage
> TALL BOY, a proud young Navaho warrior who becomes Bright
>   Morning's husband
> RUNNING BIRD, a friend of Bright Morning
> NEHANA, a young woman from the Nez Percé tribe who helps Bright
>   Morning and Running Bird escape from the Spaniards

Form and Content

Sing Down the Moon is a fictionalized retelling of a little-known and shameful part of American history. Told in the first person through the character of Bright Morning, a Navaho girl on the verge of adulthood, the novel relates the crushing of the spirit of the Navaho people at the hands of white people. The Navahos had been settled for generations in Canyon de Chelly in what is now northeastern Arizona. There they raised corn, melons, and peaches and herded sheep. This life ended in 1864, when the U.S. Army ordered them off their land, burned their crops, and chopped down their trees. The Navahos were marched on a three hundred-mile trek to Fort Sumner in New Mexico. This forced migration, known as the Long Walk, brought death to the weakest and broke the spirit of even the strongest. Nevertheless, the Navahos survived.

Scott O'Dell's novel revolves around two major disruptions in Bright Morning's happy existence in the canyon occupied by her tribe. The first trauma occurs as she herds sheep in an isolated mountain pasture with two friends, Running Bird and White Deer. They are teasing her about Tall Boy, her future husband, when they are surprised by two Spaniards. The men are slavers who kidnap Bright Morning and Running Bird, take them to a distant town, and sell them as domestic workers to the wives of the soldiers stationed there. Bright Morning and her friend are able to escape through the help of Nehana, a member of the Nez Percé tribe who, having attempted escape once before, is more knowledgeable about their captors' habits. As the three girls are about to be recaptured by the pursuing Spaniards, Tall Boy and two of his friends come to their rescue. Tall Boy kills the leader of the Spaniards and is shot in the back by one of the others. The young Navahos return to their village, but Tall Boy has lost the use of his right arm because of his injury.

A bridge between the two major parts of the novel is Bright Morning's womanhood ceremony. For four days, she is kept busy, taking orders from the many relatives and friends who have gathered at her parent's hogan for the event.

The second major event of the novel occurs with the evacuation orders from the Army, known as the "Long Knives" because of the bayonets attached to the rifles that the soldiers carry. The leaders of the tribe decide that they do not have the strength to fight the Long Knives, so they elect to move all of their people to an almost inaccessible mesa in the high country. From their vantage point, the Navahos watch the soldiers destroy their homes and their food supply. The tribe is cut off from food and water, and the elders decide that they have no choice but to surrender when it appears that the soldiers will not leave the canyon.

After their surrender, Bright Morning and her people set off on an agonizing forced march to Fort Sumner. Once they arrive at their new home, an arid reservation outside the fort called Bosque Redondo, conditions continue to be harsh. Many other tribes occupy the camp as well, and not all of them are friendly. Food is not only scarce but also is mainly wheat, a grain to which the Navahos are not accustomed. Despite these hardships, Bright Morning and Tall Boy are married. They are soon separated, however, when Tall Boy is imprisoned in the fort after an altercation with a surly Apache.

When Tall Boy escapes from prison, Bright Morning knows that they must leave Bosque Redondo immediately. Escaping in the middle of the night, they are able to survive on the supplies that Bright Morning has been storing for months. At a temporary campsite far off the trail, Bright Morning gives birth to their son. At last, they return to Canyon de Chelly, abandoned except for a few sheep that had been part of Bright Morning's original flock. They are ready to begin again.

Analysis

As a work of historical fiction, *Sing Down the Moon* offers the reader valuable knowledge of two little known segments of U.S. history: the practice of enslaving young American Indian women and the forced relocation of the Navahos. The sufferings of the Navaho people are the sufferings of Bright Morning as she watches the old and weak die and the men lose their will.

The plot of the novel is episodic rather than causally related, and the unity of the book comes through the personality of the main character rather than through a tightly structured plot. Through Bright Morning, the reader learns about Navaho customs and way of life. Bright Morning reflects the beliefs of her people and explains her role in the womanhood ceremony and the marriage ceremony. Her love of her land is evidenced by her description of the canyons, mesas, and rivers. The historical and cultural import of the novel, however, is superseded by the development of Bright Morning from a girl to a woman. It is her strength of character that sustains her through the hardships of her two captivities and her hope that ultimately brings her back to the land that she loves.

Although Tall Boy is the strong character at the beginning of the story, his injury and his powerlessness in captivity weaken him. Bright Morning, on the other hand, gains strength and determination through her experiences. Her first escape is arranged by Nehana, but the second escape Bright Morning carefully plans herself. When Tall Boy emerges from the fort, broken in will and unable to go further, it is Bright Morning who provides the supplies and the psychological spur to leave Bosque Redondo. Upon their return to Canyon de Chelly, after many months of travel and hiding from the Long Knives, Tall Boy recovers some of his warrior spirit. The appearance of a ewe and her lamb and the blossoming trees bring hope to the young Navaho couple. Bright Morning, by deliberately stepping on her baby's toy spear as he reaches to touch the new lamb, indicates her hope of a life of peace for her son.

Bright Morning's narrative embodies the humor as well as the deep feelings of her people. The dialogues are sparse, sometimes teasing, and often imply more than the words express. Bright Morning, like the rest of her people, rarely displays her emotions. She explains early in the story that the gods punish those who show their feelings. Despite the terrible deprivations that they endure, the Navahos seldom cry. Likewise, the love between Bright Morning and Tall Boy has little outward manifestation.

The title of the book is puzzling because it is not found within the novel itself. The moon, however, receives frequent mention as measurement for time and as light for escape. Critics have pointed out that the Creation myths of the native peoples of the Southeast refer to the creation of the mountains as "singing up the mountains" and that "singing down" has a reverse significance.

Critical Context

Scott O'Dell has long been recognized as a first-rate writer of historical fiction for children and young adults. His first novel for children, *Island of the Blue Dolphins* (1960), was awarded the Newbery Medal in 1961. *Sing Down the Moon*, *The King's Fifth* (1966), and *The Black Pearl* (1967), have been named Newbery Honor Books. As in all of his novels of the American Southwest, in *Sing Down the Moon* O'Dell provides the reader with a realistic description of the setting and a sympathetic portrayal of the culture of the people who lived there. O'Dell has been criticized for inaccuracies with regard to Navaho dress and hairstyle. The inaccuracies, however, are quite minor and do not detract from the dignity of the people he brings to life.

O'Dell's most important contributions to fiction for children and young adults are his strong female characters. Bright Morning embodies in her character the joy in life, the suffering, and the determination to survive of the Navaho people. The note of hope on which the novel ends is the hope that Bright Morning has fostered in her soul through all the hardships that she has undergone.

Mary H. McNulty

A SLIPPING-DOWN LIFE

Author: Anne Tyler (1941-   )
First published: 1970
Type of work: Novel
Type of plot: Domestic realism
Time of work: The late 1960's
Locale: A small town in North Carolina
Subjects: Arts, coming-of-age, family, and love and romance
Recommended ages: 15-18

Evie Decker, a teenager in search of herself, seeks the attention of a local musician but finds instead that she can be strong and self-reliant.

> *Principal characters:*
> EVIE DECKER, a nondescript seventeen-year-old trying to gain attention through a sudden, shocking act
> BERTRAM (DRUM) CASEY, a nineteen-year-old local singer and the object of Evie's affections
> DAVID ELLIOT, Drum Casey's drummer and the person through whom Evie and Drum come together
> VIOLET HAYES, Evie's only friend
> CLOTELIA, the Deckers' maid and a mother figure to Evie
> SAM DECKER, Evie's father

Form and Content

A Slipping-Down Life is a realistic tale of the awkward and sometimes painful movement of a teenager, socially handicapped by the stigmas of shyness and obesity, to a moment of decision to end her obscurity, which ultimately leads her on a true journey to maturity and a strong sense of self-worth.

From the moment that Evie Decker, a seventeen-year-old from the small town of Farinia, North Carolina, hears the disembodied voice of nineteen-year-old local musician Drum Casey sounding his need to get out of Farinia for good, Evie is called to action. After years of endlessly waiting for her colorless existence to be touched by drama, Evie hears something in the voice of this stranger on her radio that inspires her to seek him out in the hope of finding the answer to changing her life. Author Anne Tyler has created a situation that could easily occur in any town or city across the United States: A teenager, unsatisfied with her life, searches for someone to show her a better way of surviving. While Tyler's protagonist, as with many heroines of realistic young adult literature, does not live "happily ever after," the novel is ultimately positive because Evie survives her journey through adolescence and learns much along the way.

The story of the novel, while dealing with the complex feelings and unpredictable actions of adolescence, is straightforward and easy to follow. Evie has no mother, an amiable but distant father, and only one friend. She is lonely and interested in changing her life, but she takes no concrete steps to do so. One day, however, when she hears an interview with a local musician, she decides to attend a rock-and-roll show—an act much out of character for her—in order to see him in person. This sudden fascination sets in motion the rest of the action of the novel.

After the first show, Evie begins to frequent the Unicorn, a local nightclub where the musician, Drum Casey, plays every Saturday night. Drum takes little notice of Evie, and, in a moment of rashness, Evie decides to get his attention in a shocking way—by slashing the name "Casey" backward across her forehead with manicure scissors in the restroom of the club. The slashing does nothing but annoy Drum, who does not want to feel responsible for Evie's actions. Evie achieves her goal of closeness to Drum, however, when his manager, David Elliot, asks Evie to come to all of Drum's sets and sit in front of the stage, with the scars visible to the other audience members.

This situation continues for weeks until Drum achieves some small success and drops Evie from the show, thinking that publicity no longer needed. When things go badly wrong and Drum loses his job and his home, he turns to Evie for help and companionship. They drift into marriage, Drum looking for domesticity and Evie searching for identity and love. Their union is matter-of-fact and plagued by financial problems and Drum's immaturity. The marriage and the novel ultimately end with the sudden death of Evie's father and Evie's unplanned pregnancy, which forces her to give Drum an ultimatum: He must "get organized," moving into the house left to her by her father and making a decent life for the baby, or they must part. Although Drum maintains that he wants them to stay together, he refuses her demands and Evie leaves him.

Analysis

The meaning of *A Slipping-Down Life* is easily ascertained without being simplistic. It concerns the major conflict of adolescence—the quest for acceptance and identity. In the main character's journey in coming-of-age, this quest is clearly the central issue, but it is complicated by many other side issues: the pain of being classified as "different" from the peer group, the need for familial closeness, the problems of teen marriage, and even the stigma of physical disfigurement. *A Slipping-Down Life* is a novel of learning and growth that offers readers hope that, regardless of the level of isolation or the enormity of problems and while perfect happy endings are not reality, strength and a feeling of self-worth can be the by-products of adversity.

One of the two pivotal moments of the story is the revelation that Evie has carved the name "Casey" into her forehead. Prior to this moment, the reader has been introduced to an overweight, lackluster girl who feels awkward with herself and others and is seemingly incapable of making social connections. The carving is representative of the desperate measures to which some adolescents will resort when faced with alienation. It is the ultimate act of seeking identity through others, as well as a taking of power. (It is impossible for Drum to deny her completely with such a visible link between them.) The act is also a complete denial of self in a submersion into the identity of another person.

As time passes and Evie moves through her connection to Drum, including the unraveling of their marriage, the scars from the carving fade just as Evie's need to find identity in another person diminishes. With the death of her father and the impending birth of her child, Evie is symbolically putting away the past and stepping into maturity. Although the failure of her marriage denies a traditional happy ending, Evie has her second pivotal moment when she denies that she carved her own forehead; blaming someone else when she obviously performed the act herself implies that she sees herself as a new person, removed from that sense of desperation.

Critical Context

Although lacking the grittier bleakness of realism that Robert Cormier's *The Chocolate War* (1974) would soon usher into young adult fiction, *A Slipping-Down Life* does avoid the pitfalls of the overly simplistic juvenile story, with its easy answers, that was the norm at its time of publication. While Anne Tyler's later works are generally intended for an older audience, her books overwhelmingly explore the female search for identity, and her juvenile heroine clears the way for the strong young heroines of later 1970's young adult fiction, such as those of Judy Blume. While not choosing to remain a writer in today's realistic juvenile literature, Tyler can be said to be a pioneer in the movement.

Emma Cox-Harris

SO FAR FROM THE BAMBOO GROVE

Author: Yoko Kawashima Watkins (1933-   )
First published: 1986
Type of work: Autobiography
Time of work: The 1940's
Locale: Nanam, Tanchon, Seoul, and Pusan, Korea; and Kyoto and Aomori, Japan
Subjects: Family, race and ethnicity, social issues, and war
Recommended ages: 10-15

This riveting autobiography highlights a Japanese family's narrow escape from Korea to freedom in Japan during World War II.

Principal personages:
YOKO KAWASHIMA, the author as an eleven-year-old girl
KO KAWASHIMA, Yoko's sixteen-year-old sister, with whom she escapes from Korea and who helps her survive in Kyoto, Japan
MRS. KAWASHIMA, Yoko's mother, who leads her daughters in their narrow escape from Korea
HIDEYO KAWASHIMA, Yoko's older brother, who must escape from Korea alone
CORPORAL MATSUMURA, a friend and influential military officer who aided the Kawashima family's escape from Korea and who was reunited with Ko and Yoko in Kyoto

Form and Content

So Far from the Bamboo Grove is an autobiography that traces the Japanese author's narrow escape from Korea during World War II. In addition to the eleven chapters that tell Yoko Kawashima Watkins' story, this riveting account offers a map showing all the geographical locations mentioned in the story, a foreword by acclaimed author Jean Fritz, and historical notes from the publisher.

So Far from the Bamboo Grove tells two parallel escape stories from Korea: the escape of eleven-year-old Yoko with her sister and mother, and the separate escape of her brother, Hideyo, with his friends. Although most of the story is about the Kawashima women, several chapters are devoted to Hideyo's escape.

The setting is World War II. Yoko and her family are Japanese and living in Nanam, Korea. Korean Communists are killing the Japanese people, and many are fleeing the country. Yoko's father is away from home, serving in the Japanese military, and Yoko and her family must escape from the Korean communists without his help.

Korean Communist soldiers come through Yoko's village, ransacking her home and those of other Japanese families. When it occurs to Yoko's mother, Mrs. Kawashima, that they must escape immediately, Yoko's brother, Hideyo, is away working at a factory in another town. Mrs. Kawashima contacts a family friend and military officer, Corporal Matsumura, who assists Yoko, her sister, Ko, and Mrs. Kawashima in escaping from their village. They are smuggled aboard a Red Cross train and, after it is bombed three days later, escape through the fields.

Meanwhile, Yoko's brother and three friends narrowly escape death when the ammunition factory in which they work is blown up, and the young men journey back to their homes in Nanam. Hideyo's friends are saddened to discover their family and friends missing or dead, but Hideyo finds his mother's note and directions as to where to meet. He grabs supplies, clothing, and the bank book and begins his long journey.

So Far from the Bamboo Grove traces Yoko's escape in detail. Eventually, Yoko, Ko, and their mother arrive in Kyoto, Japan, where Mrs. Kawashima enrolls the girls in school. She leaves the girls behind to fend for themselves and travels by train to find her parents. Mrs. Kawashima returns several weeks later to report to Yoko that the town has been bombed and her grandparents are dead, and she then dies in Yoko's arms. Although devastated, Yoko and Ko continue to survive on their own, barely scraping by. A joyful reunion occurs when they find Corporal Matsumura.

Meanwhile, Hideyo continues to travel with his friends, but eventually they must separate. Hideyo continues the journey alone, facing many hardships. He almost freezes to death and is saved by a Korean family, the Kims, who own a farm near the thirty-eighth parallel. Risking death at the hands of the Communists, the Kims nurse Hideyo back to health and lovingly invite him to be a part of their family; they know it would be almost certain death for him to cross the thirty-eight parallel. Hideyo is moved by their deep kindness but chooses to swim across the Imjon River, which crosses the thirty-eighth parallel—he must find his family. Although machine-gun fire greets him with nearly every stroke, he makes it safely across the river to freedom.

The book ends as Yoko and Ko are reunited with their brother. The historical notes at the end reveal that the children waited many years before they were reunited with their father, who was in a prison camp.

Analysis

So Far from the Bamboo Grove is a moving, realistic portrayal of survival and the horrible effects of war: death, injury, crime, separation from family and friends, interruptions in schooling, and political turmoil.

The effectively told story evokes emotions on the part of young readers. They may cringe as they read about how the newborn baby in the Red Cross car must be bathed with urine because there is no water and may wince when reading about the piece of metal removed from Yoko's ear. Readers may also feel angry at the hate demonstrated by war crimes and be incensed by the callous behavior of prejudiced schoolchildren. Sensitive readers will more than likely be moved to tears when Yoko and Ko lose their beloved mother.

Each chapter of the suspenseful narrative ends with a cliffhanger or statement that moves the young reader through the novel, making it a difficult book to put down. Yoko Kawashima Watkins skillfully weaves her story, integrating the account of the perilous journey with personal and historical facts. Thus, readers are led to understand the Japanese view and experience during World War II.

The most powerful impact of this autobiography is the message of survival. The author faces the worst of circumstances, yet she does not give up. Forced to grow up early, live in poverty, and struggle to survive emotionally and physically without parental support, she continues on. She attends school, collects scrap paper on which to do her work, and excels in her academics. Although she nearly starves and is the most poorly clad child in her Kyoto school, she looks beyond her circumstances to dreams of a successful future as a writer. Staying true to her dream and working with undaunted diligence, she sees her dream come true.

Critical Context

The canon of juvenile literature contains a plethora of books offering European perspectives of World War II, such as Marie McSwigan's *Snow Treasure* (1942) or Anne Frank's *Het Achterhuis* (1947; *The Diary of a Young Girl*, 1952). Only a few juvenile books, however, describe the Asian or Asian American experiences during the war. *Baseball Saved Us* (1993), a picture book by Ken Mochizuki, tells of the Japanese American experience of being in an internment camp in the United States, and Jeanne Wakatsuki Houston's autobiography *Farewell to Manzanar* (1973), co-written with James Houston, relates for older readers the author's years in such a camp. The riveting narrative of Laurence Yep's *Hiroshima* (1995), a short novel for younger readers, simultaneously traces the experiences of twelve-year-old Sachi in Japan and the pilots of the American plane the *Enola Gay* as they drop the atomic bomb on Hiroshima, Japan, on August 6, 1945. Yep traces Sachi's painful adaptation to the devastating effects of the bomb. *Hiroshima*, if read in conjunction with *So Far from the Bamboo Grove*, offers young readers insight into what Mrs. Kawashima experienced when she found her parents dead and their town devastated by the bomb.

Yoko Kawashima Watkins wrote two other books that help the reader understand her experience. The sequel to *So Far from the Bamboo Grove* is *My Brother, My Sister, and I* (1994), which describes the attempt of the three siblings to reunite with their father, who had been in a prison camp. The introduction to *Tales from the Bamboo Grove* (1992) describes Watkins' childhood in the Kawashima household. The book includes six folktales told by her parents during Yoko's early childhood. Recording these childhood memories from supper time was essential for the author so that she could remember these joyful, secure family times before they were destroyed by war.

Watkins' memoir *So Far from the Bamboo Grove* is the first effective account of the Japanese experience in Korea during World War II that is accessible to young readers. It therefore holds a unique place in the canon of juvenile literature. Watkins is a gifted writer whose works are growing in popularity.

June Hetzel

SOCKS

Author: Beverly Cleary (1916-   )
First published: 1973
Type of work: Novel
Type of plot: Domestic realism
Time of work: The 1970's
Locale: The home of Mr. and Mrs. Bricker
Subjects: Animals, emotions, and family
Recommended ages: 10-13

The Brickers pay fifty cents for Socks, a black kitten with white paws, who becomes the pampered king of the household until Charles William is born and dethrones the cat.

Principal characters:
    SOCKS, a black kitten with white paws who sees himself as
        all-important in the Bricker family
    MARILYN BRICKER, a cat lover and the doting mother of Charles
        William
    BILL BRICKER, Marilyn's husband, who initially only tolerates cats but
        who grows to love Socks
    CHARLES WILLIAM BRICKER, the new addition to the Bricker household
        and Socks' competition
    MRS. RISLEY, the baby-sitter who restores Socks' self-esteem
    NANA BRICKER, Bill's mother, who visits and has Socks banished from
        the house
    OLD TAYLOR, a nasty tom cat who fights with Socks

Form and Content

Beverly Cleary's *Socks* explores the themes of family rivalry and jealousy in an unusual form: between Socks, the cat, and the new baby of the Bricker family, Charles William. This warm, humorously told story, which could take place anytime and anywhere, is told from Socks's perspective.

Marilyn and Bill Bricker are leaving the grocery store when they come upon two children who are selling kittens. Marilyn falls in love with Socks, appropriately named for his white paws, and Bill hesitantly agrees to pay the fifty cents. Before long, Socks is in control of the household, amusing the Brickers with his kittenish antics, soaking up their affection as he sits on their laps, and indulging himself with the abundant food. His good life begins to unravel when he is penned in the laundry room for several days. Upon his release, he sees Mrs. Bricker coming through the front door carrying a blanketed bundle. The bundle wiggles and makes strange sounds. No longer is Socks the center of attention now that Charles William, the firstborn of the Brickers, has made his entrance into the world.

Socks feels neglected and resents the little intruder. The Brickers have no time to pet, brush, and play with him anymore, and, when Mr. Bricker discovers that Socks is gaining weight from eating Charles William's leftover formula, Socks is put on a strict diet. One night, Mrs. Risley, a true cat lover, comes to baby-sit. She fusses over Socks, allowing him to sit on her lap, feeding him morsels of her snacks, and talking to him all the time. He is comforted by the fact that someone has come who apparently loves him more than Charles William. Socks sleeps his best sleep since the baby entered the house.

Not too many days later, Nana Bricker comes to visit. She does not like cats and is not sure that it is safe for Socks to be around the baby. After Socks attacks and almost destroys her wig one evening and nips Mrs. Bricker's ankle the next morning, he is banished from the house. Only after Nana returns to her own home and Socks is beaten by Old Taylor, the neighborhood tom cat, is he restored to the living quarters. Upon seeing Socks, Charles William calls him "Ticky," his first word, which thrills the Brickers. The cat and boy begin a new relationship.

One day, Charles William pushes his crib in front of the door, making it impossible for Mrs. Bricker to enter his bedroom. To compound the problem, Socks is in the bedroom with the baby. Mrs. Bricker has never left the two together unsupervised. Charles William picks at the bumper pad in his crib and removes cotton batting, which he throws to Socks. The two make a game of playing with the batting. By the time that the panicked Mrs. Bricker finds a ladder and climbs in the bedroom window, the boy and cat are exhausted from their play and are both sound asleep side by side in the crib, friends at last.

Analysis

This book has a wholesome theme and characters and is great fun. Cleary is known for a lively writing style that includes much dialogue and action-packed plots, and *Socks* is no exception. While *Socks* can be categorized as an animal story, much of the emphasis is on the interactions between the cat and humans. Socks remains true to the characteristics of his species, except for his ability to think and reason as a human.

In this fast-paced, entertaining, and easy-to-read story, young readers will be able to relate to the antics of Socks and his jealousy toward Charles William. Most children have experienced the emotion of jealousy, if not in family situations then in the classroom. Socks learns to deal with his feelings of neglect and dislike of the new "furless" rival through one mishap after another. In a humorous manner, Cleary allows Socks to move from the comfort of pampering and having the total attention of his owners, to the discomfort of being thrown out of the house, and to shared attention with Charles William. Thus is found a positive resolution to Socks's problem.

While Socks is the central character, the story also reveals much about human nature. It points out how people often move on to new experiences without thinking of how they may be neglecting what was once important to them and in so doing bring harm into their own and others' lives. Mr. and Mrs. Bricker become consumed with their new baby and begin to see Socks as a nuisance. Socks is removed from the house at the suggestion of Nana, a visitor to the Bricker home. It is only when Socks becomes injured, is returned to the household, and becomes a source of amusement for Charles William that Marilyn and Bill realize how much they missed Socks.

In *Socks*, Cleary develops characters with distinct personalities. Nana Bricker is presented as an unpleasant character because she is critical of the cat. When Socks scratches, Nana is certain that he is covered with fleas. She is fearful of his being in the room with the baby, reminding Marilyn that some babies are allergic to cats. She also has concerns that the cat might scratch Charles William. Warm, caring Mrs. Risley, in contrast, recognizes that Socks feels alienated since the arrival of the baby. She cannot wait to settle in a chair with Socks on her lap and lavish attention on him. Mr. Bricker is a person who aims to please, giving in to his wife's pleas for a kitten and appeasing his mother by throwing Socks out of the house. Ultimately, he pleases Socks by allowing him back into his comfortable home. Cheerful Mrs. Bricker loves babies and cats but does not handle problems well. This trait is evident in the way in which she avoids arguments with Nana and panics when she cannot reach the baby in the locked bedroom. Charles William grows into a cheerful, playful toddler, while Socks remains an attention-loving, frolicsome kitten.

Critical Context

In more than forty years of writing, Beverly Cleary published more than forty titles and distinguished herself as a clear favorite among both children and adults. This success is evidenced by the sales of her books, the high circulation of her titles in libraries, and the numerous awards and honors attributed to her work, including recognition from at least seventeen different state library associations, frequent Young Reader's Choice Awards from the Pacific Northwest Library Association, and the Laura Ingalls Wilder Award and the Newbery Medal from the American Library Association. She received the William Allen White Award and the Golden Archer Award from the University of Wisconsin for *Socks*.

Humans dominate Cleary's writings; Ramona Quimby is undoubtedly the most memorable character in her realistic stories for young readers. Henry Huggins was her earliest creation, and Leigh Botts, an adolescent from a divorced family, is the protagonist in *Dear Mr. Henshaw* (1983) and *Strider* (1991), books for a slightly older audience. Ralph S. Mouse, a motorcycle-riding mouse and the friend of Keith Gridley, appeared in three Cleary fantasy books, and Ribsy, Henry Huggins' dog, had a book of his own prior to the publication of *Socks*, Cleary's second animal story.

Cleary writes from her childhood desire to read amusing books about children like herself. While some critics fault her lack of stories with a racial mix of characters or books that deal with serious childhood problems, Cleary has remained true to her personal goals and provided several generations of children with appealing, entertaining reading.

Carol Ann Gearhart

A SOLITARY BLUE

Author: Cynthia Voigt (1942-   )
First published: 1983
Type of work: Novel
Type of plot: Domestic realism
Time of work: The 1970's
Locales: Baltimore and the Eastern Shore, Maryland, and Charleston, South Carolina
Subjects: Coming-of-age, family, and friendship
Recommended ages: 13-15

Abandoned and betrayed by his self-absorbed mother, Jeff Greene learns to trust himself, his father, and his friends.

> *Principal characters:*
> JEFF GREENE, an only child who is deserted by his mother at the age of seven
> THE PROFESSOR, Jeff's father, an introverted academic
> MELODY, Jeff's charming and beautiful mother, whose avowed concern for social problems conceals a selfish nature
> BROTHER THOMAS, the monk who befriends the father and son
> DICEY TILLERMAN, Jeff's honest and outspoken school friend who shares his pain of abandonment

Form and Content

A Solitary Blue explores the psychological damage inflicted upon an only child by deficient parents. Spanning approximately ten years, the novel begins when seven-year-old Jeff Greene comes home from school one day to find a note from his mother, Melody, explaining that she has left him to continue her serious social work. Abandoned by the mother that he adores and fearful of losing his remaining parent, Jeff withdraws. Over a period of four years, Jeff and his father, the Professor, assume an orderly and mirthless routine, broken only by the occasional visits of the Professor's colleague, Brother Thomas. An invitation to spend the summer in Charleston with his mother promises to change everything.

The summer is a magical one for Jeff. He is captivated by his mother's warm, spontaneous charm and by the music that she plays on the guitar. After a few days, however, Melody is again busy with her "causes." Jeff is largely left to fend for himself until the end of the summer, when Melody exchanges his airline ticket for a bus ticket and sends him back to Baltimore without any traveling money. Nevertheless, Jeff adores his mother so much that he overlooks her self-centered behavior.

In Baltimore for another school year, Jeff writes Melody numerous letters, to which he receives no reply. Her rejection is softened somewhat by the friendship of Brother Thomas, who provides guidance and good humor to both Jeff and the Professor. In his own awkward way, the Professor attempts to reach out to Jeff by taking an interest in his music and by contacting Jeff's great-grandmother to arrange a second summer in Charleston.

Jeff finds a different Charleston when he returns. Melody is preoccupied with Max, a journalist whom she accompanies as a photographer. Great-grandmother Gambo, who has suffered a stroke, seems annoyed by Jeff's presence; only Opal, the aging African American housekeeper, seems not to notice Jeff at all. Jeff survives the summer by exploring a remote island, where he identifies with the aloneness of a great blue heron. As a result of Melody's second betrayal, Jeff withdraws to the point of near madness upon his return to Baltimore.

The second half of the book details Jeff's recovery over the next five years. The Professor uses the extra money that he receives from the publication of his book to buy them a proper home on the Eastern Shore in Maryland. Under his father's caring concern, Jeff responds to the beauty and solitude of his surroundings. As he gains confidence at home, he begins to thrive in school, realizing that he is intelligent and strong. Ultimately, it is his friendship with a young girl named Dicey Tillerman and her family that awakens his spirit. When his mother tries to reenter his life, Jeff sees her shallowness and selfishness, and he realizes that he is no longer dependent on her approval.

Analysis

A Solitary Blue is an important, realistic novel that deals with the complex problems of family relationships. With a keen yet sympathetic eye, Cynthia Voigt looks at the dysfunctional Greene family: a timid and remote father, a self-centered and restless mother, and a confused and lonely son. The theme of abandonment drives this novel, but subthemes stress the value of solitude, commitment, friendship, and resilience. *A Solitary Blue* is significant for young adult readers because it confronts vital issues, such as independence, academic achievement, and mental illness; it is a memorable book because of Voigt's precise and powerful writing.

Abandonment is a frequent theme in young adult literature. Formula fiction regularly gets rid of the parents so that the young person will be the focus of all the action and accomplishments of the book; unlike such formula fiction, *A Solitary Blue* explores in depth the effects of abandonment, both profound and subtle, on the development of Jeff Greene and his interaction with his parents. As Jeff grows and gains self-reliance, his perceptions of his parents also sharpen. He realizes that Melody deserves neither the adoration that he felt as a young child nor the contempt that he felt five years later when she abandoned him a second time to follow her own whims. "Poor Melody," he thinks to himself with more compassion than anger. Jeff also changes his perception of his father, appreciating the Professor's intelligence and commitment. Gradually, as Jeff comes to value him more, his father's inner qualities surface to reveal a kind and generous man with a wry sense of humor. He, too, has been wounded by Melody; together, he and Jeff learn to rise above their pain and find pleasure in the world.

Beginning with the title and continuing throughout the book, the theme of solitude is explored. Jeff is left alone much of the time even before Melody deserts him because she is self-absorbed and the Professor habitually retreats to his office. Jeff learns to be unobtrusive and apologetic. The first words that he speaks when dealing with adults are often "I'm sorry." Yet, solitude also offers solace. Jeff is at peace with himself when he rows through the marshes around Charleston and identifies with the lone blue heron. He draws close to nature during the solitary times that he spends at home on the Eastern Shore.

Music and water serve as recurring metaphors in the novel. Jeff loves to hear Melody play the guitar and sing when he visits her in Charleston. The name Melody itself reminds the reader of the connection that Jeff has with his mother and with music. Music also breaks down the barrier between Jeff and his father when the Professor, prompted perhaps by the wise Brother Thomas, takes Jeff to a concert, encourages his guitar lessons, and gives Jeff a fine Martin guitar as a Christmas present. It is music that initially attracts Dicey to Jeff. When she hears him playing his guitar outside the school building, "she didn't want to be drawn over to him, but she couldn't do anything to stop herself." Music is a metaphor for Jeff's reaching out to other people. Water is the second metaphor that reveals characters. In order to push away his feelings of rejection when Melody ignores him, Jeff rows to a remote island in a patched-up boat. Dicey and Jeff discover freedom and profound friendship when they are sailing together.

Young adult readers will recognize the truth to be found in *A Solitary Blue*. Voigt renders realistic dialogue and believable people in often-powerful writing. Subtle irony is another strong point of the novel. For example, when Melody puts Jeff on the bus without any money for meals, he in fact becomes one of the "starving children" that she so grandly wants to save. Yet, the authenticity and irony do not preclude an optimistic, upbeat conclusion. The novel leaves readers eager for further encounters with these memorable characters.

Critical Context

Continuing a trend that began with the 1970's new realism, *A Solitary Blue* is a coming-of-age novel that profiles a dysfunctional family. When adults are absent, preoccupied, or flawed in some way, a child's inner conflict develops naturally. This motif of self-sufficient and resilient orphans is found in fairy tales such as "Hansel and Gretel" and biblical stories such as Joseph and his coat of many colors; it has guided several of Cynthia Voigt's young adult novels, such as *Homecoming* (1981); *Dicey's Song* (1982), the winner of the Newbery Medal; *The Runner* (1985); *Sons from Afar* (1988); and *Seventeen Against the Dealer* (1989). Constituting what might be called the Tillerman series, these books share common characters—specifically, the Tillerman family of Dicey, James, Sammy, Maybeth, and Grandma Tillerman. *Homecoming*, which was inspired by a car full of kids left to wait in a supermarket parking lot, became the springboard for the other five novels. *A Solitary Blue*, although self-contained, is considered a companion book, not a sequel, to *Dicey's Song*.

Praised for their realism, Voigt's novels stress the need for understanding and harmony between generations. She provides compelling characters who change and grow as they communicate openly with one another. Voigt has an ear for the dialogue of adolescents and an optimistic eye for the innate resilience of her protagonists. They may not all live happily ever after, but her characters teach young people that understanding themselves and others is possible if they make the effort.

Esther Broughton

SOMETHING WICKED THIS WAY COMES

Author: Ray Bradbury (1920-   )
First published: 1962
Type of work: Novel
Type of plot: Adventure tale and fantasy
Time of work: The mid-twentieth century
Locale: A small town in Illinois
Subjects: Friendship and the supernatural
Recommended ages: 13-15

Two boys encounter a sinister carnival capable of granting them their most secret wishes, but they learn that there is a terrible price to pay for succumbing to the carnival's temptations.

Principal characters:
  WILL HALLOWAY, a bright, somewhat naïve thirteen-year-old
  JIM NIGHTSHADE, Will's more worldly-wise best friend, who is also thirteen
  CHARLES HALLOWAY, Will's aging father, a library janitor
  G. M. DARK, the coowner and proprietor of the carnival who is covered with tattoos
  J. C. COOGER, the coowner of the carnival who takes on the guise of a twelve-year-old boy in order to infiltrate the town
  MISS FOLEY, the boys' seventh-grade teacher
  THE DUST WITCH, a blind witch, one of the members of the carnival

Form and Content

Something Wicked This Way Comes is a richly imaginative story of good overcoming evil. Will Halloway and his next-door neighbor, Jim Nightshade, see themselves almost as twins. Born only minutes apart in the same hospital on Halloween, they have grown up like brothers, but now, at the age of thirteen, personality differences have begun to emerge. Will is naïve and almost reluctant to let go of each moment. Jim, whose father is dead, is much more streetwise and curious; he is anxious to become the man he never knew in his father. Will's aloof and world-weary father, Charles Halloway, at fifty-four, feels too old to be a suitable father for a teenage boy. He senses that he has failed as a father and fears death and the effects of age.

Late one October night, a mysterious carnival, Cooger and Dark's Pandemonium Shadow Show, sets up on the edge of town. The carnival is peopled by menacing freaks and is run by G. M. Dark, a heavily tattooed ringmaster, and J. C. Cooger, a huge, red-haired man. With a mirror maze, a carousel, and sinister sideshows, the carnival seduces the weak-willed and vain by catering to their human cravings and frailties.

Will and Jim watch secretly as Mr. Cooger rides the carnival carousel backward. With each revolution, Cooger becomes a year younger. When the carousel finally stops, he emerges as a twelve-year-old boy and enters the town, posing as the nephew of Miss Foley, one of the town's teachers. Will and Jim follow the boy. (Later, when Cooger is being transformed by the carousel back into his adult self, they damage the carousel's machinery and make it spin faster and faster, transforming Cooger into an ancient, feeble man on the brink of death.) Jim becomes secretly obsessed with the carousel's ability to add or subtract years, seeing it as a way of instantly making himself the grown man he longs to be.

Mr. Dark begins a methodical search of the town for the two boys. He first sends the Dust Witch, a blind crone who navigates by sense of smell, over the town's rooftops in a balloon. When that plan fails, he begins a physical search of the town, in the guise of a parade, but Will's father intervenes to protect the boys. The boys tell him about their predicament. By searching old newspapers and books in the library, Charles Halloway discovers that the carnival has visited the town many times over the centuries, tempting people with the fulfillment of their most secret wishes and feeding off their corrupted souls. When Mr. Dark confronts Charles in the library, where the boys are hiding, he tempts the older man by promising to make him young if he will only betray the two boys. The boys are abducted by Mr. Dark, but Charles rescues them when he discovers that the evil of the carnival can be overcome when humans find the strength to laugh at what they most fear.

Analysis

Something Wicked This Way Comes incorporates many of the themes of Ray Bradbury's earlier work and all of his stylistic strengths and weaknesses. The novel is written in Bradbury's richly figurative language, with countless similes and metaphors, which are at times breathtaking in their originality and at other times simply puzzling. While this sometimes inspired, sometimes contrived style of expression is likely to frustrate the novel's target age-group, the fast-paced plot is visceral and unrelenting.

One of the novel's clear themes concerns the importance and strength of friendship. Throughout the novel Will and Jim are portrayed as twins, yet there are some personality differences that strain their relationship. The differences are minor, but they hold the fearsome potential of forcing a wedge between the two. Illustrative of this theme is the fact that Will was born one minute before midnight and Jim one minute after. Although only two minutes actually separate their ages, Jim is technically a day older than Will, and the resulting sense of hierarchy has had profound effects on the ways in which the boys have developed. Jim is aggressive, impulsive, and impatient to be grown; Will is more introverted, deliberate, and patient. Jim yearns to be older, despite the effects that age would have on their friendship; Will fears being left behind. Jim recklessly blunders into danger; Will follows, reluctant and cautious.

The character of Charles Halloway embodies the theme of lost youth, the fear of the effects of age, and ultimately the fear of death. He is unwilling to surrender the unfulfilled promises of his youth. Paradoxically, the same attributes of youth that Jim shuns in his craving to be older are the very ones that Charles covets. He yearns nostalgically for the energy, vibrancy, and possibility of youth, while Jim longs to cast these same things off. The story's fascination with the cycle of life and the passage of time is represented by the circular motion of the carousel and by frequent references to clocks and time. Both Jim and Charles are tempted by the promise of the age-altering carousel, and both can only find happiness by overcoming their desire and finding satisfaction in their lot. When Charles Halloway enters the Hall of Mirrors and sees his body aging in each of the successive mirror reflections, the experience amounts to a revelation of his greatest fear. It is only when he literally laughs in the face of this mortality that he is able to overcome the specter of death.

The clearest theme of *Something Wicked This Way Comes* deals with the nature of goodness and evil. As the novel progresses, the inhabitants of the carnival come to appear purely evil, but none of the other characters is purely good. Cooger and Dark represent lives given over completely to evil, and Charles Halloway sees in himself the potential to follow in their footsteps, if not for his continued personal commitment to decency and his eternal vigilance and introspection. After the evil carnival is destroyed and the story arrives at its resolution, Charles Halloway warns the two boys, "We got to watch out the rest of our lives. The fight's just begun." When the boys ask him where the evil ones will come from next, he answers, "Maybe they're here already." Bradbury suddenly moves the battleground against evil inside humanity. The potential for evil is as inescapable a part of the human condition as the aging process. It is only when the story's protagonists accept and embrace all the weaknesses of human flesh by confronting their mortality and their personal evil and by laughing in its face that the villains in the book are vanquished.

Critical Context

As was the case with his first novel, *Fahrenheit 451* (1953), *Something Wicked This Way Comes* is a greatly expanded and much more sophisticated version of one of Ray Bradbury's earlier short stories. "The Black Ferris," published in *Weird Tales* (1948) and never reprinted in any of Bradbury's story collections, tells of two boys who visit a carnival and witness the owner, Mr. Cooger, ride the Ferris wheel backwards and emerge from it a twelve-year-old boy. That story, greatly expanded, becomes the foundation for chapters 18 through 23 of *Something Wicked This Way Comes*.

Charles G. Finney's novel *The Circus of Dr. Lao* (1936), which Bradbury championed and helped raise to cultlike status, also greatly influenced this work. In Finney's novel, a mysteriously advertised circus appears in a small Arizona town. The very vagueness of the group's identity enables the townspeople to identify with it, each on his or her own primal level. In a series of vignettes, various visitors to the circus find there curious reflections of their own vanities and fears. Bradbury's sinister carnival and the individual temptations that it offers each of its visitors is a clear offspring of Finney's circus, as is the small town setting and its cast of vain and troubled citizens.

Curiously, the parallels between the two stories are even more clearly drawn in the film version of *Something Wicked This Way Comes* (1983), from the screenplay that Bradbury adapted himself.

Paul Buchanan

SOMEWHERE IN THE DARKNESS

Author: Walter Dean Myers (1937-   )
First published: 1992
Type of work: Novel
Type of plot: Psychological realism and social realism
Time of work: The early 1990's
Locale: Various homes and hotels in New York, Chicago, and Arkansas
Subjects: Coming-of-age, crime, family, health and illness, and race and ethnicity
Recommended ages: 13-18

Jimmy Little and his father, an escaped convict, struggle to establish a father-son relationship and to cope with Crab's illness during a cross-country journey from New York to Arkansas.

> *Principal characters:*
> JIMMY LITTLE, a fourteen-year-old boy who is reunited with the father he has never known
> CEPHUS "CRAB" LITTLE, Jimmy's father, who has escaped from prison and who is dying of kidney disease
> MAMA JEAN, the woman who reared Jimmy while his father was in prison
> RYDELL DEPUIS, the Arkansas man who presumably can confirm Crab's innocence in a robbery
> MAVIS, a female friend whom Crab visits in Chicago
> FRANK, Mavis' sixteen-year-old son
> HIGH JOHN, the "conjure man" to whom Crab goes in Arkansas for relief from his pain

Form and Content

Somewhere in the Darkness revolves around both a literal and a psychological journey for fourteen-year-old Jimmy Little and his father, Crab. In the last days of his life, Jimmy's father searches in desperation for what has been missing in his life, a closer relationship with his son. He also attempts to regain a sense of self-respect by using his last days to attempt to clear his name in the crime for which he was convicted, in the hopes that at least Jimmy will have proof of his innocence. Crab assumes that both objectives can be accomplished by taking Jimmy with him on a journey from New York to Chicago and finally back to Crab's hometown of Marion, Arkansas, where Rydell Depuis, the man who probably committed the crime, could tell Jimmy the truth. The novel unfolds through a third-person point of view told from Jimmy's perspective as he alternately pities and hates the man who claims to be his father but with whom he has never had a close relationship. Gradually, the reader, along with Jimmy, begins to understand Crab.

Crab reenters Jimmy's life at a time of uncertainty for the young man. Jimmy feels both physical and mental exhaustion as he copes with academic and personal troubles during his sophomore year of high school. He is intelligent, but his grades are slipping, and he has begun to cut class and to make excuses. His peers refuse to take personal responsibility for their actions, and Jimmy is beginning to be like them. "I didn't do nothing," one boy says, "I just got picked." Mama Jean, the woman who has reared Jimmy since his mother's death and his father's imprisonment, struggles to convince him of the importance of education and personal responsibility, but Jimmy seems to be drifting toward a dead end.

Jimmy comes home one day to find his father waiting on the stairs. Crab takes Jimmy away with him, presumably to a new life and a new job in Chicago. Jimmy, sick and bewildered at the sudden disruption in his life, is strangely attracted to and repulsed by the father he has never known. He is curious to find out more about Crab and about his family. Crab, in constant pain and dying from kidney disease, takes Jimmy on a journey from New York to Chicago, renewing old acquaintances, trying to revive a faded career as a jazz musician, and funding his travels through car theft and credit card fraud. Crab reveals that he has escaped from prison so that he will not die in a prison hospital before the truth of his innocence has been revealed, at least to Jimmy. He does not want to go to his grave with his son thinking that he had a part in shooting someone. Jimmy returns with Crab to Arkansas in a search for Rydell Depuis, Crab's last hope to clear his name.

Crab finds him, only to have Depuis alert the police. As the police are closing in on Crab, he and Jimmy dramatically confront each other and realize that they have become father and son again, but that the relationship is complex and ambiguous and is far from ideal. Crab collapses and is hospitalized after his arrest, dying in a hospital in Arkansas. Jimmy returns to New York and Mama Jean, changed by his experience, but clearly still confused about what it means to be a man, especially an African American man, and with a resolve to be a different kind of father to his own son, if he should ever have one.

Analysis

In *Somewhere in the Darkness*, Walter Dean Myers writes an unsentimental, realistic story of the obstacles that thwart understanding between people, even two people seemingly as close as father and son. Both Jimmy and Crab enter the relationship warily, but at the same time with a hope that lies just below the surface of doubt and suspicion. Jimmy wants to know his father but at the same time cannot automatically trust a man he has never known. He wants to reach out to Crab in the older man's pain and need, but he cannot fully believe in a man who claims to want to clear his name of the crime for which he has been convicted and yet who funds his quest through car theft and credit card fraud.

Both men have needs, and often in the novel those needs are selfish. Crab admits that he wants Jimmy to come with him because Crab needs to have resolution before his death. Jimmy feels physically ill as he leaves Mama Jean's sheltering love, but, at the same time, he also needs to know what it means to have a father and to be a man. The younger man and the older man circle each other for most of the novel, until a final confrontation occurs at the dramatic climax of the work when the police are closing in to capture Crab. Crab reaches out to Jimmy for acceptance as his father, but Jimmy is not able to accept Crab's selfishness, his failure as a father, and his false conception of what it means to be tough in a hostile world. Jimmy looks to Crab for answers to the problems that torment his own life and finds only the same weaknesses. With Crab's death, Jimmy runs out of time to find answers through his father. As he says near the end of the novel, "There wasn't time enough or world enough to piece together their prison dreams." As Crab is captured, he apologizes to Jimmy for his failures.

Myers handles Crab's death scene in the hospital with restraint and a lack of sentimentality. There are no death-bed revelations, no epiphanies. Crab mumbles words of regret about a failed life, and his last communication with Jimmy is an ambiguous smile. After Crab's funeral, Jimmy meditates on that smile: Had it been a smile of sympathy and recognition for their shared experience, or had it been a scornful laugh at Jimmy's inexperience and lack of toughness? The choice and the ambiguity reflect the lack of resolution with which the novel ends. Jimmy is left alone with the knowledge that he must answer his own questions and take responsibility for his own life. He is also convinced that if he ever has a son of his own, that their relationship will be based on honesty and a shared commitment. Jimmy must determine the outcome of his own life and must take personal responsibility in order to make his hopes something more than prison dreams.

Critical Context

Somewhere in the Darkness contributes to Walter Dean Myers' growing reputation as a novelist particularly attuned to the complexities of the relationships among young men and within families. Several of Myers' works explore the African American experience, but the overriding issues in the novels concern the complexities of growing up and coming to terms with how one lives responsibly in a dangerous and uncertain world. Myers comes to no easy resolutions.

Myers' novels feature young men from a variety of racial backgrounds and ages. For example, in one of his best-known novels, *Scorpions* (1988), he explores the friendship between two twelve-year-olds, one African American and the other Puerto Rican, both of whom must make difficult choices about gangs, drugs, and violence. Another well-known novel, *Fallen Angels* (1988), takes a seventeen-year-old boy out of Harlem to Vietnam, where he copes with the dangers of war and issues of bigotry and interracial tension. Myers' young men must make increasingly difficult choices in a world full of danger and ambiguity. These novels are psychologically stark, but certainly not hopeless, landscapes.

Ann Cameron

THE SONG OF HIAWATHA

Author: Henry Wadsworth Longfellow (1807-1882)
First published: 1855
Type of work: Poetry
Subjects: Nature, religion, social issues, and the supernatural
Recommended ages: 13-15

> *By virtue of his heroic adventures and conquests, Hiawatha serves as prophet,*
> *teacher, and peacemaker among his tribesmen.*

Form and Content

The Song of Hiawatha is a long narrative poem that, in its twenty-two sections,
recounts the adventures of an American Indian hero. The setting is on the southern
shore of Lake Superior, where Hiawatha is reared among the Ojibwas. The poem
presents a series of encounters and contests that enable Hiawatha to bring progress
and blessings to his tribe and to help create peace among the other tribes. During the
course of the narrative, Henry Wadsworth Longfellow weaves together many aspects
of American Indian mythology concerning life, nature, and ritual.

The narrative begins when Gitche Manito, the Great Spirit, calls the warring and
vengeful tribes together, rebuking them for their childish behavior and informing
them of a prophet who will come to guide and teach them. Hiawatha, the prophet
mentioned by Gitche Manito, is born after Mudjekeewis, the West-Wind, seduces
Wenonah, the daughter of Nokomis, and then leaves her to die deserted and heartbroken after giving birth to Hiawatha. Reared by Nokomis, Hiawatha grows to
manhood and obtains magic gifts and powers that will enable him to perform his great
deeds.

Through supernatural adventure tales of his building a canoe, fishing for sturgeon,
and using a picture language, readers are told how American Indians learned these arts
and are blessed by them. In one account, Hiawatha's concern for his people is shown
as he fasts and prays on their behalf. As a result of his experience, he begins to wonder
why life depends on the killing of animals for survival. Hiawatha then meets an
angelic young man dressed in green and yellow named Mondamin, who challenges
him to wrestle, and, although he is exhausted from his fasting, Hiawatha miraculously
receives renewed strength through the ordeal. After the hero defeats Mondamin and
buries him according to instruction, corn grows from the grave, providing the sought-
after supplement to animal flesh.

Soon, Hiawatha becomes a peacemaker when he woos and weds Minnihaha, the
beautiful maid of the Dacotah tribe. Their marriage cements peace between these
traditionally hostile tribes and ushers in a time of peace and harmony. Their wedding
party is celebrated in a manner that establishes a pattern to follow, with beautiful
songs and tales. In time, fever and sickness kill many, including Hiawatha's bride,
and the poem ends with the dramatic departure of Hiawatha into the sunset and with

his farewell teachings about the impending arrival of the white race and its new religious teachings.

Analysis

Although virtually unread today, there is still much in *The Song of Hiawatha* to appeal to young readers. In addition to the conventional epic features of heroic action, supernatural event, and thrilling adventure, *The Song of Hiawatha* is an entertaining source of American Indian lore. The epic story of Hiawatha is as much a rhetorical excuse for narrating tales of American Indian mythology as it is important for its own sake.

These tales are highly imaginative and interesting, such as how the lonely Wabun, the East-Wind, yearned for a lovely maiden, whom he wooed with "sighing and singing," eventually changing her into the star of morning that is visible each dawn as the East-Wind gently blows. Many of the tales are mighty adventures of bravery and magic. In order to fight off a fever plaguing his people, Hiawatha challenges Megissogwon, the powerful magician who is the cause of the fever. After striding a mile per step in his magic mocassins, Hiawatha arrives in the land of the magician, where he battles poison serpent guards. When finally face to face with Megissogwon, Hiawatha finds that his expert bowmanship is of no avail because the magician's wampum shirt is enchanted and protects him. A woodpecker reveals to Hiawatha the magician's vulnerable spot, which enables Hiawatha to vanquish Megissogwon and save his village from the fever. To reward the woodpecker, Hiawatha dyes the bird's head red with the magician's blood as an everlasting token of his service.

In addition to the physical prowess demonstrated by Hiawatha and others, the tales emphasize how intelligence is highly valued among the American Indians in the poem. Hiawatha depends as much on his wit as does the Greek hero Ulysses. For example, he taunts Nahma the sturgeon into swallowing him so that he can kill the giant fish from the inside. When battling his father, Mudjekeewis, Hiawatha fools him into thinking that the bulrushes are his weakness. Most important, however, in demonstrating his intelligence in useful ways, Hiawatha builds a canoe, invents picture writing, and develops corn production, making him a hero because of his mind as well as his brawn.

The poem is also a wonderful source for young readers of American Indian perspectives on nature and human life. In the world of the poem, the animals represent different tribes, in many ways equal participants with the people in the grand spectacle of survival. When Mudjkeewis defeats Mishe-Mokwa, the Great Bear, he taunts the creature for crying and whimpering and for thus disgracing his bear tribe. Wind and cold, moon and stars, waterfalls and cornstalks are all given human qualities; thus, Longfellow succeeds in suggesting the indeterminacy of human character typical of American Indian mythology. For example, the four winds behave as human beings as well as natural phenomena, baffling human efforts to distinguish living beings in nature.

Critical Context

Originally intended for a broad, popular audience, *The Song of Hiawatha* was standard school fare for generations of adolescents who could recite such familiar unrhymed trochaic tetrameter lines as "By the shores of Gitche Gumee,/ By the shining Big-Sea-Water. . . ." It soon became the most popular book-length poem ever written, selling forty-five thousand copies within five years. With Henry Wadsworth Longfellow's ebb in popularity, however, the poem has become increasingly obscure, although its value for young readers could be rediscovered in the wake of a revival of interest in American Indian oral literature in literature classes. In this regard, Walt Whitman, whose *Leaves of Grass* (1855) was published the same year as *The Song of Hiawatha*, praised Longfellow as the "universal poet of . . . young people." His poetry in general is accessible to young readers and has proven a reliable resource for teaching prosody.

Longfellow's interest in American Indians seems to have at least two known sources. First, he personally witnessed a delegation from the Sauk and Fox tribes, which included chief Black Hawk, on Boston Common in 1837. In addition, Longfellow was influenced by ethnologist Henry Schoolcraft, whose many works on American Indian life and legend fascinated a generation and created a new field of study. Longfellow was much impressed with the picturesque quality of the American Indians' "beautiful traditions" and ignored the harsher realities of their life. While he bases the legends of the poem on the work of Schoolcraft, he purges them of their more cruel and grotesque aspects. Even Hiawatha becomes a gentler hero than Manabozho, the hero on whom he is modeled. Like other legendary folk heroes, Manabozho has a dark side to his character, occasionally as destructive as he is constructive of tribal welfare.

Modeled on the Finnish epic the *Kalevala*, *The Song of Hiawatha* is as famous for its sometimes tedious versification as for its American Indian lore. Although it was a popular success, with its picturesque and imaginative tales, some reviewers panned the book's monotonous verse and its idealized characters. Even Longfellow himself admitted that while writing his American Indian epic he was not entirely sure of its value, worrying that he was too close to the subject to see it clearly. In time, he would have to suffer the myriad parodies that the poem spawned among humorists. Despite its flaws, *The Song of Hiawatha* remains a fascinating source of American Indian mythology and virtually the only memorable American Indian epic written in the nineteenth century.

Dennis R. Perry

SONG OF SOLOMON

Author: Toni Morrison (1931-   )
First published: 1977
Type of work: Novel
Type of plot: Psychological realism and social realism
Time of work: 1931-1963
Locale: Mercy, Michigan; Danville, Pennsylvania; and Shalimar, Virginia
Subjects: Coming-of-age, family, race and ethnicity, sexual issues, and social issues
Recommended ages: 15-18

Morrison uses a young African American man's coming-of-age to explore concepts of family and history, as well as the social implications of race, gender, and class.

> *Principal characters:*
> MILKMAN (MACON DEAD III), a thirty-one-year-old African American
> MACON DEAD II, his father
> RUTH FOSTER DEAD, his mother
> MAGDALENE (LENA) DEAD, his sister
> FIRST CORINTHIANS DEAD, his sister
> PILATE DEAD, Macon Dead's sister and Milkman's aunt
> REBA, Pilate's daughter
> HAGAR, Reba's daughter
> GUITAR BAINES, Milkman's best friend, who is six years older

Form and Content

Song of Solomon is a novel whose third-person, limited omniscient narrator is sympathetic to the protagonist, Milkman Dead. To illustrate Milkman's journey to self-knowledge as specifically African American, Toni Morrison uses Magical Realism, a worldview incorporating a culture's myths, religion, and superstitions as natural, believable components of reality. The plot resembles a gothic detective story centered on four generations of one African American family, the Deads. At the age of thirty-one, Milkman knows little of his family history; he is caught in limbo, isolated from his past and uncertain about the future. His father tells him nothing of his own boyhood in Pennsylvania or about their relatives in Virginia; his aunt Pilate tells him a bit more, but her knowledge is limited. To become a man, Milkman needs to understand his heritage.

A former slave, Milkman's grandfather received his name from information incorrectly recorded on a form. When asked his place of birth, he replied "Macon"; when asked about his father, he replied "Dead." A careless clerk entered both words on the line marked "name," so that the man's name became Macon Dead. Such "accidents" impede Milkman's quest for history. His grandfather became a successful farmer by cultivating wild forest into fertile farmland, but white neighbors coveted his land, offered to buy it, and killed him when he refused to sell, leaving Macon II and Pilate orphans. Pilate roamed from state to state, job to job, and man to man. Macon II finished high school, became a successful businessman, and married the daughter of the only black doctor in Mercy, Michigan. It was a loveless marriage, but it produced three children: Lena, First Corinthians, and Macon Dead III (Milkman).

Milkman's motives for searching out his ancestors are not noble. Through a series of events involving his friend Guitar Baines's political activities, Milkman learns a Dead family legend about bags of gold supposedly hidden in a Pennsylvania cave. He wants to find the gold and claim it for himself. To do so, however, he must return to the birthplaces of his father, grandfather, and great-grandfather. Milkman is soon hooked on finding the missing pieces to his family tree. In Danville, Pennsylvania, he meets his father's old friends and hears pleasant stories that almost make the son proud. Milkman also visits Circe, the old woman who took care of Macon II and Pilate after their father died. Circe tells Milkman where the cave is, but when he gets there, he finds not gold but bones. Thinking that Pilate might have moved the gold elsewhere, he remembers rumors of family members in Virginia and searches there. In Shalimar, he hears children singing a song about Solomon and Reena, his great-grandparents. Although he never finds any gold, Milkman pieces together his family history. Yet, the novel does not end well for Milkman. His friend Guitar, with whom he had agreed to share the gold, believes he was betrayed and kills Milkman.

Morrison's use of time is complex. As the story progresses chronologically, Milkman traces his family history further into the past. The beginning of the novel is set in 1931, the year of Milkman's birth; at the end of the novel, Milkman is physically in 1962, but he has psychologically joined his great-grandparents in the late days of slavery. Milkman's location changes as he traces his family history: He travels from a Michigan city, to a small Pennsylvania town, and finally to rural Virginia. Morrison divides the novel into two unequal parts with a total of fifteen chapters. Chapters 1 through 9 take place in Mercy, Michigan, and deal with the background of Milkman's immediate family, as well as his sexual initiation with his cousin Hagar. Chapters 10 through 15 deal with Milkman's quest for gold and his extended family history.

Analysis

Although not intended for a young adult audience, *Song of Solomon* does have several themes useful for mature teenage readers. Most important for this audience is Milkman's coming-of-age as he learns to understand his sexuality, his relationship to his parents and family, his role in society, and his position on important social issues.

Incest is a prominent theme in the book and greatly affects Milkman's sexual identity. Readers learn that his mother and her father had an intimate sexual relationship. Milkman received his nickname because someone saw his mother breast-feeding him during his late preschool years. His first sexual experience is with his cousin Hagar, and their relationship lasts for several years until he breaks it off and she becomes violent toward him and herself. Evidence also suggests improprieties between Macon II and Pilate: He cared for her as an infant, and his intimate knowledge of her body holds a permanent place in his imagination.

The strained relationship between Milkman and his parents provides a related theme. As a child and young man, he worships his mother and cannot understand his father's seemingly cruel treatment of her. When his father tells him about her incestuous relationship with her father, Macon remembers the breast-feeding incident and comes to reject both of his parents—his father for telling the truth, and his mother for her role in the truth. Milkman seeks surrogate parent figures: As a paternal confidant, he turns to his friend Guitar, and, as a mother figure, he relies on Pilate. Milkman must also learn his role in his sisters' lives by recognizing that they are women with human desires and that he has no right to hinder their relationships with men.

While many of Milkman's family issues are settled during the novel, he never fully understands his position in society. At the age of thirty-one, he works only sporadically for his father and spends most of his time loitering with Guitar. Milkman does not know what it means to be a mature, responsible adult. Morrison suggests reasons for this failure in themes relating to race and class. The most prominent of these is black exploitation of other black people. Milkman's mother is the daughter of Mercy's only black doctor. An ether addict, Dr. Foster is not a good doctor: He is elitist and racist, and he fools people into respecting him. Macon II owns most of Mercy's black housing and is a slumlord; he extracts high rents but does not maintain the houses. Macon II does not reinvest his profits into existing black working-class neighborhoods; instead, he builds a lakeside resort community for rich black families. Milkman cannot accept this aspect of his father's business. A more political issue is introduced with Milkman's friend Guitar, who is a member of the Seven Days, a group of seven black men who seek to even the score between black and white people. When white crimes against black victims go unpunished, members of the group commit identical crimes against white victims. While Milkman recognizes racism in the white legal system, he cannot commit himself to helping to change the way things are, at least not in Guitar's manner. Milkman must come to terms not only with his family history, but also with his role in society.

Critical Context

Toni Morrison was awarded the 1993 Nobel Prize in Literature, and *Song of Solomon*, her third novel, is one of her best works. Young adult protagonists coming to terms with their African American culture are common to all of her novels, but especially *The Bluest Eye* (1972) and *Beloved* (1988). Similar themes can be found in works by other African American writers. The gothic use of family history to explore generations appears in Gayl Jones's *Corregidora* (1975) and Gloria Naylor's *Linden Hills* (1985) and *Mama Day* (1988). Critiques of African American class systems and black landlords also appear in *Linden Hills*, as well as in Richard Wright's *The Long Dream* (1958). In its historiographical reassembling of a dislocated past—as a cultural detective story—*Song of Solomon* resembles Ishmael Reed's *Mumbo Jumbo* (1972). If one interprets Milkman's journey to self-knowledge as a growing connection with his extended family and the larger African American community, his story is the converse of Ralph Ellison's *Invisible Man* (1952), in which the protagonist severs all ties with society. Morrison's use of Magical Realism to narrate a family history disrupted by slavery and racism has much in common with such postcolonial fiction as Gabriel García Márquez's *Cien años de soledad* (1967; *One-Hundred Years of Solitude*, 1970) and Salman Rushdie's *Midnight's Children* (1981).

Song of Solomon is taught primarily in college literature classes, but it would also be appropriate for mature high school readers and in African American culture classes.

Geralyn Strecker

THE STORIES OF RAY BRADBURY

Author: Ray Bradbury (1920-   )
First published: 1980
Type of work: Short fiction
Subjects: Emotions and the supernatural
Recommended ages: 13-18

In one hundred tales of science fiction, both fantasy and nonfantasy culled from nearly forty years of writing, the author examines the light and dark sides of human experience.

Form and Content

The Stories of Ray Bradbury collects one hundred tales that span Ray Bradbury's four decades as a writer up to 1980. Although the author is best known as a writer of fantasy and science fiction, this omnibus volume also features his early horror stories and a generous sampling of his nonfantasy fiction. In contrast to earlier Bradbury story collections from which this compilation draws, the contents are not assembled according to a specific thematic or stylistic scheme. This arrangement allows the reader to explore ideas that pervade all of Bradbury's work and transcend any one genre in which he writes, most notably the marvelous possibilities in everyday life and the persistence of fundamental human behaviors in the face of change and progress.

Bradbury's tales of horror and the supernatural feature ordinary people who stumble upon the fantastic in the course of their mundane lives. In "The Scythe," for example, a migrant worker looking to support his family takes up residence on an abandoned farm and discovers from the unusual behavior of the wheat he mows by hand every day that he has become the incarnation of the Grim Reaper, harvesting his daily ration of lives. In "Skeleton," a plain young man develops devastating feelings of self-loathing upon realizing that he carries inside him a skeleton, "one of those jointed, snowy, hard things, one of those foul, dry, brittle, gouge-eyed, skull-faced, shake-fingered, rattling things that sway from neck chains in abandoned webbed closets." These stories can be read as the grim flip side to a handful of lighter fantasies—"Uncle Einar," "The Traveler," "The April Witch," and "The Homecoming"—all of which feature a family of benign supernatural creatures who resemble ordinary human beings in their emotions and interactions with one another.

Bradbury wrote most of the science-fiction stories collected in this volume in the 1940's and 1950's. Whether they are set on Earth or in outer space, they contrast sharply with the mostly forward-looking science fiction of their day. Earthbound tales such as "The Rocket Man," about the family left behind by a space traveler, and "The End of the Beginning," in which a husband and wife ponder the impact that space travel will have on their world, offer elegiac reflections on what humankind has given up in its pursuit of the stars. Likewise, stories set on other planets are more concerned with exploring timeless human needs than alien worlds. Complications in "The Off

Season" and "The Long Rain" develop from the psychological problems that people face adapting to new environments. In "The Blue Bottle," a quest for a legendary Martian talisman comes to symbolize the human tendency to strive for ideals. "The Fire Balloons" and "The Man" both examine humankind's unquenchable religious yearnings in a universe that has displaced humans from its center.

Bradbury's nonfantasy stories abound with eccentric characters and quiet moments of private revelation. Their concerns are indistinguishable from those of his supernatural and science-fiction stories. "The Big Black and White Game," in which a baseball game draws out the racial tensions smoldering beneath the placid veneer of a small midwestern town, is as potent a study of the dark side of human nature as any of his horror tales. The characters in "A Picasso Summer" and "Power House" experience epiphanies that transform their lives as powerfully as would any encounter with the supernatural. "The Wonderful Ice Cream Suit" and "The Anthem Sprinters" each are parts of story cycles in which Bradbury uses, respectively, Latino and Irish characters to explore the universality of hopes and dreams across cultures, much the same way that he uses alien civilizations in his science fiction as a sounding board for insights into the human condition.

Analysis

In his introduction to *The Stories of Ray Bradbury*, the author discusses how childhood memories have shaped his writing and describes himself as "the man with the child inside." Many of Bradbury's stories feature child protagonists, but even those centered on adult experiences display his youthful outlook on life through their exuberant prose and emphasis on the basic lessons that life teaches. Big events take place in these tales—first contact with alien species, time travel to the prehistoric age, and even the end of the world—but it is always in the quiet moments of self-discovery on the periphery of these events that characters learn what is important about life. "The Homecoming" is set during the bustle of a large family reunion of supernatural beings. Timothy, a young family member who was born mortal, spends most of the story failing miserably to imitate the behaviors of his relatives in the hope of earning their respect. At the story's end, Timothy's mother comforts him with the assurance "We all love you. No matter how different you are." In trying to be someone he is not in order to fit in with the larger world, Timothy discovers the importance of being true to himself.

"Life was full of symbols and omens," thinks a character in "The Golden Kite, the Silver Wind." In Bradbury's stories, the richness of life is defined by the symbolic value of its individual moments. The simplest of experiences always proves pregnant with a deeper meaning that ensures that no moment in life is superfluous or insignificant. In "The Night," family worries over an older brother's late return home result in the younger brother's first intimations of mortality. The mere changing of seasons in "The End of Summer" teaches its young protagonist the meaning of death.

A fine line separates Bradbury's genuine fantasies from stories that celebrate this magical portentousness of the commonplace. As a result, his stories often have the feeling of fables or parables, whether they approach their themes from a fantastic or a nonfantastic angle. In his supernatural tale "The Lake," a man returns to a beach where a beloved childhood playmate drowned years before and finds a half-built sand castle waiting for him to complete. In "A Story of Love," a grown man visits the grave of a schoolteacher on whom he had an unrequited adolescent crush and is comforted by the knowledge that he is now a respectable three years older than she was at her death. Both stories end with characters realizing that the platonic loves of their youths are the purest loves that they have known. "The Last Night of the World" and "Yes, We'll Gather at the River" are each concerned with the end of the world—one literally, the other symbolically—and how people will face it. In both, characters show quiet dignity in the face of an event they are powerless to change.

Bradbury's concern in all of his fiction is with the fundamental values that make people human, the ties that bind together not only childhood and adult selves but also the past and present as a species. This approach is most evident in his science-fiction stories that, although set in the future, have the same nostalgic feel as stories set in the rural Midwest of his childhood. "The Wilderness" portrays the concerns of women in the year 2003 traveling to Mars to meet their future husbands as little different from those of mail-order brides relocating to the frontier of the American West in 1849. In several stories that Bradbury incorporated into *The Martian Chronicles* (1950), a novel about the human colonization of Mars, his depiction of Martian civilization varies widely—it is alive and thriving in "Mars Is Heaven" and "The Earth Men" but long dead and disappeared in "The Million-Year Picnic" and "Dark They Were, and Golden-Eyed," even though only a relatively short interval exists between the events in the stories—but his rendering of human civilization is unremarkably the same. Earth people tend to replicate in their new environment the world that they left behind. They bring to their new world the same problems that have beset humanity since time immemorial, as well as the time-tested means for solving those problems. For Bradbury, the shifting frontier of outer space is simply a context for exploring the unchanging inner space of the human psyche. It is this consistency of subject matter that gives his stories their enduring appeal.

Critical Context

The Stories of Ray Bradbury includes much of the best work from the short-fiction collections that established Bradbury's literary reputation: *The Illustrated Man* (1951), *The October Country* (1955), *The Golden Apples of the Sun* (1953), and *A Medicine for Melancholy* (1959). First published at a time when fantasy and science fiction were separated from the literary mainstream as "popular fiction," many of these stories helped draw attention to the way in which genre fiction could serve as a vehicle for the same themes and ideas found in so-called serious literature. Bradbury's novels *The Martian Chronicles* and *Dandelion Wine* (1957) both were assembled from short stories. *Fahrenheit 451* (1953) and *Something Wicked This Way Comes* (1962) each began as a short story before evolving into full-length novels.

Bradbury published little short fiction after *The Stories of Ray Bradbury* appeared, but some of his later novels—*Death Is a Lonely Business* (1985), *A Graveyard for Lunatics: Another Tale of Two Cities* (1990), and *Green Shadows, White Whale* (1992)—elaborate ideas first tackled in his short stories and show how the timeless themes of his earlier writing continue to shape his mature work.

Stefan Dziemianowicz

THE STORY OF MANKIND

Author: Hendrik Willem Van Loon (1882-1944)
First published: 1921; illustrated
Type of work: History
Time of work: Prehistory to 1920
Locale: Major centers of human civilization, especially in Europe
Subjects: Arts, religion, and war
Recommended ages: 13-15

>   *This survey of human civilization from the earliest times to just after World War I is told in a familiar, first-person style.*

>   *Principal personages:*
>   BUDDHA, an Indian religious leader
>   CONFUCIUS, a Chinese moralist and philosopher
>   MOSES, a Jewish moral and religious leader
>   ALEXANDER THE GREAT, a Macedonian conqueror
>   JULIUS CAESAR, the founder of the Roman Empire
>   JESUS CHRIST, the founder of Christianity
>   CHARLEMAGNE, the first Holy Roman Emperor
>   FREDERICK THE GREAT, a king of Prussia
>   LOUIS XIV, a king of France
>   NAPOLEON, an emperor of France

Form and Content

Hendrik Willem Van Loon's *The Story of Mankind* follows a chronological pattern in which each chapter addresses a specific event or series of events in human history. Each chapter is given a highly descriptive heading that provides a brief summary of its contents. The work begins, appropriately enough, with the chapter "The Setting of the Stage," which briefly outlines the theory of the development of life on Earth and the eventual arrival of humans on the scene; the volume ends with an epilogue.

In between, Van Loon covers ample material with a considerable amount of detail, but in a briskly moving fashion and deft, quick characterizations of major figures that makes the volume read more like an adventure story—which, in a sense, it is—than academic history.

The style of the book, while historical in approach, is personal and even conversational in tone. Van Loon often pauses to address his young readers directly in order to explain his meaning in more detail, correct possible misconceptions, or provide additional examples. He frequently points out certain "lessons" of history, which are almost invariably commonsense conclusions drawn from the facts—such as that glory abroad often means misery at home for nations and that personal liberty, if it does not degenerate into license, is a good thing.

Van Loon envisions human history and civilization as moving in an ever-increasing arc from East to West, starting with ancient Egypt, then finding a second beginning in Mesopotamia ("the land between the rivers," in a literal translation from the Greek), and after that moving into the wider ranges of first the Aegean Sea, then the Mediterranean Sea, and finally to the Atlantic Ocean. Although he wrote within the context of his times and therefore believed that European civilization had "conquered the world," Van Loon was certainly not purely Eurocentric in his views: He saw that the civilizations and cultures of the East, in particular India and China, made important contributions. It is significant, however, that he believed he had discharged his duty to them with a single, relatively brief chapter and scattered references throughout the rest of his work. *The Story of Mankind* is clearly the history of Western peoples.

Nevertheless, given its limitations, the book has considerable power and value. From ancient Egypt onward, the story moves with almost irresistible force, relying on a combination of interesting incident (such as the conflicts between the Greeks and the Persians) and Van Loon's explication of what those incidents mean (such as the importance of individual freedom over mass conformity) to give the reader a sense of direction and progress in human affairs. Those who, in Van Loon's view, created this history, whether the great figures or the mass of individual men and women, are presented in sharply defined and characterized portraits.

Van Loon ends his work on a rather somber, yet hopeful note. Following the debacle of World War I and the failure of the League of Nations, the book had to admit that many of the mistakes of the past seemed destined to be repeated. He claimed, however, that he was "enough a believer in the ultimate fate of Man" to forecast a new era in which human beings would rid themselves of their worst enemies: "wilful ignorance and abysmal spiritual cowardice."

Analysis

In the foreword to *The Story of Mankind*, Van Loon, writing to his young relatives Hansje and Willem, tells a typically personal story of how he came to be such a passionate student of history. One day, when he was about twelve, his uncle took him to the top of an old church tower in Rotterdam. From there, the young boy could see the sweep of the Dutch countryside and sites from the history of the Low Countries: where the Prince of Orange had cut the dikes to save Leyden; the leaning tower of Delft; and the church of Gouda, where the early Renaissance scholar and humanist writer Erasmus had been taught his first lessons.

Van Loon uses the tower and the vision as a metaphor of what history is and what it does. "History is the mighty Tower of Experience," he writes, "which Time has built amidst the endless field of bygone ages." He imagines history as a vantage point from which the student can make some sense and order of the tangled confusions of the past and draw experience and courage for the tasks of the present and future. This spirit is the one in which Van Loon presents *The Story of Mankind*.

Van Loon clearly believes that history is, at least for young readers, a series of object lessons that teach fundamental human and moral truths and that it is his role, as a historian, both to present the actors and actions of the past and to underscore the meaning of past events. Furthermore, he makes his presentation in an intimate, familiar style, more as if telling the story than recording it on the page. Writing of the fall of the Roman Republic, for example, Van Loon emphasizes the value judgments explicit in his version: The Republic "became a land of rich people ruled by rich people for the benefit of rich people. As such it was doomed to disastrous failure, as I will now tell you."

Yet, Van Loon's morals and teachings, while plainly evident, are not simplistic and always relate clearly and directly to the historical message. Further, they are drawn from the record, rather than imposed upon it, and represent realistic and logically defensible interpretations of events. The collapse of the Roman Republic, for example, was in large part caused by the concentration of excessive wealth in the hands of a few families, followed by a consequent decline in the traditional standards of public and political life. Most young readers appreciate the clarity and directness of Van Loon's assessments.

Another appealing feature of the work to its readership are the numerous illustrations, pictures, and maps prepared by the author. Van Loon, an exuberant and prolific artist, lacked certain technical skills, but he made up for them with enthusiasm and an individual style that manages to suggest more than it shows. In a sense, young readers are encouraged to use their imaginations to complete Van Loon's sketchy drawings, thus making the illustrations even more engaging than more "artistic" designs.

In the end, however, it is the combination of solid historical fact with a highly engaging and personal style that makes *The Story of Mankind* an acknowledged classic of juvenile and young adult literature.

Critical Context

Hendrik Willem Van Loon was one of the most popular authors of books for young readers during his time. His works on geography, the arts, and the history of the United States, written and illustrated by the author, went through multiple reprintings and later appeared in cheaper, often paperback, editions. *The Story of Mankind* proved to be one of his most enduring works.

Recognized for its merits by being named as a winner of the Newbery Medal, *The Story of Mankind* was primarily important for three major reasons. First, it demonstrated that history for young readers did not have to be overly simplified or simplistic. Van Loon conveys a considerable amount of information in his work, often in fairly elaborate detail that requires concentration and attention by his readers. Second, Van Loon's work showed that young readers could be interested in history as history, rather than history disguised as the story of fictitious children living on the fringes of great events from the past. Third, and perhaps most important, *The Story of Mankind* proved that juvenile and young adult readers could be interested in a serious subject, approached in a serious fashion, when presented to them in an extended format. For these reasons, as well as for its inherent merits and considerable appeal, *The Story of Mankind* stands as a landmark work.

Michael Witkoski

THE STRANGE CASE OF DR. JEKYLL AND MR. HYDE

Author: Robert Louis Stevenson (1850-1894)
First published: 1886
Type of work: Novel
Type of plot: Allegory and thriller
Time of work: The nineteenth century
Locale: London
Subjects: Science and the supernatural
Recommended ages: 15-18

> *Dr. Henry Jekyll concocts and drinks a chemical potion in an attempt to separate his dual nature of good and evil and learns the terrible consequences of such an endeavor.*

Principal characters:
> DR. HENRY JEKYLL, a Scottish doctor who leads a double life, one of a respected and learned scientist and the other of a self-serving monster
> GABRIEL JOHN UTTERSON, Jekyll's friend and lawyer, in whom all the other characters confide
> DR. HASTIE LANYON, a lifelong friend of Jekyll, who is the first to discover the truth about Jekyll
> RICHARD ENFIELD, Utterson's cousin
> POOLE, Jekyll's butler

Form and Content

The Strange Case of Dr. Jekyll and Mr. Hyde is a disquieting story about the efforts of an individual to escape his own nature. The novel offers an account of Dr. Henry Jekyll, a Scottish scientist who, after years of attempting to accommodate both his moral side and his pleasure-seeking side, becomes convinced that a separation of the two would be desirable.

In his laboratory, Jekyll develops a chemical potion that is designed to accomplish the separation and drinks it. After a "grinding of the bones" and a horrible nausea, he begins to feel "incredibly sweet" and free. Looking in the mirror, Jekyll observes not himself but Edward Hyde, a smaller and younger person than himself. Jekyll delights in the division of himself and in his new liberty, but he soon begins to lose control of Hyde, who can assume Jekyll's form at will. The novel follows Dr. Jekyll's struggle with Mr. Hyde, who becomes increasingly evil and whom Jekyll refuses to acknowledge as a part of himself.

The enormous popularity of *The Strange Case of Dr. Jekyll and Mr. Hyde* has aided the perpetuation of a persistent view that it is a simple fable of the division between the good and evil that exists in everyone. The complexity of Robert Louis Stevenson's imaginative story of an individual's conflict with himself, however, is evident in its multiple narratives. Through the presentation of various points of view, Stevenson escalates knowledge of events from the peripheral to the more intimate and at the same time deepens the insight into the psychology of Jekyll.

The first narrative, Richard Enfield's horrified reaction to Edward Hyde's trampling of a little girl, provides the first evidence of the existence of Henry Jekyll and Edward Hyde. Enfield, a "well-known man about town," finds Hyde unaccountably detestable. He also relates the reactions of others present: the women, whom the sight of Hyde makes "wild as harpies," and a doctor, who like Enfield is sickened by Hyde and wants to kill him. Enfield confides his narrative to his cousin, Gabriel John Utterson, an attorney who is a friend of Jekyll and who practices self-denial in order to strengthen his own moral fiber. Utterson, through whose perspective the story is told, listens to accounts of Jekyll and Hyde told by other characters and sometimes observes Jekyll and Hyde directly. A tolerant person, he believes that Jekyll has perhaps been guilty of some foible in his youth and is being blackmailed by Hyde. Upon meeting Hyde, he too feels disgust and nausea.

The third narrator is Dr. Hastie Lanyon, who has written a letter to Utterson. A bold Scottish doctor, Lanyon has become estranged from Jekyll because of Jekyll's "fanciful" theories. Dr. Lanyon is the first to ascertain that Jekyll is Hyde and that Jekyll is in Hyde's control. His observation of Jekyll's transformation into Hyde literally shocks Lanyon to death.

Jekyll's narrative, a letter read after his death, is the one for which all others have been preparation. The most subjective account, the letter reveals his concerns that led to his experiments and the conclusions that he reached about them. Of great interest is his personal reaction to Hyde.

Analysis

One of the earliest and most enduring criticisms of Stevenson—that he wrote only children's books—has perhaps arisen from confusion about his method. Although his essays, adventure and travel stories, and poems all demonstrate an ambition to produce serious and important art, the childlike imagination that infuses all of his works has been misperceived by some as merely childish. The fact that Stevenson, as an adult, had the ability to recapture the emotions and sensations of childhood and at the same time explore the ambiguities of human motivation made him a powerful and imaginative writer.

The Strange Case of Dr. Jekyll and Mr. Hyde is a serious romance, a genre usually intended for the instruction of the young. As a writer of romances—nineteenth century stories depicting the truth of the human heart—Stevenson successfully adapts a novel about adults into a thriller that challenges young people to consider the ambiguity of human nature. He was interested in psychology, and he excels at penetrating façades and exposing the ambiguities underneath them. The several narratives that tell the story of Jekyll and Hyde present differing views of reality and prepare the reader for the chief ambiguity in the novel—Jekyll's attitude toward Hyde. Stevenson uses extensively the idea of the double, or *Doppelgänger*—the theory that an individual's character is composed of two parts, a reasonable self and evil twin or shadow, which are constantly at war—that forms the split center of *The Strange Case of Dr. Jekyll and Mr. Hyde*. Yet, Jekyll and Hyde (Jekyll's double), although split, are not two. Sharing one body and one brain, they do not separate but assume a change in form in which Jekyll is replaced by Hyde, who was within Jekyll.

Jekyll, whose existence makes Hyde possible, has rejected Hyde for more than twenty years—the chemical potion representing only his most dramatic step. Hyde is slowly transformed from one who tramples a child impersonally and without conscience to a selfish, cruel creature who is consumed with malicious hatred of Jekyll. Meanwhile, Jekyll continues his dissociation from Hyde. He considers the possibility of destroying Hyde altogether, accelerates his performance of altruistic deeds, and refuses to acknowledge Hyde as a portion of himself. Hyde is enraged at his treatment by the person to whom he owes his life, and he becomes increasingly evil. He assumes control at will, and Jekyll, failing to understand that what he had attempted was an impossibility, continues to believe that the experiment could succeed if he could only obtain pure powder for the potion. In desperation, Hyde commits suicide, thus destroying both men.

To strengthen his theme—the essential ambiguity and unknowable nature of the self—Stevenson layers contrasts within the various points of view that form the narrative. The friendship of Enfield, the first narrator, and Utterson is mysterious, because they are almost polar opposites. The motif of the double, suggested by their regular and almost compulsive walks through the fog-shrouded streets of London, continues in their responses to Edward Hyde. Although both regard Hyde himself with intense disgust and nausea, the mystery of Hyde's identity provides a mere anecdote for Enfield, while Utterson finds it very troubling. For Dr. Lanyon, who is more closely associated with Jekyll, the knowledge of Jekyll and Hyde is fatal.

The phrase "Jekyll-and-Hyde" does not merely denote a kind of split personality, but rather refers to Jekyll's intense conflict within himself. Stevenson presents to young readers an extreme case that nevertheless illustrates the dangers of refusing to accept duality as a fact of human nature.

Critical Context

The Strange Case of Dr. Jekyll and Mr. Hyde, although one of the most popular, is not the only romance novel that Robert Louis Stevenson wrote. *Treasure Island* (1883), following several essays and travel books based on Stevenson's own journeys seeking health, was his first successful novel of this kind. The romance, as Stevenson fashions it, concentrates on adventure, a distinctive narrative style that involves one or more participants in the action, and a strong sense of moral concern throughout. After *Treasure Island*, an adventure story for boys that is also keenly observant of human character, he then published *The Black Arrow* (1888), intended as a sequel to *Treasure Island*. *Kidnapped* (1886), a comic epic about David Balfour's efforts to claim his inheritance, has been connected with Mark Twain's *The Adventures of Huckleberry Finn* (1885). Both stories concern a young boy who, despite the dictates of his conscience, joins an outsider from his own society, and the two become friends in flight. *The Master of Ballantrae* (1889), the last novel that Stevenson completed, is a sequel to *Kidnapped*. It too delves into Scottish history and describes the breakup of an ancient Scottish family. Stevenson produced vivid, compelling adventures about young protagonists whose quests for identity depend on an understanding of the world as well as themselves. As Stevenson shows repeatedly, an understanding of oneself is difficult but necessary.

Mary Hurd

A STRING IN THE HARP

Author: Nancy Bond (1945-   )
First published: 1976
Type of work: Novel
Type of plot: Domestic realism and fantasy
Time of work: The early 1970's
Locale: A small Welsh village
Subjects: Death, family, nature, and the supernatural
Recommended ages: 10-15

Peter Morgan, an unhappy twelve-year-old whose family has moved to Wales for a year after their mother's death, finds an ancient harp-tuning key that teaches him about Welsh folklore and helps him learn to live with himself and his family.

Principal characters:
PETER MORGAN, an American boy spending a year in a Welsh village
while his father teaches at the University of Wales
JENNIFER MORGAN, Peter's older sister
BECKY MORGAN, Peter's younger sister
DAVID MORGAN, the father of Peter, Jennifer, and Becky
GWILYM, the Morgans' Welsh neighbor
RHIAN, a Welsh girl
DR. RHYS, a colleague of David Morgan at the University of Wales
DR. OWEN, a curator at the National Museum of Wales

Form and Content

The Morgan family has moved from Massachusetts to Wales for a year while the father teaches at the University of Wales. The family is recovering from the tragic death of the mother in an automobile accident. When the story opens, David Morgan is immersed in his work, twelve-year-old Peter is unhappy and withdrawn, ten-year-old Becky is doing her best to adjust, and sixteen-year-old Jennifer, who has stayed behind in Massachusetts to finish high school, is just arriving for her Christmas vacation.

The narration is in the third person, with some chapters from Jennifer's point of view and some from Peter's. Jennifer's concerns are keeping the family together, learning responsibility, and realizing that adults do not have all the answers. Peter is bitterly unhappy with the year in Wales and hopes that Jennifer will be able to persuade their father to leave. Becky, the youngest child, has adapted to life in this new country, but she desperately wants the family to work smoothly.

A String in the Harp changes from a simple contemporary problem-solving novel into a time-shift fantasy when Peter finds a strange object on the beach. The object turns out to be a harp-tuning key that once belonged to the sixth-century Welsh bard Taliesin. It has the power to show Peter scenes from Taliesin's life. As Peter becomes immersed in the ancient legends that the key makes real for him, his discontent gives way to involvement in Welsh folklore and natural history. Unfortunately, he with-draws even more from the family and the present. His sisters learn about the key as time begins to shift in weird cross-overs between the present and the sixth century. Peter finds remnants of an ancient sea dike, and then a severe rainstorm in the present merges with the legendary flooding of the Low Hundred. Later, contemporary sheep farmers hunt and kill a wolf, an animal long extinct in Wales.

The Morgans learn from the Welsh characters. Becky strikes up friendships with Gwilym, a shy boy who has much local knowledge of natural history, and Rhian, a cheerful girl whose farm family is in touch with the land and its legends. Dr. Rhys, a scholar of Welsh language and folklore, and Dr. Owen, who is curator of the National Museum, contribute to the children's knowledge of ancient history and artifacts.

By the end of the story, the members of the Morgan family have all come together to answer some important questions: Why has Peter been chosen to find the key? What should he do with it? What is magic? How does the past influence the present? While working out the mysteries of the key, they have learned to talk to one another and to live together. They have also learned to appreciate the Welsh country, its natural history and folklore.

Nancy Bond lends authenticity to the novel by including an author's note about the bard Taliesin and the Welsh landscape and a map of the part of Wales where the events of the novel, both ancient and contemporary, occur.

Analysis

Setting is an important element in *A String in the Harp*. The weather, geography, natural history, and archaeology of Wales become as immediate as the characters and the action. The Welsh characters are guides for Peter and his sisters as they explore notions of folklore, superstition, and the nature of magic. In the presence of the timeless landscape of the novel and of modern people who live among ancient things, it is easy to believe that Peter can slip back in time and witness the events of the sixth century. Through the action of the novel, Bond is able to express the feeling that ancient history is alive in a place as old and wild as Wales.

Bond fills the book with observant details of contemporary life in a small seaside town in winter. The summer cottage with its garish lounge and drafty bedrooms, the food that the Morgans' housekeeper cooks for them, the cadence of Welsh speech, the dismal rainswept town, and the dripping wellies (boots) and mackintoshes (raincoats) are all vividly pictured. The physical details and sensations of the Welsh atmosphere trigger the time-shifts—as when the rainstorm that is so severe that Rhian cannot return to her farm blurs into the ancient flood, or when the modern family walking along the beach, alone with the birds and the sea, scans the horizon and sees the sails of the boats of the Irish raiders that have kidnapped Taliesin.

Bond uses the Welsh characters of Gwilym and Rhian to link the two worlds, the contemporary and the ancient. It is significant that Gwilym is present when the Irish boats are spotted, when the old coracle and the weir are found, during the wolf hunt, and especially when he brings Peter to Taliesin's grave in the climactic scene. Rhian's father is willing to accept that ancient magic still exists in the wild Welsh hills and, along with Dr. Rhys, supplies important information about the past.

The issues that the Morgan family must solve are handled realistically and sensitively. The children, especially Jennifer, must learn to take over their mother's responsibility for running the household. David must learn to talk to his children and trust them. The children must learn that their father cannot solve every problem. They all must learn to work together, to overcome their individual grief and isolation from one another.

The character of Dr. Owen raises issues of ownership of ancient artifacts, as Peter must struggle with the decision of what to do with Taliesin's harp key. Should artifacts remain on the land where they are found, or do they belong in the sterile environment of a museum? Can an important historical artifact belong to an individual, or does it belong to the public? Will an object lose its magic character in a museum? What is the nature of magic, if modern adults such as Dr. Rhys and Rhian's father can believe in it while others label their belief superstition?

As the novel draws to a close, Peter must decide what to do with Taliesin's harp key. Should he give it to Dr. Owen and the National Museum of Wales? Can he keep it? Why has he been chosen to find the key?

In the course of solving this dilemma, the Morgans touch a piece of Welsh history. They come to trust one another, to listen to one another; they all grow up. As a result of the key's presence in their lives, they look outside their individual concerns and learn to live and work together.

Critical Context

A String in the Harp is a time-shift novel in the tradition of C. S. Lewis' *The Lion, the Witch, and the Wardrobe* (1950). In both books, three children on their own in the country slip into another time. Time merges in simultaneous layers as events occur in the same place in different times. Folklore comes alive as the old songs and legends become real for the children. *A String in the Harp* is a fine rainy day book in which young readers can lose themselves. Both stories, that of Taliesin and of the Morgans, are engrossing. The outcome, what Peter will do with the key, is in doubt until the final pages, adding suspense to the tale.

Nancy Bond studied at the College of Librarianship in Wales and has written a novel that expresses her love for the setting, its folklore and its natural history. *A String in the Harp* is a long novel, with space for developing minor characters and themes along with the rich local color. The story of the modern family is fully developed, with the time-shifts so skillfully woven in that the fantasy of the past coming alive is easy to accept.

A String in the Harp, Bond's first young adult novel, was named a Newbery Honor Book. She is respected for writing sensitive, original books that portray realistic characters who deal with serious life issues, as well as for novels that emphasize colorful settings.

Susan Butterworth

THE STRONGHOLD

Author: Mollie Hunter (Maureen Mollie Hunter McVeigh McIlwraith, 1922-   )
First published: 1974
Type of work: Novel
Type of plot: Adventure tale, historical fiction, and social realism
Time of work: Around 50 B.C.
Locale: The Orkney Islands, Scotland
Subjects: Religion and war
Recommended ages: 13-18

Despite the fact that he is lame, eighteen-year-old Coll risks his life to unite his tribe against their Roman adversaries by helping to expose a traitor, saving the life of the chief's daughter, and devising a plan to build strongholds to protect them.

> *Principal characters:*
> COLL, an eighteen-year-old lame architect who becomes "Master" of the Stronghold
> NECTAN, the chief of the Boar
> ANU, Nectan's wife, whose marriage to Nectan made him chief
> DOMNALL, the chief of the Druid priests
> CLODHA, Domnall's eldest daughter, whose husband will become the new chief of the Boar
> NIALL, Coll's friend who is courting Clodha
> FAND, Clodha's younger sister, whom Coll loves
> TARAN, a member of the Boar who was captured by the Roman raiders thirteen years earlier
> BRAN, Coll's younger brother, whose mother saved him from the raiders and who was reared by Druid priests
> DAGGART, a member of the Council of the Boar, whose place Taran takes after killing him

Form and Content
    The Stronghold is a fascinating historical novel focusing on the unknown creator of the many "brochs," or strongholds, built on the islands off Scotland's northern coast to protect its inhabitants from Roman attacks during the first century B.C. The story centers on eighteen-year-old Coll, a member of the Boar, one of the tribes living on the Orkney Islands.
    Almost yearly, the Boar must fend off attacks by Roman slave traders who kidnap or kill members of the tribe. Years before the novel begins, during a Roman attack, Coll was crippled and his mother sacrificed her life to save his younger brother, Bran, who is now being reared by the Druid priests. Now, the Boar are divided over how to deal with the threat of invaders. Nectan, the chief of the Boar, is tired of bloodshed and believes that his tribe should flee to safety instead of fighting the raiders when

they come. Domnall, the chief of the Druid priests, is convinced that they should show their bravery and confront the invaders. The conflict between Nectan and Domnall tests the members of the tribe, who are torn between loyalty to their leader and religious superstition. Meanwhile, Coll is developing a plan to build stone towers, strongholds in which the Boar can safely fight off the Romans and that will serve as a compromise for Domnall and Nectan.

The arrival to the island of Taran, who had been kidnapped by the Romans thirteen years earlier, further complicates the situation. Taran is hungry for power and sides with Domnall, hoping to become the tribal chief by marrying Nectan's daughter, Clodha. Secretly, Taran tries to create a dangerous alliance with two other tribes on the island, the Raven and the Deer. When Nectan and Domnall confront each other in front of the Boar, the priest threatens to cut off the tribal members from reaching the Otherworld when they die. Domnall determines that Fand, Nectan's younger daughter, whom Coll has loved for years, will be sacrificed to atone for the tribe's behavior. When Coll tries to save Fand, falsely suggesting that she is no longer a virgin and that he has spoiled the sacrifice, his younger brother, Bran, saves Coll's life by throwing himself in front of Domnall's knife.

Finally, Coll is allowed to explain his idea of the Stronghold to the Boar, who are convinced that it will work. Coll directs the construction of the first tower, which is completed shortly before the next attack by the Romans. The tower allows the Boar to retreat to relative safety and to kill any of the Romans who try to enter it. During this attack, Coll comes to respect the priest, Domnall, who is wounded by the Romans. Taran, who tries to betray the Boar to the Romans, is killed by Clodha with the same javelin that hits Domnall. Coll has gained the respect of his tribe and will marry Fand, while Niall, his best friend, will finally marry Clodha and become the new chief.

Analysis

In addition to introducing the reader to life in the British Isles in the first century B.C., *The Stronghold* explores a number of important themes, such as the value of imagination, the nature of true loyalty, the importance of the individual (as opposed to honor gained through battle), and the destructive nature of power. The novel's protagonist, Coll, lives in a society in which physical strength and beauty appear to be valued more than intelligence or artistic imagination. Because Coll is lame in one leg, he is sometimes ignored and, it appears, is not seen as a serious suitor for Fand, one of the chief's daughters. When Coll attempts to share his ideas about the Stronghold, no one is willing to listen until he proves himself by saving Fand's life. Yet, it is Coll's ideas that save the tribe, bringing together two enemies, Nectan and Domnall. The book clearly suggests that through using one's imagination and intelligence, it is possible to triumph over disabilities, although not without a struggle. This theme is further reinforced when the Boar use stratagem to make the Romans think that they are vulnerable after they have been attacked.

One of the attributes that helps Coll along the way is his sense of loyalty to his chief and adoptive father, Nectan. Unlike the traitorous Taran, Coll is loyal to his tribe, ultimately willing to risk his life to save those he loves. In addition, it is Bran's familial loyalty to his brother, despite the fact that they have been reared apart, that saves Coll from Domnall's knife. Through the conflict between Domnall and Nectan, the novel explores characters who are torn between loyalty to their political and religious leaders. Domnall represents the old heroic traditions; he believes that honor is more important than individual safety and that the tribal members should risk their lives against the Roman invaders. Nectan, however, believes that bloodshed is not necessary and desires to protect his people. Through Coll's strongholds, the novel suggests that a true leader needs to compromise between both of these points of view, that individuals are more important than honor but that there are times in which the enemy must be confronted.

Another important theme of the novel is the way in which a desire for power can corrupt. Taran, the villain of the novel, is loyal to no one but himself and is willing to sacrifice anyone to gain more power. He kills the drunken Daggart to obtain his seat on the council and helps to ensure that Fand is Domnall's choice as a sacrifice to the gods. He further tries to betray the Boar to the invading Romans. In sharp contrast, time and again Coll asserts that he has no desire for personal power, that the Stronghold is intended to help his people and not merely to bring him honor or position. In the end, Taran's desire for power destroys him, while Coll's love for his people saves them.

Critical Context

Mollie Hunter, whose books are equally popular both in her native Scotland and in the United States, has been called Scotland's most distinguished modern writer for children. Although she has written in a variety of genres, many of her books, such as *The Stronghold*, treat the history of Scotland. *The Stronghold*, her novel set at the furthest point in the past, grew out of her own conjectures as to the nature of the unnamed genius responsible for the "strongholds" that she had observed at first hand on a visit to the islands off Scotland's northern coast. When first published, the novel received widespread critical acclaim in a number of reviews, including those by two other award-winning children's novelists, Eleanor Cameron and Susan Cooper. In 1974, *The Stronghold* won the prestigious Carnegie Medal for the Children's Book of Outstanding Merit from the British Library Association.

The novel's treatment of the development of the artistic imagination and the value of individual loyalty is similar to many of Hunter's other novels, including her autobiographical stories *A Sound of Chariots* (1972) and *Hold on to Love* (1984) and her historical books *The Ghosts of Glencoe* (1966) and *You Never Knew Her as I Did!* (1981). Hunter's historical fiction draws on the tradition of Scottish historical romances established by Sir Walter Scott and has undoubtedly influenced the work of Rosemary Sutcliff, another award-winning writer who specializes in British and Celtic history, in particular in the novels *Sun Horse, Moon Horse* (1977), in which a boy saves his people from Roman slavery, and *Song for a Dark Queen* (1978), in which a queen leads her tribe against Roman invaders.

Joel D. Chaston

STUART LITTLE

Author: E. B. White (1899-1985)
First published: 1945; illustrated
Type of work: Novel
Type of plot: Adventure tale, allegory, and fantasy
Time of work: The 1940's
Locale: New York City and points north
Subjects: Animals, coming-of-age, friendship, and social issues
Recommended ages: 10-15

Stuart Little is a small mouse with big dreams; his adventurous spirit leads him through a series of escapades as he searches for a lost friend in a stoic quest for unattainable perfection.

Principal characters:
STUART LITTLE, a two-inch-tall mouse who is a member of the Little family
MARGALO, a foundling bird who captures Stuart's heart and his imagination
FREDERICK C. LITTLE, Stuart's father
MRS. LITTLE, Stuart's loving but shallow mother
GEORGE LITTLE, Stuart's creative, caring, but distractible brother
SNOWBELL, the Little family's pet cat, who is Stuart's nemesis
DR. PAUL CAREY, a surgeon-dentist who is Stuart's friend and a facilitator of his adventures
HARRIET AMES, a tiny girl from a socially prominent family

Form and Content
   Stuart Little is an episodic adventure tale reminiscent of novels in the picaresque style. It is also a fantasy relayed through omniscient third-person narration. The story unfolds in chapters describing significant incidents or adventures. The cleverly detailed illustrations by Garth Williams, although dated, complement the text and allow for complete acceptance of the fantasy. The story is timeless, with universal appeal.
   Stuart Little is a mouse living in a human family. The Littles make allowances for his size and physique with creative engineering and adaptations, and they are sensitive to his differences in appearance and stature. Although they love Stuart, the family members sometimes exploit his small size. He is sent down a slimy drain to retrieve his mother's lost ring, and he later retrieves lost Ping-Pong balls from beneath hot radiators. He must share his home with Snowbell the cat, a mouse's natural predator. Stuart learns early that survival is a difficult struggle.
   Outside of home, Stuart is forced to contend with the bustling activity on the streets of New York City, a difficult task for a mouse who stands only two inches tall. Stuart

is too small to board a bus without assistance. He lives in mortal fear of wayward dogs. Too small to carry standard change, he offers his own specially made tender when paying his fare. He dresses according to the popular fashion of his day, and his conduct is typical of a gentleman living in New York. Stuart yearns for adventure and excitement in Central Park. There, he befriends Dr. Paul Carey, a surgeon-dentist, and secures a position on his model schooner. He endures an exciting and heroic boat race on the lake, emerging unscathed and victorious. Later that evening, when his family asks how he spent his day, he replies, "Oh, knocking around town," without further explanation.

Stuart's adventures continue. One day while recovering from a cold brought about by his being accidentally trapped in the refrigerator, Stuart meets Margalo, a foundling bird given refuge by Mrs. Little. Stuart saves Margalo from Snowbell's advances in a chivalrous manner, and she later returns the favor when she is able to save him from certain death on a smelly garbage scow. Stuart loves the bird dearly. When she unexpectedly takes her leave, Stuart is heartbroken and takes it upon himself to find his trusted friend. His transportation is a six-inch-long, invisible automobile given to him by Dr. Carey.

Thus, Stuart begins a new series of adventures beyond the boundaries of New York City. Off to seek his dreams, he begins his exploration of the unknown. He works briefly as a substitute teacher, reminding his students that "a law has to be fair to everybody." Stuart next moves on to Ames' Crossing, where he meets a girl named Harriet Ames. Although she is young, attractive, and exactly his size, Stuart is not yet ready to settle down. He moves on, fueled by his need to continue searching for Margalo. Finding the elusive bird becomes Stuart's quest as he resumes his journey north in search of his dream.

Analysis

Stuart Little is a novel about conflict, coping, persistence, and hope. Stuart Little, so small a creature in so large a society, brings into focus the major theme of the individual versus a larger, hostile environment. Stuart personifies the positive aspects of the human spirit. He is unrelenting in the face of seemingly insurmountable odds. Secondary themes include an awareness of individual differences, the dynamics of interpersonal relationships, and the impact of societal conventions on the quality of life of individual members. These themes are crucial for young people coming of age. White masterfully mixes humor, satire, and concerns about social justice, allowing the characters to present specific issues without proselytizing.

Stuart is challenged by his size and must struggle to complete even the simplest tasks that most people take for granted. Yet, the struggle has made Stuart resourceful, not cynical or bitter. In some ways, he becomes the personification of the American hero as he overcomes adversity and seeks adventure. Unlike the typical American hero, Stuart elects to travel north instead of west. In yet another digression from tradition, he leaves young Harriet behind, choosing to continue his search for Margalo, his symbol of perfection and the embodiment of the unattainable goal.

White uses anthropomorphism, the giving of human qualities to animals, to advance his themes. This approach enables the fantasy to come to life, allowing him the artistic freedom to develop the characters and their dialogue as the story unfolds. Stuart barks nautical terms at the helm of the *Wasp*; he quotes romantic poetry as he waits to save Margalo. Later, he sheds his "motoring togs" for the more professional attire of a substitute teacher. Satirical humor shines through as a two-inch-tall mouse successfully leaps to ring a tiny desk bell, commanding the attention of the class. Stuart is able to persuade his students to think about the important issues of fairness and inequality.

Although Stuart seems to conform to each situation that he encounters, he never does fit into society, no matter how hard he or others try to help him adapt. His father forbids all mention of mice in their home, out of apparent concern for Stuart, masking the family's inability to accept Stuart as he is. Although they do love him, Stuart cannot be truly comfortable in their home. The same is true in the outside world. Stuart is constantly endangered by his size and by the bustle and constrictions of city life. Even his automobile, the symbol of post-World War II prosperity, is invisible. Stuart's social encounter with Harriet Ames is the last straw. He learns that he cannot be that which he is not. He writes Harriet an eloquent letter of introduction and follows all appropriate social conventions. Later, when he finds both his canoe and his plans in a shambles, he reverts to the simple language of youthful disappointment: "oh, gee whiz." These are simple but revealing words. He knows that he cannot stay. His immediate plans have been shattered, but not his unrelenting spirit. He resolves to leave Ames' Crossing behind him and motor north toward a new frontier. His future, although uncertain, will become a series of adventures in the vast unknown. He may be a wanderer, but he will persist because of his convictions. He believes that he is "headed in the right direction." In the spirit of the great Western heroes, and in a manner similar to Mark Twain's Huckleberry Finn, Stuart rejects society and accepts himself. He understands that perfection may not be achieved in this world. Yet, he continues on, and the journey for the happiness that comes with self-awareness becomes his ultimate goal.

Critical Context

Stuart Little was the first of E. B. White's three well-received and popular animal tales for children; the others are *Charlotte's Web* (1952), a Newbery Honor Book, and *The Trumpet of the Swan* (1970). Each book offers suspense and adventure, and White's characters come alive and seem to leap off the page. He demonstrates masterful use of dialogue and poetic language, elevating animal stories to a new dimension. The interactions and experiences shared by animals and humans invite complete absorption into the world of fantasy. Thus the adventures of Stuart—or Charlotte, Wilbur, and Fern, or Louis—are delightful reading on the literal level.

Some of his characters, such as Stuart and Charlotte, are well rounded. Others, such as the superintendent and the repairman in *Stuart Little*, only serve to advance the story line. Each of the characters has a unique personality, with foibles and virtues.

They mirror human experiences. Although these texts were written for children, they are not for children alone. In *Stuart Little* and the other novels, White stretches the genre of the animal tale to the level of modern allegory, exploring human nature and the role of humankind in the natural environment. These novels encourage introspection and the examination of the motives underlying interpersonal relationships. They challenge readers to find their own directions and to follow the paths best-suited to their needs and dreams.

Kathleen Schongar

SUGARING TIME

Author: Kathryn Lasky (1944-   )
First published: 1983; illustrated
Type of work: Social science
Subjects: Family, jobs and work, nature, and science
Recommended ages: 10-13

Text and photographs describe how family members in Vermont work together to collect maple sap and process it into syrup.

Form and Content

Divided into seven short chapters, Kathryn Lasky's *Sugaring Time* chronologically traces the steps used in maple sap collection and processing. Christopher G. Knight, Lasky's husband and a former photographer for *National Geographic*, clearly illustrates each stage of the maple syrup process with black-and-white photographs.

The setting of the book is Alice and Don Lacey's sugar bush on their Vermont farm. The third-person narration describes Alice and Don's children and parents as the three generations work together to harvest their sugar. Every detail of the harvest process is covered. They use their Belgian workhorses for "breaking out" trails in the snow after a cold winter. Once the trails are trod, they tap each tree with a special drill and bit. Spouts are inserted to collect the sweet sap that gathers just beneath the bark, and buckets are placed below the spouts to catch the sap. Lids, or "hats," are placed on the buckets to keep out rain and snow. The sap begins to "rise," seeping out of the tree in long drips, when the sun passes the vernal equinox.

When the Laceys go out to collect the sap, each child and adult enjoys his or her role. They delight in lifting the hats off the buckets to see how much sap there is to collect from each tree. According to Lasky, "Bark shimmers, branches quiver, a whole sky with clouds and sunbursts is reflected in the tree's sweet water. It is a bucketful of life that Jonathan cannot resist. He dips a jar into the sap for the first real taste of spring, and then begins gathering." The children enjoy tasting the sweet sugar from the bucket, as well as sneaking tastes of the sap as it runs downhill to their storage tank.

Boiling is the next and most important step after gathering. Forty gallons of sap makes only one gallon of syrup, so the family boils it in large quantities. Visitors come and go in the sugarhouse where the boiling takes place, taking advantage of the maple syrup cloud to clear away a winter's cold. They also enjoy drinking sap tea, made by steeping tea bags in cups of hot sap. The family monitors the temperature of the sap as it continues to boil and skims the foam from the surface. After it is skimmed of foreign matter, the sap flows into the evaporator pans.

At 219 degrees Fahrenheit, the sap turns to syrup. When the syrup "aprons" or "sheets," they open the spigots and save the syrup. The syrup is then bottled, graded, and sold. All members of the family enjoy their first taste of the syrup. The children delight in sugar-on-snow parties: Warm syrup is poured onto the snow, where it immediately hardens and then can be eaten like candy. Sugaring time passes, and the Lacey family enjoys the food and money gained from processing and selling their syrup. They look forward to sugaring time next year.

Analysis

Lasky takes a complicated subject in nature and industry and simplifies it for young readers. The combination of third-person narration and intermittent dialogue, along with the portrayal of tender and supportive familial relationships, makes the process of sugaring seem both homey and matter-of-fact. Even dangerous stages of sugaring, such as boiling, are explained carefully. Knight's photography evokes warm emotions on the part of readers. The Lacey children participate in all stages of the sugaring process, even in skimming the foam from the boiling sap. At each step, Lasky describes the simple joys of the children: letting their Belgian workhorses taste the sap, placing their mouths in the sap flow, sipping sap tea, and throwing sugar-on-snow parties with neighborhood friends.

The book revels in familial relationships, as children fall asleep in their grandmother's arms, stand side-by-side with their father while tapping the trees, and securely sit close to their mother on the sled. The black-and-white photographs affectionately depict these relationships. The incredible harmony in this three-generation family can provide escape and fantasy for young readers in homes where little sense of harmony exists. Readers are shown model working relationships in which each person has defined roles and tasks. *Sugaring Time* can be used as a springboard for vocational discussion, as well as a model for work projects where family and community effort is emphasized.

Scientific concepts are explained using vivid imagery. For example, Lasky describes the vernal equinox: "Finally, after a freezing cold night, the next morning is sunny. It is not the pale, thin, low-angle sunlight of November, but the direct, strengthening light of a sun that has passed the year's equator, the vernal equinox. It is the sun of longer days that feels warm on the cheeks, makes birds sing, and helps all things loosen up and stretch." Her easy-to-understand style includes not only visual but auditory and tactile sensory descriptions as well: "This snow of early spring is called corn snow because the crystals are big and granular, like kernels of corn. But it is really more sugary in its texture, and when Jonathan skis it sounds as if he is skimming across the thick frosting of a wedding cake."

A drawback of the text is that no conflicts or problems are shown among the family and community during the arduous task of maple sap collection. The narrative and photographs are so perfect that the story seems unrealistic. Difficulties in any agricultural endeavors can and will arise, and a more authentic portrait would help prepare young readers for future pursuits themselves. When discussing the book with young readers, it may be important for parents or teachers to include "what if?" questions, such as "What if the sap boiled over?" or "What if the quality of this year's maple syrup is less than that of last year's syrup?" Such questions, which are not addressed in *Sugaring Time*, can help young people learn problem-solving and the analysis of potential problems in business ventures.

Critical Context

Kathryn Lasky is a versatile author who has written adult fiction, juvenile fiction, and nonfiction. *Sugaring Time* has a unique place in the canon of juvenile literature because it appeared during the early 1980's, when children's publishers were just beginning to expand the selection of nonfiction materials for young readers. Prior to this time, the majority of books published for children were fiction. The success of *Sugaring Time* showed the potential of information books in the juvenile marketplace.

Sugaring Time is a valuable book portraying the spirit of an American family as it harvests maple sap. This ecologically sound book demonstrates how family members can benefit financially from their environment without damaging it, an excellent example of a home business. The strength of the book is the simplicity of its text and the family unity that it displays.

The text is used widely in elementary classrooms; it was adapted as a filmstrip by Random House in 1986, for audio cassette in 1986, and for videocassette in 1988. The photographic essay format of *Sugaring Time* is useful in portraying social studies subjects, such as family, work ethics, working relationships, and industry. The book also explains many scientific concepts and can easily be integrated with units on weather, weather measurement, seasons, and photosynthesis. It could be integrated with mathematics units on temperature measurement, volume measurement, and the analysis of finances, such as balance sheets of profits and losses.

Miracles on Maple Hill (1956), a Newbery Honor Book by Virginia Sorensen, is a novel for middle-school readers that reinforces the content of *Sugaring Time*. Although the novel describes the emotional healing and reunion of a family after the father spends time in a prison camp during World War II, the backdrop to the story is their move to the country and the miracle of their maple sugar harvest. This novel would make a good companion book for *Sugaring Time*.

June Hetzel

A SUMMER TO DIE

Author: Lois Lowry (1937-   )
First published: 1977; illustrated
Type of work: Novel
Type of plot: Domestic realism and psychological realism
Time of work: The 1970's
Locale: Rural Maine
Subjects: Coming-of-age, death, family, and health and illness
Recommended ages: 10-15

During a year spent in rural New England, thirteen-year-old Meg Chalmers comes to terms with the illness and death of her older sister, develops her talent as a photographer, and learns to see beauty both in herself and in others.

>   *Principal characters:*
>   MEG CHALMERS, a thirteen-year-old budding photographer who must face the illness and death of her older sister
>   MOLLY CHALMERS, Meg's seemingly perfect fifteen-year-old sister, who develops leukemia
>   DR. CHARLES CHALMERS, their father, an English professor who has temporarily moved his family to the countryside in order to finish writing a book
>   LYDIA CHALMERS, their mother
>   WILL BANKS, the owner of the house that the Chalmers are renting for the summer, who befriends Meg
>   BEN BRADY, a student from Harvard University
>   MARIA ABBOTT, Ben's wife
>   HAPPY WILLIAM ABBOTT-BRADY, Ben and Maria's infant son
>   MARTIN HUNTINGTON, Will's nephew, a lawyer

Form and Content

Lois Lowry's first novel, *A Summer to Die*, was inspired by her relationship with her older sister, Helen, who eventually died of cancer. The book is narrated by thirteen-year-old Meg Chalmers, an artist and budding photographer, and treats the events of a pivotal year in her life. During that year, Meg is forced to confront jealousy and guilt, death and grief, as she comes to terms with the loss of her sister. At the same time, she begins to discover her own self-worth by developing her talents and making new friends.

As the novel begins, Meg feels inadequate compared to her seemingly perfect fifteen-year-old sister, Molly, an attractive cheerleader for whom everything seems to come easily. When their father, an English professor, moves the family to a small farmhouse in the country, both girls are unhappy. Meg must give up her Saturday morning photography classes, and Molly must quit cheerleading. In addition, the two girls are forced to share a room for the first time, which creates further tension, provoking Molly to draw a line down the middle of their room.

In February, Meg finds some consolation in helping her father build a darkroom so that she can develop her own photographs. One day in March, after Molly and Meg have had another argument, Molly begins to feel very ill and is rushed to a hospital in Portland, Maine. When Molly returns home, she seems weak and depressed. When Molly is hospitalized again, Meg blames herself for telling their mother that her sister's legs are covered with red spots. Eventually, Meg's parents reveal that Molly has acute myelogenous leukemia. When Meg visits Molly in the hospital to tell her about the birth of their neighbors' infant, she feels older than her sister, who is too weak to respond with more than a smile. Two weeks later, Molly dies, and Meg believes that things will never be the same again.

During Molly's illness, Meg learns to appreciate her sister and grows both as an individual and as an artist. In part, this change is the result of her friendship with three adults. These friends include a young married couple, Ben Brady and Maria Abbott, who are renting a house while Ben works on a thesis for a degree at Harvard University. Meg shares in their joy when she photographs the birth of their baby, Happy William Brady-Abbott, which takes place while Molly is hospitalized.

Even more important, however, is Meg's friendship with Will Banks, the seventy-year-old owner of the house that the Chalmers are renting. Will encourages Meg's interest in photography, lending her an old camera and lenses. As Meg teaches Will what she knows about photography, she learns to look more closely at the world around her. At the end of the novel, after Molly has died, a photograph that Will has taken of Meg appears in an exhibition at her father's university. Meg sees some of her sister in her own image and realizes that Molly will live on through her and her memories. When Meg tells Will that he has made her feel beautiful, he responds that she was beautiful all along.

Analysis

As in many of Lowry's later works, *A Summer to Die* deals with the joys and pains that come from memories and treats characters who are initiated into a world in which they experience grief and loss. While the novel deals with a serious subject, a family coping with the death of one of its members, the book is not depressing. The book's hopeful tone is attributable to Meg's close relationship with her parents, her friendships with kind and nurturing adults outside her immediate family, and her own personal growth. In addition, Meg's feelings and her family are portrayed in a believable way, probably because parts of the novel, especially Meg and Molly's relationship, are autobiographical.

Lowry introduces one of the novel's important topics, memory, through a patchwork quilt that Meg's mother is making from pieces taken from the family's old clothes. For Meg and Molly, the quilt reminds them of some unpleasant memories that Meg suggests are better off forgotten because enough time has not elapsed. Her parents share a similar attitude when they refuse to consider renting the same house the next summer because it reminds them of Molly's illness and death. As time passes, however, Molly is able to keep her sister alive through the memories that are prompted, in part, by the photographs that she and Will have been taking. At the end of the novel, Meg is able to "see" her sister standing in the grass with her arms full of flowers and remarks that somewhere it will always be summer for Molly.

Perhaps even more important is the novel's exploration of the relationship between Meg and Molly, as well as Meg's subsequent grief and sense of loss. Meg's jealousy of Molly derives, at least in part, from her own sense of inadequacy. Everything seems to come easily to Molly, who is pretty, popular, and neat. Through the course of the novel, Meg gradually realizes her own talents, particularly her abilities as an artist and photographer. She is able to teach Will how to take photographs and show Molly how to improve the brides that she likes to draw. In addition, Molly reveals her own insecurities by suggesting that she has nothing but her good looks.

As Molly becomes ill, Meg, who has had a relatively sheltered existence, moves from innocence to experience as she learns about both the tragedy and the joy of life. When Ben Brady tries to tell Meg that life will be easier if she admits that bad things happen, she becomes angry. Eventually, however, she realizes the truth of Ben's remarks and is willing to recognize that one day her friend Will Banks will be gone as well. Yet, Meg is not left without hope. She has also learned about the beauty of life through the natural world around her and through the birth of Ben and Maria's baby—which brings a smile to Molly even as she is dying. Similarly, at the end of the novel, when Meg returns to the country to see Will, he shows her his favorite flower, fringed gentian; it is symbolic that these flowers bloom in the autumn and, like Meg, do not care whether anyone sees them. Like the flowers, Meg has finally bloomed, and she is able to recognize her own inner beauty.

Critical Context

A Summer to Die, Lois Lowry's first attempt at writing for children, was a success with both critics and young readers and looked forward to many of Lowry's other award-winning books. It was named to the *Horn Book* Honor List and received the International Reading Association's Children's Book Award and state book awards from California and Massachusetts, and it was translated into nine languages. It anticipates Lowry's autobiographical *Autumn Street* (1980), whose young protagonist encounters both birth and death among her family and friends, and *Anastasia Krupnik* (1979) and *The Giver* (1993), which deal with the both the pain and value of memory. While the plot of *A Summer to Die* recalls other juvenile books about death published in the early 1970's—such as Doris Buchanan Smith's *A Taste of Blackberries* (1973), Constance C. Greene's *Beat the Turtle Drum* (1976), and Katherine Paterson's *Bridge to Terabithia* (1977)—its focus on terminal illness and a close, loving family is distinctive. Much of the continued popularity of *A Summer to Die* comes from its spare and simple style, its likable and believable protagonist, and its honest treatment of sibling rivalry, grief, and friendship.

Joel D. Chaston

TALES

Author: Edgar Allan Poe (1809-1849)
First published: 1845
Type of work: Short fiction
Subjects: Crime, death, and the supernatural
Recommended ages: 13-18

This collection contains twelve of Poe's tales, including his detective stories and his most famous gothic fable, "The Fall of the House of Usher."

Form and Content

Edgar Allan Poe's *Tales* is his most representative collection, containing a wider variety of stories than the earlier *Tales of the Grotesque and Arabesque* (1839). The dozen stories in the book include his metaphysical fables "The Colloquy of Monos and Una," "The Conversation of Eiros and Charmion," and "Mesmeric Revelation"; two of his dark tales of obsession and isolation, "The Black Cat" and "The Man of the Crowd"; one of his best-known literary parodies, "Lionizing"; his chilling gothic adventure "A Descent into the Maelstrom"; his four innovative tales of ratiocination and detection, "The Gold Bug," "The Murders in the Rue Morgue," "The Mystery of Marie Roget," and "The Purloined Letter"; and his most famous masterpiece of romantic alienation, "The Fall of the House of Usher."

In "Mesmeric Revelation," Poe uses hypnotism to explore his own metaphysical views about the nature of reality as being design and form rather than simple matter. Under a hypnotic trance, the character Vankirk responds to questions about the nature of God and material reality with theories that Poe later develops in his philosophic poem *Eureka* (1848). "The Conversation of Eiros and Charmion" is a dialogue between Charmion, an aged spirit from the netherworld, and Eiros, a new spirit whom he inducts into the realm of Edenic reality. The same theme is continued in the dialogue "The Colloquy of Monos and Una," in which the Fall of Man is described as a fall from the life of concrete reality into the life of science and abstraction.

"The Black Cat" is one of Poe's best-known stories of the perverse, a psychological motivation he calls a "prime mover" of the human soul that makes characters feel compelled to act in a way that they know they should not. The obsession in this story centers on a man who kills his wife because of his unreasonable fascination with a black cat. In "The Man of the Crowd," the narrator of the story becomes so fascinated with an old man whom he sees in a crowd one evening that he follows him all night and the next day until he discovers that the old man is an emblem of human loneliness.

"Lionizing" and "A Descent into the Maelstrom" are examples of two types of fiction popular in Poe's time; the first is a satiric parody of the habit of making some writers into idolized stars (something that always eluded Poe in his lifetime), and the second is a version of the typical *Blackwood* magazine adventure, in which Poe presents the stereotyped gothic tale of a man who undergoes a quasi-supernatural science-fiction adventure—this time in a giant whirlpool in the North Atlantic—and survives it.

Poe invented the modern detective story, creating in his sleuth Dupin the model for the amateur detective that millions of readers have loved in such characters as Sherlock Holmes and Hercule Poirot. Although "The Gold-Bug"—Poe's most-famous story during his lifetime—does not feature a detective or a crime, it does depend on the kind of careful observation and deduction that characterizes his detective Dupin. Most of Poe's contributions to the detective story genre are introduced in "The Murders in the Rue Morgue" in which the "criminal" is an escaped orangutan; Dupin's methods were so popular that Poe applied them to a real-life murder of a woman named Mary Rogers in "The Mystery of Marie Roget." Yet, Poe's story of an incriminating letter hidden paradoxically in plain view is the detective story that most appeals to connoisseurs of the form, for it sums up its intellectual and aesthetic complexities.

"The Fall of the House of Usher" has become Poe's most well known story, for in it he transforms the plot of the pot-boiler gothic romance into a probing study of isolation and the dangers of an obsessive fascination with art. Isolated within himself and his house, Roderick Usher has come to stand for the ultimate disintegration of the nineteenth century Romantic artist-hero who dares to cut himself off from the world around him.

Analysis

It is a mistake, made by many teachers and critics, to dismiss Poe as a hack writer of horror tales, a sort of nineteenth century Stephen King, who has nothing of importance to say and who says it in a popularized, best-seller fashion. While it is true that Poe's stories were written in conventional forms that he thought would make them popular with the general reading public, his genius transformed the gothic pot-boiler into a probing exploration of the romantic imagination and the isolated human psyche.

The central theme in all of Poe's works is the concept of unity, an idea that he explored in most of his works—from his simplest stories to his ambitious philosophic poem *Eureka*. For Poe, aesthetic and philosophic truth is determined not by measuring a work's correspondence to external reality but by its own internal consistency. As he says in *Eureka*, "A thing is consistent in the relation of its truth—true in the ratio of its consistency. A perfect consistency, I repeat, can be nothing but an absolute truth." Based on this conviction, Poe believed that the function of language was not to mirror external reality but to create a self-contained realm of reality that corresponds only to the basic human desire for total unity. In such metaphysical fantasies as "Mesmeric Revelation," Poe asserted that the highest form of existence was what he called "unparticled matter," by which he meant mind, spirit, and ultimately God. Arguing that the universe was a perfect plot of God, Poe thought that it was the task of the artist to strive to create perfect plots—self-contained aesthetic worlds.

Similarly, it is the God-like ability of Poe's detective Dupin to unravel the mystery of a hidden pattern, to find a unity in what seems to be random and unrelated events, that makes him the model of the creator/explicator that has fascinated readers of the detective story. As the narrator of the Dupin stories (a model for Sherlock Holmes's commonsense companion, Watson) notes in "The Murders in the Rue Morgue," Dupin has a "Bi-Part Soul," made up of both the "creative and the resolvent."

Poe's most-famous character, Roderick Usher, also seems to have a double reality, embodied both in his own artistic imagination and in his more material twin sister, Madeline. Whereas Dupin is primarily the resolvent part of the self, the ideal reader who masters the seemingly meaningless material around him and perceives in it a revealing and meaningful pattern, however, Roderick is the creative soul who has retreated so far into his own imagination that he cannot tolerate any input from the world outside. Roderick's obsession is that the house in which he lives is like a palace of art that has sentience or sensibility because of the order and arrangement of its stones. At the end of the story, his bodily twin Madeline falls in upon him, Roderick falls in upon the house, and the house itself falls into the tarn to return Roderick's reality back to the artist's nonmaterial imagination whence it came. "The Fall of the House of Usher" is in many ways the complete Poe paradigm because it pulls together so many of his basic themes and embodies so many of his innovative fictional techniques.

Critical Context

Although Edgar Allan Poe is among the most widely read of all American writers, he has not always been taken seriously by critics. T. S. Eliot once said that Poe had the intellect of a "gifted young person before puberty," and the great novelist Henry James remarked that an "enthusiasm for Poe is the mark of a decidedly primitive stage of reflection." Whereas it is true that Poe has often been more admired by adolescents than by adults, Poe may have influenced more young people to become writers and teachers of writing than any other American author. Jorge Luis Borges, the South American master of Magical Realism, and John Barth, America's best-known practitioner of fabulism, are only two of the many writers who have admitted as much.

Recent literary studies have finally begun to justify what loyal readers of Poe have always believed—that Poe understood the nature of narrative better than any other nineteenth century writer. His stories, once dismissed as simple gothic thrillers, are now being analyzed for their self-conscious manipulation of narrative devices and their darkly existential view of reality. Poe, plagued during his life by debts, tragedy, and depression, is finally being recognized as a master of fictional technique and his works as the precursors of modern existential vision.

Charles May

TALES FROM SILVER LANDS

Author: Charles Finger (c. 1869-1941)
First published: 1924; illustrated
Type of work: Short fiction
Subjects: Animals, nature, and the supernatural
Recommended ages: 10-13

These folktales, fairy tales, and origin stories filled with witches, giants, strange creatures and enchanted humans were gathered at first hand from South American Indian tribes and are charmingly retold in this collection.

Form and Content

These tales are distinctive, not only for their appealing stories but also for the rich, descriptive language that Charles Finger uses to pass them on to his readers. While traveling throughout South America, the author collected legends at first hand from South American Indians; nineteen of these stories are featured as separate chapters in *Tales from Silver Lands*. Finger retells the legends in a direct and charming manner, elaborating on details that appeal to the senses, much as the original storytellers must have done. Each story is retold with respect, and many are prefaced with descriptions of the persons who told them. Woodcuts by Paul Honore are found at the beginning of each chapter, contributing to the magical flavor of the stories. These tales of origin and enchantment describe the native creatures and natural settings of South American countries and reflect the traditional values of those who tell them. The weaknesses and foibles of humans are writ large, with greed, avarice, sloth, gluttony, and selfishness vividly portrayed. Traditional values are demonstrated in the persons of virtuous heroes who are brave, strong, faithful, persistent, and unselfish.

The origin tales include "A Tale of Three Tails," from Honduras, which tells how the rabbit, deer, and rat came to have short tails and why the armadillo has a thick, leathery skin. Other stories explain the origins of seals, llamas, and monkeys. The quests of brave young men are chronicled in "The Calabash Man," "The Magic Dog," and the Hero Twins trilogy. In the latter stories, two clever brothers trick destructive giants into killing themselves. Some tales feature stories inside of stories, such as "The Tale That Cost a Dollar," which tells how the author came to receive the tale from a Chilean storyteller. This enchanting story of a boy who has never seen night and a girl who has never seen day was a favorite of the author's daughters. Other tales are stories of enchantment and involve wicked witches, wizards, and gigantic or mysterious creatures that change shape.

In "The Hungry Old Witch," an evil witch is undone by her gigantic appetite. A tar baby ploy is used to free hostages from a giant evil bird in "The Magic Knot," and "The Wonderful Mirror" is a delightful tale reminiscent of "Snow White" that involves a terrible spell and a wicked stepmother.

Many of the stories are direct in making moral statements, such as a comment in

"The Hero Twins": "Evil things must be laid low if the world is to be fair." In "The Bad Wishes," the narrator observes that "no one in the world was wise enough to wish things as they should be wished" and "no man knows the thing that is best for him." The substance of true courage is explored in "The Cat and the Dream Man," when the storyteller notes that "the brave one is not he that does not fear, but rather he that fears and yet does the thing that he has set out to do."

Analysis

Readers of all cultures will immediately recognize the classic elements of folktales in these stories: the courageous and pure-hearted protagonists; the impossible tasks, undertaken with the help of seemingly defenseless creatures; and magic spells that both assist and impede the hero. These are stories of great opposites, where characters are unfailingly good or unredeemably evil. The heroic men and women are unfailing brave, strong-hearted, fleet of foot, excellent marksmen, persistent at impossible tasks, and skilled in communicating with creatures in nature. The villains are cruel, ugly, tattered, flawed, cowardly, or possessed of terrible tempers. The characters' behavior reflects the values of the culture in which they were created, and the rewards given to the heroes are those considered to be the just rewards of the righteous: long life, peace, and happiness.

In addition to these standard elements of folktales, each of these stories is infused with descriptions of nature, similar to those found in the folk literature of North American Indian tribes. Wild creatures, water, flowers, and birds are richly described and spoken of with awe and respect. The language of the stories is rich in metaphor and simile; the descriptions of settings and persons are vivid and compelling. Readers are drawn immediately into such stories as "The Magic Ball" with the first sentence: "A cold-eyed witch lived in the Cordilleras and when the first snow commenced to fall she was always full of glee, standing on a rock, screaming like a wind-gale and rubbing her hands." One can easily imagine the rage of the "Calabash Man," whose anger was so great that "he rushed out and bent trees as though they were reeds and bit rocks as a man bites a crust of bread," or picture in the mind's eye the bird in "The Magic Knot," which was so strong that "it could bear away a llama in each claw and another in its beak."

The strange beings, mythical overtones, and grand adventures found in these stories will stir the imagination of young readers. In the process of entering adulthood, they too will embark on quests, face obstacles, and be called upon to defend good and defeat evil. Like the heroes and heroines of old, they must contend with the dualities of life—good and evil, strength and weakness, bravery and cowardice—and examine the shadings between these extremes. Folktales chronicle change and growth in their characters, and the protagonists in these tales embark on a quest and return as changed, strengthened, or more insightful people. Readers will look for signs of themselves in the heroes and hope not to find too much that is familiar in the less desirable characters.

In most, but not all, of the tales, Finger identifies the setting at the beginning of the story. Locations range from north to south on the continent, including Tierra del Fuego, Cape Horn, Columbia, Uruguay, Argentina, Brazil, Bolivia, Paraguay, Honduras, Guiana, and the Cordilleras. In the retelling of many of these stories, Finger describes the protocols observed by both the native storytellers and their audiences. For example, in Honduras, there is an appropriate way to ask persons to tell a story and equally appropriate ways for the audience to indicate their respect for the storyteller by the manner in which they respond as listeners. Instead of asking directly for another story, one of the listeners should simply ask a question about a detail in the story being told. In almost ceremonial fashion, the storyteller will then admonish the listener for not paying attention and will begin the narrative. In addition, when objects are involved in the telling of the story, members of the audience should examine them as if for the first time, although they may be quite familiar with them.

Critical Context

Charles Finger was born in England and traveled extensively throughout the world before settling in the United States. Although he wrote books for adults and children, he is best remembered for *Tales from Silver Lands*, which received the Newbery Medal in 1925, and another collection of folktales, *Tales Worth Telling* (1927). *Tales from Silver Lands* was one of the first collections that made South American Indian folktales accessible to young readers, and it is still among the few in print; others are Natalia M. Belting's *Moon Was Tired of Walking on Air* (1992), a collection of traditional South American Indian creation myths, and *The Mythology of South America* (1988), by John Bierhorst, a more scholarly volume that includes references and notes on sources.

The stories in this collection can be enjoyed by a wide range of ages, but they are quite appropriate for young readers because of the various levels at which they are written. Each tale is an entertaining adventure story, but they can also be explored in terms of the context of the storyteller, which includes the particular geography, life-forms, weather, and traditional values of particular regions. The maxims on which the stories are based are worth examining, because they reflect not only regional values but ancient wisdom about life as well. These are stories told to the young people of a culture to direct their ways, to create reflection on behavior, and to caution. Yet, they also reflect the concerns of contemporary young readers with questions such as "How should I live my life?" "What goals should I seek?" and "What values are worth having?"

Marcia Brown Popp

TALES FROM THE BAMBOO GROVE

Author: Yoko Kawashima Watkins (1933-   )
First published: 1992; illustrated
Type of work: Short fiction
Subjects: Family, nature, health and illness, jobs and work, and social issues
Recommended ages: 10-13

These Japanese folktales, recalled from the author's childhood, explore family relationships, nature, justice, vanity, and the struggle between good and evil.

Form and Content

Tales from the Bamboo Grove contains Japanese folktales told by the parents of Yoko Kawashima Watkins during her childhood supper times. Gathered in a room with twelve tatami mats and eating from lacquered trays, the author and her siblings treasured the cherished stories passed down by their parents through oral tradition. The book includes an introduction and six tales: "Dragon Princess, Tatsuko"; "The Fox Wife"; "Why Is the Seawater Salty?"; "Yayoi and the Spirit Tree"; "Monkey and Crab"; and "The Grandmother Who Became an Island." Each tale includes a full-page, black-and-white illustration created with brush and ink on bristol board by Jean and Mou-sien Tseng. The Japanese title of each folktale is incorporated into its accompanying drawing, written by the author in calligraphy.

"Dragon Princess, Tatsuko" tells the story of a lovely young maiden who discovers her beauty and wishes to remain young eternally. She sacrifices her humanness to become a dragon, bringing great emotional turmoil to both she and her mother.

"The Fox Wife" recounts the story of a poor farmer who saves a maiden who has fallen unconscious. After nursing her back to health, she repays the farmer in service, and they eventually marry and have a child. When wife and child fall ill, the husband spends so much time caring for them that he fails to plant his rice crop in a timely manner. The wife performs a miraculous feat to save her husband from financial ruin and plants his entire rice crop. When the husband observes that the rice seedlings are planted upside down, he tells his wife, who, in the form of a fox, quickly replants them. During the replanting, he discovers his wife's true identity, and she returns to her life as a fox.

"Why Is the Seawater Salty?" explains why the ocean contains salt. A young man and his wife obtain a hand mill that performs any miracle they ask, including producing rice and gold. They use it to bring about good for themselves and the people of their village. The man's greedy older brother, however, hears about the mill and steals it, escaping by sea. During his escape, he asks the mill to produce salt but does not know how to make it stop. Eventually, the boat fills with salt, and the greedy brother drowns. To this day, the mill continues to produce salt at the bottom of the sea.

"Yayoi and the Spirit Tree" recounts the tale of a poor, hardworking daughter who cares for her ill mother. The Spirit Tree repays the daughter's kindness by giving her specific instructions that, if followed exactly, will bring her rewards. She follows the instructions exactly and receives doctor's services and food for a lifetime for her ailing mother.

"Monkey and Crab" is a lesson about greed, punishment, penance, and justice told by way of a greedy monkey and the crabs that he victimizes. "The Grandmother Who Became an Island" is a nature story explaining the origin of summer island rainy days and winter island snow.

Analysis

Tales from the Bamboo Grove reflects the values of the Kawashima household and—in a broader sense, of Japanese culture—as handed down through oral tradition. Good versus evil is the underlying theme of many of the stories, such as "Monkey and Crab," and "Why Is the Seawater Salty?" Good wins in the end and evil is punished: The greedy older brother drowns at sea as a direct result of his avarice, and the sly monkey is crushed, pinched, burnt, and stung by the other characters in the story as a punishment for stealing the crabs' persimmons. Reflecting harsh consequences for evil deeds, the tales nevertheless reveal the willingness to forgive within Japanese culture. After the monkey is punished, confesses, and asks Mrs. Crab for forgiveness, he is allowed to live with the others in peace, and harmony returns to the community. These tales reveal the shame that selfish deeds bring in Japanese culture and the importance of honesty, fairness, and harmony within the community.

Hard work and loyalty to family are other important values reflected in these Japanese tales. In both "Yayoi and the Spirit Tree" and "The Fox Wife," the main characters devote themselves completely to the service to their loved ones. Although both characters are materially poor, their selfless devotion is miraculously rewarded, and they receive material blessings to meet the physical needs of their family. In contrast, the main character in "Dragon Princess, Tatsuko" concentrates her energies on self-devotion and vanity and ends up spending the rest of her life as a dragon, causing great pain to her devoted mother.

Folkloric explanations of physical aspects of nature is another characteristic of these Japanese tales. For example, "The Grandmother Who Became an Island" explains the origin of island weather patterns, and "Why Is the Seawater Salty?" explains how the oceans became salty and why they remain in this state. Similar to American Indian folklore in their explanations of physical events and geographical phenomena, such as earthquakes and the Creation, these nature folktales lend themselves to both language arts and science integration in the classroom.

Critical Context

Tales from the Bamboo Grove offers young readers an exciting glimpse of Japanese culture and tradition and an opportunity to consider the value of oral tradition. Although there are many single-title traditional Japanese folktales in the canon of juvenile literature, few publications offer a collection of tales with such poignant points of cultural reflection. Many folktales are simply stories of intrigue. For example, Yoshiko Uchida's *The Magic Purse* (1993) tells the story of a poor young farmer who wanted to go with his friends to the Iseh Shrine. His passage (and more) is paid by the mysterious maiden in the swamp who wears a silvery blue kimono. They carry on a long-distance romance; he sends gifts of wine and rice cakes to her, and, in return, she sends a gift of a tiny flower and a shiny green leaf floating on a tray down the river. *The Magic Purse* entertains and intrigues the reader but does not offer the depth of Yoko Kawashima Watkins' collection. Watkins' tales not only invite readers to enjoy well-told stories but also encourage them to ponder morality, honesty, hard work, and family values.

The introduction to *Tales from the Bamboo Grove* describes Watkins' childhood in the Kawashima household. Watkins' father, who played an important role in the Japanese military service, was separated from the rest of the family, which lived in Korea during World War II. For Mrs. Kawashima, the physical and emotional demands of the family's narrow escape from Korea and the shock and horror of finding her own parents and their city completely destroyed were more than she could take, and she soon died in the author's arms. Even after the war ended, Watkins and her brother and sister were separated from their father, who was still in a prison camp. Thus, it was essential for the author to preserve her childhood memories of the joyful, secure family times around the supper table before the family was torn apart by war.

Two other companion books by Watkins can be read after *Tales from the Bamboo Grove*. *So Far from the Bamboo Grove* (1986) and its sequel, *My Brother, My Sister, and I* (1994), describe her early childhood in the Kawashima household. In *So Far from the Bamboo Grove*, Watkins gives an autobiographical account of her family's flight from Korea during World War II, telling the story of the war that destroyed the close-knit family's "story time" where the author heard the stories recorded in *Tales from the Bamboo Grove*. *My Brother, My Sister, and I* describes the attempt of the author and her siblings to reunite with their father, who had passed down to them these treasured folktales.

In the 1990's, classroom instructors were starting to discover the impact and power of Watkins' writings as they reflect the love of Asian culture and tradition. *Tales from the Bamboo Grove* will undoubtedly become a classic collection of folktale literature.

June Hetzel

TALES MUMMIES TELL

Author: Patricia Lauber (1924-   )
First published: 1985; illustrated
Type of work: Science
Subjects: Crime, death, health and illness, and science
Recommended ages: 10-13

Lauber explains how scientists unlock secrets of the past by studying mummies, using scientific methods, medical equipment, and investigative intuition.

Form and Content

In *Tales Mummies Tell*, Patricia Lauber presents the mystery of mummies in detail and with scientific exactness. She avoids the traditional discussion of mummification as seen in the Egyptian culture by approaching the subject universally to include frozen, mummified mammoths and peat bog graves containing alleged miscreants preserved since the Iron Age. Moving the reader from twelve thousand years ago, when woolly mammoths roamed the earth, to the early seventeenth century, the author documents several mummy excavations and accurately defines the scientific value of the findings at each site. The amassed information gained by scientists from mummified bodies verifies knowledge about ancient cultures that otherwise could be only surmised. Authorities on mummification thoroughly examine the bodies to discover diseases suffered by the populace, the tools of the culture, mummification techniques, sociological data, and causes of death.

The book categorizes well-documented mummy sites according to methods of burial and geography. Lauber also includes animal mummification, both accidental (as with mammoths) and intentional (as with Egyptian mummies). The book displays more than seventy black-and-white photographs and several artistic renderings in order to augment the well-drafted text; a credit page indicates the sources of the photographs. Younger readers may be alarmed by the realism of the photographs because many mummies, particularly the bog-buried bodies, depict graphic, lifelike human forms. X rays and schematics further clarify the research. Lauber moves around the world presenting mummies from the former Soviet Union, Peru, Egypt, and Europe, with each area appropriately constituting its own chapter, seven chapters total. The author concludes her text with a succinct bibliography as a guide for those youths who seek more detailed information on mummification. The four-page index will assist the average reader; while it could be more expansive, it will aid most youthful researchers. In all, the book is attractively presented and formatted for easy reading.

Lauber affirmed in this book her reputation for detail and a scholarly approach to scientific subjects. She explains the carbon 14 dating principle in a manner that most young people will comprehend. X-ray images offer an amazing look into the past and Lauber reveals some secrets of the mummies unknown until the scientists examined crypts. One X ray revealed a baby's head buried between her mother's thighs; another disclosed a small, female baboon encased in bindings buried with a human previously thought to be its mother. X rays also divulged evidence of parasitic plague suffered by many Egyptians. Mummies hold the key evidence concerning the diseases, diets, and life spans of ancient civilizations. Sociologists are able to expand on the physical information provided by mummies to extrapolate lifestyle choices of the societies that offer up their preserved dead. Several discussions in the book center on types of death, particularly those experienced by alleged criminals. Bodies buried in peat bogs have leather thongs tightly encircling their necks, suggesting a painful form of death. Mummies with broken bones and crushed skulls represent accident victims or executed criminals. Lauber does not always offer explanations, which may inspire readers to research the causes of these individuals' fates. Thus, the book contains the elements of a good mystery among the scientific data found in each chapter.

Analysis

Lauber usually approaches her subject in a scientific manner. She presents mummification—the process of body preservation from either natural or artificial actions—as a phenomenon that was practiced worldwide. The author records anecdotes in the daily life of animals and humans that eventually lead to their mummification. She begins with a woolly mammoth near the Arctic Circle. A young wandering mammoth falls into a natural pit, cannot reach the top, and freezes to death; the walls collapse to form its tomb. The frozen body remains in place for thousands of years until it is accidentally discovered in 1977. Until then, scientists had found few intact mammoths, only incomplete bodies with deteriorated torsos or limbs scattered by scavengers. This specimen, named Dima, became the pet project of a prestigious alliance of Russian scientists. The animal's stomach contained milk, dirt, and a few summer grass seeds, so the researchers knew that the animal had probably died in desperation in late summer. Carbon 14 dating, which is precisely defined for young readers, found the mummy to be nearly forty thousand years old.

Mummification requires specific conditions in order to preserve bodies successfully. Lauber clarifies the primary natural mummification processes: salting, freezing, drying, and embalming. Because oxygen deprivation accompanies mummification, many bodies suffer a combination of these effects. The author provides examples of these methods by citing specific mummies that scientists have discovered. In a South American copper mine in the Atacama Desert, the drying air and natural salts froze a miner—his slight, statuelike frame still in a working position, with his hair braided and his loincloth covering intact. The so-called Copper man relayed information to the scientific community not only from his body but also from the tools surrounding him. In 400 A.D., an Inuit woman attempted to escape a landslide that rolled down her hillside. The earth crushed her and preserved her frozen body, which was decorated with tattoos and the marks of disease. A Scythian king who reigned over a territory bordered by Siberia and Mongolia was found lying with one of his queens, personal servants, and several of his finest horses—all of them embalmed. The heads of the corpses were chiseled so that the brains could be pulled out, the internal organs were removed, and salts filled all body cavities. A smooth coating of wax encased each figure.

The author describes unique methods for preservation as she continues her geographic tour of mummification. The Jivaro Indians living in the High Amazon River Basin perfect the shrunken-head art called *tsantsas*. The hair remains the same length, while the head shrinks from the precise process of skinning the face from the skull. The result launches a tribal celebration.

Often, liquid preparations can adequately suspend the deterioration of bodies. The body of John Paul Jones remained in identifiable condition as a result of friends encasing him in a lead coffin filled with alcohol. A Chinese woman more than two thousand years ago floated in a slightly acid solution containing mercury. Egyptian mummification processes varied from century to century and reign to reign. Priests learned two important aspects of mummification during the Old Kingdom, around 2600 B.C.; they removed all organs and used natron, a salt, to dry the tissues. Lauber traces in detail the Egyptian methods of preservation.

Archaeologists unearthing mummies of all types allowed other scientists to glean historical information concerning diets, clothing styles, hairstyles, methods of punishment, diseases, parasites, body sizes, and social disfiguration such as tattooing. Animal mummies often accompany human forms, giving archaeologists additional information concerning husbandry and the social importance of what are presumed to be pets. Researchers often heavily rely on the tales that mummies tell to explain cultural changes initiated by cruel invasions like that of the Incas by the Spaniards.

The Peat Bog mummies of Denmark represent the most accurate forms of natural preservation. Bodies suggesting a violent death, with thong nooses and bashed heads, were maintained in near-perfect condition buried in the depths of peat bogs, which lack oxygen. Peat is a source of heat for inhabitants of this cold northern country; while digging blocks for making fires, workers discovered bodies dating to 500 A.D. Researchers christened one of these the Tollund man, from the name of the small village nearby. They determined his age by several key components: the seeds and grain found in his stomach, the known age of a type of spade found near his body, and the leaf type of the sphagnum moss constituting the peat base. Mummies of both sexes have been uncovered from these dark, acid rainwater graves. Bodies suffered crushed skulls, wrung necks, and scalping; these were unceremonious burials compared to those of Egyptian priests and rulers.

Critical Context

Patricia Lauber considers herself a serious author of informative juvenile literature. She has written for *Scholastics Magazine* and has moved in scholarly circles, with staff positions at *Science World*, *The New Book of Knowledge*, and *Scientific American Illustrated Library*. Lauber has published books on volcanoes, dinosaurs, earthquakes, glaciers, rivers, and icebergs and such creatures as earthworms, penguins, dogs, bats, and mice. She also documents nations—their people, scientists, and environment.

Volcano: The Eruption and Healing of Mount St. Helens (1986), received several prestigious awards. *Tales Mummies Tell* received the New York Academy of Sciences Honor Book citation in 1986. Lauber is the author of many other books with archeological themes, such as *Dinosaurs Walked Here and Other Stories Fossils Tell* (1987), *The News About Dinosaurs* (1989), and *Living with Dinosaurs* (1991).

Lauber began writing in a lighthearted manner; she first wrote of her dog Clarence in a series of humorous misadventures. Editors soon realized that she had the ability to surprise and fascinate adults while explaining information to intermediate readers. Lauber suggests that her ability to write emanates from her love of hearing others read. She writes of those subjects that interest her, and, judging by her long list of books, curiosity has served her well.

Craig Gilbert

TEX

Author: S. E. Hinton (1950-   )
First published: 1979
Type of work: Novel
Type of plot: Psychological realism
Time of work: The late 1970's and early 1980's
Locale: Garyville, a small town in the Midwest
Subjects: Coming-of-age, family, and friendship
Recommended ages: 13-18

> *Rambunctious ninth-grader Texas McCormick struggles to come to terms with his own immaturity, his highly disciplined and college-bound older brother, and his absent father, in the process discovering the family secret that they have kept from him.*

Principal characters:
> TEXAS "TEX" MCCORMICK, a fifteen-year-old boy who loves horses and
> pulling pranks in school
> MASON MCCORMICK, Tex's brother, a disciplined star basketball player
> and college-bound high school senior
> POP, their father
> JOHNNY COLLINS, Tex's best friend
> JAMIE COLLINS, Johnny's twin sister and Tex's love interest
> LEM PETERS, Tex's and Mason's drug-dealing friend

Form and Content

The story in this short novel is episodic but tied together by Texas McCormick's struggle with the changes in his life. It begins when Tex comes home from school one day and discovers that Mason, his older brother, has sold their horses in order to pay the household bills. Because their father is off riding the rodeo circuit and their mother has been dead for twelve years, Mason has taken responsibility for the household and his brother's well-being. Tex has never quite realized that the money their father left with them would not last long and that Mason's discipline in running the house is vital for their survival. The loss of his horse, however, begins to awaken him to these facts.

Tex spends most of his free time with his friend Johnny Collins, who has a motorcycle they ride together, and Jamie, Johnny's twin sister, with whom he is falling in love. His feelings for Jamie create conflicts with Johnny and, later, with Jamie when she tells him that their relationship will not last.

Mason plans to attend college on a basketball scholarship, but the stress of being the head of a household causes him to develop an ulcer that is diagnosed at a hospital in the city. While in the city, the brothers visit Lem Peters, Mason's former classmate who lives there with his wife and new baby. Lem is working at a gas station, and they discover that he is dealing drugs for extra money.

On the way home, the brothers pick up a hitchhiker who orders them at gunpoint to drive to the state line. Tex saves them in a risky maneuver that ends in the hitchhiker being killed by the police. The media attention provokes a call from the boys' father, who finally comes home. Tex is overjoyed, but Mason is still angry that Pop has been so irresponsible. Pop has a history of irresponsibility; he once served a stretch in prison for alcohol bootlegging, and he frequently forgets promises that he makes to the boys. Pop promises to buy back Tex's horse and then forgets about it, but the new owners will not sell the horse back anyway. This fact, combined with Mason's resentment of Pop, hardens Tex against Mason.

When Tex and Johnny get in trouble for pulling a school prank, Tex first learns that his behavior at school puts him at risk of being expelled. When Pop and Mason confront each other in the principal's office, Mason lets it slip that Pop is not actually Tex's father. Tex runs out of the school and joins Lem in a drug deal that goes wrong and ends in Tex getting shot. Tex calls Jamie from a pay phone for help, which arrives in time to save him.

In the hospital, Tex comes to a new understanding about his relationship with Jamie and his changing friendship with Johnny. Pop also tells Tex the family secret, that Tex's father was a rodeo rider who had an affair with Tex's mother while Pop was in prison. His story explains why Pop, although he loves Tex, has always treated him differently from Mason. The novel ends with Tex reconciling with Mason and encouraging him to go to college. Now that Tex understands his family history, he feels ready to take on the changes and new responsibilities that are coming in his life.

Analysis

Tex is a coming-of-age story that deals with a young person's attempts to adjust to the changes in his life and his relationships. It is not until he understands his own history and his place in his family that he is able to sort things out. Narrated by the good-natured Tex, the novel has a generally optimistic tone, but there are some disturbing qualities about it. Tex is young and, in many ways, innocent—almost to the point of being an unreliable narrator. For example, although he and his brother live in near poverty without any adult supervision, Tex does not seem to be disturbed or saddened by the situation. He also takes risks, such as pulling pranks at school or trying to jump Johnny's motorcycle over a creek, without realizing the potential consequences of his behavior. Tex's growth in the novel comes when he realizes that his behavior also has consequences for other people.

Tex must learn that as people grow and change, they also move on. In an early chapter, Tex goes to the fair with Johnny and Jamie and a gypsy tells their fortunes. She tells Tex that "there are people who go, people who stay. You will stay." The question of who is going and who is staying returns to Tex over the course of the novel: Johnny is staying, and Lem Peters is someone who should have stayed. Jamie and Mason, however, are going.

The novel also depicts a young person's struggle with complex relationships. Tex's friendship with Johnny is simple but also shallow; when Tex is injured, he does not call for Johnny. Tex's friendship with Jamie becomes sexual and romantic and much more complicated. When she tells Tex that they have no future together, he is angry and shuts her out until he realizes that they can still have a close friendship that is probably deeper than his friendship with her brother. Throughout much of the novel, Tex and Mason have a tense relationship: Tex hates Mason for selling his horse, and Mason is angry that Tex's behavior is so irresponsible. After Tex is shot, however, he learns that Mason beat Lem Peters savagely for endangering Tex and then wept openly, worrying about his brother. Tex begins to understand how much Mason loves him when Mason is willing to sacrifice his chance at college for Tex.

The novel is brought to its climax by the revelation that Pop is not Tex's father. To Tex, this news means that neither Pop nor Mason really love him, and he runs away. Suddenly, he sees how differently Pop has always treated him, that Pop never paid as much attention to him. Tex wonders if his mother ever loved him and if every good thing that he believed about his family was a lie. When Pop finally tells Tex the whole story, it replaces his illusions and fears with truth.

The coming-of-age plot of the novel relays a clear message: Without an understanding of their place in the world, young people cannot begin to make the transition to adulthood. The knowledge may not be pleasant, but it is better than living with illusions in a stage of arrested development. One of the compelling aspects of the novel is that Tex does not even realize what it is that he lacks.

Critical Context

All of S. E. Hinton's novels deal with young male protagonists struggling with a coming-of-age crisis in world populated by teenagers who are trying to survive without effective adult guidance. In *The Outsiders* (1967), she depicts a world of street violence and brutality. This novel broke new ground for young adult literature and paved the way for authors such as Paul Zindel, Paula Danziger, Richard Peck, and Robert Cormier. *Rumble Fish* (1975) has an even darker vision, incorporating themes of betrayal. In *That Was Then, This Is Now* (1971), Hinton explores the world of drug abuse and a protagonist struggling with an ethical crisis caused by his friend's involvement in drug dealing. *Taming the Star Runner* (1988) deals with many of the same issues as the previous novels but is written with special subtlety, prominently featuring horses (of which the author is especially fond) and a young novelist. Her novels often depict adults as, at best, uninvolved and, at worst, cruel to adolescents. Because her young protagonists are sympathetic, their casual involvement in violent criminal activity is often disturbing. Despite her treatment of grim subjects, Hinton's novels are always grounded in a strong sense of right and wrong, and they often illustrate how difficult it may be to do the right thing.

Daniel A. Clark

THANK YOU, JACKIE ROBINSON

Author: Barbara Cohen (1932-1992)
First published: 1974; illustrated
Type of work: Novel
Type of plot: Domestic realism
Time of work: 1947-1949
Locale: Winter Hill, New Jersey; and Ebbets Field, Brooklyn, New York
Subjects: Death, friendship, race and ethnicity, and sports
Recommended ages: 10-13

Sammy Greene's obsession with baseball separates him from other people until he meets Davy, a father-figure who shares his interest in baseball, takes him to ball games, and helps him expand his experiences in life.

> *Principal characters:*
> SAMMY GREENE, a man who recalls his childhood relationship with Davy and their interest in the Dodgers
> DAVY, an aging black cook who works at Mrs. Greene's inn and becomes the young Sammy's best friend
> HENRIETTA, Davy's daughter, who takes care of him
> ELLIOT, Davy's son-in-law, who uses his wit and audacity to help Sammy
> JACKIE ROBINSON, the first black man to play major league baseball and Sammy and Davy's favorite player
> MRS. GREENE, Sammy's mother, a widow who supports her family by running an inn

Form and Content

Thank You, Jackie Robinson is a first-person account of a bittersweet relationship between a young Jewish boy and an aging black man. Sammy Greene looks back upon his two-year friendship with Davy and presents it as an important example of the beneficial aspects of racial toleration in personal and social relations.

The story presents Sammy Greene's recollection of his obsession with his favorite baseball team, the Brooklyn Dodgers, and his favorite player, Jackie Robinson. Whenever his school friends have questions about baseball, they can count on him for answers. His friends' interest goes no further, however, so Sammy listens to ball games, reads record books, and relives games alone until he meets Davy, the cook who comes to work at his family's inn. On the basis of their interest in baseball, the two form a close friendship. Davy becomes Sammy's surrogate father and takes him to games with Henrietta, Davy's daughter, and Elliot, his son-in-law, at Ebbets Field in New York, as well as in Boston and Pittsburgh.

Davy's health, however, is not strong, and he suffers a heart attack. Sammy decides to give Davy a baseball signed by the Dodgers, a gift that he believes worthy of their friendship and powerful enough to restore Davy's health. Sammy gathers enough money to buy a regulation baseball and to travel to Brooklyn. At Ebbets Field, however, he is not able to obtain any signatures, until he sees Jackie Robinson come onto the field and yells to him for his autograph. After listening to Sammy's story about Davy, Robinson promises to sign a ball used during the game and to have his teammates sign it as well.

On the following day, Sammy asks Henrietta and Elliot to give the ball to Davy, because only immediate family members are allowed to visit him in the hospital. Elliot insists that Sammy give the gift in person, however, and thinks of a way to sneak him into the hospital. Dressed in one of Davy's white uniforms, Elliot pretends to be a laundryman and brings Sammy, who is hidden in a laundry bag, into Davy's room. Davy is deeply touched by Sammy's gift, but the ball does not fulfill Sammy's hope that Davy will recover.

Upon Davy's death, Sammy struggles with rituals of death and feelings of loss. He does not want to view Davy's body, but he overcomes his revulsion. He sees that, in a spiritual sense, Davy is not lying in the coffin; yet, his recognition does not lessen his grief, for it confronts him with unanswerable questions regarding the fate of the soul. In his depression, he wishes that he had never been Davy's friend. Although he does not want to listen to a baseball game again, he thinks about Jackie Robinson and the Dodgers and turns on the radio. The game draws him out of his depression. Robinson hits a double as if in answer to Sammy's prayer for him to hit the ball for Davy. In his mind's eye, Sammy sees Robinson running around the bases. His interest in life returns, and his memory of Davy becomes a valued part of it.

Analysis

Thank You, Jackie Robinson is a simple story that touches on emotionally charged issues of a complex nature set during the late 1940's against a background of racial inequality.

Sammy and Davy's friendship develops as they discuss baseball in a manner that carries unusual significance for them. Sammy's short and intense experience as a Dodger fan reflects his Jewish background: When Davy asks Sammy why he chose the Dodgers rather than the Yankees or Giants, he is unable to answer because he realizes that the Dodgers chose him in a mystical way similar to God's inspiration of the prophets. Sammy's obsession with baseball manifests itself in his ability to recite complete Dodger games. Unlike the children at school, Davy enjoys listening to Sammy and talking with him about the games, both past and present.

Davy's relationship to the Dodgers, unlike Sammy's, has been long and enduring, but like the boy's, it has mystical and ethnic qualities. Davy tells Sammy that he loved the Dodgers before World War II and before the team was successful, but the Dodgers vindicated his devotion. In the struggle against racism in baseball that reflects the larger struggle in society, the Dodgers came through: In 1947, Branch Rickey, general manager of the Dodgers, hired Jackie Robinson, officially breaking the color barrier in modern baseball.

Race is not an issue between Davy and Sammy, but Davy's awareness of prevailing attitudes in society at first prevents him from asking Sammy to go with him and his family to baseball games. His daughter, Henrietta, is not as cautious. Awed by Sammy's ability to recite the play-by-play of a year-old Dodger game, she suggests that they invite him. Attending baseball games with Davy expands Sammy's geographical horizons and increases his psychological maturity. He goes to Ebbets Field, where he participates in the whole experience of the game. As true devotees, they arrive early to watch batting practice and leave at a leisurely pace after the crush has gone. Sammy and Davy decide that they will share ownership if either of them catches a ball.

When Sammy goes to baseball games with Davy and his family, people's stares remind them of the inequities of racism. On the playing field, an incident occurs during one of the games that reveals that racism still exists in the game. Ralph MacGruder slides into first to spike Robinson, who quickly steps aside. Elliot uses the incident to suggest the injustices that black people experience in everyday life.

Like Sammy's father, Davy has a heart attack. In Sammy's desperate attempt to find a cure for Davy, he proves that he has matured to the extent that he can act alone in difficult circumstances. He decides to buy a baseball and go to Ebbets Field to ask the Dodgers to autograph it for Davy. On one level, Sammy's project is more successful than he thought it would be. Jackie Robinson gives him the baseball that he hit that day and that he and his teammates have autographed. Davy appreciates the gift and its significance, but, on another level, the baseball disappoints Sammy; it does not cure Davy as he expects it to.

When Sammy's father died, he was too young to attend his funeral, but he overcomes his reluctance to go to Davy's funeral and thus fulfills his duty to Davy and indirectly to his father. He continues to suffer from depression, however, until he listens to a baseball game in which Jackie Robinson hits a double. Through Sammy's appreciation of Robinson's vitality, he regains his interest in life and is able to understand his relationship to Davy in its true perspective as an invaluable part of his life.

Critical Context

Barbara Cohen was a prolific writer of novels and picture books who found inspiration in Jewish tradition and in her experience as an outsider growing up in a small town during the 1930's and 1940's. Her highly successful first book, *The Carp in the Bathtub* (1972), is based on the celebration of Passover. *King of the Seventh Grade* (1982) tells of a boy's decision to accept his identity as a Jew and to celebrate his bar mitzvah. *Thank You, Jackie Robinson* deals with outsiders in different situations—a Jewish boy participates in the life of a black family and a black baseball star becomes a Brooklyn Dodger in the formerly segregated national pastime.

Other children's novels that have been influenced by *Thank You, Jackie Robinson* include Betty Bao Lord's *The Year of the Boar and Jackie Robinson* (1984) and Alan Lelchuk's *On Home Ground* (1987), in which immigrant youngsters from China and

Russia, respectively, are assimilated into their new country through their passionate enthusiasm for Jackie Robinson and the Brooklyn Dodgers.

Cohen's work has been well received, as attested by her numerous awards. Among them is the American Library Association Notable Children's Books citation for *Thank You, Jackie Robinson*. Another indication of the popularity of this work is the television version made in 1978 as an ABC afterschool special under the title *A Home Run for Love*.

Frank Ardolino

THAT WAS THEN, THIS IS NOW

Author: S. E. Hinton (1950-   )
First published: 1971
Type of work: Novel
Type of plot: Psychological realism
Time of work: The mid-1960's
Locale: A tough neighborhood in Tulsa, Oklahoma
Subject: Coming-of-age, drugs and addiction, education, friendship, and poverty
Recommended ages: 13-18

As best friends and foster brothers, Bryon and Mark struggle to survive in spite of poverty, violence, and ignorance; Bryon learns to accept responsibility and reject drugs and fighting, while Mark descends into drug dealing and vengeance.

> *Principal characters:*
> BRYON DOUGLAS, a sixteen-year-old hustler, who reflects upon the events of the previous year and examines how his decisions have changed his life
> MARK, Bryon's best friend, orphaned when his parents killed each other in a domestic dispute, who lacks an awareness of consequences
> M&M, a thirteen-year-old hippie whose pacifist beliefs and intelligent sensitivity make him vulnerable to brutal beatings from hoods and harsh criticism from his father
> CATHY, M&M's older sister, whose relationship with Bryon causes friction between Bryon and Mark

Form and Content

That Was Then, This Is Now chronicles the experiences of Bryon, the first-person narrator, and Mark, his best friend and foil, as they grow up in a tough, low-income neighborhood during the turbulent 1960's. Charlie's Bar, where the novel's flashback begins, provides the setting for much of the action, and Bryon's frequent foreshadowing comments create a tone of expectation and foreboding. The opening chapter moves quickly to a scene of violence, as members of the bullying Shepard gang jump M&M. Bryon and Mark rescue him, but M&M's victimization continues throughout the novel, reinforcing S. E. Hinton's depiction of the lack of justice on the streets, as does the story told by hospital patient Mike Chambers, a white youth who is beaten by black toughs when a girl he tries to rescue falsely identifies him as an attacker. Bryon understands why Mike does not hate black people as a result of his beating, but Mark considers him "stupid" for trying to help.

Despite their bond, Bryon and Mark have distinctly different ethical systems; Mark is on probation for hot-wiring cars, yet he ironically steals the principal's car each day in order to meet his probation officer. Talking his way out of that situation, Mark leads a seemingly charmed life; Bryon marvels at Mark's ability to get away with anything and admires his lionlike beauty and daring resourcefulness. For example, when Bryon and Mark owe Charlie three dollars, and Bryon worries about paying the bill before Charlie beats it out of them, Mark conveniently picks three dollars from the pocket of one of M&M's assailants. Mark rationalizes his actions, and, when Bryon's mother is hospitalized, Mark brings home money that Bryon suspects is either stolen or poker winnings. Since they cannot live without it, however, Bryon asks no questions.

While Mark seeks quick, dangerous solutions to their financial crisis, Bryon gets a job at a supermarket bagging groceries and develops a serious relationship with M&M's sister, Cathy. The divergent reactions of the boys to the increasing tension of their lives emphasize that people change. Bryon examines his decisions, often pondering the "what if" questions that are impossible to answer. Mark, on the other hand, does not want to consider difficult questions; his is a practical existence, and his decisions are based more on immediate need than on the ultimate outcome. Even Charlie's death, which haunts Bryon throughout the entire novel, is dismissed by Mark as "just one of those things that happen." Charlie dies because Mark and Bryon hustle two armed Texans who decide to take revenge, yet Mark feels no sense of responsibility or guilt.

Both Mark and Bryon end up in the hospital for stitches as a result of brutal beatings. Mark is hit in the head with a bottle at a school dance because a jealous Angela Shepard sends someone after Ponyboy Curtis (a character from Hinton's 1967 novel *The Outsiders*); Bryon is badly beaten by the Shepard gang because he is blamed for Mark's cruel prank against Angela (cutting her hair while she is drunk). In each case, the violence is senseless and mistaken, yet the injustice cannot be undone. Their different reactions to their experience, however, reflect the growing rift in the boys' relationship: When Mark wants to retaliate against the Shepard gang for Bryon's beating, Bryon makes him promise not to seek revenge. Bryon wants to break the "circle" of violence, but Mark feels frustrated by his inability to impose his own justice.

As Bryon's relationship with Cathy intensifies, he spends less time with Mark, who continues to supply the household with more money than could possibly be won or stolen. Mark becomes openly antagonistic toward Cathy, and she, too, does not hide her disapproval of him. When M&M runs away, Mark knows that he is hiding out at the hippie commune, but he does not tell Bryon until after the Shepard beating. When Bryon and Cathy go to the commune to bring M&M home, they find him in a delusional state, fearfully trapped in a nightmarish LSD reality.

Bryon and Cathy rush M&M to the hospital, but the cynical doctor offers little hope for a full recovery. Bryon's love for Cathy and her family overwhelms his loyalty to Mark, and, when he discovers Mark's stash of pills that same night, facing for the first time the truth about Mark's drug-dealing activities, he panics. In his worry and anger over M&M's bad trip, Bryon calls the police. Mark's subsequent arrest destroys the bond of brotherhood and friendship that sustained the two, and both are miserable in the final outcome. At the end of the novel, Bryon has only questions and self-pity upon which to reflect: Cathy is seeing Ponyboy, and Mark is a hardened inmate of the state reformatory. Mark has become a "dangerous caged lion" who is unable to get away with anything, and Bryon is a straight-A student who longs to return to a simpler, idealized past.

Analysis

While Hinton's works are often characterized as "problem" novels, *That Was Then, This Is Now* focuses on individual personal morality and ethical choices against a backdrop of social controversies. When Charlie gets his draft notice, for example, his bad temper reflects the seriousness of the call, but no protests or demonstrations, no statistics or images of the war intrude into the narrative. Conflict is frequently internal, since the lives of these teenagers revolve around day-to-day dilemmas that have life-or-death consequences. Hinton's characters reveal the importance of decisions about drug and alcohol use, family, work, and school, but she does not moralize. The destructive outcomes of events such as M&M's running away from home, his involvement with an older crowd, and his use of LSD suggest that these activities need to be reevaluated. Yet, the sympathy created for M&M as a character prevents total condemnation of his behavior. Readers understand his need to escape the painful reality of his father's criticism and the violence of his peers, but his ultimate loss of innocence and intellect teaches that these choices are costly.

Mark, too, eventually must pay for his choices, but Hinton evokes sympathy even for this drug-dealing car thief. As a nine-year-old, Mark witnessed his parents' fatal dispute over his true parentage; other than Bryon and his soft-hearted, economically devastated mother, Mark has no one. It is understandable that he would struggle to maintain these connections, even by illegal means. Nevertheless, the implicit warning about the moral responsibility of the dealer for the user, when Bryon and the readers associate Mark's actions with M&M's dangerous experience, suggests that good intentions alone cannot justify illegal risks. Young readers will recognize, too, the illusion of invincibility that sustains Mark throughout most of the story; his eventual arrest reveals that even if the consequences are not immediate, they may be harsh and irrevocable.

Bryon's choices, on the other hand, while they do not always have a happy outcome, do reflect a growing awareness of responsibility and consequences. When he compares the decency of Cathy's family to the violence of Angela Shepard's house, he makes a value judgment that rejects the tough ways of the street. He recognizes that violence tends to perpetuate itself, and, in choosing to prevent Mark from taking revenge on the Shepards, he hopes to break the cycle. When Bryon chooses to turn Mark in, however, he faces his most difficult internal conflict: a sense of betrayal. He turns his guilt upon himself and rejects his possible happiness with Cathy as a self-imposed punishment. Even when ethical, responsible decisions are made, Hinton implies, the consequences may not be altogether positive.

Critical Context

Although some critics have accused S. E. Hinton of sensationalism and glorification of rebellious antisocial behaviors, her work has received acclaim for its innovative use of symbolism, literary allusion, and diverse narrative techniques. *That Was Then, This Is Now* continues in the tradition of Hinton's first book, *The Outsiders*, building an atmosphere of violence and hostility in which her young protagonists must constantly struggle to survive. As Hinton herself has said, it is the people of her novels that concern her most, and her subsequent works, such as *Rumble Fish* (1975), *Tex* (1979), and *Taming the Star Runner* (1988), contain memorable characters facing authentic problems that have no pat solutions. Her first four novels have been adapted successfully into popular films.

Kathleen M. Bartlett

THEIR EYES WERE WATCHING GOD

Author: Zora Neale Hurston (1891-1960)
First published: 1937
Type of work: Novel
Type of plot: Psychological realism
Time of work: Around 1900
Locale: Florida
Subjects: Gender roles, love and romance, and race and ethnicity
Recommended ages: 15-18

Challenging the material standards of society, Janie Crawford finds love and personal fulfillment in her brief marriage to a poor but fun-loving younger man.

Principal characters:
JANIE CRAWFORD, who seeks personal fulfillment in three marriages
NANNY, Janie's grandmother and guardian, a former slave
LOGAN KILLICKS, Janie's first husband, a gloomy older man
JODY STARKS, Janie's second husband, the mayor of the first all-black town of Eatonville, Florida
VERGIBLE "TEA CAKE" WOODS, Janie's third husband, who is handsome, fun-loving, and passionate
PHEOBY WATSON, Janie's friend who listens to her life story

Form and Content

By introducing each chapter of *Their Eyes Were Watching God* with a thematic image, Zora Neale Hurston artistically changes the focus of the novel from an emphasis on Janie Crawford's linear chronology of her life to her internal development. For example, the "far horizon" to which ships sail and from which they return identified in the first line of chapter 1 becomes the protagonist's standard in evaluating the imaginative vision of each of her three husbands. By the concluding chapter, Janie reveals that she herself has traveled to and returned from the "far horizon," thus expressing her personal voyage of internal discovery.

Their Eyes Were Watching God begins as weary black workers sit on their porches and witness the return of Janie to her hometown of Eatonville, Florida. Expressing the superficial standards of society, these people believe that the widow of their deceased mayor, in returning alone and wearing overalls, has been financially exploited and abandoned by the young man with whom she had departed. When Janie's best friend, Pheoby Watson, questions the circumstances of her return, Janie responds that Pheoby can only understand if she knows the whole of Janie's life. It is within this framework that Janie proceeds to tell her story.

Janie's grandmother, a former slave, is determined to leave her granddaughter with a protector, in the hope that Janie can avoid the black woman's experience of being "the mule of the world."

At the age of sixteen, Janie marries her grandmother's choice, an older, lugubrious owner of a farm, Logan Killicks. Ironically, when Killicks expresses his intention to buy a mule, "gentle enough for a woman," Janie foresees a future very like the one from which her grandmother had sought to save her, and she leaves him to marry Jody Starks.

Although Janie knows that Jody is not the "dust-blossoming bee" of her dreams, he does speak of "far horizons," the word "horizon" expressing Janie's intention of fulfilling her dreamed destiny. While Jody fulfills his own dream of fortune and importance by setting up a general store and becoming the mayor of Eatonville, he relegates his wife to a lonely, subordinate position. At Jody's death, Janie savors the freedom of making her own decisions.

Her independent lifestyle is disturbed by the arrival of Vergible "Tea Cake" Woods, whom she intuitively believes to be the "dust-blossoming bee" of her dreams. In spite of the difference in their ages and fortunes and the criticism of the townspeople, Janie leaves Eatonville with Tea Cake and marries him. They travel south to the Everglades to work as migrant workers on the Muck. To all appearances as Janie works beside her husband in the fields, she would seem to be the "mule of the world" that her grandmother decried. The difference is that Janie works in the fields not because she has to, but because she and Tea Cake prefer to be together as much as possible.

Unfortunately, a hurricane destroys their idyll, and Tea Cake, in trying to protect Janie from a rabid dog, is himself bitten. In a hydrophobic rage, he attacks Janie, who shoots him in self-defense. After a brief trial that exonerates her, Janie returns to Eatonville.

At the conclusion of Janie's tale to Pheoby, her friend is so impressed that she claims to feel magnified by hearing the tale. Pheoby's response universalizes Janie's personal defiance of conventions into a challenge to all women to satisfy their personal dreams.

Analysis

Their Eyes Were Watching God appeals to readers of all ages because the primary conflict is so universal: the feeling of division experienced when the world (society, parents, friends) offers standards of happiness that do not satisfy the individual's personal needs. Listening to Janie's narrative, the reader realizes that life is not fair, as Janie suffers criticism from her first two husbands and the townsfolk in spite of her efforts to concede to their demands. In the end, Janie's loyalty to her own needs makes her indifferent to the townsfolks' comments. Likewise, young adults who are facing conflicting decisions can empathize with Janie's original concessions to security and her ultimate decision to sacrifice security in favor of a loving relationship.

As one example of the hollowness of society's standards of happiness, Zora Neale Hurston highlights the value ascribed to home ownership. As a child, Janie is taunted by her schoolmates because she does not live in her own home: She grew up in a small cottage erected in the yard of the white people who employed her grandmother. When she marries Logan Killicks, who provides her with her own home, she finds that it is isolated, "like a stump in the woods." In a similar way, her second husband provides her with a new white house where she can sit on a high white porch. Yet, she finds that this larger house, with its elevated place in society, only isolates her all the more. In contrast, in her third marriage, Tea Cake and Janie live in whatever room or small house they can rent. Because Tea Cake's personality attracts people to come into their house, however, Janie enjoys these fulfilling personal relationships much more than the lonely experience of owning her own home.

Clothes are another external status symbol that the author uses. Although Jody wants his wife dressed in fine clothes, he advertises his dominion over her by making her wear a head rag, worn by slaves and, later, by older women. After his death, Janie declares her freedom by doffing her head rag. Janie's feelings for her two dead husbands are also expressed in her clothes. After the death of Jody Starks, she wears expensive black-and-white dresses, the prescribed colors worn by a mourning widow. In contrast, after Tea Cake dies, Janie is so grief-stricken she is totally indifferent to society's conventions and wears overalls to his funeral.

Contrasting natural symbols are also used to devalue civilization's artificial icons. The lyrical description of the bee carrying pollinating dust to the blossoms of the pear tree expresses Janie's empathy with nature. This natural sympathy is emphasized when she luxuriates in the fecundity of the Muck.

Although *Their Eyes Were Watching God* is not a novel of protest against the unfair treatment of African Americans, Hurston does satirize racial discrimination, both white people's treatment of blacks and color discrimination within the black community. After the hurricane, black workers are instructed to put white bodies in coffins but black bodies in mass graves. Tea Cake observes wryly, "Look lak dey think God don't know nothin' 'bout de Jim Crow Law." The author equally criticizes black people who attempt to emulate the lives of white people. For example, Jody Starks sees himself as superior to the other black townsfolk. When he becomes mayor and financially successful, he builds a white house like those owned by white people. Another example of white envy is expressed in the character of Mrs. Turner, the black wife of a restaurant owner in the Muck. She despises people with darker skin like Tea Cake's and idolizes people with lighter skin like Janie's. In contrast, Janie finds her freedom and independence in the company of those who enjoy their black culture.

Critical Context

When Zora Neale Hurston's *Their Eyes Were Watching God* was first published, some critics praised the work's affirmation of women and black culture, while others criticized it as expressing a view of African Americans as happy and carefree, the stereotype generated by the black minstrels. For thirty years, the novel was out of print. It was the influence of novelist Alice Walker that propelled the work into prominence in the civil rights era. Walker particularly praised the use of black dialect and the emphasis on one woman's narrative influencing her listener. Other twentieth century works that emphasize acceptance of racial identity, a woman narrating stories, and a listener reacting to a narrative include *The Kitchen God's Wife* (1991), by Amy

Tan; *The Woman Warrior* (1976), by Maxine Hong Kingston; *Beloved* (1987), by Toni Morrison; and Walker's own *The Color Purple* (1982).

Some of Hurston's other novels, such as *Jonah's Gourd Vine* (1934) and *Seraph on the Suwanee* (1948), are written in dialect and contain strong female protagonists. Like the blossoming of the pear tree in *Their Eyes Were Watching God*, the mountain in Hurston's *Moses, Man of the Mountain* (1939) is a natural symbol expressing something greater than the pyramids of Egypt. Hurston, an anthropologist, laced her fiction with elements of the folklore and sermons of the black South, capturing for the reader the essence of this culture.

Agnes A. Shields

THEN AGAIN, MAYBE I WON'T

Author: Judy Blume (1938-   )
First published: 1971
Type of work: Novel
Type of plot: Domestic realism and psychological realism
Time of work: The early 1970's
Locale: Rosemont, Long Island, New York
Subjects: Coming-of-age, emotions, and family
Recommended ages: 10-15

Thirteen-year-old Tony Miglione struggles through a difficult year as he faces the onset of puberty and significant changes in his family's circumstances.

> *Principal characters:*
> TONY MIGLIONE, a thirteen-year-old boy experiencing puberty and dramatic changes in his family's situation
> RALPH MIGLIONE, Tony's older, married brother
> ANGIE MIGLIONE, Ralph's wife
> VIC MIGLIONE, Tony's father, whose tinkering results in new wealth and status for his family
> GRANDMA, Tony's grandmother, who has lost her larynx to cancer and can no longer speak
> MRS. MIGLIONE, Tony's mother
> JOEL HOOBER, Tony's next-door neighbor, his best friend in Rosemont
> LISA HOOBER, Joel's attractive sixteen-year-old sister

Form and Content

Then Again, Maybe I Won't is a short, fast-paced account of thirteen-year-old Tony's efforts to cope with the onset of puberty and the tremendous upheavals in his world occasioned by his family's sudden affluence. The account of Tony's ambivalent feelings about both his changing body and his altered circumstances provides an insightful examination of the daily disruptions and contradictions inherent in adolescent life.

As the novel opens, life is good for its narrator, Tony Miglione, whose days in Jersey City are routine and predictable. Somewhat apprehensive about starting junior high and annoyed by the cranky customers on his paper route, he nevertheless believes that he can handle whatever life has to offer. His parents both work hard to support their family, which also includes Tony's brother, Ralph, a seventh-grade teacher; Ralphs' wife, Angie, who attends teacher's college; and Tony's grandmother, who lost her larynx to cancer and cannot speak. Tony idolizes Ralph, known as the "Wizard of Seventh Grade Social Studies" at the local junior high, and he admires both his brother and sister-in-law for their dedication to education. He has a loving relationship with his grandmother, who cooks for the family, and respects his father for his knowledge of electronics, even though he does not share this interest.

Angie's unexpected pregnancy, however, precipitates a series of changes in the Miglione household. Fearful of being unable to provide for the growing family, Tony's father works hard to complete the project with which he has heretofore spent only his spare time tinkering in their basement. His completion of a new type of electrical cartridge earns for him the offer of a partnership in a large corporation, accompanied by a dramatic change in income and status. The family that was barely making ends meet in Jersey City launches a new life in the affluent Long Island suburb of Rosemont, and Tony immediately faces more changes than he had anticipated.

Tony's mother hires a housekeeper, who soon kicks his grandmother out of the kitchen and takes over the cooking, causing the old woman to take to her room, refusing even to attend Mass. Ralph gives up teaching to join his father in the electronics business, in which he had previously evinced no interest, and Tony's mother worries incessantly about being accepted by their new neighbors. Tony makes friends with the boy next door, Joel Hoober, whose occasional bouts of shoplifting make Tony uncomfortable. As if these major alterations were not enough, Tony must also deal with the changes taking place in his body. He spies on Joel's sixteen-year-old sister when she undresses at night, worries about wet dreams, and endures his father's bumbling attempts to talk to him about sex.

Tony's mounting concern over his own, and everyone else's, problems results in his hospitalization, as ever-increasing stomach pains finally become too serious to ignore. As his diagnosis reveals no physical problem, he begins to see a therapist, to whom he divulges the concerns that he has been internalizing for so long. Having an unbiased, understanding adult in whom to confide helps Tony gain some perspective, and he puts his difficult thirteenth year behind him and looks forward to life at fourteen.

Analysis

Even the title of *Then Again, Maybe I Won't* expresses the contradictory nature of adolescence, the confusing state of simultaneously wanting to be autonomous adult and dependent child, while awkwardly hovering somewhere in between. Judy Blume does a remarkable job of getting inside a teenage boy's mind and employing a believable adolescent voice to express the worries, fears, and confusion of this difficult age.

Blume thoroughly understands young people, and her juvenile characters ring true. Unlike many adults, she appreciates the seriousness of adolescent concerns. Tony internalizes everyone's problems, assuming responsibility and worry for events over which he has absolutely no control. He is anxious about money, afraid that at the rate his parents are spending their newfound wealth they will soon have nothing left. He mentally girds himself for the day when the money will run out and worries constantly about his grandmother's exile from the kitchen and how terrible she must be feeling. He worries about getting caught making crank phone calls with Joel, and he agonizes over whether he should report Joel's shoplifting to the police. The adults around him, wrapped up in their own concerns, have no inkling of what is going on in Tony's head. When Mrs. Miglione learns that Tony needs to discuss his problems with a psychiatrist, she responds, "What problems? A thirteen-year-old boy doesn't have any problems."

Tony possesses the typically adolescent tendency to focus on his parents' faults, to the exclusion of their virtues, and he develops an unerring sense of radar for adult hypocrisy. After the move to Rosemont, he begins to see his mother and father as people rather than as parents for the first time, and he is terribly upset by the revelation that they are flawed. He comes to the conclusion that all adults are phonies and is particularly critical of his mother, who begins to lose her own identity in her quest to fit in among the families in Rosemont, and his brother, whose seemingly easy rejection of his dedication to education hurts and puzzles Tony.

Blume's frank treatment of Tony's budding sexuality, although it may offend some adults, does not skirt the issues and feelings that are crucial to young people. Unlike most authors of juvenile fiction, she writes openly of wet dreams, of embarrassing situations involving unwanted erections, and of peeping in a neighbor's bedroom. She accurately portrays how all-consuming sexually related thoughts can be in a teenage boy's life, dealing with these thoughts humorously and honestly.

Blume is equally skillful at describing the often-complex dynamics of family life, conveying to young readers the reassuring notion that families are all different and none of them is by any means perfect. Tony feels let down by his mother's betrayal of his grandmother, his grandmother's refusal to leave her room, and his brother's defection from teaching, but he realizes that the Hoobers next door are even more "messed up." Joel Hoober gets caught shoplifting, Lisa smokes cigarettes and crashes her brand-new Corvette, and Mr. and Mrs. Hoober spend more time at the golf course and country club than at home.

Then Again, Maybe I Won't, although presumably taking place in the early 1970's, has a timeless appeal. Blume places her characters in a richly detailed, believable world without employing time-specific details, so that one boy's story can be relevant and meaningful to young readers for years to come, as if it were written yesterday and just for them.

Critical Context

Then Again, Maybe I Won't has all the familiar hallmarks of a Judy Blume novel: an honest portrayal of less-than-perfect children and their parents, a blunt approach to sexuality, and an authentic voice. This novel bears particular similarity to Blume's *Are You There God? It's Me, Margaret* (1970), which captures the same moment between childhood and adolescence in a young girl's life that *Then Again, Maybe I Won't* captures in a young boy's life. Both novels address similar concerns about sexuality, adjusting to a new town and school, and dealing with family tensions.

Then Again, Maybe I Won't also resembles J. D. Salinger's classic novel *The Catcher in the Rye* (1951). Tony, like Holden Caulfield, sees the world in black-and-white terms, holds adults up to impossibly high standards, and abhors hypocrisy. Each character relates best to a person outside the realm of adult "phonies"; Tony can find comfort only from his elderly grandmother, while Holden relates only to children.

Then Again, Maybe I Won't, although considered neither a juvenile classic nor likely required classroom reading, nevertheless occupies a highly regarded place in the young adult canon because it speaks so effectively and honestly to teenagers and preteens about what really matters to them. Blume is a master at exploring the minds and hearts of adolescents, presenting life from their perspective. While being neither judgmental nor didactic, she manages to teach valuable lessons about honesty, family, and growing up.

Mary Virginia Davis

THE THIRD WAVE

Author: Alvin Toffler (1928-   )
First published: 1980
Type of work: Social science
Subject: Social issues
Recommended ages: 15-18

In the wake of the agricultural and industrial "revolutions," society currently stands
at the threshold of a new revolution in both lifestyle and philosophy—a "third wave"
of human development spurred on by rapid and monumental technological advances
that are directly and significantly affecting the ways in which people work, interact,
and view their world.

Form and Content

The works of sociologist Alvin Toffler have been read and cited by sources as widely divergent as Richard Nixon and Mikhail Gorbachev. Appearing in 1970, *Future Shock* was a profoundly influential book dealing with the social neuroses created by the technological advances that characterized the mid-twentieth century. Adopting what Toffler called a "sociology of the future," this book introduced the concept of futurism into popular culture, asserting that these advances were having such a broad and perhaps threatening effect on humanity that a new value system must be developed in order to deal with the daunting phenomenon of continuous and radical change. *The Third Wave*, written some ten years later, is a more seasoned, optimistic sequel to its somewhat disquieting precursor. Although it does not abandon the assumption that technology is changing the way people live and work more rapidly and profoundly than most realize, *The Third Wave* confidently asserts that humanity can retain control over its future if society realizes that humankind currently stands at the dawn of a new historical epoch of similar proportions to the agricultural and industrial revolutions (what Toffler dubs the first and second "waves") that have traditionally defined the development of human civilization. Considered, as it should be, as a companion to *Future Shock*, *The Third Wave* confidently attempts to reclaim humanity's future, offering a vision of the twenty-first century that is markedly less "shocking" than that of Toffler's previous work.

Whereas *Future Shock* primarily examines the social and psychological transformations imminent in the coming decades, *The Third Wave* seeks to provide a historical context for Toffler's view of the future and provide what he refers to as a more "prescriptive" set of projections concerning how current technological development will invariably impact future growth. Roughly the first third of the book (chapters 1 through 10) is devoted to describing the three major historical epochs through which the civilized world, in Toffler's model, has advanced. The first wave of technological transformation arose and reached fruition between 8000 B.C. and A.D. 1650. This period is primarily characterized by the rise of subsistence farming and agriculture, which liberated humanity from its "primitive" beginnings as a nomadic culture of hunter-gatherers. The dominant movement of the second wave, which began in the mid-seventeenth century, was the Industrial Revolution. In a matter of decades, rampant industrialism transformed most of the world's population from agrarians into wage-laborers. Technologies developing around the extraction and use of fossil fuels, the proliferation of advances in mass-production techniques, and the rise of the consumer culture profoundly affected human life in ways that were as dramatic as the swiftness with which the Industrial Revolution took hold.

Toffler devotes the second two-thirds of *The Third Wave* to describing the epoch into which he believes the world is presently entering. This segment of the book maintains that the underlying tenets on which the Industrial Revolution was founded, and continues to be fueled, are no longer conducive to social or economic progress. In the light of the rapid depletion of nonrenewable energy sources and the development of new approaches to interpersonal communication, the workplace, and global economic interdependency, Toffler depicts the current generation as being in the throes of a major philosophical, economic, and sociopolitical metamorphosis that promises to be even more dramatic and monumental than the two that have preceded it.

Analysis

Although *The Third Wave* attempts to present a thorough, detailed historical synthesis and prescriptive forecast of near-future socioeconomic trends to a general audience, it can prove to be a difficult book for juvenile readers, as it assumes at least a cursory familiarity with the major technological forces that have characterized civilized history. It is a valuable book, however, for the young adult audience because it provides a candid but optimistic view of trends that will invariably affect occupational opportunities, economic philosophies, political dynamics, and lifestyle options in the coming decades. Since Toffler's main premises revolve around the assumption that humanity now stands at the beginning of a distinctive period in history, many adolescent readers should find *The Third Wave* to have an immediacy and urgency not often found in the literature of technological change, as its message is neither as bleak nor as cerebral as most contemporary literature that addresses this subject.

Toffler's style is most commonly characterized by his penchant for aphorisms and catchphrases, making him one of the most widely quoted social thinkers of the twentieth century. Yet, even Toffler's pithiest generalizations are backed by sound erudition; thus, his ideas are compelling without eluding the grasp of the average reader. Toffler is responsible for a number of words and phrases that have carved distinctive niches in the popular vernacular and consciousness: "future shock," "sociology of the future," and "the throw-away society," to name only a few. *The Third Wave* provides the world with at least two new catchphrases, both of which refer to concepts central to the book's primary thesis. Chapter 16 concerns "the electronic cottage," a home-centered work environment that may have been regarded as a novel, fanciful concept as recently as 1980 but that has become a more commonplace work option in the industrialized world as the rapid development in global telecommunications has begun to redefine traditional conceptions of "the office." Subsequent writers have adopted Toffler's phraseology of the work-at-home movement that has swept much of the West as high-tech computers and the Internet have continued to reach more households throughout the world.

A number of the middle chapters of *The Third Wave* attempt to explain how and why technological change has contributed to the dissolution of what many refer to as "the nuclear family." Curiously enough, Toffler views the traditional Western model of this primary social unit as an anachronism whose existence he attributes not to any naturalistic or evolutionary tendencies but to the factory-centered, producer/consumer society that was spurred on by the Industrial Revolution. Toffler argues that a new society of "prosumers" will develop as industrialism is surmounted by the ability of smaller, community-oriented groups, enabled by new task-specific technology, to generate products and services tailored toward their own needs rather than those created by the obsolete culture of mass production. *The Third Wave* asserts that the advent of "prosumption," which is actually more similar to preindustrial ways of thinking than to more modern ideologies, will probably define both economic and social development throughout the twenty-first century.

Critical Context

All three installments of Alvin Toffler's trilogy on how current trends promise to affect future development—including *Future Shock*, *The Third Wave*, and the volume that appeared ten years after it, *Power Shift: Knowledge, Wealth, and Violence at the Edge of the Twenty-first Century* (1990)—continue to be among the most widely read and influential works of contemporary popular sociology. Initially banned after its appearance in mainland China, *The Third Wave* later became the second most widely distributed book there, next to a volume of the speeches of Deng Xiopeng. *Future Shock* received the French award Prix du Meilleur Livre Étranger in 1972, and all three of the above-mentioned works have been translated into more than fifty languages. Toffler has been a visiting professor at a number of universities, including The New School for Social Research and Cornell University. Likewise, in the wake of the overwhelming success of his books, he has served as a consultant to a number of major international corporations.

The Third Wave particularly stands out as a work making large-scale historical synthesis both useful and relevant to the general reader, which perhaps serves as the basis for its broad international appeal. Its optimistic blueprint for constructively surmounting the demons of "future shock" and tackling society's most basic fears about the march of technological progress lend to its appeal as well, as Toffler seems at times to express a singularly hopeful vision of what is more often characterized as a daunting, doom-ridden twenty-first century socioeconomic landscape. Many young adult readers will find the view of the twenty-first century in *The Third Wave* both objective and passionate, making it a fresh and rewarding reading experience—one that makes social science more relevant, accessible, and exciting.

Gregory D. Horn

THISTLE AND THYME

Author: Sorche Nic Leodhas (Leclaire G. Alger, 1898-1968)
First published: 1962; illustrated
Type of work: Short fiction
Subjects: Love and romance, race and ethnicity, and the supernatural
Recommended ages: 15-18

This collection of tales and allegories examines the traits that unite the Scottish people.

Form and Content

In a collection of eighteen short stories, Leclaire G. Alger, writing under her Scottish name, Sorche Nic Leodhas, explores the character traits that define Scottish people. Written in the third person, some of the stories are illustrated with line drawings. Eight of the stories in this collection first appeared in *Heather and Broom: Tales of the Scottish Highlands* (1960), an earlier anthology by the same author.

One of the themes that is explored in the stories of *Thistle and Thyme* is that of love and the sacrifices or dangers that often come with it. When the daughter of the king of Scotland is kidnapped, the brave knight who promises to rescue her must undergo a series of trials before he can set her free. The beekeeper, who is one the central characters in one of the tales, must combat the powers of evil to liberate from an enchantment the young woman who will become his bride. The English lady who falls in love with a Scottish nobleman must pretend to be dead in order to escape her father, who has forbidden her to marry the man she loves. All the romances related in this work end happily, despite episodes of tragedy or loss. The lord of the Isles wins the love of Fionna, the seal king's daughter, only to lose it because of his quick temper. After a lifetime of repentance, however, the lovers are reunited.

In each tale can be found a clue to the character of the Scots. When these pieces are joined like the parts of a puzzle, a fairly accurate picture of the Scottish people begins to emerge. They are indeed canny, but the Scots are also brave, loyal, fearless, self-sacrificing, and, at times, reckless. They regard the supernatural and the miraculous with awe, and most of the tales in this collection feature enchantment. Some characters, such as the red-haired lass who drove the ghosts from the home of the man she eventually married, live to tell of their encounters with that other dominion, while others, such as the old woman who angered St. Cuthbert, are punished. Likewise, the pirate captain who steals the consecrated bells from the abbey of the glen perishes with his entire crew. Scots often see the work of mystic beings in unexplained phenomena, and this trait is an important component of Scottish myths.

Analysis

In *Thistle and Thyme*, Leodhas uses a number of Gaelic terms and words in the Scottish dialect that may confuse readers who are not familiar with these colorful, expressive, and complicated languages. While some terms may be defined by their use in context, a good dictionary that includes words from Gaelic and Broad Scots will prove an essential tool for the complete enjoyment of this work.

Strengths and weaknesses are assigned equally to men and women, and, although Scottish folklore celebrates the cult of the warrior, it also praises women who triumph over adversity. There is a rough but honest equality among the Scots that is ably illustrated in this collection of stories. The fisherman who allows a young woman to work for him as a servant discovers after a year that he loves her more than the haughty maiden he had sought as his bride. The servant girl adored him from the day that she first sought refuge under his roof, and her patient devotion is rewarded in time. The paradox of love that brings both bliss and woe is a common theme, and love that demands sacrifice is also a favorite device of Scottish bards. The young lass who risks her own life to deliver her sister from an enchanter finally breaks an evil spell, which frees both her sibling and the man with whom she falls in love.

The stories in *Thistle and Thyme* that concern fairies and the other supernatural beings who frequent the mountains and glens may be dismissed by the careless reader as mere superstitious nonsense invoked by an illiterate people terrified by their environment. When these tales are regarded as allegories, however, their great value as agents of instruction becomes immediately apparent. Those characters who arouse their anger have ignored or broken the rules of courtesy, taken unwarranted risks, or committed thoughtless acts. When a young mother boasts of the virtues of her baby, the infant is stolen and a changeling takes his place. It is only with the help of a wise woman that she is able to rescue her lost child. A Scottish housewife whose cakes are justly famous finds herself the prisoner of the fairies, who demand that she bake only for them. Using her wits, she wins her freedom, but she does not forget "the little people": For the rest of her life, they regularly receive offerings of cake from her. The lairdie with the heart of gold who shows great kindness to a family of homeless brownies has his generosity returned a hundredfold. This tale ably illustrates the Scottish adage that propitiation of the supernatural is essential to true happiness, if not survival.

Scottish society is based on the clan, a group composed of members of related families who vow allegiance to one leader and to one another. By counting kinship to forty generations, they are able to maintain a social cohesion that is truly remarkable. The unity and stability of the clan are threatened, however, when respect and traditional values are forgotten or social codes are disregarded. The evil lord who kidnaps the King of Scotland's daughter is destroyed, along with all of his followers, because he has violated the basic tenets of Scottish society. Bravery and physical prowess are not enough; loyalty and trust are also needed.

Critical Context

Several anthologies of traditional Scottish stories have been published, for various audiences. Some books, such as Barbara Ker Wilson's *Scottish Folk-Tales and Legends* (1954), are intended for younger people. Sorche Nic Leodhas' *Thistle and*

Thyme, however, requires an understanding of the structure of the clan system and a familiarity with a number of basic Gaelic words and expressions, and younger readers may be discouraged by the necessity of mastering these elements before sampling the rich cultural heritage of Scotland. Therefore, this anthology is probably better suited to the needs of older readers, who will find these stories entertaining and an excellent introduction to the rich canon of Scottish literature.

These stories have been used for generations to entertain people of all ages, regardless of social rank, and some have even been set to music. Their most enduring quality, however, is their ability to impart the concepts, principles, and modes of behavior that provide the foundations of Scottish society.

Clifton W. Potter, Jr.

THE TIGER'S WHISKER AND OTHER TALES AND LEGENDS FROM ASIA AND THE PACIFIC

Author: Harold Courlander (1908-   )
First published: 1959; illustrated
Type of work: Short fiction
Subjects: Nature, politics and law, religion, and social issues
Recommended ages: 13-15

Simple as well as sophisticated folk tales from the East provoke laughter, teach homely lessons and describe heroic feats.

Form and Content

Harold Courlander's *The Tiger's Whisker and Other Tales and Legends from Asia and the Pacific* consists of thirty-one tales complemented by twenty-two pen-and-ink illustrations. Seven of the tales are taken from ancient sources, eleven of them are taken from collections published between the mid-nineteenth century and 1948, and the remaining thirteen were collected by Courlander himself from oral sources. The stories vary between one and ten pages in length in a small-page format and also differ in level of sophistication in both style and message. The tales are grouped by place of origin: five tales from Burma; four each from India and China; three each from Indonesia (specifically Java) and Kashmir, which lies largely in northwestern India on the border with Pakistan; two tales each from Korea, Japan, and Arabia (the desert peninsula in southwest Asia that includes Bahrain, Oman, Qatar, Saudia Arabia, Kuwait, Yemen, and the United Arab Emirates); and one tale each from Malaya (in the Republic of Malaysia), Ceylon (Sri Lanka), Persia (Iran), Laos, Polynesia, and Yap. The difference in sophistication is explained in part by the area of origin, the more complex tales originating in India, China, Japan, Persia, and Arabia.

The three tales from Indonesia are all fool tales, featuring the comedic team of Guyo and Kono, who demonstrate how not to approach the problems of life. By their nature as fool tales, they are among the least sophisticated of the collection, entertaining in the manner of a short Laurel and Hardy film and whimsical in the solutions to their problems, which invariably underscore the value of ordinary common sense.

The lessons of other tales are imparted with a gentle and subtle humor. Typical of this type is "The Spotted Rug," from Arabia. A merchant who is desperate to save his daughter's life promises anything to the doctor who heals her. When the doctor is in need years later and requests a substantial but not unreasonable fee, however, the merchant's feelings have cooled and he finds a reason not to pay. What makes this tale of crass ingratitude so poignant is the reaction of the impoverished old medical man, who smiles sadly and says "Yes, I understand." The story, like others, is also the source of a proverb, in this case, defining ingratitude.

Human foibles are parodied also in politicians in "The Tiger's Minister of State," from Burma, and in scholars in "The Scholar of Kosei," from Korea, and "The

Scholars and the Lion," from India. Still other tales teach a sharp lesson in courtesy or common sense. "The Ambassador from Chi" tells of a king, who—apparently out of arrogance—decides to humiliate the ambassador of a neighboring land and of how the ambassador is able to turn each of the calculated insults back on the king.

The collection also features trickster tales from Japan, China, India, and Arabia, as well as two lengthier tales describing the exploits of Krishna in India and Maui in Polynesia that are excellent short examples of the heroic epic.

Analysis

The most notable characteristic of this collection, other than its great geographical range, is the diversity in the complication of plots and the subtlety of styles. The lighthearted humor of the Guyo and Kono stories is balanced by the admirable feats of Krishna and Maui and by the gravity and wisdom of didactic tales such as "The Tiger's Whisker," in which a young woman who despairs of her marriage learns that she has the capacity to save it. With some exceptions, this variation also holds true within the tales from individual areas, such as China. Even a reader acquainted with other folklore collections or legendary cycles will find it refreshing to move from the cosmopolitan battle of wits in "The Ambassador from Chi" to the simple fun of "The King of the Forest," in which the quick-witted fox takes advantage of the gullible tiger.

A number of the tales are edited for content. Courlander is careful to note that his version of the exploits of the god Krishna—taken from the *Harivamsha*, a supplementary book to the great Indian epic the *Mahabharata*—makes no mention of Krishna's divine connection as an avatar of the god Vishnu or as a reincarnation of the god Narayana. In other words, the author has adapted these tales of Krishna to the context of his collection, where one might expect to find subtlety and sagacity as well as adventure and humor, but not a mythological pantheon and its cultural apparatus. The Krishna section, like the Maui section, is entertaining in the manner of a heroic epic told in its simplest form, comparable on an elementary level to the labors of Hercules, and should thus be suited to the young reader whose inquisitiveness may lead to further reading in mythology proper. This adaptation seems to typify Courlander's approach: offering a variety of folk tradition forms in the hope that the young reader will be inspired to investigate one genre or nationality more closely.

Like many of the stories themselves, some of Courlander's "Notes on the Stories" at the end of the volume betray his interest in the lessons of truth and morality that may be drawn from oral traditions. One such interpretive comment is the note to "The Hidden Treasure of Khin," which reads: "A tale of typical Asian character, in which the father bequeaths a riddle to his son, that results in contentment and prosperity." In this context, it is not surprising to find truth named as the most powerful thing in life in "The Philosophers of King Darius" or knowledge as the sixth weapon in "The Prince of Six Weapons."

As in his other collections, Courlander also carefully explains the source of each tale, including his oral sources. The reader learns, for example, that the oral version of "The Philosophers of King Darius" from an Arabian informant employs an anonymous ruler instead of the Persian monarch as its central figure and that the literary version that names Darius is probably from an Oriental Jewish source. This fact accounts for the placement of the literary tale in Persia and its emphasis on the rebuilding of a temple in Jerusalem as the reward for winning the contest. Typically, Courlander chooses to amalgamate the two versions to create a tale that identifies Darius but tells of a readily comprehensible reward of gold and jewels, thus combining a more recognizable form of the theme with a famous and often-encountered figure from antiquity.

For the reader with no prior exposure to folkloric tales, the notes offer a number of comparisons and connections to other traditions and universal motifs. The description of Maui, which speaks of the coincidence of the trickster and the culture hero in one legend, points the way to a further investigation of the trickster-provider figure as described by Paul Radin, among others, in his prefatory note to *The Trickster* (1972). Notes on "The Tiger's Minister of State" and "The Prince of Six Weapons" suggest connections to the Brer Rabbit figure made famous by Joel Chandler Harris in *Uncle Remus and His Friends* (1892) and adapted and made famous again by Walt Disney Studios in the animated film *Song of the South* (1946). Other notes describe motif similarities with tales from Poland, Egypt, and West Africa and in the biblical judgments of Solomon.

Critical Context

Although Harold Courlander has published far more on African, African American, and related oral traditions and noticeably more on the Hopi of the American Southwest than on Asian oral traditions, he was based in Bombay, India, with the U.S. Office of War Information during World War II, and is conversant especially with Indonesian folk tradition. His acquaintance with Arabic tradition is complemented by his knowledge of Somalia, Ethiopia, Mali, and the Hausa peoples, where Arabic and specifically Islamic influence is significant.

This compilation is one of comparatively few English-language collections of Eastern folk tradition, one of which is Courlander's own *Kantchil's Lime Pit and Other Stories from Indonesia*, published in 1950. *The Tiger's Whisker and Other Tales and Legends from Asia and the Pacific* lies approximately in the middle of his most active publishing career of forty-six years (from 1936 to 1982). Like other of his collections, it enjoyed a renaissance in the 1990's, being republished by Henry Holt in 1996.

For those interested in the folklore and legends of Asia, this collection offers an eclectic introduction to a wide variety of lands. As a basic element of ethnic tradition, folklore is also the beginning of understanding different cultures, both their similarities to others and their unique characteristics.

James L. Hodge

TO ALL GENTLENESS
William Carlos Williams, the Doctor-Poet

Author: Neil Baldwin (1947-   )
First published: 1984; illustrated
Type of work: Biography
Time of work: 1883-1963
Locale: Rutherford and Paterson, New Jersey; New York City; Philadelphia; Paris; and Geneva
Subjects: Doctors and poets
Recommended ages: 13-18

Unlike his more bohemian friends, Williams determined to have a career and family as well as to be a groundbreaking poet.

Principal personages:
WILLIAM CARLOS WILLIAMS, a New Jersey family doctor who wrote poetry in his spare time
WILLIAM GEORGE WILLIAMS, his father, a hardworking British immigrant
RAQUEL HOHEB WILLIAMS, his mother, an artistically inclined Puerto Rican immigrant
EDGAR WILLIAMS, his younger brother and constant playfellow
FLOSSIE HERMAN, Williams' long-suffering wife
EZRA POUND, a poet who would both help and betray Williams
ROBERT MCALMON, the founder with Williams of *Contact* magazine

Form and Content

To All Gentleness: William Carlos Williams, the Doctor-Poet, tells the life story of one of the creators of modern American poetry. Neil Baldwin offers the portrait of a man who juggled a demanding medical practice with a literary career, making a success of both callings.

Williams was born in 1883, the son of a British immigrant father and a Puerto Rican immigrant mother, in Rutherford, New Jersey. Aside from his fourteenth year, which he spent with his younger brother Edgar at school abroad in Geneva, Williams remained rooted in Rutherford, loving the surrounding countryside and the quiet atmosphere. Therefore, it was no surprise, at college in Philadelphia, that although he wanted to be a writer, he did not side with his friend, poet Ezra Pound, who believed that an American writer should live in Europe as a footloose bohemian. Williams decided to stay put, making this decision as part of his belief that a poet's true subjects lay ready to hand. The aspiring poet enrolled to become a doctor, believing that such an occupation would give him ample literary material.

Both Williams and his brother set their caps for the same girl, Charlotte Herman. When she agreed to marry Edgar, William, out of pique, proposed to her sister Flossie, who unexpectedly accepted. She would become the ideal helpmate for him in their fifty-year marriage.

In 1910, Williams embarked on a dual career, setting out his doctor's shingle in Rutherford and becoming a denizen of avant-garde salons in nearby New York City. In one of these gatherings, in 1920, he met Robert McAlmon, a younger poet, whom he joined in setting up *Contact* magazine. This was a short-lived venture, but it introduced the doctor-poet to many other modernist writers.

Williams' course was not an easy one. His patients were generally poor and slow to pay. His ascent to recognition as a writer was also slow, much tardier than that of his friends abroad. Pound kept urging him to move overseas, where Williams would be better appreciated; but Williams, although he did visit Paris once, responded particularly with a set of essays, *In the American Grain* (1925), defending the unique qualities of civilization in the United States. To document further the artistic possibilities of his native place, in 1927 he began *Paterson* (1958), an epic poem portraying the history and significance of a New Jersey industrial town.

The outbreak of World War II brought even more activity, as the older Williams took on the caseloads of drafted doctors. Despite his patriotism, he was scandalized to find himself under surveillance by the Federal Bureau of Investigation (FBI) because of the fact that his erstwhile friend Pound was broadcasting anti-American diatribes from fascist Italy.

In 1948, Williams suffered a heart attack and soon retired from medicine. Having nothing to do except write, he was bored and took up lecturing. By this time, his importance as a writer had been acknowledged. He had little time, however, left to bask in this well-earned adulation. In 1956 and 1957, he suffered strokes and could function only in a severely diminished way until his death in 1963.

Analysis

Readers that come to this book through a love for Williams' poetry may be surprised to find that poetry is not always at the center of the story, not because no attention is paid to his writings but because Baldwin has set himself to portray the whole man. This biography brings Williams to life as a doctor and family man as well as a sincere writer.

It is the story of an unassuming man who possessed the strength to live two lives—fulfilling, as it were, both the practical ideals of his father and the artistic aspirations of his mother. The biographer shows that these parallel careers proved symbiotic. Williams' observation of his patients and family were poured into his writings, and this writing, grounded in thought about the continuities of America's hybrid life, helped him to empathize with his immigrant clientele.

It is not that Williams had no regrets. During World War II, with both his sons in the service, the poet began to think that he had neglected them as they grew up. Moreover, he later envied Pound the freedom that his friend had to write. Indeed, the friendly rivalry between these poets provides an important counterpoint in the biography. Pound was rebellious and sophisticated; Williams opted for conventionality (in lifestyle if not verse) and simplicity. Williams chose to write about common things in a simple language, while Pound came to write in a heavily allusive, elliptical style. In the end, there is an underlying, if unpronounced judgment against Pound, the apostate. After all, the freedom to write of which Williams was jealous was what Pound gained in an insane asylum, where he was put after a trial for his treasonable radio talks. Most would see freedom of this sort as hardly desirable.

This story of the two poets is especially valuable because it leads to reflections on compelling questions. The first is whether a writer's personal and political activities should be taken account of in an evaluation of the author's life. A second question would be "How was it that, after World War I, so many writers who seemed most representative of their nations, such as the Irish novelist James Joyce or the American writer Ernest Hemingway, lived, by choice, most of their adult lives outside their homelands?" Did this fact indicate that exile was necessary for authors to draw a bead on their native land?

For the first question, in Baldwin's opinion, the whole individual must stand or fall together. Hence, Williams, who tried to be decent in all realms, receives the highest marks. Baldwin rejects the idea that writers should be judged by their literature alone, claiming that what an author wrote is only one of the criteria for the type of evaluation that an enterprising biographer will set down.

On the second question, a less decisive answer is presented. The fact that an exiled writer can be true to his or her original roots is not questioned, but it is established that some writers, such as Williams, need to nurture their creativity on a single soil. Williams not only spent his whole life in the one place about which he wrote but also dipped into historical studies to deepen his understanding of that locale. The power of Williams' writing to unfold lyrically the happenings of everyday life and the beauties of the pastoral landscape certainly stem from how he steeped himself in his surroundings.

Critical Context

To All Gentleness avoids the traditional sins of biographies of writers that are meant for young adults: It neither downplays the faults of the subject nor overestimates that subject's achievements. The rather tawdry circumstances of William Carlos Williams' marriage, on the rebound from another woman, are presented. At the same time, Williams' literary triumphs are not glamorized. This is not the heroic story of an unorthodox writer's fight for recognition or of the dramatic creation of some singular masterpiece. Williams struggled for recognition over decades without making any sudden breakthrough. Moreover, he created not one towering work but rather a large body of exceptionally creative literature.

One might guess that Neil Baldwin's ability to write a biography that is engrossing without whitewashing or exaggeration grows from his own life and relation to the writer. He first became excited about Williams when, as a student, he took on the job of cataloging the poet's papers at a university library. Working for three years, he studied not only drafts and poems but also letters and diaries. Thus, he was able to see all sides of the doctor-poet. After graduating, Baldwin became a teacher of poetry in public schools. In 1981, he published *The Poetry Writing Handbook* out of this experience. Working with student writers, he could see the flow of creativity as a process, thus avoiding a fixation on unique monuments as the keys to understanding literature.

Readers can thank these two experiences, as well as Baldwin's thoughtfulness and taste, for preparing a work for young adults that, in the way that Williams' poetry did, shows that a life presented unvarnished and unromantically can yield the most well grounded truths.

James Feast

TO BE A SLAVE

Editor: Julius Lester (1939-   )
First published: 1968; illustrated
Type of work: Biography
Time of work: From the seventeenth century to the 1860's
Locale: Western Africa, the Jamestown colony, and the antebellum South
Subjects: Race and ethnicity
Recommended ages: 10-15

Drawing from a variety of sources and a plethora of quotes from slaves and former slaves, Lester illuminates some of the darkest annals of United States history in order to discover what it was to be a slave.

Principal personages:
    CHARLES BALL, an American-born slave
    JOSIAH HENSON, a former slave
    SOLOMON NORTHUP, a black man who was born free in the North but
        who was kidnapped and enslaved before regaining his freedom

Form and Content

Decades after its publication in 1968, *To Be a Slave* remained among the relatively small number of books that draw heavily from primary sources to provide young people with history of the African American experience.

The dedication, a brief note quoting an unnamed former slave, a table of contents, an author's note, and a prologue precede a text which is so moving that readers who skipped these introductory features will probably be compelled to go back and read them as well. Similarly, the epilogue is also likely to be read and the bibliography studied. All these components contribute greatly to the text itself by providing background, authenticity, and documentation.

In seven chapters, *To Be a Slave* presents verbatim transcripts of disclosures made by Africans and African Americans who were enslaved in the antebellum South and a few others who were firsthand observers of slavery. All these contributors are specifically identified when possible, immediately after their words are presented. Background information and commentary are offered by Julius Lester and are presented in italics so that they are easily distinguishable from the transcripts. These vivid threads of history are woven into a most revealing tapestry made more compelling by the fact that these are the first-person narratives of minor figures who were, in the view of Lester, the true movers of history, the bedrock of black history—those whose actions are symbolically represented by the famous. The accounts are dramatic—sometimes bitter, always poignant.

In the author's note, Lester avers that one of the greatest overlooked sources of information about slavery has been the slaves themselves. He explains how he drew from the words of those who had been enslaved to create the book, using two large databases. Before the Civil War, narratives of former slaves became a literary genre through the efforts of abolitionists who wrote down the stories of thousands of those who had escaped. After the Civil War, interest in such narratives dwindled until the 1930's, when workers for the Federal Writers Project took down the stories of those former slaves still living. Lester also explains that these databases differ in one significant way: language. The abolitionists sometimes rewrote the stories to meet literary standards and to avoid giving the opposition fodder, based on the former slaves' language, for the grist mill on black inferiority. In contrast, Federal Writers Project workers were as interested in preserving the former slaves' speech patterns and language as the stories themselves. Lester notes that in order to make his book more readable, he modernized punctuation and the dialect spellings that resulted from white writers' attempts to transcribe the former slaves' speech.

Analysis

Lester's first trip to Mississippi was in 1964; he stood alone in a field and tried to know what his slave ancestors felt standing there 150 years before. That experience was the genesis of *To Be a Slave*, *Long Journey Home* (1972), and *This Strange New Feeling* (1985). Clearly, these are personal stories for him.

The most moving aspect of the book are the accounts of former slaves. Their narratives are compelling beyond description, impossible to ignore or forget—whether in their own words or those of an abolitionist. There is no fictionalizing. Physical, emotional, and socioeconomic truths are raw; little is spared or softened. Through Lester's meticulous selection of the former slaves' narratives, his own commentary, and the artful compression of time, the strong character and resilience of those enslaved is realistically and dramatically shown, as is the willful inhumanity of those who enslaved them.

The accounts relate the slaves' experiences, from their abduction from Africa through their presence on slave ships, auction blocks, and plantations. They relate their efforts to escape and their experiences with the Civil War, emancipation, and the Ku Klux Klan. Most of the accounts are wrenching: babies drowned by mothers not wanting them enslaved, babies drowned as a result of the greed of plantation owners, beatings, suicides, and brainwashing.

Without mitigating the slaves' horrors and hopelessness, Lester also includes some happier accounts, such as of sneaking away at night for church or parties and of Christmas—one of four holidays generally celebrated on the plantations. One humorous account is of how a slave in Mississippi had his owner believing he was too blind to work—until emancipation came.

Lester does a beautiful job of providing a multidimensional picture of slaves and, to a lesser extent, their owners. Among slaves, significant differences are revealed in such matters as how field and house slaves were treated, saw themselves, and treated one another; the attitudes and behaviors of those born free in Africa or the United States and then enslaved and those born into slavery in the United States; the acceptance of servitude; and loyalty to slaveholders and the reasons for it. Slaveholders are shown to have varied in attitude, behavior, and socioeconomic station. The slaves are the heroes in this book, and a few of the traditional American heroes are somewhat diminished by the truths told of them. A Polish poet who once stayed at Mount Vernon for two weeks reveals the pitiful conditions in which George Washington kept his slaves. An excerpt from an essay by Thomas Jefferson on the inferiority of black people is presented. Several slaves' accounts reveal some disappointment with the way in which Abraham Lincoln handled emancipation. Others express resentment or hatred for Harriet Beecher Stowe, the author of *Uncle Tom's Cabin* (1852).

In a few cases in Lester's commentary, generalizations are offered that should have been avoided for complete accuracy. On balance, however, the work is objective.

Tom Feelings, an African American who has received numerous awards for his art, including the Caldecott Medal and the Coretta Scott King Award, drew the art for *To Be a Slave*. Most of the thirteen illustrations (all full-page spreads) show dark, somber figures and scenes. All perfectly match the tone of the text. It is interesting to note that Feelings' almost wordless volume *The Middle Passage: White Ships/Black Cargo* (1995), although graphic and violent, is a perfect complement to the first part of *To Be a Slave*. Indeed, the illustration preceding the title page and those on some of the other pages could easily fit in either book.

Critical Context

To Be a Slave, one of Julius Lester's first books for young people published by a major publisher, is a milestone. Prior to its publication, few books on the subject that provided such documentation existed for young people. With it, Lester became one of the few African Americans writing for young people in the 1960's to enjoy mass marketing and high literary acclaim.

In 1968, when *To Be a Slave* was published, Lester also had published *Look Out, Whitey!: Black Power's Gon' Get Your Mama!*, a history and explication of the Black Power movement in the United States, and was serving as the field secretary of the Student Nonviolent Coordinating Committee (SNCC), an organization about which the Establishment and much of the American public had strong reservations.

Attesting the veracity of the literary community, critical response to *To Be a Slave* was good. In 1969, it was a runner-up for the Newbery Medal. Major textbooks on literature for young people and literature reference sources have consistently praised the work. It is often described as forceful, well constructed, and important.

Subsequent works by Lester continue to illuminate the African American experience in varied ways. In *Long Journey Home*, which tells the stories of six slaves and freedmen, Lester again drew from primary sources, interviews, and such footnotes to history as letters, bills of sale, and marriage registers. Lester's work for young people conveys much about the African American experience, and his sense of morality speaks to all.

In an educational context, Lester's *To Be a Slave* and *Long Journey Home* correlate beautifully with Paula Fox's Newbery Medal-winning *The Slave Dancer* (1973), Feelings' profoundly moving wordless book *The Middle Passage*, and the volume of Milton Meltzer's trilogy *In Their Own Words: A History of the American Negro* (published in 1964, 1965, and 1967, respectively) that covers the years from 1619 to 1865. Also worthy of note is that Caedmon produced a sound recording derived from *To Be a Slave*, with Ruby Dee and Ossie Davis in the roles of various slaves telling their own stories and Lester himself presenting the narrative framework to make the work whole.

Sandra F. Bone

TO TAKE A DARE

Authors: Crescent Dragonwagon (1952-   ) and Paul Zindel (1936-   )
First published: 1982
Type of work: Novel
Type of plot: Domestic realism and social realism
Time of work: The 1980's
Locale: The small town of Excelsior Springs, Arkansas
Subjects: Coming-of-age, family, jobs and work, and sexual issues
Recommended ages: 13-18

Chrysta Perretti runs away from home at the age of thirteen but turns her life around when she realizes that she cannot run from herself and her past.

Principal characters:
> CHRYSTA PERRETTI, a teenage runaway from Chicago trying to make a new life for herself in a small Arkansas town
> LUKE BEAUFORD, a college student and the assistant kitchen manager at the General's Palace Hotel
> DARE WILKIE, an abandoned twelve-year-old whom Chrysta takes in to live with her
> LISSA DANFORTH, another runaway who becomes Chrysta's best friend
> NETTIE CARLISLE, Luke's aunt, a cook at the General's Palace Hotel
> HUGH DEWLING, the owner of the General's Palace Hotel
> HOWIE SNOODGRASS, the kitchen manager at the General's Palace Hotel, who sexually harasses Chrysta
> MR. and MRS. PERRETTI, Chrysta's parents

Form and Content

To Take a Dare is the disturbing yet inspiring story of a young girl who runs away from home at the age of thirteen. Chrysta is a bookish and an only child; her mother eats obsessively and will not leave the house, and her father refuses to address the situation, maintaining the family in an uneasy coexistence. Chrysta endures her strange home life until she suddenly undergoes a rapid physical development and appears to be much older and more sexually mature than her thirteen years. Unable to deal with Chrysta's development, Mr. Perretti withdraws even further from the family. Alone and confused, Chrysta falls in with a crowd that experiments with drugs, alcohol, and sex. When her father finds out that Chrysta has contracted gonorrhea, his hatred and anger become so intolerable that Chrysta finally runs away.

After spending a few years on the road, Chrysta decides to settle down in a small Arkansas town and make a new start in life. Although she is still an underage runaway, she easily passes as a young woman in her twenties and gets a job as a cook at the General Palace's Hotel in Excelsior Springs, Arkansas. At first, Chrysta simply works and keeps to herself, but as she gets to know the town's kind inhabitants, Excelsior Springs begins to feel like home.

Many people come into Chrysta's life, and all have a profound effect on her. She meets a twelve-year-old boy named Dare Wilkie whose father has essentially abandoned him, leaving him in the care of various acquaintances. When Chrysta discovers that Dare has been sneaking into a local school to sleep at night, she decides to take him in, recognizing that he is at a turning point similar to that which Chrysta experienced herself. Chrysta also meets Luke Beauford and Nettie Carlisle, who also work in the restaurant kitchen; Luke is a college student, and Nettie is the aunt who reared him when his parents died in a car accident. Although Chrysta initially dislikes Luke because his quiet seriousness is so foreign to her, they eventually fall in love, and Chrysta is able to share her past with him. She earns a job promotion and eventually even decides to try to make peace with her parents. The ending, however, is not entirely happy; Dare becomes hostile toward Chrysta, and she realizes she is powerless to help him.

Written from Chrysta's first-person perspective, *To Take a Dare* is a particularly warm and personal story. At Luke's urging, Chrysta writes down her experiences so that she can come to understand how she has developed from a rebellious runaway into a mature young adult capable of holding down a job with considerable responsibility. The story is told in retrospect, with occasional present-tense passages in which Chrysta expresses the pain of reliving her past through her writing. Although the book is not illustrated, a distinctive touch is added in the form of a postcard and a letter that are typeset to appear as though they were handwritten.

Analysis

To Take a Dare is an entertaining and heartwarming story that also conveys several messages to the reader. The main theme is that people with problems eventually reach a crossroads where they either learn to take responsibility for themselves, perhaps by accepting help when they need it, or grow more hostile toward the world and reach a stage that may be beyond help. The authors drive this point home by drawing obvious parallels between Chrysta's and Dare's thirteenth birthdays. This was one of the most miserable days in Chrysta's life: Her dog was hit by a car—and Chrysta suspects her mother left the gate open on purpose, letting the dog escape—and Mr. Perretti does nothing to comfort her. In shocked numbness, Chrysta loses her virginity that night, deciding that she may as well do what her father assumes she has been doing anyway. Although Chrysta does not run away from home that day, she recognizes her thirteenth birthday as a turning point when she realizes that she will have to fend for herself, without assistance from her parents. Chrysta later reaches two more turning points: first, when she stays in Excelsior Springs rather than continuing to "run," and, second, when she accepts help from Luke and other residents of Excelsior Springs when her earlier case of gonorrhea necessitates an expensive operation.

Dare's thirteenth birthday is as miserable as Chrysta's. At this point, Dare has been staying with Chrysta for some time, but their relationship has been steadily declining, in part because of Chrysta's growing feelings for Luke. Chrysta issues Dare an ultimatum: He must decide to make an effort and work things out with her, or he must leave. Belatedly, Chrysta realizes that the day that she has chosen for this deadline is Dare's birthday. When His father does not arrive for a promised visit, Dare turns on Chrysta, becoming violent and destructive before walking out. She can only watch him leave, knowing that he has chosen his path.

This novel also addresses the issue of sex. When Chrysta begins sleeping with the boys in her school crowd, she decides that there is nothing special about sex—it is simply another sensation, neither good nor bad. She does not understand why her rapid physical development resulted in a sudden popularity at school, when before she was considered a quiet loner. When Chrysta falls in love with Luke, however, she discovers for the first time why sex with the right person can be a special and meaningful experience. Without preaching, the novel clearly conveys that sexual relations are not to be taken lightly. In addition, when Chrysta's operation results in the loss of her ability to have children in the future, she is greatly saddened but gains a new wisdom about the complex connections between love, sex, and the responsibility of having children.

Finally, the novel touches upon the issue of personal guilt. In spite of her anger toward her parents, Chrysta feels guilty because she could not get along with them, wondering if the situation was somehow her fault. Similarly, when Dare leaves, Chrysta cannot help but wonder what she could have done differently to help him. Yet another instance occurs when Chrysta is sexually harassed by her supervisor, Howie Snoodgrass. At first, Chrysta believes that perhaps her behavior or appearance are responsible for Howie's unwelcome advances. She learns from Luke, however, that even people as responsible and serious as he is can be very sensitive, experiencing guilt and regret over things that they cannot always control. This realization helps Chrysta to attain a sense of closure for the tumultuous period in her life and to believe that she is a good and valuable person.

Critical Context

To Take a Dare is a frank, honest examination of circumstances that can lead a teenager to run away from home. Chrysta, Dare, and Lissa have all suffered parental abuse of some form, whether physical, emotional, or mental, yet they all deal with their problems in different ways. When first published, this novel was one of a growing number of works that attempted to address serious issues, some of which had been considered "inappropriate" for young readers, instead of merely trying to entertain. It is similar in content to Norma Klein's novels, particularly *It's OK If You Don't Love Me* (1978), which portrays teenagers as sexual beings, struggling with their new identities while dealing with divorce and their parents' own insecurities.

Although Crescent Dragonwagon had published several children's picture books, this was her first young adult novel. Paul Zindel, on the other hand, had written many young adult novels dealing with subjects such as teenage pregnancy and parental pressure to succeed. Although these books are also well written, the added talents of

Dragonwagon give *To Take a Dare* a somewhat softer style and more sympathetic characters. In addition, by writing from her own surroundings in a small town in the Ozarks of Arkansas, Dragonwagon has created a vivid and memorable setting for this novel.

Amy Sisson

TONGUES OF JADE

Author: Laurence Yep (1948-   )
First published: 1991; illustrated
Type of work: Short fiction
Subjects: Animals, family, and nature
Recommended ages: 10-15

These seventeen folktales collected from Chinese immigrants who came to the United States in the nineteenth century not only offer young readers remarkable insights into Chinese culture but also provide storytellers with excellent multicultural materials.

Form and Content

Like its companion volume, *The Rainbow People* (1989), *Tongues of Jade* is a collection of folktales retold by Laurence Yep. Sixteen of the seventeen stories originally appeared in *The Golden Mountain*, a book of Chinese folktales collected in the 1930's in Oakland's Chinatown by Jon Lee, and the last story, "The Ghostly Rhyme," is a story gathered by Wolfam Eberhard in San Francisco's Chinatown. These were tales recalled by Chinese immigrants who came to work in the United States in the nineteenth century who called themselves "guests of the Golden Mountain." As a leisure activity, they told one another stories that illustrated aspects of Chinese culture with which they identified. Following the Chinese idea of jade as a preserver, the book as a whole suggests that by telling stories, the storytellers' jade tongues maintain part of the group's cultural heritages.

Through the use of simple and concise language, Yep artfully retells the stories in third-person narrative form and organizes them into five sections according to the following themes: "Roots," "Family Ties," "Wild Heart," "Face," and "Beyond the Grave." At the beginning of each section, a brief introduction links the theme to Chinese culture. These introductions assist readers in understanding the meaning and significance of the stories. The attractive black-and-white watercolor illustrations by David Wiesner preface each story and augment the simple retellings beautifully.

The first section, "Roots," contains three earthy tales with strong connections to China. "The Green Magic" is a story of two brothers. Emerald, the older boy, is happy with his green thumb, while Jade, the younger brother, wants to create great magic in the world. "The Guardians" is a tale about the relationship between the farmer and the earth. In "The Cure," a boy finds a magic melon in which three pretty fairies reside.

Four tales in the second section, "Family Ties," portray the sense of responsibility to one's family. The title character of "The Little Emperor" is spoiled and does not see the love and effort that his mother spends on him; ironically, his mother dies before he can demonstrate his change of heart. The "Royal Robes" tells how the peacock's first performance of his duty brings a splendid reward of beauty. "Fish Heads" is a story of how an undutiful daughter-in-law is turned into a monkey because of a trick that she plays on her mother-in-law. A wife's love leads her to seek assistance in defeating the dark supernatural force portrayed in "The Phantom Heart."

The third section, "The Wild Heart," has four tales. Charity as a virtue is emphasized in "The Snake's Revenge" and "Waters of Gold." "The Foolish Wish" is a humorous ghost story, and "The Tiger Cat" relates an interesting story of how tigers and cats became what they are today.

The fourth section, "Face," is divided into three stories. "The Rat in the Wall" humorously illustrates the lesson learned by a rich man who takes too much pride in his wealth. "The Fatal Flower" is a moral story of a young girl who craves physical beauty and, because of her intense desire, almost loses her life. "The Teacher's Underwear" facetiously depicts a teacher who falls into disgrace and exile because of his pride and poverty.

The last section, "Beyond the Grave," contains three more stories related to magic and supernatural forces. In "The Magic Horse," a fascinating flying horse comes alive in a poor painter's last painting and brings fortune to the man's son. In "Eyes of Jade," the jade collector is sent to the underworld because of his greediness. "The Ghostly Rhyme" is a humorous tale about a ghost who is a poet and is unable to rest until he remembers the last line of a poem.

Analysis

Tongues of Jade is an important collection of folktales for young readers because it serves not only as a vehicle for understanding immigrant history but also as a tool for teaching American students about the ethnic minorities in the United States. The tales provide insight into Chinese culture and unveil the heritage and values that many Chinese Americans prize and pass on from generation to generation. The sections cover a broad range of subject areas, and subthemes such as the ethic of hard work, self-sacrifice, perseverance, filial piety, responsibility, charity, and modesty emerge.

Hard work, responsibility, self-sacrifice, and the dutiful performance of one's role are emphasized through several tales, such as "The Guardian," "The Little Emperor," "Royal Robes," and "Fish Heads." The hardship that farmers experience is depicted in a lively manner in "The Guardians." Furthermore, self-sacrifice is emphasized as a virtue, one that glorifies those who go beyond their social roles. The idea of what should be valued and how one should behave in Chinese culture provides non-Chinese readers the opportunity to learn about Chinese and Chinese American cultures and to gain different perspectives about things that they know in their own cultures.

Filial piety and respect for elders are important traditions in Chinese culture. Being disrespectful, even to the extent that one does not take care of one's parents or elders, is almost considered a crime. For example, the little emperor is despised by the villagers because of his disrespectful attitude toward his mother. Later, he dies of grief as a punishment for his deeds. In "Fish Heads," the deceitful daughter-in-law is turned into a monkey as a result of her actions. This kind of behavior is so serious that the author indicates that she would have "made a far better pet than human being." Filial piety is based on the concept that children respond to the effort and love that their parents have shown in rearing them. This concept is strongly emphasized in Chinese culture, but it is not so easily recognized in American culture. Reading about the Chinese view would offer a valuable learning experience to many young readers.

Yep believes that living in a strange and oftentimes hostile land requires cooperation and charity among Chinese immigrants. In a land that was not their own, these immigrants needed to depend on their own people. For example, in "The Snake's Revenge," a hunter's life is spared from the lethal bite of the evil snake because he has helped an old woman. Also, Auntie Lily in "Waters of Gold" obtains gold from a bucket of dirty water because she is generous in helping other people, even strangers and beggars. Her charity is well rewarded, and it has helped to change her mean neighbor into a good person as well. Auntie Lily's spirit is inspiring; she is never discouraged by the fact that she lost her wealth in helping others and that she must work as a cheap laborer in order to support herself. She continues to help people whenever she can. Stories such as these are not only fun to read but also encouraging for young readers.

Modesty is a virtue greatly valued in the Chinese tradition. Taking too much pride in one's wealth, as the rich man does in "The Rat in the Wall," somehow will result in misfortune. "The Teacher's Underwear" is a comical story of one arrogant teacher who takes too much pride in his social status. The teacher who is too haughty to show his poverty to the villagers not only loses his job but also is forced into exile. Without thorough consideration, following norms as to the proper thing to do or say according to one's social role is oftentimes not wise, and it can cause unnecessary misunderstanding and misfortune.

Critical Context

Laurence Yep has written many works related to his Chinese American heritage and experience. His novels *Dragonwings* (1975) and *The Dragon's Gate* (1993) were both named Newbery Honor Books. In digging into his culture, Yep has done a exceptional job in turning his cultural heritage and experience into exciting, imaginative, and entertaining works for young readers.

Both *Tongues of Jade* and *The Rainbow People* are intended to introduce Chinese and Chinese American culture to young readers. They are excellent collections of Chinese folktales that reveal those things valued by many Chinese and Chinese Americans and passed down through the generations. This kind of work is extremely important in moving young adult literature into the direction of multicultural education. Young readers in a culturally diverse society such as the United States will certainly benefit from books that offer different cultural perspectives. More important, such works can cultivate cultural awareness and sensitivity among young readers.

Shwu-yi Leu

THE TRAGEDY OF PUDD'NHEAD WILSON

Author: Mark Twain (Samuel Langhorne Clemens, 1835-1910)
First published: 1894
Type of work: Novel
Type of plot: Social realism
Time of work: 1830-1853
Locale: Dawson's Landing, a fictitious Missouri village on the Mississippi River
Subjects: Crime, family, race and ethnicity, and social issues
Recommended ages: 15-18

For two decades, the citizens of Dawson's Landing regard David Wilson as a "pudd'nhead"—until he brilliantly unravels a murder mystery and proves that a slave and a free man were switched in infancy.

Principal characters:
> DAVID WILSON, a lawyer whose brilliance is misunderstood by the residents of Dawson's Landing
> PERCY DRISCOLL, a prosperous businessman whose wife dies shortly after bearing his son in 1830
> ROXY, Driscoll's mulatto slave, who switches her own baby with Driscoll's
> TOM DRISCOLL (the true CHAMBERS), Roxy's natural son, who grows up as the son of Percy Driscoll
> CHAMBERS (the true TOM DRISCOLL), Percy Driscoll's natural son, who grows up as the slave Chambers
> JUDGE YORK DRISCOLL, the chief citizen of Dawson's Landing and the brother of Percy Driscoll, whose son he adopts
> ANGELO and LUIGI CAPELLO, Italian twins who settle in Dawson's Landing in 1853

Form and Content

With twenty-two chapters, *Pudd'nhead Wilson* is half the length of Mark Twain's *Adventures of Huckleberry Finn* (1884). Unlike that vernacular masterpiece—which is narrated by Huck—*Pudd'nhead Wilson* is a plain third-person narrative set mostly in one place—Dawson's Landing, a Southern village modeled on Twain's boyhood hometown. The novel begins on February 1, 1830, when Percy Driscoll's wife and his slave Roxy both deliver sons. A week later, Driscoll's wife dies, leaving Roxy to rear both babies. Around this time, a young lawyer named David Wilson comes to town. An odd remark that he makes immediately gets him branded a "pudd'nhead." Never able to get a legal case, he makes his living as a surveyor and dabbles at collecting fingerprints—a hobby that makes him appear even more foolish.

Roxy is one-sixteenth African by parentage and could easily pass for white, except for her strong slave dialect. Chambers, her son by a white man, so resembles Driscoll's son that only she can tell them apart. When the babies are several months old, something happens to make Roxy fear that Chambers might be sold "down the river." To ensure that this never happens, she decides to drown her baby and herself. A better idea occurs to her, however, and she switches the babies. No one else will guess their true identities for twenty-three years. From this point in the narrative, the boys are known by their false names. Roxy's son grows up as "Tom Driscoll"; unaware of his true identity, he treats Roxy badly and abuses "Chambers"—the white slave whose place he has taken.

Through the novel's first five chapters, twenty-three years fly by. Percy Driscoll dies in 1845; on his deathbed, he frees Roxy, who then leaves to work on steamboats. Tom is adopted by Percy's brother, Judge York Driscoll. Later, Tom attends Yale University, returning home with drinking and gambling habits that get him into serious trouble. By 1853, he is burglarizing houses to pay his gambling debts. That year, aristocratic Italian twins, Angelo and Luigi Capello, arrive in town. When Tom publicly insults them, Luigi kicks him. Tom responds by taking Luigi to court, outraging Judge Driscoll because he has not settled the affair "honorably." The judge challenges Luigi to a duel himself, but no one is seriously hurt. Afterward, the twins' popularity soars, as does that of Wilson, who has acted as Luigi's second in the duel. Tom gets revenge by telling his uncle that Luigi is a confessed assassin, turning the judge against the Italians, with disastrous results.

Meanwhile, Roxy returns home, eager to see Tom, but is distressed to hear about his bad habits. After he greets her rudely, she reveals the truth of his parentage and threatens to expose him as a slave if he does not obey her. Demanding a share of his allowance money, she insists that he clear his debts to avoid jeopardizing his inheritance. Eventually, however, Tom's financial situation becomes so desperate that Roxy lets him sell her into slavery, until he can buy back her freedom. Tom betrays his mother by selling her down the river, but she escapes from a plantation and makes her way to St. Louis to confront him again. Her fierce insistence that he purchase her freedom immediately drives him to rob his own uncle. While committing this crime, he kills the judge with a knife that he stole earlier from the Capellos, who reach the murder scene immediately after he flees. Charged with murder, the Capellos engage Wilson as their attorney.

The murder trial finally brings Wilson to the fore, letting him demonstrate his true brilliance. The evidence against the twins is overwhelming, but Wilson uses fingerprints to prove that Tom Driscoll handled the murder weapon. Even more sensational is his use of prints to prove that Tom is actually the slave Chambers. Tom is later convicted of murder, but he is pardoned so that he can be sold down the river to pay old debts. Chambers is restored to his place as Judge Driscoll's heir, but his slave conditioning has left him unable to cope with freedom.

Analysis

Twain did not write *The Tragedy of Pudd'nhead Wilson* for young readers, but his book has many ideas that are particularly stimulating to young adults. On its simplest level, it is an exciting tale of a mystery, which David Wilson—the village misfit—brilliantly solves with fingerprint evidence (something not done previously in a novel). Twain had a lifelong interest in exceptional people whose genius is not recognized by their own neighbors. It is an idea that many adolescents can easily appreciate, and the novel's conclusion is gratifying: After years of snubbing Wilson, the villagers finally admit that they are the true "pudd'nheads."

Wilson's own story is not, however, the true center of the book. This character was almost an afterthought to Twain, who at first was writing a quite different novel. His original story was to be a farce about Siamese twins with contrary personalities. As he developed this story, other characters—notably Roxy—intruded, pushing him in new directions. Eventually, he dropped the farcical elements, separated the Siamese twins (the Capello brothers), and allowed Roxy and her son to come to the fore. Wilson was merely a device to pull the diverse characters together. Although the finished novel shows signs of its patchwork origins, it is rich in complex role reversals and difficult social questions. Its importance lies primarily in its exploration of identities—in particular, what it means to be black or white, slave or free.

For the gimmick of switching babies to work, Twain made Roxy only one-sixteenth black and her son one-thirty-second black. He understood that by any rational physical definition, both characters should be considered white. He also knew, however, that the social conventions of American society—particularly those of the Old South—were anything but rational in such matters. Of Roxy, he wrote: "The one sixteenth of her which was black outvoted the other fifteen parts and made her a negro. . . . Her child was thirty-one parts white, and he, too, was a slave, and by a fiction of law and custom a negro." Although Tom has spent his life as a white man, he never questions that he is actually a "negro," once his mother convinces him of his true parentage. He asks

> Why were niggers *and* whites made? What crime did the uncreated first nigger commit that the curse of birth was decreed for him? And why is this awful difference made between white and black? . . . How hard the nigger's fate seems, this morning!—yet until last night such a thought never entered my head.

The other side of this identity switch is the true Tom Driscoll, who has spent his life believing himself to be the negro slave "Chambers." Even after being freed and made wealthy, he remains psychologically enslaved:

> He could neither read nor write, and his speech was the basest dialect of the negro quarter. His gait, his attitudes, his gestures, his bearing, his laugh—all were vulgar and uncouth; his manners were the manners of a slave. Money and fine clothes could not mend these defects or cover them up; they only made them the more glaring and the more pathetic. The poor fellow could not endure the terrors of the white man's parlor, and felt at home and at peace nowhere but in the kitchen. . . .

Writing at a time when few Americans challenged the notion that white and black people were fundamentally different, Twain dared to suggest that social conditioning, not heredity, separated the races. The key to his argument is not so much Tom Driscoll—who is, after all, essentially a white person "passing" for white—but Chambers. A purely white person living in a black world, Chambers is conditioned to have all the attributes of a black slave except skin color. If his entire social identity can be inverted, could not the same happen to anyone?

Critical Context

Although *The Tragedy of Pudd'nhead Wilson* has long been classified as part of Mark Twain's "Mississippi Writings," which include *The Adventures of Tom Sawyer* (1876) and *Adventures of Huckleberry Finn*, it has also long been regarded as untypical of his best work. Its somber tone has doubtless contributed to its comparative lack of popularity. Moreover, its frank treatment of the evils of slavery and its tacit admission of miscegenation (Roxy's implied sexual liaison with a white man) have also contributed to its past neglect. During the mid-1950's, a resurgence of interest in the novel began, with one scholar even calling the book a "neglected classic." Since then, it has found its way increasingly into literature courses, while earning recognition as an important contribution to understanding American identities.

R. Kent Rasmussen

THE TREES STAND SHINING
Poetry of the North American Indians

Editor: Hettie Jones (1934-   )
First published: 1971; illustrated
Type of work: Poetry
Subjects: Animals, nature, and race and ethnicity
Recommended ages: 10-18

These North American Indian songs, presented as poems, represent the attitudes, beliefs, and values of sixteen native groups scattered throughout the United States.

Form and Content

The Trees Stand Shining: Poetry of the North American Indians, selected by Hettie Jones with paintings by Robert Andrew Parker, includes prayers, short stories, lullabies, and a few war chants that were passed down orally from one generation to the next over hundreds of years. While the authors of these songs are lost in the swirl of history, their words and lyrics have remained intact. Because native groups had no written documents, it was not until the nineteenth century that their oral history began to be translated and written down. The songs, presented as poems, reveal their attitudes and values toward the earth and their beliefs about their relationship with nature.

Parker's full-page illustrations face each page of text. No more than three poems are situated on any given page, and they are surrounded by white space. This layout would seem to draw the focus mainly to the illustrations, but the opposite appears to be true. Text and illustration support each other; on many facing pages, Parker's watercolors speak to multiple poems. In other instances, his softly hued, impressionistic paintings feature a subject of one of the poems. Mysteriously, this approach remains true to the spirit of the poems. Both author and illustrator portray subtleties of mood and expression, as exemplified in this Teton-Sioux poem: "Friend,/ My horse/ Flies like a bird/ As it runs." The facing page features a young man astride a swiftly moving horse. Parker conveys rapid motion so effectively that movement is almost felt. The artist paints poems with his deft brush and the colors of nature; blues, grays, greens, yellows, browns, reds, and their variations dominate *The Trees Stand Shining*.

The subjects of the poems include the sun, the day, rainbows, birds, the woods, animals, the sky, the moon, seasons, insects, people, and Father. Each is addressed anthropomorphically, which accounts for the tone of reverence permeating each poem. The poems are not unlike haiku in their choice of topic and yet are less formulaic than this ancient Japanese verse, in which the first and third lines contain five syllables and the second line contains seven syllables. Arching over this body of selected poetry is a relationship with the immediate world, as well as one with the spiritual world. Both words and pictures capture the uniqueness of native groups. The representation of sixteen different tribes dispels the myth of a single American Indian culture. In fact, there are at least five hundred such cultures, each with its own language, views of life, and political, social, and economic systems.

The Chippewa and Arapaho-Comanche poems near the end of the book are perhaps the most poignant as they tell about the interactions with white people. The facing images are ones of Sioux women gathering up their wounded men. The Arapaho-Comanche song reads:

> My children,
> When at first I liked the whites,
> I gave them fruits,
> I gave them fruits.
>
> Father have pity on me,
> I am crying for thirst,
> All is gone,
> I have nothing to eat.
>
> I'yehé! my children . . .
> The whites are crazy—Ahe' yuhe' yu!
>
> We shall live again.
> We shall live again.

Analysis

This collection of poetry provides more than a glimpse of the mores and folkways of sixteen native groups: Tewa, Nookta, Mescalero Apache, Zuni, Acoma, Nez Perce, Iroquois, Cochiti, Teton Sioux, Crow, Chippewa, Papago, Kwakutl, Cheyenne-Arapaho, Pima, and Arapaho-Comanche. The native groups, although disparate in several identifiable ways, sing about similar topics. One major theme of these songs recognizes the elements of nature and offers praise to those aspects that bear directly on well-being and survival: Good weather derives from the sun and sky; animals provide food, clothing, and transportation; trees provide shade and shelter; day and night make beginnings and endings; the owl closes the day and the mockingbird announces it; and, when it grows light, the trees stand shining. Inherent in these songs, presented as poems, is the steady rhythm of birth, growth, love, and death.

The mystical quality of these native songs inspires contemplation about what the singers felt as well as curiosity about the content of the poems. Most of the topics of the songs are universal. Peoples throughout the world share the same sky, sun, and moon and experience birth, growth, love, and death. A higher power is a central theme of countless cultures. Moreover, many cultures throughout the world have known invading armies, conquest, hunger, thirst, rape, pillaging, and loss of territory.

The illustrations add significantly to the understanding of the native people from these sixteen groups. The sparseness of the text belies the eloquence of the songs, for much is said between the lines. Their lyrical quality begs for countless renditions. *The Trees Stand Shining* serves as a reminder of humankind's role in relation to the earth that it inhabits. The earth needs caregivers now, just as it did long ago. The ancestors of North American Indians knew this, and their legacy is passed on in this collection.

Generally, literature of the oral tradition reflects the words, feelings, and actions of the culture that it represents. In some cases, American Indian cultures are reported by well-meaning but ill-informed writers and speakers. Too few instances of native people's own words, feelings, and actions have been available for juveniles and young adults between the ages of ten and eighteen. In Jones and Parker's impressive collaboration, readers hear American Indians speak, learn what they are thinking and feeling, and discover a little about their lives. Illustrations portray each person as a genuine individual.

Father, a higher power, is a secondary theme implied in many of the songs and stated explicitly in at least six of them. Among the beliefs attributed to him are unlimited abilities, recognition as the Creator, a continuing and constant presence acknowledged and unseen, and determination of life and death; he is a rescuer in times of tribulation and the deliverer of justice. The relationship between the people and Father appears to be accepted with neither doubts nor denials.

Another secondary theme speaks to the interdependence between animals and nature. One of the very brief songs shows this: "At the rainbow spring/ The dragon-flies start . . ." In other selected songs, the coyote sings before the west wind roars; the eagle speaks with the sun's rays; the prairie gets ready for summer through the course of spring; little red spiders and the gray-horned toad make the rain fall; and the butterfly learns to walk among the flowers. The title of this book comes from a Papago tribute to day: "At the edge of the world/ It is growing light./ The trees stand shining./ I like it./ It is growing light."

The success of the illustrator's use of line, space, and color cannot be overemphasized. The unity of these elements creates a style that is compatible with the text and has great appeal for the eye. On some pages, the picture truly is worth a thousand words.

Critical Context

Before 1971, few specialized collections of American Indian poetry were available for juveniles and young adults. Consequently, *The Trees Stand Shining*, collected by Hettie Jones and illustrated by Robert Andrew Parker, has a rightful place in the canon of juvenile and young adult fiction. When there is no written document of a culture's history, the oral one must be preserved for the children of that culture to learn about their heritage. Young people can come to know, understand, and respect peoples of American Indian cultures through the prayers, short stories, lullabies, and war chants that constitute *The Trees Stand Shining*.

This collection assumes its place in the canon for other reasons as well. The unfortunate practice of lumping together all native people is avoided by including selections from sixteen different groups. There is neither an implied nor a stated reference to "them" or "us." The unity among the peoples, nature, and animals is evident throughout the book. Each of the people portrayed in Parker's illustrations is a unique individual, with different facial characteristics, and it is easy to imagine their feelings from their vivid expressions.

This book informs its readers accurately. This is no small feat when one considers how much misinformation circulates about any given culture or group at any given time. The questions that it inspires can serve as a springboard to continuing inquiry about American Indians. The elegance of the text, matched only by the beauty of the illustrations, sets a standard for quality that may be difficult to surpass.

Joan S. McMath

TROPICAL RAINFORESTS
Endangered Environment

Author: James D. Nations (1947-   )
First published: 1988; illustrated
Type of work: Science
Subjects: Nature and science
Recommended ages: 13-18

Nations describes the complexities of the tropical rainforest and discusses how this ecosystem is being destroyed.

Form and Content

James D. Nations' *Tropical Rainforests: Endangered Environment* gives young readers detailed and thorough information about the world's rainforests. The book's first chapter defines tropical rainforests, the oldest and most complex of ecosystems existing in Latin America, southeast Asia, and Africa. This overview introduces subsequent chapters which provide in-depth looks at specific aspects of rainforests. For example, the second chapter focuses on the rainforest's three layers—the canopy, the understory, and forest floor—and emphasizes the role that each of these layers performs in making the rainforest such a diverse ecosystem, rife with so many species of plants and animals.

The third chapter provides a sophisticated discussion of the products derived from rainforests. In addition to the foodstuffs commonly associated with this ecosystem, such as bananas, coffee, and pineapple, Nations discusses lesser-known rainforest crops such as corn, guavas, and cloves. He examines the possibility of as-yet undiscovered food sources as well as ones that have been newly found, such as the feijoa, the rambutan, and the naranjilla. In addition to being a kind of huge grocery store, the rainforest is a well-stocked drug store. Nations discusses plant-derived medicines that are used in the treatment of cancer, sickle-cell anemia, Parkinson's disease, hypertension, and heart disease, and he stresses, especially in chapter 4, that the properties of these plants were originally discovered by indigenous peoples. Other rainforest products that Nations addresses in this chapter include wood (such as mahogany, teak, and balsa), fibers, latexes, resins, waxes, acids, alcohols, flavorings, sweeteners, dyes, bug killers, and petroleum products.

Tropical Rainforests also focuses on the human residents of the rainforest. Nations discusses the indigenous tribal people, with their wealth of ancient knowledge about the rainforest, as well as the people who immigrated to this ecosystem beginning in the early 1960's. These outsiders, who are lured to the rainforest by the hope of owning their own land and having a better life, do not have the knowledge and do not receive the necessary training to live in such a delicate and difficult environment.

The book's final three chapters shift from a description of rainforests to their disappearance. The first of these chapters discusses why rainforests are in danger, the second focuses on what is being done to protect them, and the last chapter in the book focuses on what young readers can do to help save rainforests.

Throughout the book, Nations frequently acknowledges the experts whose work has helped people understand the rainforest. For example, he cites biologist Terry Erwin's attempt to number the species of plants and animals actually living in the rainforest, chemist Melvin Calvin's discovery that liquid hydrocarbon similar to diesel oil can be drained from some rainforest trees, and ethnobotanist Mark Plotkin's studies of the use of plants by tribal peoples. These scientists' productive work has helped people to realize how devastating the destruction of the rainforest would be.

The book's diagrams, maps, and numerous black-and-white photographs depicting the plants, animals, and people of the tropical rainforest help young readers to imagine a distant ecosystem that most will never visit. A list of organizations working to conserve tropical rainforests, a glossary of terms, and a bibliography conclude the book.

Analysis

The subject of Nations' book is the world's tropical rainforests, but the lens through which he views his subject is reflected in the subtitle *Endangered Environment*. After convincing his readers of the importance and wonders of rainforests, Nations wants to show them that this ecosystem is in grave trouble.

This agenda is reflected at the beginning of the book with a fictitious story about future astronauts returning home from a long space expedition and seeing the tropical rainforests that were damaged in the twentieth century. This environmentalist slant, which frequently punctuates the first four chapters, overtakes the book in chapter 5 as Nations explains why humans destroy rainforests (for example, road construction, logging, colonization, cattle ranching, and development projects) and the problems that are caused by deforestation (such as the extinction of plants and animals, soil erosion, decreased rainfall, and changes in the global climate).

Nations' presentation of the devastation of the rainforests is sobering and worrisome, but it does not always place the blame on those who are responsible for this destruction. Several times in the book, Nations mentions that much of this damage has been done unknowingly: both by those unaware of the importance of this ecosystem and by those who have no other alternative but to clear the rainforest and farm the poor soil in an attempt to survive.

The book is also filled with hope. Nations wants to make it clear that serious damage has been done to the rainforests, but he also points out that not all the world's tropical rainforests are doomed to disappear—at least not yet. The rainforests in the western Brazilian Amazon, for example, should stand unharmed for at least another fifty years. Furthermore, Nations praises people for beginning to realize the importance of this ecosystem and acknowledges the national wildlife reserves, biosphere reserves, and new methods of logging and farming that have helped to preserve the rainforests. He believes that the destruction of tropical rainforests could best be stopped by implementing programs that both protect species and wildlife and serve human beings. He also subtly offers a solution: a slowing of the population growth that many environmentalists suggest is at the heart of many environmental problems.

More than anything, perhaps, the book is a cry for help to the younger generation, especially in the United States. (Nations chooses to study the rainforest of Central America in depth because it lies closest to the United States.) By making the book highly anecdotal and by portraying the rainforest as a fascinating and unexplored ecosystem, Nations hopes to educate young readers, to capture their imaginations, and to win their support in helping to solve a problem that older generations have caused.

Critical Context

Since the middle of the twentieth century, scientists have been measuring an environmental crisis: The world is running out of resources such as water, wood fiber, and minerals, and much of what remains is becoming contaminated and ruined beyond repair. Rachel Carson's *Silent Spring* (1962), which chronicles the dangers of pesticides, was one of the first books to warn the public about environmental hazards. Writers such as Bill McKibben, Dixy Lee Ray, Marc Reisner, and Al Gore have followed in Carson's footsteps as they too draw attention to specific environmental problems, such as the greenhouse effect, nuclear waste, acid rain, overpopulation, a disappearing water supply, and the depletion of the rainforest. The works of these environmental writers and others have been institutionalized; many college courses are offered that focus on studying environmental writing and the problems affecting the environment.

This emphasis on environmentalism has filtered down to the juvenile and young adult literary canon. *Tropical Rainforests*, with its warning about the hazards of depleting the rainforests and its call to young people to help solve this specific environmental problem, is a simplified but sophisticated version of the environmental crisis books for adults. *Tropical Rainforests* and other works that focus on environmental issues—Kathlyn Gay's *Acid Rain* (1983), *The Greenhouse Effect* (1986), and *Silent Killers: Radon and Other Hazards* (1988), as well as Gene B. Williams' *Nuclear War, Nuclear Winter* (1987), Michael H. Sedge's *Commercialization of the Oceans* (1987), and Malcolm E. Weiss's *Toxic Waste: Clean-up or Cover-up?* (1984)—help young audiences realize that environmental issues are complicated and that it is necessary for all people to think harder and deeper about the ecology of the earth than they have in the past.

Cassandra Kircher

THE TRUE CONFESSIONS OF CHARLOTTE DOYLE

Author: Avi (Avi Wortis, 1937-   )
First published: 1990
Type of work: Novel
Type of plot: Adventure tale and historical fiction
Time of work: 1832
Locale: The North Atlantic Ocean
Subjects: Coming-of-age, gender roles, and travel
Recommended ages: 13-15

Charlotte Doyle's transatlantic voyage teaches her crucial lessons about appearances, loyalties, and self-reliance as the crew mutinies and she is cast into a maze of choices.

> *Principal characters:*
> CHARLOTTE DOYLE, a thirteen-year-old schooled in England, traveling alone on a sailing ship to her home in America
> CAPTAIN ANDREW JAGGERY, the captain of the *Seahawk*, a refined man of seeming respectability
> ZACHARIAH, a decrepit old black sailor who serves as cook and surgeon on the ship
> HOLLYBRASS, the first mate on board the *Seahawk*
> KEETCH, the second mate on board the *Seahawk*
> CRANICK, a stowaway

Form and Content

The True Confessions of Charlotte Doyle is an adventure story set on the high seas that begins with "an important warning" in which Charlotte explains to the reader: "If strong ideas and action offend you, read no more." She goes on to explain that as a result of her voyage on the *Seahawk*, she is a much different young woman from the one who stepped aboard the ship in England.

Because her father and the rest of Charlotte's family have had to return home to Providence, Rhode Island, before Charlotte was finished with her schooling at the Barrington School of Better Girls in England, he has made arrangements for Charlotte to travel on one of his company's ships, along with two other American families. The two families are delayed, however, and the *Seahawk* sets sail promptly as appointed. Charlotte finds herself the only girl in the company of a crew of ruffians.

She is somewhat offended by the familiarity of the old black cook, Zachariah, who early on befriends her. When he offers her a small dagger—"in case you need it"— Charlotte is convinced that he is not someone with whom she should spend time. Nevertheless, she accepts the knife and hides it under her mattress. Charlotte knows that she is in a worrisome situation and that there is something amiss on the ship.

When she is introduced to Captain Jaggery over a cup of tea in his quarters, however, Charlotte is pleased to find him a refined and charming gentleman, someone worthy of her trust. Jaggery explains to her that a sea captain must be stern and that his actions may even sometimes appear to be harsh. He also requests that she be on the lookout for anything in the crew's behavior or conversation that would suggest trouble.

Soon enough, Charlotte makes unsettling discoveries. In the hold of the ship looking through her trunk, she thinks that she feels the presence of another person in the dark; later, on deck she witnesses Captain Jaggery's severe treatment of the crew. She also catches a glimpse of a "round robin," a piece of paper bearing the names of crew members intent on mutiny, and she discovers that one of the sailors has a gun in his possession. Charlotte believes that she is obligated to inform Captain Jaggery.

Within minutes after she has told the captain, the crew rushes onto the deck, and in their midst she sees a stowaway. Jaggery meets the desperate crew with guns drawn, and, in the ensuing confrontation, he shoots the stowaway Cranick and whips Zachariah unmercifully, leaving him for dead. The captain also explains to the crew that it was Charlotte's observation of their actions that prompted his awareness of their planned mutiny. From that point on, Charlotte recognizes that the captain is a treacherous and sadistic villain; she also sees that her foolish actions have put her at odds with the crew.

Charlotte decides to prove to the crew that she can be trusted, and, in open defiance of the captain, she "joins" the crew. She works heroically in the riggings during a hurricane, but, when the first mate is found murdered after the storm, Jaggery blames the crime on her. Cast into the brig, she is comforted by Zachariah (whose burial at sea has been staged by the crew), and the two plot to overthrow Jaggery before she is tried for murder and executed.

Through several reversals of action, Charlotte survives the voyage and is reunited with her family, who offer a cool reception to her tale of adventure. She determines that she cannot accept a life of stifled propriety and sneaks out one night to join the crew of the *Seahawk* as it sets sail.

Analysis

Told in the first person some time after Charlotte's voyage, the story is presented much like the travel narratives popular during the nineteenth century. Early in the novel, Charlotte explains that she is telling the truth as she lived it, suggesting an air of authenticity that adds to the reader's enjoyment of the melodrama. Charlotte tells her tale using a hyperliterary style common to the writing of that time period. In doing so, she joins the well-established tradition of the woman's travel narrative, whose roots go back to Sarah Kemble Knight's *Private Journal of a Journey from Boston to New York* (1704-1705) and in many aspects to Mary Rowlandson's *Narrative of the Captivity and Restoration* (1682), which details her capture by American Indians during King Philip's War.

"Woman-in-peril," or perhaps "virtue-in-danger," is an assertive theme in many historical accounts of travel. Avi builds on this motif as Charlotte finds herself in an all-male society. The "confession" does not belabor any potential sexual threat; however, an underlying element of propriety is what fuels much of the book's appeal. From the outset, Charlotte finds herself forced by circumstances away from propriety. When she discovers that the traveling companions that her father arranged for her will not be present for the voyage, she exclaims that the situation would not be proper. Charlotte discovers, however, that there is considerably more wrong on the ship than simply traveling with sailors.

"Impropriety" is the watchword as the crew mutinies against Jaggery, who is outwardly smooth but inwardly vicious. It is Charlotte's abeyance to propriety that causes much of the conflict. She is unable to pull away from the socially correct—that is, the way things ought to be—that results in savage authority and tragedy. Charlotte at first refuses to accept the fact that things may not be as they seem. When she alerts Jaggery to the planned mutiny, she sets into motion a series of events that show her the captain's treachery. It has become too late for her to rectify the situation, to restore propriety, and she becomes an outcast. She no longer can approach Jaggery, and she is no longer trusted by the crew.

At that point in the novel, the heroine herself takes a turn from propriety. In an attempt to show her solidarity with the crew, she becomes one of them—but only after a great struggle to be accepted. Her defiance against the captain eases her into the crew's acceptance, but it is her willingness literally to learn the ropes and her increasing antagonism toward the captain's authority that eventually win her the crew's uneasy approval. Charlotte deliberately rejects a proper woman's proper place in favor of danger and revenge. She dons sailors' clothing and, at the height of a hurricane while she is dangling by ropes, she shears her hair short so that she can see to cut the billowing sails.

Charlotte's move away from all that is acceptable and proper is fully realized once she has safely arrived in America, although her parents do not accept or allow this change. To please her parents, she pretends to acquiesce to their wishes. The night before the *Seahawk* is set to leave Providence, however, she is drawn to the gangplank and smuggled aboard. While the novel explores gender roles, it more succinctly inspects the power of authority and propriety. Charlotte's move away from expected behavior offers an additional dimension to the traditional genre of the woman's travel narrative. It is this element of self-reliance that makes the story significant to young adult readers.

The True Confessions of Charlotte Doyle also functions as a classic quest story. Charlotte delineates the change that she undergoes as she rejects appearance for reality. Her metamorphosis from a sheltered schoolgirl to an independent young woman is a winning exploration of self-realization.

Critical Context

The True Confessions of Charlotte Doyle was named a 1991 Newbery Honor Book. Avi, whose writing has received numerous awards, is a popular author of historical and realistic fiction. His work for young adults includes such novels as *A Place Called*

Ugly (1981), *Devil's Race* (1984), *S.O.R. Losers* (1984), *Wolf Rider: A Tale of Terror* (1986), *Romeo and Juliet—Together (and Alive!) at Last* (1987), *The Man Who Was Poe* (1989), and *Nothing but the Truth: A Documentary Novel* (1991).

Douglas A. Jones

THE TRUMPET OF THE SWAN

Author: E. B. White (1899-1985)
First published: 1970
Type of work: Novel
Type of plot: Fantasy
Time of work: The 1970's
Locale: Billings and Red Rock Lake, Montana; Ontario, Canada; Boston; and Philadelphia
Subjects: Animals, family, friendship, love and romance, and nature
Recommended ages: 10-13

> *Louis, a trumpeter swan, struggles to live within his world without a voice.*

Principal characters:
    LOUIS, a trumpeter swan without a voice
    LOUIS' FATHER, a swan who loves his son so much that he steals a
        trumpet to give Louis a "voice"
    SAM BEAVER, an eleven-year-old boy who befriends Louis
    SERENA, the beautiful swan whom Louis loves

Form and Content

The Trumpet of the Swan is an enchanting story about Louis, a trumpeter swan without a voice, and his plight to fit in with nature. At one point in time, Louis thought that "fate is cruel to me," and not being able to speak led him to believe that he was "defective." With his father's help and his own creativity, however, Louis becomes a famous and happy swan.

Louis is born without a voice, a definite disadvantage for a trumpeter swan. He is befriended by Sam Beaver, an eleven-year-old boy, who is camping with his father. Sam tries to help Louis and takes him to school so that he can learn to read and write. Louis is a fast learner and spends the rest of his life with a slate and a piece of chalk around his neck. This works well when Louis wants to communicate with humans, but, unfortunately, swans do not know how to read. This situation becomes a problem for Louis when he falls in love with the disinterested Serena. Serena is used to her suitors saying "ko-hoh," and Louis is not able say "I love you" in that manner.

Louis' father decides to fly to Billings, Montana, to secure a trumpet for his son so that the horn can be Louis' "voice." Since he does not have any money to pay for the horn, he is forced to steal it from the music store and put his honor aside for the love of his child.

Louis learns to play the trumpet, but he is upset that the instrument has not been paid for. Again, with the help of Sam, Louis acquires a summer job at Camp KooKoosKoos in Ontario, where he is paid one hundred dollars to play his trumpet.

During this experience, Louis saves the life of a camper and receives a medal. Louis leaves the camp to travel to Boston, where he has secured a job on a swan boat. He flies to this next adventure with not only a slate, a piece of chalk, and a trumpet around his neck but also a money bag and his medal.

Louis becomes famous as he plays his trumpet on the swan boat and is paid one hundred dollars a week. He is then asked to perform at a nightclub in Philadelphia where he is paid five hundred dollars a week. It is at Bird Lake in the Philadelphia Zoo where Louis is reunited with Serena, the love of his life. Using his trumpet, Louis plays the song, "Beautiful Dreamer, Wake Unto Me," and, when he plays "Ko-hoh," Serena responds with "Ko-hoh." Each feels drawn to the other by a mysterious bond of affection, and they both know that never again will they be parted.

When the zoo officials attempt to pinion Serena, Louis once again requests Sam's assistance. Sam then speaks with the administrator of the zoo, and an agreement is reached whereby Serena is allowed to leave the zoo with Louis. In turn, Serena and Louis agree to donate one of their cygnets to the zoo, as needed. The two swans return to Red Rock Lake to give Louis' father the $4,691.65 that Louis has earned.

Louis' father returns to Billings to pay the owner of the music store the money that he owed from stealing the trumpet, so that he can redeem his honor, but he is shot on his way into the music store. It is only a superficial wound, however, and he returns to his family with his honor intact.

Serena and Louis return each spring to the pond, nest, and have their young. They donate a cygnet to the zoo, as promised, and never forget about their adventures and friends, especially Sam Beaver.

Analysis

After writing *The Trumpet of the Swan*, E. B. White stated, "I think it was extremely inconsiderate of my characters to lead me, an old man, into such unfamiliar territory. At my age, I deserve better." White leads his readers into a fantasy world of unusual characters in some unique situations.

Louis is a mute cygnet born to a family of trumpeter swans. This condition evokes many terms including "handicaps," "speech defects" and being "defective." Although this handicap is not the primary theme of the book, it probably would be dealt with differently in today's world than it was in 1970. The term "handicap" is now referred to as a "disability" and would probably be handled with more sensitivity.

The book teaches a little about geography as Louis travels to Canada, Montana, Boston, and Philadelphia. The reader also gains some knowledge about science and nature, including some detailed information about cygnets and trumpeter swans. The word "pinion" is introduced and defined so that readers of all ages should be able to understand the term.

Although some of Louis' adventures seem a little bit far-fetched, readers who can suspend their disbelief are able to stretch their imaginations. Fantasy can lead one to visions of worlds beyond the one at hand, and *The Trumpet of the Swan* is a wonderful example of the power of this genre.

Critical Context

E. B. White is the author of many books of prose and poetry that were written for adults. He also wrote three books specifically for children. White's first book for a younger audience was *Stuart Little* (1945), the story of a tiny mouse who leaves home to find his true love, Margalo, a pretty wren. Through his many adventures in New York City, Stuart learns about both friendship and love. This book was followed by *Charlotte's Web* (1952), the story of a little girl named Fern who cares deeply about a pig named Wilbur. Wilbur is also friends with a special spider named Charlotte. The three characters share many adventures, and, in the end, Charlotte is able to save Wilbur from his impending death in a creative fashion. Fern, Wilbur, and Charlotte, too, learn much about both friendship and love.

All three of White's children's books share many commonalities. Stuart Little has adventures in different locales, just as Louis spends time in Canada, Montana, Boston, and Philadelphia. The many relationships in *Charlotte's Web* are not unlike the love between Louis and his father and Louis and Serena. The friendship between Stuart and Margalo in *Stuart Little* and the friendship between Wilbur and Charlotte in *Charlotte's Web* parallels the relationship between Louis and Sam Beaver in *The Trumpet of the Swan*. The themes of all three books include friendship, loyalty, honesty, and love.

These three books are children's fantasy at its best. To leave reality in the company of a tiny mouse, a spider who writes messages, and a swan who plays a trumpet is a delight for children of all ages.

Ellen Garfinkel

UNDER ALL SILENCES
Shades of Love

Editor: Ruth I. Gordon (1933-   )
First published: 1987
Type of work: Poetry
Subjects: Coming-of-age, emotions, friendship, and love and romance
Recommended ages: 15-18

Sixty-six poems anthologized that offer truths and insights about love, emotional bonds and sexuality; poetry gleaned from differing times and cultures.

Form and Content

In the anthology *Under All Silences: Shades of Love*, Ruth I. Gordon compiles sixty-six poems and songs about love in which the emotional strength of each poem is linked to the sum of the whole. The collection explores diverse cultures and insights as the author draws on the works of ancient Egyptian, Chinese, and Persian poets and medieval Japanese poets to create a geographical and historical representation of deep thought and warm feelings. The structure of the anthology links these carefully selected poems to themes that may be carried from poem to poem or merely connect two of them in an understated union. The silences of all times and cultures speak in this collection, the kind of silence that only poets can allow the reader to experience. Love, as defined among these verses, travels from its inception at first meetings, through discovery, passion, and knowledge, and then beyond.

The format of the book allows easy reading. Each poem is isolated, having its own page, its own space. The reader can dwell or move on at leisure. When possible, the name of the poet and other pertinent data such as translation information and country of origin are provided. An extensive acknowledgment section cites sources and serves as an excellent reference tool for readers who want to research further works by a particular poet. For quick reference, Gordon provides both an index of authors and an index of titles. For those with a penchant for memorization, the first line of all poems are indexed at the end of the book.

The titles of the poems often express the content, and readers can make the transition from the song "The First Time Ever I Saw Your Face" to the poem "As We Are So Wonderfully Done with Each Other." Some poems speak of love from a distance—sometimes of the love of youths who are too timid to allow their paramours secret winks or soft words. Suddenly, but not too suddenly, the focus of the poems becomes more sensual. Physical togetherness and celebration of the human body sing from the pages. Occasionally, one reads of love unrequited, of a lover leaving. The full circle of emotions is reached with the maturity of relationships that have borne out time and trials; the poets speak of a union that not all know. Gordon ends with E. E. Cummings asking whether "lovers love."

Analysis

Gordon credits her youthful audience with having the maturity to experience love through the beauty of other people's words. The gentle affection that is portrayed in the early poems soon warms to passion and intimacy that only a lover can know. Such a lover, however, may be one who has loved in the flesh or in the heart—and these poems assure readers of both the difference and the sameness. Gordon prefaces her book with a comment about being struck dumb by strong emotions, the ones felt in all stages of love. She lets the reader know that she has chosen these poems so that feelings can find release, expressing the love that is under all the silences.

In exploring these poems, readers will notice several themes. Composed as a popular song and made popular by Roberta Flack, "The First Time Ever I Saw Your Face" begins the book with the rapture of initial love—the experience of love at first sight. Next, folksinger Joan Baez offers a gentle love song: She does not want to be told of eternal love; she simply wants to know of passionate strangers, of a selfishness in wanting but not giving. Then, a Hebrew poem allows the reader to compare the love of a woman to the beauty of an apple.

Several short, sweet Japanese poems reveal deeper meanings than the few phrases representing their thoughts. A seventh century Greek poem wonders at a lover's presence and laments her absence. A series of poems speaks of the bliss of two being together and of the memories of nights of lovemaking. Another poem peeks at one lover in wakefulness, thoughts spinning through his mind as his mate sleeps. Intense feelings of lament, fear, and joy are carried through a series of poems describing the power of a lover, particularly when distance separates.

Love among married couples is celebrated in a Chinese poem that describes two mates as sharing the clay that molds their figures; the clay of each is broken into small pieces and mixed together, reformed to make the individual who now carries parts of the other. Poet John Holmes describes his wife as "Quick-tempered as fire crackers, scornful, clean;/ A spiritual materialist, Eve with clothes on." Then a Persian poet, Rumi, tells of the next step after being in love—responsibility. He advises his readers to be lovers in a way that they will know their beloved and to be faithful in order to learn of faith. He writes, "Lovers don't finally meet somewhere,/ They're in each other all along." Another poet, Rika Lesser, speaks of simple lives, not extraordinary ones, that harbor the silence of their union: "Our silence seals/ a deeper silence."

Gordon expects poetry to be learned, but she contends that it cannot be taught. Her blend of poems, her choice of poets, and her careful assembly of these love poems all express her ideals. Generations separate these poems, which clarifies the universal appeal of poetry and love. E. E. Cummings abstractly addresses love and relationships. The Persian poets seem to dwell more on the physical, while the Japanese poems express tangibility. Emily Dickinson's soft touch but deep meaning may create tension in some readers, while Ewan MacCall lets his thoughts hum through his readers' minds.

Critical Context

Ruth Gordon is a highly respected librarian who received her Ph.D. at the University of California at Berkeley. She spent her early years as a professional librarian in the eastern United States and eight years as a teacher for the Department of Defense in Aviano, Italy, and she eventually settled in California. She actively writes critiques in professional journals, but, most important to her, she anthologizes poetry for younger readers. She compiled the poems for *Time Is the Long Distance* (1991), in which she strives to link mortality and time; she expresses the human need for that connection. Some of these poems revolve around unimaginable circumstances in which people find themselves, such as a definite state of doom. Gordon's *Pierced by a Ray of Sun* (1995) takes another step, another route to reflect the concern of time and timelessness. Again, she crosses cultural and time barriers and examines the spectrum of emotions—hope and despair, gain and loss.

Gordon merited mention as one of the Best of the 80's by *Booklist* for both *Time Is the Long Distance* and *Under All Silences*. *Under All Silences* was chosen as a Best Book of 1987 by two prestigious organizations, *School Library Journal* and the American Library Association. Reviewers expressed an open-arms acceptance of her anthology, noting that the greeting card approach to love has little comparison to the genuineness expressed by true love poetry. Gordon is adamant that young people be able to read and learn of love through the beauty of poetry.

Gordon collected other poems in *Peeling the Onion: An Anthology of Poems* (1993). Although she also writes critiques, reviews, and professional papers, creating anthologies seems to be her forte. Gordon is a member of several children's literature associations and has a strong commitment to the earth, as expressed in her association with Friends of the Earth and the Sierra Club. Both of these positions, as well as her attraction to poetry focusing on love and youth, guide Gordon in her selection process.

Craig Gilbert

UNDERGROUND

Author: David Macaulay (1946-   )
First published: 1976
Type of work: Science
Subjects: Jobs and work and science
Recommended ages: 13-18

The complex system that exists beneath the buildings and streets of a modern city is explained in detailed drawings and clear descriptions.

Form and Content

In *Underground*, by David Macaulay, the puzzle of what lies beneath cities is unraveled in clear pen-and-ink sketches that stand out against the brown earth and white background. In the text, each aspect of the underground and its construction is explored in concise, direct statements that explain various parts of the world beneath city streets.

Accurate, step-by-step explanations help readers understand the unseen structures and systems. The network of walls, columns, cables, pipes, and tunnels serves many purposes: Walls and columns support buildings, bridges, and towers, while cables, pipes, and tunnels carry water, electricity, and gas. Larger tunnels transport people on subways. Macaulay examines the maze beneath the streets by exposing a typical section of the network. He has invented a site at the intersection of two streets that serves as a prototype of any underground in an urban setting and portrays various kinds of foundation construction that support both large and smaller buildings.

The foundations considered depend on the composition of the earth's surface, which may include sand, clay, rock, water, and, at the very bottom, bedrock. Horizontal and vertical diagrams indicate the site plan and soil profile. Various methods are used to determine the exact composition of the site: for example, digging a hole, using a sounding rod, or employing a variety of methods to analyze samples of soil. Bedrock, although the best material, may be too far beneath the surface. In that case, foundations must be constructed. Macaulay shows and explains various foundations, such as spread foundation for smaller buildings, which means a concrete slab with footings. Precisely how this is done is shown in a double-page, four-panel illustration, with the text interpreting lagging, reinforcing rods, and steel ties. Macaulay's technique of guiding the reader from the parts to the whole is well demonstrated in the section in which he follows the step-by-step diagram with a full-page view from the perspective of a viewer far underground looking skyward with the busy traffic of the street suspended overhead, creating a view similar to looking through a glass-bottomed street.

Larger buildings use adaptations or combinations for four types of foundations: floating foundations, friction piles, bearing piles, and piers. Each of these types is demonstrated with diagrams and text, enabling the reader to compare and contrast the four methods. Excavation methods prior to the foundation are explained. The reader senses the seriousness of this task through illustrations that help explain the support needed. By showing life above the ground such as a pianist on the third floor of the building, the reasons are made absolutely clear.

Words such as "slurry" are explained in the text; this is helpful since not all words appear in the glossary. Guiding readers through complex vocabulary and a multiplicity of concepts is Macaulay's strength. As the intricate web of underground parts is unraveled, a periodic look at the whole reminds the reader of where the parts fit. These views often are inhabited by people (such as a boy and his dog), revealing the humanness of the environment. This is masterfully delineated lest the reader/observer get buried in the plethora of particulars.

Once the foundations are laid, *Underground* moves to the next level, portraying the structures necessary for utilities such as water, sewage removal and drainage, electricity, steam, gas, and telephone communication. Most cities have grown gradually and randomly, so that a crowded intertwined underground system is more often the case. In *Underground*, an ideal system is shown so that water, sewer, storm drain, electrical, steam distribution, gas distribution, telephone systems, and subway systems can be explained clearly. The complex technology beneath cities has been rendered significant, fascinating, and amazing in only 112 pages.

Analysis

Underground has appeal to a wide range of readers because of the unique topic of exploration, which is not addressed in other sources. Technology, scientific theory, urban development, engineering principles, and social history are included in text and illustrations that make the complex understandable. In an orderly and interesting manner, Macaulay leads the reader on a fascinating exploration below city streets, where a vast, hidden system supports the life taking place above ground.

Bedrock, being the deepest level of soil, supports sand, clay, and rock, which must be considered before excavation takes place and a foundation is constructed. A foundation is important because it transfers the weight of the building to the material below. To prevent shifting and movement, the foundation must provide uniformity and stability; this becomes even more important if the ground below the building is unstable. Thoughts about multistory buildings or earthquakes remind the reader of the significance of this principle. The reader gains greater respect for the careful construction of the foundation. The description and diagrams of spread foot construction explain how soil and water are removed, laggings are braced, concrete is poured, and steel reinforcing rods are installed, all of which takes several weeks.

Being able to read and understand diagrams and following directions in a well-organized text will be skills enhanced by Macaulay's book. Variations between the four major types of foundations for larger buildings will call upon the reader to differentiate, promoting careful observation and critical assessment. Skills found in the real world are similar to the work carried out by the engineers in this book. Orderliness, attention to detail, and the ability to synthesize information are skills inherent in the concepts presented in *Underground*.

Macaulay prevents this book from becoming a textbook through his style of writing; he is like an informed guide who addresses the reader in a clear, direct, conversational tone, never overwhelming his audience with too much information. The detailed drawings provide perspectives from a variety of angles. This refreshing change of views continually modifies the pace and keeps the reader alert. The desire to look and look again at the detailed drawings rewards the viewer: The workers are accurately portrayed, and the human activity above ground is endlessly interesting, with people and animals shown in lifelike situations.

A sense of humor, one of the trademarks of Macaulay's books, is revealed in the table of contents, entitled "What to Look for on the Street and Where to Find It in the Book." These words appear in the form of a billboard on a detailed double-page spread of a teeming city street. In this drawing, objects represent locations in the book where information can be found, indicated by a brown circle and a page number. For example, a phone box on the street indicates page 89; the reader turns to page 89 to find an explanation of the telephone system. A cable filled with thousands of wires shows wires for outgoing messages and for responses. The text explains that an average underground cable contains 5,400 wires, or enough for 2,700 simultaneous conversations. Facts of this sort are engaging and impressive.

Underground helps explain all those colored wires seen in a cable for telephones, why steam escapes from manhole covers, how subway systems work, and how the vast network of systems underground support life above ground. Macaulay enables readers to understand and appreciate this underworld because he has been there. He did the research by actually visiting the subterranean world with his notebook, sketchbook, and camera. He interviewed utility workers, engineers, and architects. He portrayed such diligence in his own research that the reader is spellbound by the unique adventure in the inner depths of a world that one cannot see but that is one of the basic support systems of modern civilization.

Critical Context

In classrooms where research in social studies, science, and technology is conducted, *Underground* provides knowledge, pleasure, and an ideal model for investigation. Previous works by David Macaulay introduced architectural monuments of civilization, enabling understanding and appreciation of the constructed environment. The three award-winning books *Cathedral* (1973), *Castle* (1978), and *Pyramid* (1975) represent a trilogy in the canon of books for young adults and for a general audience.

His previous book concerning a city represented an earlier time and a community above ground, *City: A Story of Roman Planning and Construction* (1974). This work was included in the Children's Book Showcase in 1975. The combination of text, illustrations, and format that the award recognized is a hallmark of Macaulay's work. This excellence is also evident in *Underground*, in which black-and-white drawings convey the excitement of a city and diagrams explain the most intricate details of engineering feats. A third color, brown, is introduced in *Underground*, adding contrast. The density of text is greater than in some of Macaulay's earlier books, but the information presented is no less clear and is in keeping with the subject. Thus, the most complicated concepts can be easily understood, and the whole is unified, from the introduction to the satisfying conclusion.

David Macaulay is an artist, illustrator, author, researcher, and teacher whose books teach and inform. They are picture books, but, as Macaulay has said, "Information told more through pictures than words does not necessarily have an age limit for appreciation. Picture books can be universal in their appeal and efficiency." *Underground* is such a book.

Helene W. Lang

UNDERSEA EXPLORER
The Story of Captain Cousteau

Author: James Dugan (1912-1967)
First published: 1957; illustrated
Type of work: Biography
Time of work: 1910-1956
Locale: France and the oceans of the world
Subjects: Explorers and scientists
Recommended ages: 13-18

Dugan carries the reader on an exciting journey around the world, both above and beneath the waves, along with Captain Cousteau and his crew.

Principal personages:
JACQUES-YVES COUSTEAU, a marine scientist, the captain of the *Calypso*, and the inventor of modern scuba gear
FRÉDÉRIC DUMAS, a friend of Cousteau who shared early diving adventures and later was a key member of the crew of the *Calypso*
PHILIPPE TAILLEZ, a friend and diving associate of Cousteau who helped develop diving equipment and techniques
JAMES DUGAN, the author and the first non-Frenchman to sail with the *Calypso*, who helped to make the film *The Silent World*
FERDINAND BENOÎT, an archaeologist with whom Cousteau worked, especially in excavating the undersea remains of a Roman merchant ship from the year 3 B.C.

Form and Content

Undersea Explorer is a narrative concerning the life of Jacques-Yves Cousteau, from a brief look at his pre-World War II childhood through his work as scientist and explorer into the mid-1950's. This is not a comprehensive biography containing much personal detail but rather a treatment of Captain Cousteau's life relating to his focus on the world beneath the surface of the sea. James Dugan spent time working with Captain Cousteau aboard the *Calypso*, the converted British mine sweeper that serves as a floating marine laboratory, an exploration vessel, and living quarters for Cousteau and his crew of scientists. Dugan writes in an easy-to-follow and interesting manner about his own firsthand experiences and also records stories of Cousteau's earlier life and adventures.

Interspersed within the text are twenty-eight black-and-white photographs and line drawings. These illustrations diagram details of the equipment and techniques used in underwater exploration and provide a record of the personages who appear within the text. The book also includes fourteen color photographs that provide vivid images to accompany some of the incidents discussed within the text. The author also provides an annotated bibliography for thirteen books and periodicals to which the reader can turn for additional information and entertainment about the world under the sea.

The history of modern undersea exploration began with Jacques-Yves Cousteau before World War II. As a French navy officer, Cousteau had the opportunity to visit many places. His abiding interest in exploring the sea and in seeing the beauty beneath the waves was only partially fulfilled by his ability to dive for the amount of time that he could hold his breath. He tried using some of the earliest oxygen-breathing apparatuses but found some rather serious problems with the available equipment. The arrival of World War II temporarily ended Cousteau's work with the navy. He moved to Paris and became an active member of the French Resistance. In between his somewhat daring adventures with the underground resistance, Cousteau maintained his interest and involvement in diving, especially in finding a way in which a human being could breathe underwater for extended periods of time without bulky suits and air lines to hinder movement. In Paris, he met Émile Gagnan, an expert in working with gasses under pressure. Gagnan worked from Cousteau's ideas, and together they developed the key element for what was to become the Aqua-Lung: the pressure regulator that controls the amount of air that will flow through a breathing tube, irrespective of outside water pressure. In 1943, Cousteau descended into the Marne River outside Paris using this device connected to a tank filled with compressed air. The regulator worked well, and the same basic device is still used in all self-contained underwater breathing apparatus—or scuba—devices.

Following the war, Cousteau, along with friends and fellow navy personnel and divers Philippe Taillez and Frédéric Dumas, unofficially started the Undersea Research Group of the French navy. They even managed to procure two diving vessels. When an order arrived for Lieutenant Cousteau to move to a dull desk job in Marseille, he convinced an admiral that there was a purpose for his group. With the official blessing of the French navy, Cousteau and his crew were able to expand their diving operation and requisition materials through official channels. During the following years, they made a number of advances in the science and technology of diving, including the construction of decompression chambers that helped cure the diver's malady commonly known as "the bends."

Undersea Explorer follows Cousteau and the *Calypso* through the early days of his explorations. Among the highlights of these journeys is the six-year-long project to bring to the surface the cargo and remains of a Roman merchant ship, three times larger than *Calypso*, that had lain on the bottom of the Mediterranean Sea for more than two thousand years. Other, more modern wrecks are also explored. Cousteau and his divers encounter and, for the first time ever, film sharks in a feeding frenzy. Other sea-dwelling creatures come to the attention of the crew of *Calypso*, including sea turtles, whales, dolphins, and a huge "truckfish," which turns out to be a giant wrasse. The reader joins Cousteau in a deep-sea submersible vehicle as he journeys more than a mile down into the darkness of the ocean.

The story of Captain Cousteau's life does not end with the final page of the book. This account provides a contemporary record of the early days of Cousteau's work,

an account that has not been distorted by time and legend and that brings the reader
an up-close look at this scientist and explorer.

Analysis

The author worked aboard the *Calypso*, the first foreigner to do so, and it is evident
in *Undersea Explorer* that Dugan holds Cousteau in high regard, both professionally
and personally. Cousteau appears to the reader as a man of dedication and conviction.
The portrait of his childhood shows the early independence and spirit of adventure
that characterizes Cousteau's life throughout the book. He overcomes adversity and
physical injury to become the foremost undersea explorer in history. Few glimpses
emerge, however, of Cousteau's family life. One learns that he married and had two
sons, but there is little personal detail. Instead, major events of the subject's life are
interwoven with personal stories to provide an accurate portrait of Cousteau.

The time line of this account of Cousteau's life follows his first forty-five years,
from a brief description of what appears to be a precocious childhood through his
coming-of-age as a young French naval officer and finally to his life as captain of the
Calypso. The concentration is clearly on those factors that have shaped Cousteau's
life as a diver and explorer. Consequently, there are gaps in the story, with long periods
of Cousteau's life with little or no narrative, but this does not detract materially from
the book. Much of Cousteau's personal life remains undiscussed in this record. What
the reader does obtain is an easy-to-follow account of the professional life of an
extraordinary modern-day pioneer.

Much of the sea is a mystery to scientists, even today. The story of that which
Jacques-Yves Cousteau has done and the windows that he has opened to the undersea
world should prove to be motivational and inspirational to many young people, some
of whom may aspire to follow Cousteau into the sea, either on a recreational basis or
as professional divers. The text and illustrations provide the basis for developing an
understanding of the environment in which divers operate and the processes of diving.
Many of the "hows" and "whys" of diving are explained in a clear, understandable
fashion. The relationship between humans and the animals of the oceans is also
explored, and the reader is provided glimpses of a number of species of marine
organisms.

Critical Context

Jacques-Yves Cousteau's professional life has been revealed to the public through
numerous television programs and many more films and books. Indeed, Cousteau has
provided much of this material himself, such as his first undersea film, *The Silent
World* (1956), and one of his earlier books bearing the same name. *Undersea Explorer*
provides a worthwhile portrait of the early Cousteau, penned in contemporary terms
by an author who was living some of the adventures along with him. Other historical
accounts may be more comprehensive, but this biography uncovers the more salient
parts of Cousteau's early life and exploration and keeps the young reader actively
involved in the processes of the scientist as he goes about his business. First published

in 1957, the story remains dynamic and important as an abridged biography. It provides a view of the emerging scientist that might be overshadowed in later works, which seem to focus on the accomplishments and not on the man.

Duane Inman

UNDYING GLORY
The Story of the Massachusetts 54th Regiment

Author: Clinton Cox
First published: 1991; illustrated
Type of work: History
Time of work: 1863-1865
Locale: Massachusetts, New York, South Carolina, and Florida
Subjects: Race and ethnicity, social issues, and war
Recommended ages: 10-15

The significant and heroic contributions of the members of the all-black Massachusetts 54th Regiment are traced, from the formation of the regiment in 1863 through the end of the Civil War.

Principal personages:
>   ROBERT GOULD SHAW, the officer who first declines and then accepts command of the all-black Massachusetts 54th regiment
>   EDWARD N. HALLOWELL, the officer who assumes command of the 54th regiment after the death of Shaw
>   JOHN ANDREW, the Massachusetts governor who champions the formation of the 54th regiment
>   ABRAHAM LINCOLN, the U.S. president, who makes key decisions regarding black soldiers
>   FREDERICK DOUGLASS, a black abolitionist who recruits black soldiers to the 54th regiment through the power and persuasion of his speaking and writing
>   LEWIS DOUGLASS, Frederick Douglass' son and the first recruit for the 54th regiment
>   CHARLOTTE FORTEN, a black teacher who works with former slaves in a model project
>   ROBERT SMALL, a black riverboat captain who provides vital service to the army and navy in Charleston
>   STEVEN A. SWAILS, the first member of the 54th regiment to be promoted to officer
>   WILLIAM H. CARNEY, a recipient of the Medal of Honor who rescues the colors during the assault on Fort Wagner

Form and Content

Undying Glory: The Story of the Massachusetts 54th Regiment is a well-researched account of the first all-black regiment recruited in the North during the Civil War. In a narration rich with anecdotes, Clinton Cox presents a historical account of events surrounding the formation of the regiment and chronicles the contributions of those who helped make an all-black regiment a reality. He also describes the obstacles presented to men of color who wanted to serve their country, including policies that initially forbade their service and later denied them equal pay and promotion.

From the beginning of the war, African Americans petition to join the Union Army but are refused. John Andrew, the governor of Massachusetts, leads the effort to create an all-black regiment, assisted by abolitionist leader Frederick Douglass, who uses the power of his newspaper and his considerable speaking eloquence to attract recruits. When the roster is complete, the Massachusetts 54th regiment will have drawn recruits from twenty-two states, including the sons of Frederick Douglass and Martin Delaney and the grandson of preacher Sojourner Truth.

Initially, black troops are used as laborers and are denied equal pay and promotion. When the regiment is ordered to Charleston Harbor in South Carolina to assist in the assault on Fort Wagner, however, the courageous performance of the black soldiers in this engagement generates a positive response from government and civilians alike, and, within six months, sixty black regiments exist within the Union Army. As Cox notes, "None but the most biased now questioned the ability of black men to fight or the wisdom of using them to save the Union." Tragically, as black soldiers are engaged in battle, rioters burn black homes and attack black men, women, and children in the streets of New York City. Troops fresh from battle at Gettysburg are sent to New York to restore order.

After the first failed assault on Fort Wagner, troops spend months preparing for a massive artillery bombardment, and the 54th regiment eventually guards the fort as part of the victorious army. Thanks to their initial efforts, nearly 216,000 black soldiers will fight in 449 engagements and 39 battles. President Abraham Lincoln will declare that "without the help of black freed men, the war against the South could not have been won." Although the epilogue acknowledges the eroding of the rights that these men fought to obtain, it also emphasizes the significance of the contribution made by the 54th and other regiments, noting that "largely because of their fulfillment of that work, slavery had been abolished and the foundations laid for a nation where all men might one day live as equals."

Cox makes extensive use of primary documents in his research for this book and includes an impressive bibliography of historical and contemporary texts, from which he draws historical interpretation, quotations, and battle descriptions. Photographs of major participants, statistics from governmental publications, recruiting posters, banners, telegrams, letters, and newspaper excerpts effectively complement the narrative.

Analysis

This account of events surrounding the Massachusetts 54th regiment offers readers an opportunity to explore the moral deliberations of both black and white participants. As Cox explores the backgrounds and motivations of the persons involved, he brings them to life through their own words, excerpted from letters, diaries, journals, essays, and speeches. He also provides details within the narrative that help the reader visualize the experiences of the soldiers and grasp the significance of events. For example, he describes the role of the flag bearer in such a way that the reader understands the importance of the flag as a military marker and the danger that attends the flag bearer in battle.

Cox also observes details of historical location, noting that the newly formed regiment marches over the death site of Crispus Attucks on its way to board a ship in Boston harbor and that the poet Henry Wadsworth Longfellow comments on having seen the new regiment in his diary. He connects events with other historical figures, observing that Clara Barton, the founder of the American Red Cross, treats the wounded at Fort Wagner and that the 54th regiment serves alongside the son of John Quincy Adams, who leads an all-black cavalry unit.

Although Cox shows obvious admiration for the achievements of the 54th regiment, his credentials as a journalist are evident. He neither vilifies nor glorifies the participants in these events, but reveals the doubts and concerns that each has about the decisions that must be made and leaves the evaluation of these choices to the reader. For example, Cox notes that Lincoln was slow in his decisions regarding black participation in the war and their fair treatment as soldiers, but he also suggests reasons that Lincoln might have delayed these decisions. This balance in reporting is also evident in his descriptions of the antiblack riots in New York, where white people rescue, hide, and comfort victims of white mob violence.

Cox puts a human face on statistics, sharing the touching records of those who found a dead boy in a Confederate uniform, "almost a child, with soft skin and long fair hair," whom they buried with great care. In other notes, he ties the regiment's casualties to specific persons, such as "Corporal Henry Dennis, a laborer from Ithaca, New York, who drowned after being forced into the river," or "Private Caldwell, Sojourner Truth's grandson," who "was one of the missing." Cox quotes from the writings of Barton, who treated many of the 54th regiment's wounded and would later found the American Red Cross. He also notes that Colonel Robert Gould Shaw is buried in a mass grave with his troops, a resting place that his father decides not to change when the fort is occupied by Union troops later in the year, believing where Shaw fell with his men to be an appropriate grave.

The historically informed reader will find the research sound and the treatment of subjects and events fair and balanced. Readers with extensive background knowledge of the Civil War will realize that much of the suffering endured by black soldiers was also common to white soldiers, who died more often from disease than from bullets, could be shot for desertion without a hearing, and were often starved, poorly clothed, horribly abused in prison, and subjected to horrors of war past describing. What is important to note, however, is that black soldiers not only shared these hardships but also faced execution or return to slavery if captured and were subject to the additional injustice and indignities that arose from prejudice. That they were able to overcome these additional challenges to perform with exceptional competence and valor makes this a story worth telling.

Critical Context

Undying Glory is the first notable book for young adult readers to focus specifically on the participation of black troops in the Civil War. It is a significant contribution to this largely untold history, providing African American readers with heroic models and nonblacks with the opportunity to identify with these unheralded participants in the war. Hailed for its contribution to the history of the Civil War and described as moving, articulate, and thought-provoking by major reviewers, this book has found a place of regard on the bookshelves of both the newly interested and the historically informed. Young adult readers will find that it serves as a excellent introduction to other volumes from which it was drawn, such as *A Brave Black Regiment* (1894, 1968), Luis Emilio's eyewitness account of the 54th regiment. The motion picture *Glory* (1991) draws on the same events, and, although somewhat lacking in historical accuracy, it has helped develop interest in black Civil War soldiers and motivated many readers to take advantage of Clinton Cox's well-researched and exciting account of the same events.

Cox was twice nominated for the Pulitzer Prize, and his journalistic background is evident in this well-written, balanced, and carefully researched book. As a child, Cox listened to his father tell about his experiences in World War II. He developed an interest in writing about black Civil War soldiers because, like the stories told to him by his father, they were a part of "untold history."

Marcia Brown Popp

VOLCANO
The Eruption and Healing of Mount St. Helens

Author: Patricia Lauber (1924-   )
First published: 1986; illustrated
Type of work: Science
Subjects: Animals, nature, and science
Recommended ages: 10-13

Lauber's dramatic story of the volcanic eruption of Mount St. Helens in 1980, presented using vivid documentary photographs, focuses on nature's profound healing capabilities.

Form and Content

In *Volcano*, Patricia Lauber rekindles the fires that drove Mount St. Helens to its eruption during three dramatic months, March through May, 1980. Through a well-documented text and spectacular color photographs, the author relays the events that led to the eruption, the enormous explosion itself, and the story of phenomenal recovery of the mountain and surrounding terrain.

Lauber first provides a scientific explanation of the volcanic process and of how Mount St. Helens began its explosive venture to become one of the most significant geological events in the twentieth century in the United States. All scientists' eyes were on the mountain from the first minor quake on March 20, 1980. The mountain awoke with shaking and rumbling, and then the big blast on May 18, 1980, inspired members of the geophysical community to head for southwest Washington State, where the volcano loomed amid the beautiful mountain chain whose snow and glaciered peaks dot the Cascade Range. Lauber also details the survivors of the eruption, such as plants grabbing the slightest impressions to begin new life in a barren landscape. The final chapter connects Mount St. Helens to the cosmic picture of volcanoes as the purveyors of destructive and reconstructive geological processes.

The photographs paint the story with beautiful colors and offer a unique perspective. The author gleaned most of the U.S. Forest Service files for these vivid, almost-alive images that were recorded as close to the action as possible. A series of before-and-after photographs dramatically expresses the power of this major volcanic explosion and the influence that it had on its surroundings. The photographs are linked directly to the text in most parts of the book, so that readers have little distance to travel from a textual description to a visual image. Accompanying the photographs are literate, descriptive illustrations explaining specific scientific concepts, such as the three-part color series showing the influence of plate tectonics on volcanic eruptions. Several maps allow those readers not familiar with the beautiful Northwest to visualize the location.

The book is only sixty pages, its five chapters packed with accurate details and descriptive scientific data and written in a language easily read by the average ten-year-old. The index could be more expansive, but it will serve as a useful reference for the curious researcher. Even adults will cherish this exploration over ashen earth alive with new energy. Scientists vow that the entire area will return to its once-pristine beauty—unless humans choose to interfere.

Analysis

Volcano: The Eruption and Healing of Mount St. Helens examines natural phenomena—in this case, trauma to the environment that the author elegantly relates in language for the average juvenile reader. The full impact of this volcanic eruption may not be known for years, but it is significant that geologists, seismologists, paleolimnologists, and other specialists within the scientific community had this opportunity to study the event at first hand. Consequently, Mount St. Helens may prove to be the most substantial outdoor laboratory of the twentieth century. Accurate photographs show the devastation to an area, a community, and the entire Pacific Northwest. In a matter of minutes, 230 square miles of land changed; fifty-seven people were incinerated or buried in avalanches of mud, dirt, and trees; and the economy of a region was altered. More animals and plants than can be counted were extinguished from the earth, and yet much life survived.

In *Volcano*, Lauber presents the systematic destruction and rebuilding of the mountain. The volcano awakens from its slumber, spitting and smoking, rumbling back to life. Scientists sense the impending signs and come to the mountain en masse. When the largest recorded volcanic explosion in history finally occurs, it produces a "stone wind"—a tremendous, 200-mile-an-hour blast that propels stones, some as big as cars, snaps trees, and flattens all in its path. An avalanche rumbles down the stripped side of Mount St. Helens, striking a ridge that splits it in two; one flow fills Spirit Lake with 180 feet of rock and dirt, while the other streams into the Toutle River. Ash spews into the air, unleashing fine particles that will darken the sky as the cloud begins to circle the earth. Pumice and ash flow profusely from the widened gap in the mountain. Finally, vast mud flows careen down the slopes. Six minor eruptions ensue in the next couple of months, a crusty dome building in the newly formed crater. The scientists know that it is safe to swarm in with their instruments to begin the next phase—finding the survivors and studying the colonizers.

The rebirth of the mountain furiously begins. Surviving plants hid under heavy snow, and plants with bulbs and significant root systems lost only that part of life above ground level. Chunks of soil scattered with their plant inhabitants intact. Burrowing animals stayed indoors, wise not to venture out during the first mountain rumblings. Insects and their eggs and larvae held fast inside their small caves. Small seeds now take hold, whipped by the wind and caught in a minute whirlwind above a hoofprint of a fallen elk. The power of nature and the embrace of life come together as the morning mist soothes seed pods with their first drink and causes them to take root and grow. Thus, the healing process begins. Survivors include bacteria, fungi, algae, weeds, insects caved underground, spiders protected in their lairs, and pocket gophers holed up, perhaps in fear of the rumbling earth. The beginnings of a new forest as hardy silver firs and mountain hemlocks spring from crevices in the eroded soil, blanched by the warm spring sun, melting snow trickling over parched earth—the laboratory teems with life.

Curiosity drew the scientists, and curiosity guided the author to this story. Nature encourages survival, and the cycle of life begins. Plants protect aphids, who suck their sap; the sap is then nursed by ants, who will be trapped for dinner by spiders. Bacteria, encouraged by the heat of the event, take hold in the droppings of animals, the fallen timbers, and the defeated wildlife. Fish surviving the massive blast share oxygen with algae growing in their home.

The author opens one chapter with an explanation of how plate tectonics can force glowing magma to flow to the surface. Volcanic eruptions create soil, add gases to the atmosphere, and build mountains. The force of nature that erupted in violence now lay at peace to build a new home for life.

Critical Context

Patricia Lauber loves science, and this book continued her role as a writer of instructional, descriptive books for young readers. Early in her career, Lauber wrote for *Scholastic Magazine*, the science foundation for many children, and held staff positions with *Science World*, *The New Book of Knowledge*, and *Scientific American Illustrated Library*. The nature subjects that she has covered include earthworms, penguins and other birds, glaciers and rivers, dogs, bats, and mice. She also documents nations, their peoples, their scientists, and their natural backyards.

Volcano, lauded by the critics, documents this most significant geological event in a manner that all readers will comprehend. The miraculous power of the volcano, the irony of nature's destructive force wiping the slate clean so that new life can begin, the detailed scientific explanations, and the vivid color photographs to augment the well-written text—all these qualities make this a required factual text for any child's library. *Volcano* was named a Newbery Honor Book and received the *Horn Book* Fanfare Book Award and a New York Academy of Sciences Honorable Mention.

The author trusts a story line to carry the message of her science books—linking events, discoveries, and learning as part of the experience. Lauber has written several books with related themes that will assist the young reader to comprehend the immensity of a volcanic eruption and the ever-changing force of the planet. *All About the Ice Age* (1959), followed by *All About the Planets* (1960) and *Icebergs and Glaciers* (1961), start the student on a learning tour of geology. Her 1965 book entitled *Volcanoes*, in the Junior Science Book series, is certainly a precursor to this 1986 book. Lauber documents another significant earth event in *Summer of Fire: Yellowstone 1988* (1991).

Lauber studied a photograph of a hardy green plant pushing its way through a crusty crack in Mount St. Helen's surface. Fascinated, she began to compose this book. She knew her mission—to explain this phenomenon in a way that young readers could understand and in order to awaken their curiosity—and she accomplished it.

Craig Gilbert

WAITING FOR THE RAIN
A Novel of South Africa

Author: Sheila Gordon (1927-   )
First published: 1987
Type of work: Novel
Type of plot: Social realism
Time of work: The 1980's
Locale: South Africa at a farm on the veld and in Johannesburg
Subjects: Coming-of-age, education, race and ethnicity, and social issues
Recommended ages: 13-18

Tengo, a black boy on an Afrikaaner's farm, leaves the veld and his childhood friend, Frikkie, who will inherit the land, to find his destiny in Johannesburg, where a desperate struggle for education and against apartheid await him.

Principal characters:
TENGO, the ten-year-old son of the "boss-boy" on Oom Koos's farm
FRIKKIE, the nephew of Oom Koos, also ten years old, who loves the farm that he will inherit
OOM KOOS, the white owner of the prosperous farm established by his grandfather during the previous century
TANT SANNIE, Frikkie's childless aunt, who welcomes the boy's visits to the farm, where he spends all his school holidays
SELINA, Tengo's mother, a housemaid and cook for Tant Sannie
TIMOTHY, Tengo's father, the "boss-boy" for Oom Koos
JOSEPH, Tengo's Johannesburg cousin, a young member of the outlawed African National Congress who is committed to change

Form and Content

Sheila Gordon's *Waiting for the Rain* is a realistic account of the doomed friendship of Frikkie and Tengo in South Africa in the turbulent decade of the 1980's when apartheid, the long-standing forced separation of the races maintained by the reactionary government of P. W. Botha, controls the lives of both black and white people. Activist Nelson Mandela has not yet been released from prison, where he has languished for more than twenty years because of his founding of the African National Congress (ANC), which in Mandela's mind was to be a nonviolent resistance to an unjust authoritarian regime. Apartheid, with its cruel, inhumane policies, has kept black people in inferior positions, denying them decent jobs, education, and living conditions.

Apartheid also tears apart the close friendship of Frikkie and Tengo, who have played together since they were three years old. At the beginning of Gordon's novel, they are ten years old. It is then that Tengo notices the differences between them. Why are his mother and father called by their first names when Frikkie's uncle and aunt are called "Master" and "Mistress"? Why do all the black farm workers live in the kraal, a dusty, stench-filled area of small mud huts with no running water and no trees, while Oom Koos and Tant Sannie live in the long white farmhouse surrounded by green grass, jacaranda trees, and flower beds? Why does his family eat only mielie (corn meal) porridge when Selina, Tengo's mother, cooks for Master and Mistress delicious roast beef, chicken, or lamb served with many vegetables and all kinds of mouth-watering desserts?

The real break with Frikkie comes when Tengo, who wants more than anything else to study, goes off at age fourteen to live with his aunt's family in a township outside Johannesburg in order to attend school, to pass his matriculation examinations, and to enter a black college on a scholarship. Frikkie, on the other hand, hates school and lives for the holidays, which he spends on the farm. He hopes that life will never change and that Tengo will be his "boss-boy" some day, just as Tengo's father is the "boss-boy" for Oom Koos.

In town, Tengo's cousin Joseph has joined the ANC. Tengo, who wishes desperately for enough time to study and pass his matriculation exams, is drawn against his will into the struggle for equality that he nevertheless knows must come before his own desires. Meanwhile, Frikkie barely passes his "matrics" and enters the army for compulsory service. He is stationed near Johannesburg.

Gordon's most dramatic scene comes at the climax of her novel. The two boys, now eighteen, unexpectedly confront each other in one of the violent riots in the townships—Tengo as a protester fighting inequity and Frikkie as a soldier protecting the status quo. Alone at the edge of a township in the twilight, Tengo gets control of Frikkie's gun just as the two recognize each other, enemies now. Yet, the childhood bond is strong; neither can kill the other. They go their separate ways in the dusk.

Analysis

Waiting for the Rain dramatizes the disturbing events of South Africa in crisis. Gordon does not show all white people as evil and all black people as good. For example, in the townships, the "tsotsis" are young, lawless black men who rob and kill indiscriminately. Likewise, Frikkie's uncle, although narrow-minded, is considered a kind boss. Although he may threaten his workers with the sjambok (a metal-tipped whip), he has never used it. The British family for whom Tengo's aunt works discusses openly the unfair treatment of black people and sends the sons overseas to avoid serving in the army, whose main mission is to keep black people "in their place." The white minister who helps Tengo study is also sympathetically portrayed.

Yet, it is with the two believable boys, childhood chums who grow and change, that Gordon is at her best. The youngsters race, swim, and play ball together. In one scene in the barn, they furtively drink fresh warm milk from the same cup, laughing at the white mustaches on their faces. Frikkie only superficially notices the differences in their relations; like his uncle, he wants no changes, a situation that the reader finds untenable.

Dialogue sets the tone of inequity. Frikkie is called "Little Master" (Kleinbaas) by the black farm workers, whom he addresses by first name only. Tengo's grandmother is "Lettie" to him. Oom Koos is "Old Master" (Oubaas). Yet, the oubaas refers to his adult male workers as "boys." A derogatory term that he uses for the black children is "piccanin." "Kaffir" is another insulting term for black people. When Tengo informs the oubaas that he wants to study in the city, he is called "cheeky" by Tant Sannie. Language thus emphasizes inequality.

Frikkie, a mediocre pupil, accepts without question the biased historical account of the "Great Trek" of his ancestors when the Boers left hated British rule at the Cape of Good Hope to set up their homeland on the veld. In reality, supremacy over the black people came about when their lands were bartered away for a few beads or cooking pots. The guns of the Boers were powerful persuaders. Frikkie believes that the advantages he has in a secure future on the farm are his birthright.

For black children, there is no such security. With no schools on the farms, Tengo studies in a township and gains an understanding that Frikkie never will have: "None of the Afrikaaners wanted to think about the unfairness, the hardness, the bitterness, the hopelessness of life for the blacks." In the township schools, black people pay for their tuition and books, while education is free for white children. Black people live in crowded slums where garbage accumulates in huge dumps, where the smell of burning tires is constant, and where threats from the tsotsis are a real danger. Bad air, poor food, and disease are daily facts of life.

Tengo has only a few short years to concentrate on his school work. Then, by government decree, Afrikaans is designated as the only language to be used in black schools. The children themselves organize peaceful boycotts carrying signs declaring that they will return to school when they are assured that they will study in English, not in hated Afrikaans. Here, Gordon relies strictly on historical fact in her fair, balanced account.

The army is called to break up the boycotts, but confrontations only increase the violence. Many children are killed, wounded, tortured, or jailed, as their sticks and stones are no match for the rifles, bombs, and tanks of the soldiers. This world has turned ugly and brutal. Yet, the children will not give up, and adults, desperately afraid at first, begin to join them in their crusade against all that apartheid represents.

Crucial to Gordon's story is her phrase "waiting for the rain," a reality that becomes a symbol. A drought of several years threatens the farmers. In their churches every Sunday, they pray for rain.

In addition, in the cities of South Africa, for black people, along with many white people who have joined the movement to end apartheid, "waiting for the rain" is the symbol of what must come, a storm that will bring freedom from oppression. Gordon ends her powerful novel with all her characters "waiting for the rain."

Critical Context

Waiting for the Rain is one of the few realistic novels available describing accurately the turbulent 1980's in South Africa. Its riveting story is often used in classes that stress multicultural literature. *The Middle of Somewhere: A Story of South Africa* (1990) is Sheila Gordon's other novel set in the same period, but it is written for younger children, omitting the violence found in *Waiting for the Rain*.

Two similar dramatic accounts are Beverley Naidoo's *Journey to Jo'burg* (1985) and its sequel, *Chain of Fire* (1989), in which Naledi, her brother Tiro, and her friend Taolo are courageous young protesters. Mark Mathabane's autobiographical *Kaffir Boy: The True Story of a Black Youth's Coming of Age in Apartheid South Africa* (1986) is another gripping account. *My Name Is Not Angelica* (1989) is Scott O'Dell's historically accurate treatment of the slave trade along the southeastern coast of Africa in the eighteenth century. Based on historical fact, it makes superb background reading for stories of this troubled land. Lesley Beake's inspiring *Song of Be* (1991) is another realistic work in which a young bushwoman tells her own story of freedom turned into terror, of recovery and love in postcolonial Namibia.

Although violence and tragedy are themes in these well-written books, the terror that they portray nevertheless leaves young readers with a feeling of hope because in these works the youthful characters act bravely to bring about change. In Gordon's compelling novel, Tengo and his cousin Joseph are two of the many youths whose voices, like Be's, ring true. They will survive as they struggle for peace and understanding.

Paula Kiska

WALK TWO MOONS

Author: Sharon Creech
First published: 1994
Type of work: Novel
Type of plot: Psychological realism
Time of work: The 1990's
Locale: Euclid, Ohio; Bybanks, Kentucky; and various places along the route between Ohio and Lewiston, Idaho
Subjects: Coming-of-age, death, family, and friendship
Recommended ages: 10-13

> *On a trip from Ohio to Idaho with her grandparents, Salamanca Tree Hiddle learns to accept the death of her mother as she tells the story of Phoebe Winterbottom.*

Principal characters:
  SALAMANCA ("SAL") TREE HIDDLE, a thirteen-year-old struggling with her mother's disappearance
  CHANHASSEN ("SUGAR") PICKFORD HIDDLE, Sal's mother
  JOHN HIDDLE, Sal's father
  GRAN and GRAMPS HIDDLE, Sal's grandparents, with whom she is traveling
  PHOEBE WINTERBOTTOM, Sal's friend
  NORMA WINTERBOTTOM, Phoebe's mother
  MARGARET CADAVER, John Hiddle's friend and Phoebe's neighbor
  MRS. PARTRIDGE, Margaret Cadaver's mother, who leaves notes on Phoebe's doorstep
  BEN FINNEY, Sal's friend

Form and Content

Walk Two Moons is a story within a story. Salamanca Tree Hiddle entertains her unique and charming grandparents on a trip from Ohio to Idaho with the story of Phoebe Winterbottom. Sal's story about her experiences with Phoebe is intermingled with her first-person narrative of the trip's events. Sharon Creech presents a deeply moving story told in a simple, straightforward fashion liberally sprinkled with picturesque phrases.

Sal's mother left their farm in Bybanks, Kentucky, in April; a short time later, they learned that she is never returning. Unable to bear the memories that the farm evoked, Sal's father moves them to a small house in Euclid, Ohio, where he sells farm machinery and, to Sal's resentment, spends much of his spare time with his friend Margaret Cadaver. Phoebe Winterbottom, Margaret's next-door neighbor, soon becomes Sal's friend and confidante. Later that year, Sal's grandparents arrive to take her by car from Euclid to Lewiston, Idaho, where her mother is "resting peacefully."

As they begin the trip, Gram Hiddle asks Sal to entertain them with a story, so Sal spins the "extensively strange story" of Phoebe Winterbottom.

Phoebe's very ordered life with her highly respectable family begins to change the day that a strange young man appears on their doorstep. He asks to see her mother, who has gone shopping. Phoebe, who has been warned about strangers, is convinced that he is a lunatic, and, when her mother disappears sometime later, Phoebe decides that she has been kidnapped by him. Phoebe's father points out that her mother has left notes for each family member and that the freezer is filled with neatly labeled meals, but Phoebe persists in her belief. Meanwhile, Sal finds herself attracted to Ben, the cousin of another friend, Mary Lou Finney. Ben is staying with Mary Lou's family, and his mother, too, is missing. Sal and Phoebe trace the "lunatic" to a nearby university, where they see Phoebe's mother kiss him gently on the cheek. Sal flees and tracks down Ben, who has traveled on the same bus to the university town, at a hospital. Here, she meets his mother, a psychiatric patient. When Phoebe arrives home, she discovers that her mother is returning the next day and is bringing someone with her. That someone turns out to be the "lunatic," her illegitimate son.

Sal's story about Phoebe progresses slowly as she and her grandparents drive across the country. Sal is anxious to arrive in Lewiston by her mother's birthday, but, a hundred miles east, Gram Hiddle has a stroke and is hospitalized. Gramps gives Sal money and the car keys, and Sal drives carefully, as Gramps had taught her, to Lewiston Hill. It is there that her mother's bus left the road, killing her. A kind sheriff helps Sal find her mother's grave, and finally Sal can accept that her mother is dead.

Analysis

In *Walk Two Moons*, Mrs. Partridge, Margaret Cadaver's mother, leaves messages on Phoebe Winterbottom's porch. The first of these messages reads, "Don't judge a man until you've walked two moons in his moccasins." As Salamanca tells Phoebe's story, she walks in Phoebe's moccasins, and she learns not only about Phoebe but about herself as well. She declares that "beneath Phoebe's story was another one. Mine."

The two primary themes in *Walk Two Moons*, separation and love, are strongly intertwined. The first theme, separation, reflects the basic developmental task of adolescence: separation from the mother. Creech clarifies this theme for readers with Sal's memories of her dog, Moody Blue. She remembers how Moody Blue would not let anyone touch its litter of puppies during the first week after their birth. Gradually, the dog allowed its puppies to be touched but would always carefully herd them back. When they were six weeks old, however, Moody Blue pushed them away. Sal thought that Moody Blue was terrible, but her mother explained the dog's behavior by telling Sal, "They have to become independent. What if something happened to Moody Blue? They wouldn't know how to survive without her."

Walk Two Moons examines the related themes of separation and love through the stories of Salamanca, Phoebe, and, to a lesser extent, Ben. Their mothers have all left home, either temporarily or permanently, and, as Salamanca gives voice to her own thoughts and experiences or tells her grandparents the story of Phoebe, readers come to understand why these young people react as they do. Sal remembers how, after Phoebe's mother left, Phoebe showed her things such as a handmade birthday card and a photograph of Phoebe and her mother, and how she explained that she and her mother had painted the violet wall in Phoebe's room. Sal had clung to memories of her own mother in much the same way. She knew why Phoebe, all evidence to the contrary, insisted that her mother had been kidnapped. Phoebe could not allow herself to believe that her mother would voluntarily abandon her. To do so would be to admit that her mother did not love her.

As the story progresses, Sal and Phoebe learn that their mothers' reasons for leaving were personal and unrelated to their relationships with their daughters. Both left to discover their identities apart from their families. Phoebe's mother returned, and perhaps Sal's mother would also have returned, had she not died. As Sal finally realizes, "Maybe my mother's leaving had nothing whatsoever to do with me. It was separate and apart. We couldn't own our own mothers."

For children around Sal's age, the issues surrounding separation, so realistically portrayed in this novel, are particularly relevant. Preadolescent children are beginning to crave independence, yet they are still young enough to need mothering and to believe that things happen because of them. By walking in the moccasins of Sal and Phoebe, young readers begin to see their mothers as separate from them, with their own lives and their own needs. Children come to recognize that they are neither responsible for—nor can they control—the actions of their parents.

Walk Two Moons is about people who love and care for others under trying circumstances. The love between Sal and her grandparents is strong and shines out of every page, as does the love between Sal's parents. Phoebe and her father come to realize, during Mrs. Winterbottom's unexplained absence, how much they love her. Thus, Mr. Winterbottom is able to accept his wife's illegitimate son into their family. Love is reflected in the friendship between Sal's father and Mrs. Cadaver and in the caring between Ben and Sal that blossoms into first love. Creech's poetic prose weaves her two themes of separation and love into an unforgettable story.

Critical Context

Walk Two Moons won the 1995 Newbery Medal, presented annually by the American Library Association to the author of the most distinguished contribution to literature for children published in the United States during the preceding year. Until its publication, Sharon Creech, who lives most of the year in England and whose three preceding novels were published there, was unknown as a writer of American juvenile novels. *Walk Two Moons*, although not originally intended as a book for young readers, will appeal to children between the ages of ten and thirteen because of its realistic portrayal of the young protagonists, its touches of humor, and its warm descriptions of the places and events experienced by an unforgettable thirteen-year-old heroine, Salamanca Tree Hiddle.

Accepting death, coming-of-age, and relationships such as those between parents and adolescents, between grandparents and adolescents, and among adolescent peers are important themes in juvenile and young adult literature, particularly in award-winning novels. These themes are all present in *Walk Two Moons*. This novel provides an interesting contrast to the 1993 Newbery Medal-winning *Missing May* (1992), by Cynthia Rylant. Both deal with a similar theme: accepting the death of a loved one. While each novel depicts colorful characters and uses poetic and picturesque language, Creech has successfully woven a far more complex tale from the same basic story. With *Walk Two Moons*, Creech assumes an important role in the field of juvenile literature.

Constance A. Mellon

THE WATER-BABIES
A Fairy Tale for a Land-Baby

Author: Charles Kingsley (1819-1875)
First published: 1863; illustrated
Type of work: Novel
Type of plot: Fantasy and moral tale
Time of work: The mid-nineteenth century
Locale: Northern England and a fantasy water world
Subjects: Nature, poverty, religion, social issues, and the supernatural
Recommended ages: 10-13

After his transformation into a water-baby, Tom the chimney sweep journeys from a small stream to the ocean while developing the physical and moral cleanliness necessary for his salvation.

> *Principal characters:*
> Tom, a little chimney sweep, who is turned into a water-baby
> Thomas Grimes, Tom's cruel master
> Miss Ellie, Sir John Harthover's daughter, "the most beautiful little girl that Tom had ever seen"
> Mrs. Bedonebyasyoudid, an ugly fairy who administers justice in the world
> Mrs. Doasyouwouldbedoneby, a beautiful fairy who nurtures the water-babies, the sister of Mrs. Bedonebyasyoudid

Form and Content

Charles Kingsley's *The Water-Babies: A Fairy Tale for a Land-Baby* is an English Victorian fairy tale that traces the progress of little Tom, a chimney sweep, from a world of filth, poverty, and abuse to an aquatic fantasy world in which he eventually becomes physically and spiritually clean. The first two chapters present Tom's hard life in the North Country of nineteenth century England. The remaining six chronicle his adventures in the world of the water-babies. While the story itself is told from a third-person omniscient point of view, the narrator continually addresses his young readers directly. "Once upon a time," he begins, "there was a little chimney-sweep, and his name was Tom. That is a short name, and you have heard it before, so you will not have much trouble remembering it." Since Kingsley originally wrote *The Water-Babies* for his youngest child, Grenville, it is not surprising that this parent-to-child approach is maintained throughout. In a playful manner, Kingsley always makes sure that his readers see the point. For example, at the end he states that "we should learn thirty-seven or thirty-nine things" from the tale, but "I am not exactly sure which." *The Water-Babies* is essentially a charming fantasy with a serious, consistently developed moral purpose.

The first part of the tale is a sentimental, Dickensian account of a poor orphan facing poverty and danger. Tom's master, Mr. Grimes, is a bully and a drunkard who beats the boy on a regular basis. At Harthover Place, the estate of Sir John Harthover, his wife, and their daughter, Miss Ellie, Tom accidently stumbles into the little girl's room after getting lost in a maze of chimney flues. Looking around the room and then in a mirror, he learns for the first time the difference between being dirty and being clean. When Miss Ellie awakens and screams in fright, Tom flees, pursued by practically everyone on the estate. After an arduous trek through the country, Tom arrives at the village of Vendale, exhausted. The local schoolmistress helps him, but, with the sound of church bells ringing in his ears and an overpowering desire to be clean, he stumbles off to a nearby stream and drowns while trying to wash himself.

Tom is transformed into a water-baby, and the second part of the story treats his moral progress as he moves from the stream to the river and finally to the ocean. He encounters various aquatic creatures in his journey—from caddis flies to lobsters, from otters to whales. Along the way, he learns the moral lessons necessary for his redemption from characters such as the two sister fairies, Mrs. Bedonebyasyoudid and Mrs. Doasyouwouldbedoneby, and the creative force in nature, Mother Carey. Once in the ocean, he travels to fantasy lands such as St. Brandan's Isle (the home of the water-babies); Mother Carey's Shiny Wall and Peacepool; and the Other-end-of-Nowhere, where Tom at last does "the thing he did not like" and thus completes his moral journey. In the conclusion, he returns to St. Brandan's Isle and is reunited with Miss Ellie.

Analysis

The Water-Babies explicitly informs its young readers that there are serious problems to be faced in the world: poverty, abuse, and death among them. The work's exploration of these unpleasant subjects reveals its author's commitment, as an Anglican clergyman and Christian Socialist, to the spiritual and physical well-being of his fellow humans in an age when England was in the midst of its sometimes troubling transformation into the first industrialized nation in Europe with a colonial empire that stretched around the world. *The Water-Babies* also assures its readers, however, that there are solutions to these problems. The primary one is the individual's difficult but necessary development into an adult who is both spiritually pure and morally aware of his or her responsibility to others—even those whom one may, with good reason, find reprehensible. Thus, as the work progressively makes clear, Tom cannot really grow up until his moral choices come from an inner sense of what is right, rather than from fear of reprisal—however just—from Mrs. Bedonebyasyoudid, and until he can learn to care about Mr. Grimes, the one whom he hates and fears the most.

In addition to its major emphasis on the process of redemption, *The Water-Babies* also assures children of the continuing presence of God in the natural world. From childhood, Kingsley had been an avid naturalist, and his tale shows his intimate knowledge and love of the creatures of the streams and seashores of England. The book abounds not only in a variety of species but also in concrete, specific descriptions of their appearance and habits. Kingsley is at pains to show, however, that the natural world is not merely natural but far more complex and mysterious than humans' finite minds can comprehend. In the second chapter, for example, he mounts a detailed attack against the argument that some things are "contrary to Nature," in defending the possible existence of water-babies. Unlike many of his contemporaries, he strongly believed that science and religion were ultimately compatible.

Although the narrator will often pause to tell readers that they are to look for the message in it, *The Water-Babies* is not a long lesson in morality; it could hardly have survived as a children's favorite if it were. Instead, Kingsley is successful for the most part in interweaving his message with his fairy tale. For example, the water creatures that are so accurately described are given human traits, a common characteristic in fables. Some are merely humorous, recognizable English types such as the lordly salmon, who will have nothing to do with the lower-class trout, or the mollymocks, sea birds inhabited by the spirits of whaling captains who use the colorful language of sailors. Others, such as Tom's lobster friend, learn lessons as a result of character flaws such as conceit. In addition, both of the fairy sisters, Mrs. Bedonebyasyoudid and Mrs. Doasyouwouldbedoneby, are well-drawn characters possessing a charm beyond that of the moral or theological concepts that they may represent.

Only in the eighth chapter, when Tom reaches the Other-end-of-Nowhere, does Kingsley's attempt to wed fable with message break down. To reach Mr. Grimes, Tom must pass through fifteen obviously allegorical locations. The focus of Kingsley's satire—for that is what he is engaged in here—is intellectual folly. Unfortunately, most of it is rather lame, such as "Waste-paper-land" or "the sea of slops." Although the satire can be effective at times, Kingsley appears to be cramming as many of his pet peeves into the final pages as possible. As a result, the confrontation with Mr. Grimes—the crucial point in Tom's redemption—only partly redeems the climax. Until chapter 8, however, Kingsley does a masterful job of blending message and fable, building effectively toward the conclusion by paralleling Tom's moral development with his progression through the various aquatic worlds.

Critical Context

The Water-Babies marked the beginning of a golden age of fantasy writing in English literature. It was the first of a series of fantasies offering not only an escape from the ugly complexity of adult life but also a fully realized alternate world. Lewis Carroll's *Alice's Adventures in Wonderland* (1865) and *Through the Looking-Glass and What Alice Found There* (1871), however, create such a place far more successfully than Charles Kingsley's book does. Other works in this tradition include George MacDonald's *At the Back of the North Wind* (1871), James M. Barrie's *Peter Pan* (1903), and A. A. Milne's *Winnie-the-Pooh* (1926). Though these works have retained their popularity more successfully than *The Water-Babies*, Kingsley's tale still has its readers, although their number grows smaller each year.

Kingsley's writing for children was not confined to *The Water-Babies*. *Glaucus: Or,*

The Wonders of the Shore (1855), for example, is a guidebook to natural wonders that Kingsley put to good use later in *The Water-Babies*. *The Heroes: Or, Greek Fairy Tales for My Children* (1856) is a competent retelling of Greek legends. His other works include *Hereward the Wake* (1866), and *Madame How and Lady Why* (1870).

John Bunyan's *The Pilgrim's Progress* (1678, 1684) is clearly an important influence on *The Water-Babies*, particularly in the paralleling of physical and moral journeys. Jonathan Swift's *Gulliver's Travels* (1726) was also influential. In fact, in the last chapter, Tom visits Swift's Isle of Laputa.

The Water-Babies is still worth reading—for the fascinating details of aquatic life, the wonderful characters, the work's overall spirit of fun, and even its moral.

George F. Horneker

WATERLESS MOUNTAIN

Author: Laura Adams Armer (1874-1963)
First published: 1931; illustrated
Type of work: Novel
Type of plot: Moral tale and social realism
Time of work: The early twentieth century
Locale: Arizona
Subjects: Coming-of-age, nature, and race and ethnicity
Recommended ages: 13-18

Conscious of a vocation to become a medicine man, Younger Brother, a Navajo boy, studies the ways of his people.

> *Principal characters:*
> YOUNGER BROTHER, eight years old at the beginning of the story, a Navajo boy in Arizona
> ELDER BROTHER, his brother, who marries and starts his own family
> UNCLE, a famous medicine man who gives Younger Brother his secret name (Little Singer) and trains him in the ancient ways
> HASTEEN TSO (THE BIG MAN), a white trader
> CUT FINGER, a horse thief

Form and Content

A slow-moving, lyrical story, *Waterless Mountain* follows a single character, Younger Brother, as he matures from a sensitive eight-year-old into a successful young farmer attending his first social dance. The book's thirty-four chapters, most of which can stand alone, center on traditional ceremonies ("The Basket Ceremony," "The Dance of the Maidens," a healing ceremony, an initiation) and markers of the seasons, such as the "month of Short Corn." Into these chapters Laura Adams Armer has woven many folktales of the "Navaho" (the spelling used throughout, rather than the spelling "Navajo" preferred by later scholars). These tales are retold by, and sometimes to, Younger Brother as he gradually learns more about his culture and becomes increasingly sensitive to the natural world around him.

From the opening chapters, Younger Brother is shown to be closely in tune with nature. Watching his sheep as they graze, he thinks about the grass "and how it grew after the rain," picturing its underground roots: "He thought of seeds underground, waiting in the darkness for the rain to moisten them and swell them so they could burst into leaves and roots." He communicates mystically with Pack Rat, Yellow Beak (the eagle), and Soft-footed Chief (the cougar). After seeing the dance of the Deer People, Younger Brother begins composing songs. This ability to see what others do not see, and to transform it into song, causes his uncle, a medicine man, to dub him Little Singer and begin training him in his craft, including a knowledge of the culture's legends and of sand painting. During this period, Younger Brother also expands his knowledge by going up in a small plane with a white trader known as the Big Man and a water developer.

Younger Brother's quest to become worthy to be a medicine man takes a literal form in the central section of the book, when at the age of twelve, feeling restless, he sets out for an unknown western destination on his pinto pony. Along the way, he rescues and travels with a white boy, loses his horse to thieves and reclaims it, visits a relative who tragically loses her young husband, and rejoins his family in time to travel to the coast by train. He has proved his independence and resourcefulness and has become a young man. His first view of the ocean and his experience of a big city (where his parents are exhibiting at a museum) are both mixed. The visit ends shortly after a trip to see a motion picture in which Younger Brother recognizes one of the actors as his relative's young husband, now dead. His distress is so profound that the Big Man acknowledges, "We must go back. We do not belong here."

The book closes with the return to Waterless Mountain and its timeless ways. The last immediate threat to peace in the community, Cut Finger, is arrested and removed after setting fire to a trading post. Younger Brother helps to find the tribe's missing deerskin masks, hidden long ago in a cave. The all-night Dance of the Yays is the climax of a nine-day ceremony attended by more than a thousand Navajos. For the first time, Younger Brother participates as an assistant to his uncle. In parallel fashion, soon after the ceremony he attends a "girl dance" at the trading post, and it is clear that he will be settling down before long, in a ceremony like his brother's wedding at the beginning of the book. The cycle of the seasons, as well as of the day, is again complete as Younger Brother greets the dawn "with a consciousness of new power rising within him."

Armer and her husband created more than a dozen full-page aquatint illustrations for the book, a reminder that the author's first creative works were paintings and that she had made an extensive study of sand paintings, copying many for the Rockefeller Museum in Santa Fe, New Mexico.

Analysis

Waterless Mountain is about a way of life that Armer profoundly admired. Its slow pace, its insistence on the minutiae of tribal life, and its many interpolated legends and stories all underscore the closeness of the Navajo culture to the cycles of nature. The family is the central unit. Each person has a clear role to play at every stage of life: Younger Brother herds his mother's sheep, his father makes beautiful silver jewelry, and his mother weaves as well as managing the household affairs and trading. At any important point in life, there is a ceremony—for initiation, for betrothal, for sickness, for harvest. Armer believed that exposure to the ways of the Navajo released her own creative abilities; all of her significant work in art, film, and fiction was done after she began studying the Navajo culture in her fifties.

The retellings of Navajo legends and the descriptions of Navajo ceremonies remain compelling features of the book. The plot itself, in which a young boy matures, leaves home to find himself, and returns to take his place in society as an adult, is almost submerged beneath the weight of the expository material about Navajo culture. This aspect of the book has caused it to be more popular with critics and teachers than with young readers. Armer's simple, beautifully balanced prose, however, is one of the books' strongest features.

Critical Context

When Laura Adams Armer wrote *Waterless Mountain*, she clearly intended it to portray its subject in a positive light to a reading public that knew nothing about it. In 1931, the novel was progressive in most respects. Its subject matter, fidelity to its material, and luminous prose brought excellent reviews and two awards: the Longman's Juvenile Fiction Prize and the Newbery Medal. As a Newbery-winning book, *Waterless Mountain* has remained available and is mentioned in most accounts of the development of juvenile literature in the United States; however, it has never been a favorite of young readers, and both Armer and her book have lapsed into relative obscurity. Following the success of *Waterless Mountain*, Armer portrayed another Navajo adolescent, Na Nai, in *Dark Circle of Branches* (1933). Several other books by the author about the Southwest were designed for young readers, such as *The Trader's Children* (1937) and *Farthest West* (1939). Her picture book about a Mexican boy, *The Forest Pool*, received a Caldecott Honor Book designation; otherwise, Armer's later works attracted little attention. In the year before her death, Armer described her time among the Navajos in the autobiographical book *In Navaho Land* (1963).

The relationship between Navajos and white people in *Waterless Mountain* is problematical. Unlike many authors dealing with this subject matter, Armer does not dwell on the clashes between white people and American Indians but rather portrays them as coexisting in relative harmony. Despite the fact that the book's focus on day-to-day Navajo life puts the non-Navajo characters at the periphery, it is evident that the white characters—with their cars, planes, and money—represent a threat to the very way of life being described. The benevolent paternalism of the Big Man, in particular, seems less attractive with the passage of the years. Younger Brother "could feel power shining through the blue eyes" when he first meets the Big Man who—literally—pats him on the head. The pat on the head is only the first indication of the Big Man's attitude; after giving a dollar to a young man, he "drove on, smiling at the ways of these brown people, whom he loved." Clearly, the Big Man is intended as a sympathetic character; clearly, he no longer seems quite so sympathetic. Other white characters echo this paternalism (although, like the Big Man, they seem to feel real affection).

Beginning in the 1980's, many critics have believed it important that a culture be portrayed from the inside: African American stories by African Americans, American Indian ones by American Indians, and so on. *Waterless Mountain* has, like many other books, fallen into this controversy because it is obviously written from the outside—by a white author, writing for young white readers. Feminist readers may feel concern about the extremely traditional gender roles shown in the book. Even though the book may have its detractors on such political grounds, *Waterless Mountain* is still admired for its sensitive and accurate portrayal of Navajo life in the early years of the twentieth century.

Caroline C. Hunt

WE INTERRUPT THIS SEMESTER FOR AN IMPORTANT BULLETIN

Author: Ellen Conford (1942-   )
First published: 1979
Type of work: Novel
Type of plot: Social realism
Time of work: The late 1970's
Locale: A typical suburban high school
Subjects: Education, friendship, and love and romance
Recommended ages: 13-15

Although only a sophomore, Carrie Wasserman is already the features editor for the Lincoln High School newspaper and dates the handsome editor-in-chief, a senior, but she soon discovers that she has much to learn about both journalism and love.

> *Principal characters:*
> CARRIE WASSERMAN, a high school sophomore experiencing the joys and trials of first love
> CHIP CUSTER, the senior boy whom Carrie has been dating for three months
> PRUDIE TUCKERMAN, a new student, who is beautiful, glamorous, rich, and stiff competition for Carrie
> MR. MARK THATCHER, the new faculty adviser for the student newspaper
> CLAUDIA, one of Carrie's best friends
> TERRY, Carrie's other best friend
> PETER KAPLAN, a freshman willing to help Carrie uncover a big story
> DR. WASSERMAN, Carrie's father and the head guidance counselor at the high school
> MR. NELSON FELL, the head of the school lunch program

Form and Content

We Interrupt This Semester for an Important Bulletin is a tightly plotted high school novel that takes a humorous yet sensitive look at the joys, heartaches, and confusions of teenagers trying to understand both themselves and their relationships. The setting is a generic suburban high school in an unspecified city. Ellen Conford makes no attempt to present hard-hitting social realism, but she does deal with a wide range of concerns facing most young people as they enter the world of high school.

As Carrie Wasserman, the narrator, begins her sophomore year at Lincoln High School, everything seems perfect. She is the features editor for the *Lincoln Log* and is dating Chip Custer, a senior and editor-in-chief of the newspaper. In the first chapter, Conford subtly introduces two important conflicts. When the new faculty adviser shows up, Carrie is attracted by his good looks, feeling "all melty" inside, which causes her to feel confused and a bit guilty because she has a boyfriend. Another conflict involves the seriousness with which Chip takes his job as editor. These two issues are developed over the next few chapters. Carrie interviews the "incredibly gorgeous" new biology teacher and again is confused by the attraction that she feels. When she turns in her story, Chip, as editor, tells her bluntly that it is inadequate and cannot be printed. Her second interview is better, but Chip again edits it mercilessly, and Carrie is left close to tears as she equates his rejection of her work with a rejection of her.

The novel's primary complication arises when new student Prudie Tuckerman arrives looking for a position on the newspaper staff. Prudie is beautiful in face and form, is rich, and oozes Southern charm—and she wastes no time in plying that charm on Chip. Carrie realizes that she cannot compete with Prudie, so she swears off men and dedicates herself to her career in journalism.

The rest of the novel plays out an overzealous attempt by Chip and Carrie to expose what they think is graft in the lunch program. Carrie, with the help of an adoring freshman reporter, bugs the office of Mr. Fell, the program director. In the meantime, Chip finds a "source" for further evidence of profiteering, and they rush a story into print with a joint byline. To celebrate the first issue, Prudie hosts a sophisticated dinner party at her luxurious home. Feeling hopelessly outclassed, Carrie gets drunk on Brandy Alexanders, and her breakup with Chip becomes official.

The lunch program story creates an uproar at the school, and they taste the excitement of big-time investigative reporting. Unfortunately, they also get a taste of reality as they are hauled into the principal's office and shown that they have misinterpreted comments by Mr. Fell and have used a very unreliable "source" for facts. The *Lincoln Log* staff receives a strong reprimand, issues a retraction, and is put on probationary status. Prudie, who feels no responsibility for what happened or loyalty to the others, decides that neither journalism nor Chip is for her. The story ends with Carrie in Chip's arms.

Analysis

With strong plotting, a brisk pace, and a humorous touch, Conford creates dynamic scenes through which her main character moves toward realizations about love, friendship, and herself. *We Interrupt This Semester for an Important Bulletin* is intended to be a relatively easy book with a solid story. Although it lacks the emotional intensity of tougher realistic novels, it articulates relevant themes for young adult readers, and it does so with sensitivity and sympathy.

Conford's themes resonate through the entire novel. The primary theme of young love, and the confused emotions that accompany it, is expressed through several characters and situations. At the beginning, Carrie is secure in her relationship with Chip. Why then, she wonders, does she feel so tingly in the presence of the young, good-looking teachers? She seems to recognize a rather basic sexual attraction but perhaps is not quite ready to admit it. When Chip criticizes her work, not only is her pride hurt but the security of her relationship is shaken as well. Prudie's arrival demolishes that security, and Carries feels inadequate, rejected, jealous, confused, helpless, and hopeless—all the symptoms of heartache. In other developments, Carrie's best friend also breaks up with her boyfriend because he paid more attention to football than to her, and the helpful freshman reporter, under the influence of a couple of Manhattans at Prudie's party, proclaims his love for Carrie. Conford deftly guides her characters through a gamut of emotions.

Another major theme is that of individual responsibility and the need to face the consequences of one's actions. When Carrie does a poor job on her first two stories, she wants to blame the critics, who include not only Chip but also other staff members and her mother, father, and sister. Eventually, she admits her need for improvement. Chip also discovers that he is not the perfect editor when he fails to check the accuracy and reliability of his facts and sources. His personal ambition to break the big story was stronger than his journalistic judgment. Carrie and Chip are both willing to face the consequences of their misguided actions, and they seemed to have learned and grown from the experience. Nevertheless, many readers may think that the principal's decision to give Chip another chance as editor is a bit unrealistic.

The themes of friendship and loyalty also run through the novel. Carrie exhibits a rather believable selfishness when one of her best friends calls to cry about her breakup with her boyfriend. In a nicely ironic touch, Carrie says that her friend is "too wrapped up in [her] own petty problems" to notice that other people have troubles, too. In the end, however, with her own situation resolved, Carrie is finally able to give her friend some comfort. The idea of team loyalty and unity is expressed in the way that the staff of the *Lincoln Log* sticks together when the principal and Mr. Fell call them on the carpet for the story that Chip and Carrie wrote. Even though the responsibility for the story rests directly on Carrie and Chip, the whole staff accepts the punishment—except, that is, for Prudie. Ultimately, her disloyalty to the newspaper negates her sweetness and charm in Chip's eyes and allows him to see the difference between his relationship with Carrie and the one that he was starting with Prudie.

Critical Context

We Interrupt This Semester for an Important Bulletin is a sequel to Ellen Conford's *Dear Lovey Hart, I Am Desperate* (1975), in which freshman Carrie Wasserman wreaks havoc as an advice columnist for the school newspaper. These books, and others such as *Seven Days to a Brand-New Me* (1981), a novel of self-esteem, represent Conford's move to a somewhat older audience than the one for which she had been writing. Conford began with the picture books *Impossible, Possum* (1971) and *Why Can't I Be William?* (1972). Later books such as *Dreams of Victory* (1973) and *Me and the Terrible Two* (1974) are aimed at mid- to upper-elementary students, to whom Conford continues to return in, for example, her Jenny Archer books.

Conford's high school novels have found a legitimate niche in young adult literature, and their popularity is a sign that she hits the mark pretty closely with the thirteen- to fifteen-year-old audience. Conford understands that high school life, especially the first two years, is dominated by peer relationships. While it could certainly be argued that these works are not serious literature, there is no doubt about their value for young readers. They are intended to be light reading, easily accessible with strong plots and recognizable, sympathetic characters. Although the issues are not tough and there are no hard edges to the stories, Conford's novels do focus on what, for a large number of young people, are serious concerns and problems.

Daniel Glynn

WELSH LEGENDS AND FOLK-TALES

Author: Gwyn Jones (1907-   )
First published: 1955; illustrated
Type of work: Short fiction
Subjects: The supernatural and war
Recommended ages: 15-18

Jones retells some of the more prominent Welsh legends and folktales, giving the young adult reader a thorough insight into the legendary past of the Welsh people.

Form and Content

Gwyn Jones's *Welsh Legends and Folk-Tales* is a collection of traditional legends and tales deriving from the distinctly Celtic people of Western Britain known as the Welsh. Many of the stories within the book parallel those found in *The Mabinogion*, a nineteenth century collection of Welsh legends and tales that Lady Charlotte Guest extracted from two medieval Welsh manuscripts. Jones recounts these stories from a third-person perspective in modern English prose while still preserving many of the Welsh names for people and places. The book deals with legendary Welsh leaders and folk heroes, focusing especially on their lineage, their heroic exploits, and their contributions to the legendary past. While Welsh tales are more obscure than their more popular counterparts in Irish, Scottish, and English folklore, well-read young adults may be familiar with some of the names and events, especially those pertaining to the Arthurian legends, which are still shared by most cultures throughout the British Isles and France.

The book contains three major sections—"The Four Branches of Story," "The British Arthur," and "Tales Old and New"—each of which is composed of subsections. For readers who may find some of the names difficult to read and pronounce, Jones includes at the end of the book a guide to pronouncing Welsh names. Other aspects of the book include a genealogical page, a map of Wales, and frequent illustrations by Joan Kiddell-Monroe.

The first section of the book, "The Four Branches of Story," introduces the great Welsh heroes of *The Mabinogion* and relates the various travails and deeds associated with these heroes. A common theme throughout this section is familial disharmony. A prince named Pwyll falls in love with a beautiful woman, Rhiannon, whose father intends to marry her to another man, Gwawl, whom she does not love. A king named Brân the Blest promises his sister Branwen to Matholwch, the king of Ireland, so that relations between Britain and Ireland are eased, but, because Brân's half brother, Efnisien, insults Matholwch, relations are strained to the point of war. Pryderi (the son of Pwyll) and his mother, Rhiannon, are entranced by a magical bowl. Gwydion, the son of Dôn, resorts to trickery in order to coerce the lady Aranrhod to bestow upon their son a proper name and weapons.

The second section of the book, "The British Arthur," offers a rendition of some of the exploits of the legendary King Arthur, but the tales have a truly Celtic flavor to them. The majority of these tales derive from the same Welsh manuscripts from which *The Mabinogion* was created. The first story in this section tells of Arthur's cousin, Culhwch, and his quest to marry Olwen, the daughter of the Chief Giant Ysbaddaden. The next story gives an account of the love of Trystan and Esyllt; because Esyllt is the wife of March, an argument ensues between Trystan and March that Arthur is forced to settle. The third story deals with a giant named Rhitta whose pride encourages him to steal the beards of his foes and wear them as ornamentation, until Arthur humbles him. The final story of this section recounts the strange, seemingly prophetic dream of a man named Rhonabwy.

The third and final section of Jones's book, "Tales Old and New," begins with two more stories from the Welsh manuscripts from which *The Mabinogion* was created. The first story describes the manner in which an emperor of Rome named Macsen Wledig finds himself a bride, while the second story tells of King Lludd and the way in which he rids Britain of three disturbing plagues: an invasion by a mischievous people called the Coranieid, a terrible scream occurring every May-eve, and a shortage of food and drink. Lludd succeeds in his quest because of the advice of his brother, Llefelys. Following these two stories are a handful of shorter Welsh folktales.

Analysis

Jones's book allows the young adult reader to understand the Welsh people through their legends and tales. People of all cultures have a body of knowledge and wisdom that they transmit through their stories—through myths, legends, and folktales—and the Welsh are no different. Such stories help to define the culture out of which they arise, explaining to the reader or listener (for such stories in most cultures were first transmitted orally) what values and mores that culture cherishes. In essence, myths, legends, and folktales help both to preserve a people's past heritage and to create a people's future heritage.

Readers can easily detect within the stories of *Welsh Legends and Folk-Tales* those things that the Welsh hold most dear. Marriage and family are important aspects of traditional Welsh life. Pwyll's quest for a suitable wife is a concern not only for him but also for his friends and advisers. The expectation of an heir coming from his marriage to Rhiannon is a source of anxiety for all of Pwyll's subjects until their son Pryderi eventually is born. Gwydion's efforts for a proper name for his son, Culhwch's quest for Olwen, and Macsen Wledig's curious way of finding a wife because of a dream all emphasize the place that familial relations occupy in Welsh life.

Personal honor as well is privileged in traditional Welsh society. The insults that Efnisien heaps on his brother-in-law Matholwch not only anger Matholwch and his people but also agitate Efnisien's half brother, Brân. Because of his haughtiness, Efnisien brings dishonor on Brân, on the rest of his family, and on his people, so that Brân exclaims to Matholwch's messengers that he is equally ashamed and disgusted by Efnisien's dishonorable conduct. In order to make amends, Brân gives horses, treasure, and a magic cauldron to Matholwch. The story of Pryderi and Manawydan also reinforces the importance of personal honor to the Welsh. When Pryderi is entranced by the magical bowl, Manawydan fails to lend assistance and returns to Pryderi's mother without him; Rhiannon rebukes Manawydan for his act of cowardice and for his failure to be a good comrade to Pryderi. The same type of message is stressed in the story of the boy who returned from Faerye, found in the third section of Jones's book. Elidyr spends a whole year with the fairies of the Otherworld, enjoying the best life and education that the little folk can offer. Unfortunately, Elidyr steals gold from the fairies at his mother's request and loses all of his privileges in Faerye. Because of his treacherous act, Elidyr is subject to shame, unhappiness, and the scorn of his peers. To the Welsh people, acting honorably in all situations is the most appropriate form of action.

More than anything else, however, Jones's book displays the sense of wonder with which the Welsh people view the world. Magic cauldrons, mysterious old men bearing cryptic messages, elves and fairies who populate fields and meadows, and hidden dens filled with gold and silver are all part of the marvelous legendary past of Wales. The stories in Jones's book serve the purpose of showing the reader who the Welsh people are, but they also provide pure entertainment for the reader. Such stories amuse while they instruct, which is the magic of legends and folktales.

Critical Context

As an accomplished writer and scholar, Gwyn Jones was well suited to present the best of Welsh legends and folklore to young adult readers. *Welsh Legends and Folk-Tales* is only one book in an entire corpus of Jones's works dealing with the legends and folklore of Northern cultures, works such as *Scandinavian Legends and Folk-Tales* (1956), *The Norse Atlantic Saga* (1964), *A History of the Vikings* (1968), and *Kings, Beasts, and Heroes* (1972). It is clear, however, that the most important influence on *Welsh Legends and Folk-Tales* was *The Mabinogion*, a work that Jones translated from the Welsh with Thomas Jones and published in 1949.

Popular interest in mythology and folklore grew steadily throughout the twentieth century, and the elements of Welsh legends and folklore presented in *Welsh Legends and Folk-Tales* began to arise even in mainstream young adult fiction. One need only go to Lloyd Alexander's highly successful Chronicles of Prydain series to witness the appeal of Welsh tales. Alexander openly acknowledges a great debt to the traditional Welsh tales that inspired the Prydain series. In fact, much of the fantasy fiction of the latter half of the twentieth century incorporates the same elements that make the traditional Welsh tales so enticing: heroic quests, magical trinkets, glorious battles, fairies, and antagonistic giants. The influence of collections of traditional folklore such as *Welsh Legends and Folk-Tales* is widespread, profoundly affecting readers and writers alike.

Trevor J. Morgan

THE WHEEL ON THE SCHOOL

Author: Meindert De Jong (1906-1991)
First published: 1954; illustrated
Type of work: Novel
Type of plot: Domestic realism
Time of work: The early twentieth century
Locale: Shora, a small Dutch fishing village on the edge of the North Sea
Subjects: Animals, education, and friendship
Recommended ages: 10-13

The six schoolchildren of Shora wonder why their village has no storks, which spurs them to action and even to danger but better yet to unexpected friendships, so that they can provide the wheel that the storks need for their nest.

> *Principal characters:*
> LINA, the only girl in the school and the first to wonder about the storks
> JELLA, the biggest boy in the school
> EELKA, a clumsy boy with the swift mind
> AUKA, a nice, everyday boy who helps the tin man
> PIER and DIRK, the twins who first talk to Janus
> THE TEACHER, who told the children that sometimes wondering can
> make things happen
> JANUS, the legless town terror and the owner of the cherry tree
> GRANDMOTHER SIBBLE, who remembers when Shora had storks
> OLD DOUWA, who takes Lina out to the upturned boat

Form and Content

Excitement mounts from the first page of *The Wheel on the School*, which was written by Meindert De Jong and illustrated by Maurice Sendak. When Lina reads her essay about storks, the teacher asks the class to wonder why there are none in Shora. He gives them the afternoon off to discover something about storks, telling them that "sometimes when we wonder, we can make things begin to happen." Some students take their assignment more seriously than others, but something does begin to happen when Lina learns from Grandmother Sibble both that storks had nested in Shora when she was a girl and that an old woman can be her friend. The children conclude that storks would need trees in the long run and, more immediately, since the birds are returning from Africa, a wheel so that they could nest on a sharp roof. School is again dismissed early so that the children can look for a wheel "where one is and where one isn't."

The following chapters are structured like spokes as the children fan out from Shora looking for wheels. Jella, the biggest boy, "borrows" one from a farmer but is caught by the irate man. The twins Pier and Dirk, having no luck on their road, decide that a closed-off courtyard that hides Shora's cherry tree and its mean, legless owner, who keeps boys away with his pile of stones, is "where a wheel isn't." Their scheme, failing when Janus catches them, is transformed as they learn from the man how he lost his legs. They enlist him as an ally because "Janus had become real . . . a part of the village."

Clumsy Eelka is triumphant at having found a wheel in the heights of a barn, especially knowing that Jella had failed, although he narrowly escapes with his life when he tries to remove it. Hauling its pieces back to the village, he must ask Jella to help him recover some of them from the dike. Jella falls in, only to be rescued by Eelka, whose physical prowess he has scorned. Auka arrives in the next village as he helps the tin man keep a rickety wheel on his cart. There, he persuades a villager to exchange his brightly colored wheel for the tin man's wheel.

Lonely Lina, frightened by dogs on the remote farms, stares from the dike out to sea at an upturned boat. Old Douwa assures her of her "impossibly impossible" insight: There is indeed a wheel under the boat, one that saved his father's life long ago. He tries to help Lina remove it before a storm sweeps in from the sea, but the tide cuts them off, and all the other children and adults, now firm companions, cooperate in a dramatic rescue.

The ferocious storm hits Shora, but, even in the midst of the gale, the fisherman-fathers and Janus fasten the wheel to the roof of the school. The tension continues, however, as the children worry about storks, which have been killed or scattered by the storm. After preschoolers who are lost in the village tower spot two storks stranded in the sea, the children, Janus, and the teacher attempt another rescue, successfully beginning the fulfillment of their "long dream—storks on every roof in Shora."

Analysis

When he accepted the 1955 Newbery Medal for *The Wheel on the School*, De Jong told his audience that to write this story, he had dug deeply into his own childhood in a small Dutch fishing village that hugged the dikes along the North Sea to find the "universal child" that he once was and that all children are. Perhaps that explains why this book, with its setting and plot so removed from contemporary Western culture, continues to be satisfying to young readers. Psychologist Sigmund Freud once argued that being able to work and to love are the prerequisites to maturity; readers can see in this book six children unconsciously but successfully maturing in both competence and relationships.

From the beginning, the teacher fosters this growth in his students, as good teachers will do. He allows his classroom routine to be interrupted for significant learning, first by listening to Lina's report—she will always have the satisfaction of knowing that she sparked the whole adventure—and then by giving the children the time and encouragement to learn about storks and, beyond that, to work to make their dreams become reality. His first admonition to them sets the theme of the book: "For sometimes when we wonder, we can make things begin to happen." While he worries that they might be crushed by the defeat that seems so likely, he also encourages them to think about the long term as well as the immediate present. Janus, who had been a man of action before his accident, admires the teacher, claiming that he does not simply "fool around with words. He goes and does things." Thought and action belong together, and the children as well as the adults are capable of both.

The process of their work and adventure has repercussions far beyond six individuals and two storks. Unknown to them, the children have resources upon which to draw in their seemingly dull, small village. As a result, the children not only develop unexpected but significant relationships but also cause several outsiders, particularly the elderly and the crippled, to become reintegrated into the community. In addition, Jella, the leader of the boys, learns that he must depend on Eelka for his very life and that he can enjoy friendship with this boy who has never been able to keep up in their games. Lonely Lina, the only girl among all these boys, discovers that the ancient Grandmother Sibble and Old Douwa are the source of a wealth of fascinating information and can be friends as well.

Perhaps most profound is how Janus, isolated behind his wall in bitterness after his accident, is accepted first by the twins, then by all the children, and lastly by the fisherman-fathers. He not only provides workable ideas—about rescuing children, storks, and wheels—but also physically puts them into action. During the rescue of Lina and Old Douwa, "he grunted between his teeth, 'a man can do something now and then without a lot of legs.'" Later, the fisherman-fathers learn that they can work together so intently at fixing the wheel to the dangerous school roof that they forget about Janus' condition: "They were treating Janus man to man. He was one of them again." It is no wonder then, although the townsfolk rustle in wonder, that this final integration is symbolized by Janus' return to church, the heart of the community, after years of absence. It is where all people of Shora belong, a people rooted to the land along the dike, to their history, and to their common faith. Because the children began to wonder, something indeed began to happen: Shora became whole as a community again.

Critical Context

Meindert De Jong had established his reputation for creating novels that are true to children's experiences and emotions long before *The Wheel on the School* won the Newbery Medal. Although another of his best stories, *The House of Sixty Fathers* (1956), is set in China, where De Jong served during World War II, most of his books that are still read today—for example, *Far out the Long Canal* (1964) and *Journey from Peppermint Street* (1968)—are set in The Netherlands, where the "tower rises out of Wierum right beside the dike . . . rises out of my childhood soul . . . strong and eternal, set forever." These words come from his acceptance speech for the Hans Christian Andersen Award in 1962, when he became the first American to win the international award. All of his books explore themes of friendship and family—sometimes in the negative form of rejection—or the human bonds that extend to animals, for whom De Jong also feels great empathy.

That these emotions are distilled rather than sentimentalized can perhaps be attributed to the hardships and prejudice that De Jong's family faced when it moved to the United States during World War I. Unrelenting poverty, illness, and discrimination caused De Jong to become especially sensitive to those who are mistreated. The second part of his childhood, at least, was not to be sentimentalized, although De Jong himself said in his award speech that the move also allowed him "a few more stolen years of . . . dreaming and imagining" about the years in Holland "as if set in amber."

Barbara J. Hampton

WHEN SHLEMIEL WENT TO WARSAW AND OTHER STORIES

Author: Isaac Bashevis Singer (1904-1991)
First published: 1968; illustrated
Type of work: Short fiction
Subjects: Family, friendship, poverty, and religion
Recommended ages: 10-15

The stories in this collection celebrate how the force of laughter, bonds of love, and power of memory can triumph against great odds.

Form and Content

In his preface to this collection of eight stories, Isaac Bashevis Singer explains that some are folktales with which his mother entertained him as a boy. In *When Shlemiel Went to Warsaw and Other Stories*, he has retold these tales, re-creating them in "plot, detail and perspective." The remaining stories, from his "own imagination," include "Tsirtsur and Peziza," "Rabbi Leib and the Witch Cunegunde," and "Menaseh's Dream."

Whether derivative or original, each story re-creates life in shtetls, the villages or small towns that were home to millions of Eastern European Jews prior to World War II. Margot Zemach's illustrations, notes critic Eric A. Kimmel, "capture the humor and sighs" of shtetl folk. Singer wrote the stories initially in Yiddish, the language of the shtetl, then translated them into English with his editor, Elizabeth Shub.

The title story takes place in Chelm, the legendary village of fools, and features Shlemiel, the quintessential Chelmite. When Shlemiel sets off to visit the great city of Warsaw, he loses his way and ends up back in Chelm. Perplexed over Warsaw's resemblance to his own village, he is convinced that he has discovered a Chelm Two. Chelm is also the setting for "Shlemiel the Businessman" and "The Elders of Chelm and Genendel's Key." In the former, Shlemiel, in his efforts to sell a goat, repeatedly becomes the target of swindlers. In the latter, a wife's attempt to keep her husband from speaking nonsense at community council meetings is thwarted by the foolishness of his fellow elders. In each story, Singer skillfully builds the humor by compounding misunderstandings.

"Shrewd Todie and Lyzer the Miser" is a pointedly moral, if farcical, tale. The desperately poor Todie approaches the town miser for a loan. When he is refused, he borrows a silver spoon and deceives the miser into believing that it has given birth to a teaspoon. Lyzer agrees to lend Todie not only spoons but also candlesticks. When Todie fails to return the candlesticks, claiming that they died, Lyzer drags him before the rabbi. It is Lyzer whom the rabbi admonishes, for accepting nonsense in an effort to bring profit.

"Utzel and His Daughter Poverty" is a more serious fable about the triumph of a man's love for his daughter over the laziness that has impoverished them. The powers of good also overcome the seductions of evil in "Rabbi Leib and the Witch Cunegunde," about a witch courting a saintly rabbi.

"Tsirtsur and Peziza" tells a sweet-natured tale of friendship between an orphaned imp and a cricket. An orphan is also the protagonist of "Menaseh's Dream." Menaseh's only possession is a storybook called *Alone in the Wild Forest*—which is also the title of a children's book that Singer would publish two years after *When Shlemiel Went to Warsaw and Other Stories*. Losing himself in a forest, Menaseh falls asleep and dreams of a castle inhabited by his parents and other relatives. Each room contains something of his life; in the seventh, he discovers a girl with long golden braids and other strangers who, it is explained, are people in his future. When Menaseh awakes, before him stands the golden-haired girl, who is giving him her hand to help him up. The story closes with "little people" singing a song heard "only by those who know that everything lives and nothing in time is ever lost."

Analysis

Singer dedicates *When Shlemiel Went to Warsaw and Other Stories* to the memory of his father and mother, "great and enthusiastic storytellers." Reared by adherents of Hasidism—a mystically fervent, pious sect of Judaism—Singer believed in the transforming power of stories and in the ability of children to grasp profound ideas presented imaginatively in tales. Legends and fables, known in Yiddish as *bubah meises* (roughly translated as "tales my grandmother told me"), have served to transmit lessons and values from generation to generation.

According to Canadian critic J. A. Eisenberg, Singer's fiction owes its emotional charge to the principle that the greater the fall, the more forceful the moral or message communicated. In "Utzel and His Daughter Poverty, " Utzel's redemption is highlighted by the contrast between the degraded state in which the reader finds him and the exalted state that he achieves. In "Rabbi Leib and the Witch Cunegunde," just as it appears that Cunegunde has secured Rabbi Leib's defeat, her own greed and vanity seal her destruction. The extremes that they absorb not only add to the emotional tension of Singer's stories but also invest his characters with an archetypal significance.

Because archetypal figures—from saints to fools to devils—formed a vibrant part in shtetl consciousness, the real and the mythical appear to coexist naturally in Singer's tales. By surrounding his shtetl characters with a mythology authentic to their lives, Singer keeps his work free of the artificiality and abstractions that can sap the vitality from allegorical writing, especially for young readers.

Also appealing to young readers is the triumph of the "underdog"—particularly the poor and the orphaned—in Singer's work. The despised and overlooked overcoming the odds to win fortune and fame is a popular theme in fairy tales and other folk literature. Stories such as "Utzel and His Daughter Poverty" and "Shrewd Todie and Lyzer the Miser" suggest that love and insight into human nature can triumph over worldly cares and wealth. Children find great satisfaction in stories that end with the victory of the weak and powerless, with whom they can readily identify.

Satisfying to children, too, is a good laugh. That they can laugh at a schlemiel distances them from his folly and unhappy fate. Traditionally, the schlemiel is caught in a snare of his own making, deluding himself that his mistaken notions are how things really are. As children who are learning the values of the culture in with they live understand the joke in a schlemiel tale, they gain a sense of belonging.

Orphans, for whom a sense of belonging takes on even greater urgency, are the protagonists of "Tsirtsur and Peziza" and "Menaseh's Dream." In both stories, venturing outside the familiar culminates in a kind of wholeness. Peziza leaves the secure spot behind the stove, and Menaseh wanders into the woods surrounding the village. There, in the wide world, Peziza meets the imp who is to be her mate; Menaseh, the girl who is to be his wife. The symbolism in these stories appears in myths around the world: a journey down the path through a shadowy present into a bright future; and marriage, the joining of male and female or universal opposites, whose union makes possible the continuity of life.

In these two stories, the most lyrically written in the collection, the wholeness that the characters achieve embraces the past as well as the future. The richness of love and the imagination, in memory, overcomes loss. The power of memory is very much a part of the impulse behind all the stories in the collection, as suggested in Singer's dedication of them to his parents. Memory is also important in honoring the victims of the Holocaust, who included most of the inhabitants of shtetls. Continuity is vital not only for the self and the family but also for the community and the larger civilization. Without it, meaning is confused. One becomes as disoriented as the schlemiel who can no longer recognize his home.

Critical Context

When Shlemiel Went to Warsaw and Other Stories was Isaac Bashevis Singer's second collection of stories and fourth book for children. It appeared on the *Horn Book* honor list and was an American Library Association Notable Book. Reviewers praised its period flavor, as well as its humor and insight into human nature. As *The New York Times* declared, "In this book children are getting what they deserve—some of the most imaginative stories that have been available in recent years."

According to Singer, the "same spirit, the same interest in the supernatural," is in all his tales, for adults and for young people. "No matter how young they are," he stated, "children are deeply concerned with so-called eternal questions." Singer, who would receive the Nobel Prize in Literature in 1978, considered children "the best readers of genuine literature." That it is "rooted" in folklore "alone makes children's literature so important," he claimed, adding that without folklore, "literature must decline and wither away."

The resemblance of the wise men of Chelm in Singer's stories to the wise men of Gotham in British lore has been critically noted. Additionally, folk literature the world over has its schlemiels, or typically foolish characters. As Singer himself observed, "The more a writer is rooted in his environment the more he is understood by all people." As multiculturalism became a significant trend in the United States toward the latter half of the twentieth century, *When Shlemiel Went to Warsaw and Other Stories* was joined by more books for children featuring folktales from around the world.

                                                                    Amy Allison

WHERE THE SIDEWALK ENDS
The Poems and Drawings of Shel Silverstein

Author: Shel Silverstein (1932-   )
First published: 1974; illustrated
Type of work: Poetry
Subjects: Animals, emotions, family, friendship, and nature
Recommended ages: 10-13

In this collection of poetry, Silverstein addresses, in an exaggerated and humorous way, the fears and joys of growing up.

Form and Content

Shel Silverstein is a highly popular writer of children's poetry, mainly because of his use of nonsense and humor, but he can also show a depth of feeling that encourages readers to examine their own emotions in relation to various aspects of growing up. This collection encompasses 117 poems, ranging in length from three sentences to three pages, that present various objects, experiences, and emotions related to children, their imaginations, and the realities of moving into adolescence. The humorous poems, nonsense poems, and narrative poems of *Where the Sidewalk Ends* are all interlaced with rhythm, rhyme, sound patterns, and repetition. All are written in such a way as to be timeless.

The first poem in the collection is an invitation to join the author in the world where the sidewalk ends: "If you are a dreamer, a wisher, a liar,/ A hope-er, a pray-er, a magic bean buyer,/ If you're a pretender, come sit by my fire,/ For we have some flax-golden tales to spin./ Come in! Come in!" Following this poem, Silverstein does exactly as he says: spins golden tales that are sure to entertain and delight young readers, while at the same time providing subjects for in-depth thought or enjoyment, depending on degree of intensity that the reader brings to each poem. Pen-and-ink sketches illustrate the majority of the poems and provide an introduction to each subject even before the first word is read.

The childhood world of Silverstein's poetry begins where the fictitious sidewalk ends, and the reader enters a new world, one where he or she will meet (to name only a few) Sarah Cynthia Sylvia Stout, who will not take the garbage out; a boy who turns into a television; a girl who has a giant as a best friend; Rudy, who knows how to belch better than anyone; unicorns; "humpy bumpy" camels; chimpanzees; long-neck geese; and Betsy Blue Bonnet, who has the longest nose in the world. This world is also a place where the reader can play in the rain, ride a horse, be eaten by a boa constrictor, plant a diamond garden, stand in a crocodile's mouth, and erase someone with a magical eraser. On a more serious note, the reader learns about hugs, love, looking to the future with anticipation for all the things that can happen in life, and how sometimes taking action is more important than merely thinking about things. Regardless of the subject, Silverstein presents poems that reach the reader by tapping into humor and emotions and providing genuine entertainment.

Analysis

The brevity of most of the poems in *Where the Sidewalk Ends* provides a stimulus to reading. They are less demanding than more lengthy forms of literature, and yet enough information is provided within the body of each poem to provide a complete and comprehensive view of the subject. This collection serves well as an introduction for those young readers who have not yet decided if they truly enjoy poetry or who have not previously been exposed to poetry. It entertains, informs, inspires, and tells of things that may never be as well as of things that may one day be.

The subject matter in the collection appeals to readers of all ages. It is easy to understand, and the reader need not constantly look for the hidden message of a poem. The meanings are apparent upon the initial reading and are flexible enough to communicate with a vast array of readers with differing viewpoints. In fact, some poems focus on the aspect of varying perspectives, such as "Point of View," and "Forgotten Language."

On the serious side, Silverstein has included poems such as "Hug o'War," where everyone wins when hugs take place; "Listen to the Mustn'ts," where anything can happen as one grows older; "No Difference," which presents similarities among all people; and "Love," which implies the need for several people to cooperate in order for love to thrive. All these poems examine realistic situations and present them with an understanding and empathy that immediately communicates itself with the reader.

Probably the most notable aspect of *Where the Sidewalk Ends* is the inclusion of the nonsense poem, the humorous poem, or a combination of the two. In nonsense poems, meaning takes a second place to the sound of the words and to the fact that the characters within the poem are involved in improbable situations. Readers know that these situations could not possibly happen but nevertheless enjoy the absurdity of the situations and the exaggeration that occurs. Nothing is impossible in Silverstein's nonsense poems—such as Dirty Dan, who has never taken a shower and has enough dirt in his ears to grow flowers, and Chester, who "growed another head." Perhaps this is one reason that the nonsense poems of Silverstein are so popular with adolescents.

Humor is found in the poems that deal with amusing things that might befall real people, even the readers themselves. One can consider "Homemade Boat," in which the children's boat is beautiful except for the fact that they forgot to include a bottom, or "Smart," in which a boy continually trades the money that his father has given him for change that amounts to less than the amount with which he began. A very popular poem, "Sick," tells about a girl who details how terribly ill she is and how she cannot go anywhere because of her illness—until she realizes that it is Saturday. Silverstein's humorous poems allow children to learn to laugh at themselves and to recognize that such situations occur in the course of human events. The use of rhythm, rhyme, sound patterns, and repetition combined with nonsense and humor, such as in the lines "Ickle Me, Pickle Me, Tickle Me, too,/ Went for a ride in a flying shoe," is another reason for the popularity of his poems. Reading such poems aloud enhances the humor found within them and engages the reader in learning about the magic of sound.

The poetry found in *Where the Sidewalk Ends* meets the generally established criteria for all good poetry for children. First, it shows a compatibility between sound and subject. Silverstein provides unforced rhythm and rhyme, and his poems appeal to the senses when read aloud. Second, the words within the various poems have been carefully chosen by the poet to provide sensory and connotative meaning. The words and phrases are not hackneyed or overused; rather, they are precise and memorable, and they evoke within the reader a mental picture of the action taking place. Finally, the subject matter of each poem takes what could be called the facts of everyday life and presents them with new life, providing the reader with fresh meanings and ways of looking at the world and expressing what is perhaps commonplace in a different and interesting light.

Critical Context

Where the Sidewalk Ends remains as well received and enjoyable to children, adults, and teachers as it was when it first appeared on bookshelves in 1974. Readers, both young and old, savor hearing these poems read aloud, as well as perhaps acting out the characters found in some of the longer poems. Some poems, such as "The Unicorn," have been made into popular songs. Others, such as "Smart" and "One Inch Tall," have been incorporated into the curriculum in an attempt to show that mathematics problems can be entertaining. Additionally, "Paul Bunyan" has been used in English literature classes as a point of comparison with the more traditional version of this tall tale.

In addition to several picture books for intermediate readers, Shel Silverstein published the humorous books of poetry *A Light in the Attic* (1985) and *Falling Up* (1996). Both of these collections include pen-and-ink drawings by Silverstein and provide the reader with comic and profound poems that encourage divergent and creative thinking.

Leslie Marlow

WHITE FANG

Author: Jack London (1876-1916)
First published: 1906
Type of work: Novel
Type of plot: Adventure tale and social realism
Time of work: Winter, 1893, to the early twentieth century
Locale: Northern Yukon Territory, Canada; eastern Alaska; and Santa Clara Valley, California
Subjects: Animals, death, and nature
Recommended ages: 10-15

Wolf-dog White Fang's responses to the cruelties, kindnesses, and laws of nature and of humankind result in his evolution from innocent puppy to ferocious killer to household pet.

Principal characters:
>HENRY and BILL, dogsled drivers battling an Arctic winter and wolf attacks to deliver a dead body
>WHITE FANG, a wolf-dog who journeys from the wild to American Indian, Klondike, and California cultures
>KICHE, half wolf and half dog, the mother of White Fang
>GRAY BEAVER, a Mackenzie Indian who is White Fang's first owner
>BEAUTY SMITH, a gambler who acquires White Fang
>CHEROKEE, a bulldog who fights White Fang in a near-death showdown
>WEEDON SCOTT, a California mining expert who rescues White Fang from dogfighting and domesticates him
>JUDGE SCOTT, Weedon's father, who lives in Santa Clara Valley
>JIM HALL, a convict who escaped from San Quentin and is seeking revenge on Judge Scott

Form and Content

White Fang is the tale of a wolf-dog's fierce struggle for survival against a hostile environment and cruel men. Only late in his life, only after struggle has made him profoundly vicious and an expert killer, does White Fang discover love for a man and the comforts of domesticity. The novel's twenty-five chapters have five major parts, each with its own locale, theme, rhythm, tone, and climax. The first part, chapters 1 through 3, constitutes a prologue to White Fang's journey. The tale begins with human experience of the wolf's natural habitat. Two dogsled drivers delivering a body to Fort McGurry struggle to survive the killing cold and the fierce pursuit of a pack of starving wolves, among them Kiche. Part 2, chapters 4 through 8, depicts the wolf's experience in nature. Kiche mates, finds a lair, gives birth to White Fang in the spring of 1893, and nurtures him through his first months as a hungry puppy and a novice hunter. In parts 1 and 2, first men and then wolves battle for the food and warmth necessary to survive the cruelties of an Arctic winter. The humans' horror story in the opening three chapters, although sometimes said to be only loosely attached to the rest of the novel, has an essential similarity to chapters 9 through 25, the horror story of White Fang's adaptations to an environment dominated by men.

White Fang's life with humans has three distinct locales. Chapters 9 through 15 are spent in the Yukon Territory traveling with Gray Beaver, a Mackenzie Indian. Then, captive in a cage in Dawson, White Fang is abused for sport by Beauty Smith in chapters 16 through 18. In California in the last seven chapters, the wolf-dog is tamed and willingly employs his strength and intelligence in service of men as companion, ally, and even savior. Thus, the slow evolution of White Fang's relationship to humans is outlined; his choices take him from freedom in the wild with his mother through life in three consecutive human cultures.

First, the wolf-dog comes in from the cold, choosing to live with and work for the food and fire of an Indian master. White Fang's life as leader of Gray Beaver's sled team climaxes with a long trading journey on the Mackenzie, Porcupine, and Yukon rivers. At their destination in Fort Yukon, in the summer of 1898, the wolf-dog is first initiated into the ways of white people and the world of commerce and guns. There, his special strength and intelligence make White Fang a commodity. Sold to Beauty Smith, the five-year-old wolf-dog is a captive, abused and exploited so harshly that he develops into a ferocious killer called "The Fighting Wolf." The culminating transformation of White Fang's relationship to humans occurs when he is rescued from Smith by Weedon Scott and treated for the first time with kindness. In the novel's last seven chapters, allegiance and affection for a man springs from this good treatment, and White Fang becomes "The Blessed Wolf." In the final chapter, his positive bond to Scott is proven when he risks his own life in valiant defense of the Scott family against the murderous intentions of the escaped convict Jim Hall.

White Fang's movement from the wild freedom of the Northland during the years of the Klondike Gold Rush to the tame comforts of the Scott estate in California is presented in omniscient narration. An invisible but all-knowing presence is able not only to represent what goes on in the minds and hearts of people but also to represent the nonverbal, nonrational, nonconscious experience of the wolf-dog. For example, in chapter 7, White Fang's first big kill as a puppy is interrupted with omniscient commentary:

> This was living, though he did not know it. He was realizing his own meaning in the world; he was doing that for which he was made—killing meat and battling to kill it. He was justifying his existence, than which life can do no greater; for life achieves its summit when it does to the uttermost that which it was equipped to do.

Such passages interpret actions and help establish the novel's themes, but, unfortunately, they can also create an undertow of murky abstraction and sticky sentiment.

Analysis

One reason for the popularity of this novel, especially among young readers, is its sympathetic portrayal of the life of a wild animal. Details of the wolf's mating behavior, gestation period, physical development, hunting behavior, adaptation skills, and life span constitute a capsule education. Depictions of the dangers of sledding through Arctic winters are both realistic and exciting.

The animal's years of gradual and painful integration into human society are also employed as a vehicle to expound some of Jack London's personal socialist convictions. His themes include the relationships of heredity and environment to individual development; the roles of violence, property, and love in both animal and human experience; and the pleasures and constraints of civilization. The dog's view of humankind allows London to objectify humanity's imperialism over its physical realm and the boundless inhumanities to human beings and other creatures. White Fang's individual struggle for survival, demanding all of his physical and intellectual resources, operates as a metaphor for each human's battle to realize his or her own nature while accommodating accidents of circumstance and social and natural laws. The novel's conclusion, with White Fang "the Blessed Wolf" happily drowsing in the sun with his offspring, suggests that love offers redemption and that, whatever its constraints, civilization offers contentment.

Critical Context

The Call of the Wild (1903) was Jack London's first critically acclaimed novel, riding the turn-of-the-century wave of American fascination with the Klondike, the Gold Rush, and the mysteries of the Arctic. Although intended as adult adventure with serious political and philosophical messages, the book has since become part of the canon of animal stories for young readers. *White Fang* was London's effort to capitalize quickly on his initial success. Its story was intended to be the antithesis of the earlier novel, exploring not the removal of but the acquisition of the trappings of human civilization. In *The Call of the Wild*, the dog Buck is kidnapped from California and forced to adapt to the wilds of the north; in White Fang, the wolf-dog leaves the wild and slowly adapts to humans and even to domesticity. *White Fang* is generally regarded as artistically inferior to its companion piece, but it helped to establish London as a popular American literary figure.

The first three chapters of *White Fang* resemble London's most frequently anthologized short story, "To Build a Fire." Both dramatize a fundamental law of the Arctic winter: Traveling alone at fifty degrees below zero means destruction. The laws of nature are inexorable. The laws of humans, however, are equally punishing but far more confusing, as White Fang discovers. Repeatedly, he is brought to the edge of extinction, only to recover by adapting to the laws that govern his own nature and the laws that structure his new environments. With his combination of instinct and intelligence, the wolf seems far better skilled at adaptation than does the human being. In the novel's last chapter, another innocent—the convict Jim Hall—cannot accept the mandate of the law or adapt to his captivity, and he is destroyed. A wolf's life serves to dramatize the extreme complexity of humankind's relations to nature and to the legal and moral constructs of societies.

Possessing moral consciousness makes life in this world profoundly disturbing. In 1909, London explored in *Martin Eden* the moral consciousness and education of a man struggling with the constraints and pressures of human civilization. Like the struggles of a wolf, the struggles of a strong, intelligent, and sensitive artist adapting to the complex demands of human society can be full of great horror and small satisfaction. London's rather negative views of his society produced plots full of adventure and excitement veiling a grim allegory of human imperialism, greed, and cruelty.

Virginia Crane

THE WHITE STAG

Author: Kate Seredy (1899-1975)
First published: 1937; illustrated
Type of work: Novel
Type of plot: Folktale and historical fiction
Time of work: The fourth and fifth centuries
Locale: The empire of Attila the Hun in Asia and Europe
Subjects: Travel and war
Recommended ages: 10-15

Following a prophecy, the Huns and Magyars travel westward into Europe as Attila, the leader of the Huns, leads them to their promised land.

> *Principal characters:*
> NIMROD, a mighty hunter
> HUNOR, a son of Nimrod, the father of the Huns
> MAGYAR, a son of Nimrod, the father of the Magyars
> DAMOS, a prophet
> BENDEGUZ, the son of Hunor
> ALLEETA, a Cimmerian princess
> ATTILA THE HUN, the son of Bendeguz and Alleeta

Form and Content

Kate Seredy explains in the foreword to *The White Stag* that she wrote the novel because she had felt dissatisfied with a book on Hungarian history that presented a dry "unending chain of facts, facts, facts" and argued that the Magyar (Hungarian) race was not descended from Attila the Hun. Her book, therefore, fictionalizes and romanticizes the westward drive of the Huns and Magyars and the life of Attila the Hun, using the rhythms and rhetoric of folklore as it establishes Attila as the founder of Hungary. Seredy's black-and-white illustrations depict chiefly the warriors, who, like comic book superheroes, appear noble, mighty-thewed, and glorious. These drawings also hint at a slant to the eyes to reveal the Huns as an Asiatic race.

The book traces four generations of Huns. Nimrod, a great hunter, is the leader of a tribe suffering from hunger and illness. His two sons, Hunor and Magyar, have been gone for months, following a miraculous white stag. Nimrod asks their god, Hadur, for a sign that their fortunes will improve. Hadur sends first an eagle, which plunges into his sacrificial pyre; then two more, which depart northward and westward; then a fourth; and then a great red eagle, which flies away to the west. Nimrod interprets these signs: He is the first eagle, who is soon to die, while his two sons will lead their tribe nearer to their destined home. After they are gone, there will be another leader, and it will be his son, greatest of all, who will lead them to the promised land.

Hunor and Magyar return and tell a tale of having followed the White Stag on a visionary quest to a beautiful country with food enough for all. A prophetical young boy, Damos, has a mystical dream in which Hunor and Magyar are paired with two white herons, and shortly thereafter Nimrod's sons marry two lovely "Moonmaidens."

Seredy traces the journeys of the tribe, which splits into Huns and Magyars—some choosing to travel to the less populated northern regions with the peaceful Magyar and others, fierce and wild, preferring to wage war through Europe with pitiless Hunor. Hunor's son, Bendeguz, grows into a brawny warrior who builds the Hun tribe into a restless, reckless army. Bendeguz falls in love with a captured princess, Alleeta, the daughter of King Ashkenaz of the Cimmerians; Damos, now grown old, marries them.

Worrying that Hadur has turned his back upon the tribe, Bendeguz desires to remain with Alleeta in the peaceful land where their army is encamped. Damos replies that the Huns have a destiny to fulfill and that their travels are not yet over. When Alleeta dies giving birth, Bendeguz is so angry at Hadur that he declares their son, Attila, will become the Scourge of God. Bendeguz rears Attila without love or comfort, and the boy becomes a ruthless warrior. Attila's army rampages across Europe, always seeking their foretold home. At last, the White Stag reappears during a blizzard to guide them across the Carpathian Mountains, where the Huns find a beautiful valley rich with greenery and game. Attila vows to protect this land and its people.

Analysis

Many generations of young readers have enjoyed *The White Stag* because it emphasizes drama and conflict and moves very rapidly. In fewer than one hundred pages, Seredy covers about a hundred years at a gallop. The Huns are presented as harsh and violent, but as having become so from trying to escape hardship. Nimrod worries about the welfare of his tribe, and Bendeguz's loss of his beloved wife and consequent rearing of Attila without compassion teaches a juvenile audience that adults may be harsh because they have been hurt and disappointed by life.

Although Attila is notorious in Europe as an invader and destroyer, Seredy gives little idea of what his victims suffered. Historians agree that Attila was militarily successful primarily because the peoples that he conquered were weak and unorganized. Regardless, the passages that discuss war are told vividly but with an eagle's-eye view, as it were. Seredy uses sweeping verbs and calls upon such heroic imagery as black horses and swinging swords. She describes the warriors' laughter and songs, which makes the battles seem almost like games. The author depersonalizes the victims of the Huns by calling them "the enemy," and she shows them scampering for shelter rather than being killed. She writes that the Huns left such destruction in their wake as smoking ruins and desolate fields, but young readers who have no real-life referent for such things may not visualize the real human cost of war. The passages describing battles therefore will neither frighten young readers nor cause them to lose sympathy for the protagonists. Seredy also does not explain precisely how the Huns waged war or survived in the field. Young readers instead will probably focus on the prophecy and the glorious destiny awaiting the Huns.

The major appeal of the story lies in the personalities that Seredy depicts. Nimrod is an admirable father figure who gives his life for his people. Hunor and Magyar receive less character development. They are noble and heroic, and their visionary quest and marriage to the Moonmaidens, who are essentially fairyland figures, are romantic and fantastic but not depicted in a profound way. Bendeguz, meanwhile, arouses awe as an angry, bellicose man; the volume seems to rise during his scenes. Attila, likewise, is bold and warlike, but he is shown chiefly as a youth. Because he receives no love from his father, he discovers inner resources that strengthen him. Because of the romanticization of the characters, the story works better as a folktale of gods and heroes than as a historical biography.

Children like reading about animals and will enjoy how Seredy associates each of the major characters with eagles. She also colors the Huns' journeys by describing the wild bears, wolves, and panthers they see in the wilderness, rather than by discussing the prosaic details of nomadic life. The White Stag itself is a fabulous beast that confers honor and the magic of destiny by singling out the Huns and Magyars for a promised land. Seredy's story also features many children, as well as romantic figures such as the Moonmaidens and the princess Alleeta, so that young readers will not grow bored with a steady diet of adult politics and warmongering.

As many legends do, the tale of the White Stag emphasizes personal sacrifice. In a moving scene, Nimrod sacrifices his favorite horse in order to plead for a divine sign to help his people. Bendeguz loses his beloved wife and becomes a sad and bitter man. Attila must learn to avoid all weakness, sacrificing an appreciation of the value of human life in return for human ambition. Juvenile readers will realize from these scenes that life exacts its costs.

Critical Context

In 1920, Hungary underwent a loss of more than two-thirds of its territory as a result of the Treaty of Trianon at the conclusion of World War I. All Europe had once feared the Huns, but their putative descendants believed that their glory had been diminished. Furthermore, at the time that this book was written, historians were arguing that the Magyar race was not connected with the Huns after all. Kate Seredy desired to retell the ancient legend that traces a descent from Attila to the Magyars and thus to recapture the lost glory of Hungary's legendary heritage.

Seredy calls upon biblical authority by choosing Nimrod, the biblical hunter, as the forefather of the Hun and Magyar races, which historians argue both came out of Scythia. The tale of the White Stag is ultimately an explanation of national identity, much like the myth of Romulus and Remus, the legendary founders of Rome, or the twelfth century Germanic *Nibelungenlied*. For Seredy and all Hungarians, the legend was a matter of roots. Young readers, Hungarian or not, understand that much personal strength comes from pride in one's racial and national identity.

The White Stag won the Newbery Medal and continues to be included in bibliographies for children's literature in library collections. It is unquestionably the most famous of the retellings of the legend of the White Stag.

Fiona Kelleghan

WHO LOOK AT ME

Author: June Jordan (1936-   )
First published: 1969; illustrated
Type of work: Poetry
Subjects: Arts, race and ethnicity, and social issues
Recommended ages: 13-18

Jordan, a writer and social activist, explores African American identity with a series of poetic images interspersed with paintings that challenge readers to think about the black experience in the United States.

Form and Content

In the late 1960's, when the concept of black pride enabled many African Americans to recognize and proclaim a hidden heritage of struggle and endurance, poet June Jordan collaborated with editor and publisher Milton Meltzer to design a book in which Jordan's poetry would complement and comment on pictures concerning black identity chosen by Meltzer. In explaining her intentions, Jordan commented:

> We do not see those we do not know. Love and all varieties of happy concern depend on the discovery of one's self in another. The question of every desiring heart is, thus, WHO LOOK AT ME? In a nation suffering fierce hatred, the question—race to race, man to man, and child to child—remains: WHO LOOK AT ME? *We answer with our lives.* Let the human eye begin unlimited embrace of human life.

In order to guide the majority of white Americans in an exploration of the world of African Americans, Jordan has fashioned a poem—or, more precisely, a poetic cycle—that is interwoven with twenty-seven illustrations—paintings, lithographs, posters, and a collage—by artists from both the black and the white community. Her title *Who Look at Me* is both assertive and interrogative, emphasizing both the importance of the person who is the subject of the poem or painting and the questioning gaze of the onlooker joining the observer and the subject. The artists whose work illustrate the book represent a wide variety of styles and approaches, suggesting that there is no single way to see and no single, approved manner of appearance. Significant is the inclusion of a reproduction of *Portrait of a Gentleman*, by an unknown painter, the anonymity of the artist an indication of the universal impulse to capture the essential qualities of a human being in a permanent form.

Following several pages of poetry setting the direction of the book ("Who would paint a people/ black or white?"), the first painting to be included is a vividly colorful, semicubist rendering entitled *Manchild*, indicating the range of human experience to follow. The next five reproductions are in black and white, the absence of a complete palette diminishing the color-enforced sense of difference between races. The last in this group is called *Enigmatic Foursome*, its title posing the query of a society unsure how to deal with people who are not ruled by exclusionary, superficial racial characteristics.

Jordan and Meltzer deepen the common humanity that the book stresses by offering in the next section paintings by some famous white artists, including Andrew Wyeth, Winslow Homer, and Thomas Eakins, who have chosen African Americans as subjects. The center of the book is a two-page reproduction and detail by another anonymous artist with the title *The Slave Market*—a powerful symbolic rendering of the crime against humanity at the heart of U.S. history. The remainder of the book contains an assortment of styles and subjects, concluding with a collage by Romare Bearden that fuses a traditional subject—a rural black family in a railroad shack— with a modern method that looks toward the future.

Analysis

The poems that Jordan has written for *Who Look at Me* are both a commentary on and an extension of the images. The poet and the visual artists are all concerned with the art of vision, hoping to engage the imaginative responses of their audience, and Jordan's poetry is purposely arranged on the page in different shapes and forms so as to complement the pictures with additional visual patterns, black letters on a white background. As the separate stanzas appear, Jordan follows her initial question "Who would paint a people . . . ?" with some of the specific sources of her own motivation, indicating that her inquiring intelligence has compelled her to try to understand the dimensions of human experience as a way of understanding herself. The hostile, dismissive posture of a too-frequently racist society, she believes, is partly the result of confusion, fear, and uncertainty before a mystery that she can help to explain. "Is that how we look to you," she asks, "a partial nothing . . . ?"

Her commentaries on the illustrations are designed to dispel doubt and supply some of the details of black life that have an immediate correspondence in any culture. They then touch on some of the most captivating qualities of African American citizens of the United States and their particular contributions to the richness of American life. While her poems are clearly in the mainstream of contemporary poetry of the latter decades of the twentieth century, her use of the rhythmic patterns of black vernacular speech enlivens her descriptions, and her inclusion of tonal inflections and syntactic arrangements that convey the flavor of the oral tradition of African American music and folk speech lend a distinctive voice to the book. When she wishes to make a point, usually as a kind of closure to a subsection of the book, she often employs a tight-rhyming couplet, as in the poem facing the portrait *Sylvester*, by Robert Henri: "Describe me broken mast/ adrift but strong/ regardless what may/ come along."

The dramatic focal point of the book is the painting by an unknown artist called *The Slave Market*, which explains the suspicion and guilt felt by many white Americans and illuminates the anger and resentment that many African Americans harbor, an aspect of a complex continuing form of slavery that traps both races. Jordan follows this painting with poems that speak of survival and recovery: a tribute to her father accompanying a portrait of an old, dignified black man, *Alexander Chandler*, by Andrew Wyeth; a loving evocation of her mother's ability to create a safe space ("her geography/ becomes our home"); a brief historical account of the rebel Cinque, an abolitionist freedom fighter defended by John Quincy Adams; and poetic fragments that refer to heroic ancestors whose actions enabled a people to grow amid trying conditions and to visions of religion, family, community, and other institutions instrumental in the persistence of the spirit and soul of black consciousness.

The concluding poems move toward a more abstract and philosophical presentation of African American life, the answer for which her title calls. The poem beginning "Tell the whiplash helmets GO!" is a surrealistic expression of black energy directed toward all symbols of oppression, an ingenious method of altering hard realities with imaginative language. The brief poem "we will no longer wait for want for watch/ for what we will" is set next to Charles Alson's painting *Walking*, of people advancing forward with composure and confidence; the poem is a verbal equivalent that captures in a surging line the power of common purpose. There is a degree of ambivalence in the last poems and pictures, an open-ended aspect of a history still being written, in which the positive forces that Jordan mentions are seen in conflict with "a carnival run by freaks/ who take a life/ and tie it terrible/ behind my back." The final section, however, begins "I trust . . . ," and the last line, a repetition of the title, implies that many people are capable of seeing and understanding the life that the poet has presented.

Critical Context

June Jordan expects much of her readers and justifies this demand by asking even more from herself. As in her novella *His Own Where* (1971), which renders the reality of a love between two teenagers in the language of the narrator's mental observations, Jordan assumes that young readers can respond to a creative use of form and poetic structure and an inventive use of American English. She assumes that her young readers still retain the qualities of hope, enthusiasm, openness, curiosity, and decency that can be reached by an honest presentation of a complex, difficult subject. She wrote *Who Look at Me* for those who are not frozen by bigotry or poisoned by hate, and the continuing racial division in the United States has kept her work timely and relevant, just as the pictures, painted through the nineteenth and twentieth centuries, speak both to a submerged history and to a contemporary reality.

The idea of a poet looking at a painting is a part of an established tradition in American letters, notably in William Carlos Williams' essay "Pictures from Brueghel" (1962), and it carries the thought that the conventional division of genres need not prevent a fusion of modes, an appropriate point for a work that attempts to remove artificial boundaries that separate people. Considering how many young readers are familiar with the work/text union of comic books and magazines, Jordan's efforts may not seem that unusual, and the increasing reliance on visual means of presenting information through computer technology may also make Jordan's hybrid seem simply another variant in an increasingly fluid mix.

Leon Lewis

THE WINTER ROOM

Author: Gary Paulsen (1939-   )
First published: 1989
Type of work: Novel
Type of plot: Folktale and moral tale
Time of work: Prior to the 1940's
Locale: Northern Minnesota
Subjects: Coming-of-age, family, jobs and work, and nature
Recommended ages: 10-13

Eldon uses the cycle of the seasons to describe his life and his family while growing up on an isolated, northern Minnesota farm during the period prior to the development of mechanized farming.

> *Principal characters:*
> ELDON, the eleven-year-old narrator of the novel
> WAYNE, Eldon's brother, who is two years older
> ELDON'S FATHER, a hardworking second-generation Norwegian
>   American farmer whose primary concerns are his farm and his family
> UNCLE DAVID, Eldon's great-uncle, a former logger and gifted storyteller
> NELS, Uncle David's closest friend, who is treated like a part of Eldon's
>   extended family

Form and Content

Set in northern Minnesota in the period prior to mechanized farming, this short novel is narrated by eleven-year-old Eldon, who lives on an eighty-acre farm with his parents, older brother Wayne, his father's Uncle David, and David's friend Nels. Eldon, a third-generation Norwegian American, presents a picture of a simpler way of life as he describes what he likes and dislikes about life during each of the four seasons. Gary Paulsen provides crisp and sometimes graphic descriptions of the softness of spring when the land thaws, the back-breaking work of summer thrashing, the autumn slaughter of pigs and chickens, and the camouflaging snows of winter. Work, particularly repetitive, physical labor, is the major component of the lifestyle that Eldon depicts. The love and bonds among Eldon's extended family compensates for the lack of material comforts and the isolation of the family from the rest of society. Paulsen also includes some vignettes about the pranks of Eldon and his brother, as well as vivid profiles of Eldon's father and his Uncle David. Eldon's mother, for the most part, remains a shadowy figure in the book.

Although Eldon finds some attractive elements in each of the seasons, he loves winter best without question because it is the time when Uncle David enlivens the evenings with his stories, four of which conclude the book: the story of the death of Uncle David's young wife, Alida; a Norse legend; a tall tale about a practical joker; and the story of Uncle David's superiority as a lumberjack when he was a young man.

The family gathers around the wood-burning stove in one of the four rooms in the farmhouse, in what might be called the living room, and, while Eldon's father carves and his mother sews, Uncle David recounts his wonderful stories. Eldon is spellbound by David's stories and his storytelling technique, which provide a major form of entertainment for the family. Wayne, who sees the stories as factual recollections of earlier events, ends David's stories, however, when he accuses Uncle David of lying in the story about his exploits as a lumberjack. Markedly hurt by Wayne's accusations, Uncle David revives the storytelling only after he proves to himself that he still has the physical strength to perform one of the feats that Wayne thought was a lie.

The novel is short on action, which may put off some readers accustomed to reading Paulsen's survival and action-adventure stories, and the age of the narrator makes the book more appropriate for a young audience. Nevertheless, the novel is a strong testimonial to the purpose and power of stories in the lives of young people. If the lifestyle that Paulsen presents is more idyllic than what actually existed anywhere, it does provide a model of what a family could and should be.

Analysis

Paulsen devotes a chapter to each of the seasons, allowing readers to experience the rituals of planting, growing, and harvest that marked premechanized farming. The conventions of fiction have never seemed to intimidate Paulsen, and, in *The Winter Room*, he appears to break the first unbreakable rule of elementary fiction writing: Show, instead of tell. Paulsen gets away with breaking the rule because the teller is eleven-year-old Eldon, who reports what his senses discover, and the tale is the story of a year on his family's farm. Although the life that Paulsen pictures involves repetitious and neverending hard work, the evenings, particularly during the winter, provide time for family bonding that has been lost in large segments of fast-paced, industrialized societies. Paulsen provides a vivid picture of a way of life long past, as well as the physical surroundings of the house and the farm that constitute Eldon's world.

Told in the form of a reminiscence rather than a novel, the simple language, appropriate for an eleven-year-old, nevertheless enables Paulsen to construct a text that resembles a mood poem in prose. Portions of the novel could be used as effective models of prose poems. The vivid description and poetic language make this book an excellent choice to be read aloud. In fact, hearing the language provides a greater impact than seeing it on the printed page.

The final chapters, consisting of Uncle David's stories, may at first glance seem tacked onto the novel. If the stories are viewed from Eldon's perspective, however, young readers may feel as if they are sitting with Eldon, listening to a gifted storyteller illustrate the importance of stories in their lives. Uncle David's first story is always about Alida, his wife in the old country who died in childbirth, a woman whom he loved so much that he "never remarried and never looked at another woman." Such loyalty should be attractive to even the youngest readers. Readers will be amused and entertained by Uncle David's next story, a tall tale about Crazy Alan, the practical joker whose ultimate practical joke was allowing his body to freeze spread-eagle when he died so that his friends had problems getting the frozen body through the small door of his cabin. Finally, readers should be able to relate to the ethical issue involved with the telling of "The Woodcutter." Wayne and Eldon considered it merely another story until their father mentions that Uncle David was the lumberjack in the tale. Wayne then claims that Uncle David lied when he said he "could take a four-foot piece of cordwood and swing two axes, one in each hand, swing them into the two ends and the wood would split clean and the axes would meet in the middle." Wayne's accusations end Uncle David's stories until he, with Wayne and Eldon observing from a hiding place, repeats the feat—thus proving, as Wayne observes, the truth of the story to himself. Even young readers should be interested in discussing that segment of the story.

"Tuning," a brief prologue to the story, also has a tacked on quality, but it is not as defensible as Uncle David's stories. Paulsen's point in the prologue—that readers must supply the smells, sounds, and light for a story—seems condescendingly simple even for young readers.

Finally, one of the attractions of the novel may be that Eldon's account of his extended family may provide a sharp and positive contrast to the dysfunctional families in which some of Paulsen's young readers may live. Considering how Paulsen has portrayed his own family in *Eastern Sun, Winter Moon: An Autobiographical Odyssey* (1995) and in interviews, Eldon lives in a close-knit extended family markedly different from what Paulsen experienced as a child, except for a short period in which he lived with his grandmother in northern Minnesota.

Critical Context

Although *The Winter Room* earned Gary Paulsen the third selection of one of his works as a Newbery Honor Book, the novel bears little resemblance to either of its predecessors, *Dogsong* (1985) and *Hatchet* (1987). In fact, *The Winter Room* is a prime indication of Paulsen's versatility as a writer, a quality that has enabled him to join the front ranks of juvenile and young adult writers. Whereas the two earlier Newbery Honor Books are memorable survival stories told by older narrators, *The Winter Room* is an almost actionless story told by a younger narrator, one who sometimes does not fully understand what is going on around him. If *Dogsong* and *Hatchet* are testimonials to what young adults can do if they are challenged by nature, *The Winter Room* provides a vivid picture of an almost-perfect world in which love and concern for one another are primary values.

A constant in all three of these books and in many of his other works is Paulsen's poetic use of the English language, a quality that has earned him critical acclaim in addition to a large audience of young adult readers. Reading Paulsen's books not only introduces young people to someone who tells a good story but also exposes them to someone who obviously values the written word. In a time when fewer young people read for pleasure, that becomes an important reason for introducing them to Paulsen's books.

Ronald Barron

THE WISH GIVER
Three Tales of Coven Tree

Author: Bill Brittain (1930-   )
First published: 1983; illustrated
Type of work: Novel
Type of plot: Fantasy and moral tale
Time of work: Probably the early twentieth century
Locale: The village of Coven Tree in New England
Subjects: Emotions and the supernatural
Recommended ages: 10-15

Three young people learn to be careful with their wishes when they begin to come true exactly as stated.

Principal characters:
    STEW MEAT, the owner of the Coven Tree General Store, the narrator
      and a receiver of a wish
    THADDEUS BLINN, the wish giver
    POLLY KEMP, an eleven-year-old receiver of a wish
    ROWENA JERVIS, a fifteen-year-old receiver of a wish
    ADAM FISKE, a sixteen-year-old receiver of a wish

Form and Content

The Wish Giver: Three Tales of Coven Tree begins with a discussion of the presence of witches and witchcraft in the New England states since Colonial times. This evil presence pervades the story as, one by one, three young people fall under its spell. The name of the village—Coven Tree—conjures up witches. Even the dark sketches by Andrew Glass scattered throughout the book add to the feeling of evil.

When Thaddeus Blinn sets up a tent at the Coven Tree Church Social, his advertisement states, "I can give you whatever you ask for only 50 C." Despite his enticing claim, only four people enter his tent. They include Stew Meat, the owner of the Coven Tree General Store and the narrator of the story; Polly Kemp, an eleven-year-old girl who always speaks her mind, even when her words hurt others; Rowena Jervis, a fifteen-year-old girl who believes that she is in love with a traveling salesman who has enthralled her with his stories of travel all over the world; and Adam Fiske, a sixteen-year-old boy whose family's farm suffers from drought and who must haul tubs of water from the creek to their home. Before Blinn lets them leave his tent, he warns them that each wish that he gives them "will be granted exactly as you ask for it." As soon as they leave, Blinn packs up his tent and leaves the area.

Polly only has two friends who will play with her because of her habit of speaking without thinking. She desperately wants to be friends with two girls in town and not to be shunned by others when she meets them on the street. Her wish is that people will like her and that Agatha will invite her for tea. Following her wish, every time that she starts to say something hateful, she croaks like a bullfrog. This phenomenon lasts for about thirty minutes.

Rowena's traveling salesman returns to Coven Tree for his twice yearly visit. Even though her mother warns her of his flirtatious manner, Rowena refuses to believe that he is not in love with her. Her wish, that "Henry Piper would put down roots in Coven Tree and never leave again," comes true. That night as Henry leaves her home, he slowly becomes a tree in a grove near her home.

Adam's farm continues to suffer from drought. As he takes the wagonload of tubs back and forth to the creek for water, the townspeople heckle him. Adam's father hires a dowser to locate water on the farm. Despite all of his efforts, the dowser cannot find a drop of water on the entire farm. That night, Adam wishes for water all over the farm. When his wish comes true, underground streams arise. Each time that a hole is punched in the ground, a spout of water develops. The farm floods, and the family must float their possessions and themselves to the hill overlooking their home.

The story progresses as, after each person's wish is granted, he or she thinks of the person who sat in the tent. Disaster follows disaster as all three young people use their wishes for their own gain. Their only hope rests with Stew Meat, if he has not used his wish.

Analysis

The meaning of *The Wish Giver* is easy to comprehend: People need to be careful of what they desire, for it might come true. Readers also learn another lesson: that what one wishes for is not always what one wants or what is best. Each young person learns these lessons as the wishes come true.

Polly's wish to be liked and to be invited to Agatha's house does come true, but with a heavy price. She realizes that she is doomed to a life of saying nice things unless she wants to sound like a frog. When Polly is invited to Agatha's house, she also discovers that Agatha's idea of fun is dull compared to the good times that she has in the woods with her two friends. Polly finally realizes that instead of wasting her time trying to be friends with Agatha, she could be spending her time making friends with others who would enjoy the same things that she does. Polly ultimately decides that she needs the guidance of someone older and wiser and sets out for Coven Tree.

Rowena's wish for Henry Piper to put down roots in Coven Tree takes on a bizarre aspect as he slowly turns into a tree. As Rowena tries to comfort him, she realizes that Henry has been leading her along and that his pleasantness and flirtatiousness were a thin veneer for his real self—a complainer and a liar. During her efforts to make Henry comfortable as he transforms into a tree, Rowena realizes that Sam, the young man who helps on her father's farm, has stood beside her all the way. Sam did not blame her when she confided in him about her wish. He only increased his efforts to help her, and it was he who discovered Henry's lies about being a world traveler. Sam also serves as an example of the knowledge that one can gain from reading. Rowena learns that she loves not Henry but Sam, who is dependable and helpful. The tree that bears a faint resemblance to Henry Piper, however, will always haunt her.

Adam's wish for water all over the farm has bizarre consequences. As he watches the water begin to flood the farm and his home, Adam learns that there is such a thing as too much water. Not until he overhears the people who have gathered to watch the strange occurrence of water spewing out of the ground does he realize that he has caused the disaster with his wish. Despite all of their efforts to cap the water, nothing works. Adam confesses to his father about the wish. Having feared the repercussions of this action, he is relieved when his father does not blame him and confides that had he been given the opportunity, he would have done the same thing.

All three young people not only learn to be careful in wording their wishes and to reevaluate what they wanted but also learn that selfishness and thoughtlessness can result in tragedy. The tragedy for Polly—a life in which she can only say nice things—causes her to fear that she will explode one day from being so nice. For Rowena, every time that she passes the grove of trees at the rear of her house, she will see Henry Piper's eyes and mouth in the runty sycamore. Adam must carry the knowledge that he and his family have lost their home and farm.

The many lessons of *The Wish Giver* are important to all people. Too often, people spend their lives waiting for their wishes to come true and not taking advantage of what is occurring in the present. These young people realize this fact when their wishes come true. Two of the young people—Rowena and Adam—learn the importance of confiding in someone when they have done something wrong. Polly recognizes her need for help from someone older and wiser, while Rowena seeks help from a friend. Polly also learns that people need friends with similar interests, not necessarily those whom they idolize.

Critical Context

Bill Brittain's Coven Tree books blend comedy and horror as readers learn moral lessons. He loosely based the village and its inhabitants on his acquaintances in his childhood home of Spenceport, New York. The first book in this series, *Devil's Donkey* (1981), received mention as an American Library Association's Notable Children's Book and was inspired by one of his eighth-grade students. According to Brittain, the plotting for the second book in the series, *The Wish Giver*, proved to be the most difficult that he had done. The problem centered on all three sections in the book taking part over four days in a small village in which the characters' paths would cross occasionally. His perseverance paid off, as *The Wish Giver* received praise as a Newbery Honor Book. After this book, he returned to the village of Coven Tree for *Dr. Dredd's Wagon of Wonders* (1987) and *Professor Popkin's Prodigious Polish: A Tale of Coven Tree* (1991). Brittain desires not to teach enduring lessons but to offer his readers a good story. He accomplishes this goal with a blend of fantasy, horror, and humor.

Beverly B. Youree

THE WOMEN OF BREWSTER PLACE

Author: Gloria Naylor (1950-   )
First published: 1982
Type of work: Novel
Type of plot: Social realism
Time of work: The 1970's
Locale: A dead-end ghetto street in an urban setting
Subjects: Family, poverty, race and ethnicity, and social issues
Recommended ages: 15-18

The stories of how seven African American women cope with rejection, violence, poverty, and prejudice reveal that hope, joy, and love can be maintained even in the face of tragedy when women work together in a tight-knit community.

Principal characters:
MATTIE MICHAEL, a woman in her sixties who worked for thirty years maintaining a house and rearing her son but who lost everything and had to move to Brewster Place to live out her last years
ETTA MAE JOHNSON, Mattie's best friend, who has gone from man to man, music hall to music hall, and who winds up at Brewster Place seeking out Mattie when her luck runs out and age catches up with her
KISWANA BROWNE, a young woman in her twenties from an upper-class family and neighborhood who chooses to move to Brewster Place in order to help the people there improve themselves and their living conditions
LUCIELIA LOUISE TURNER, a woman in her thirties who chooses to abort a child to help save her marriage and who then loses her only child in a tragic accident and almost dies of sadness
CORA LEE, an immature young woman who continually chooses to have children because she enjoys the experience of loving babies
LORRAINE and THERESA (THE TWO), a lesbian couple who moves to Brewster Place to find safety and peace, only to find this hope smashed by intolerance and a violent tragedy

Form and Content

The Women of Brewster Place offers a realistic account of the lives of seven African American women of various ages. Framed by opening and closing sections that point to political and economic forces affecting life in Brewster Place, the novel is a series of vignettes about the major characters and how their lives connect to one another. Although set in the 1970's in an urban ghetto, the range of lives explored offers a broad spectrum of social and cultural experiences. Gloria Naylor neither romanticizes these women nor downplays the oppressive forces arrayed against them. Instead, she reveals the dual need for social justice and personal responsibility in a wonderfully written and powerful book.

The novel proper begins with the story of Mattie Michael— appropriately, because Mattie becomes the loving mother-figure of Brewster Place. Despite being betrayed by her son, Mattie keeps her ability to love, and she offers emotional sustenance to others, especially Etta and Lucielia. Both of their stories depict the pain and suffering that are common to many black women—being rejected by mainstream society and struggling with men who are not successful or loving. Both women recoil from the world to find solace in the glow of Mattie's love.

The second half of the novel explores members of a younger generation who have had different opportunities. Kiswana, Lorraine, and Theresa are all educated African American women who have taken a degree of control over their lives and who have become relatively successful. They all stand in contrast to Cora Lee, who seems to have a pathological need to give birth continuously. As the final chapter unfolds, however, only Lorraine yearns to unite the loving, accepting quality of Mattie with the power to take control of one's life. Lorraine has both a strong sense of herself and a strong commitment to community; for her, people rise or sink together, but all must pull their own oar. Because of the prejudices against Lorraine's lesbianism, however, she becomes ostracized. When Theresa, Lorraine's lover, forces her to choose between her desire for community and her individuality, Lorraine is forced to put her vision on the line alone. Pushed into isolation by the intolerance and small-mindedness of her lover and the other women, Lorraine steps into tragedy: She is raped and killed by a gang of young punks.

Although the attack on Lorraine is horribly painful, her death is not in vain. All the women recognize how they treated Lorraine in ways they had been treated in their own lives, and they learn from this tragedy. The women come to recognize the power of community, the need to accept and love one another. At novel's end, they symbolically tear down the wall separating Brewster Place from the city, revealing their new commitment to individual agency and an understanding community.

Analysis

The Women of Brewster Place is a complex novel, and coming to terms with it may be difficult for some young adult readers. Any novel confronting racism and sexism will inspire many reactions, from uncritical acceptance to outright rejection. Naylor's book, however, is an extremely worthy novel for many reasons. First, it serves as a testament to the lives of African American women who have maintained self-respect and hope in the face of suffering and who have been the backbone of their communities; various young readers will identify with and appreciate this aspect. Second, Americans whose lives are generally left secret are represented in this book; students, especially mainstream students, should be exposed to these depictions. Most important, the book confronts significant questions of morality for a democratic, pluralistic society; young people should explore these issues in a mature and serious manner.

The first major theme that the book explores is racism, the experience of being black in America, and the ways in which people cope with and confront prejudice. Symbolized by the wall separating Brewster Place from the life of the city, racism affects all of the character's lives. Naylor does not harp on historic injustices; racism is a fact of life, a real force that these characters cannot escape, although they proceed with their lives as best they can. Some, such as Mattie, Kiswana, and Lucielia, seem to transcend racism, maintaining the ability to dream and hope and love. Others, such as Etta, rebel but never escape the effects of racism. Those like Cora internalize racist attitudes, feeling no self-worth and believing that they and their children deserve nothing. The reader is left wondering what these women's lives would have been like in a world without racism—what beauty and triumph might have been revealed.

The second and more inclusive theme that the novel explores is of the community of women. Unlike the men in their world, who deal with social injustice in violent and often self-destructive ways, the women of Brewster Place cope with the effects of racism and injustice by forming nurturing networks and strong bonds. These bonds can have both dramatic effects, as when Mattie soothes Lucielia's tragic sadness with love and caring, and subtle effects, as when Kiswana takes Cora and her children to a Shakespeare play. Here, the bonds formed within a community of women ameliorate the effects, the cynicism and the despair, of a world that devalues both African Americans and women.

The significance of this community of women is heightened when Lorraine and Theresa move to Brewster Place and Lorraine seeks acceptance into that community. Naylor here reveals limitations within the African American community itself, for the overall community and the women do not welcome Lorraine. They can accept that she is black but not that she is a lesbian, a category that seems to threaten their existence as women and mothers. Lorraine's tragedy serves both to emphasize the protection and sustenance offered by the community and to criticize the community's inability to transcend its own prejudice. Naylor's theme—that prejudice of any sort curtails the possibility of a shared and productive future—reverberates outward beyond the boundaries of Brewster Place to American society and beyond the pages of the book into the minds of those who read it.

Critical Context

The Women of Brewster Place is not a typical young adult novel. The youngest character in the book is a young woman around the age of twenty, and the narrative does not offer a single main character with whom readers can identify. Nevertheless, as the winner of the American Book Award for 1982, this book has already become one of the most widely read books about the contemporary experience of black women in America. The chapter "The Two" has been anthologized as an indictment against prejudice and intolerance. The novel opens a window to a world about which many young adults only hear in simplified media portrayals, and it poses important questions that these readers should be asked to address and consider.

Gloria Naylor's book contributes to a growing tradition of African American female novelists. Toni Morrison's *The Bluest Eye* (1970) depicts the tragedy of a young girl driven mad by lack of affection and physical abuse, and her book *Sula* (1973) explores the friendship between two black women. Terry McMillan's *Waiting to Exhale* (1992) explores the lives and triumphs of four modern black women in a mode similar to Naylor's. All the books in this tradition portray the trials and tribulations, the hopes and dreams of black women living in a tangled modern world. Although Naylor's novel contains difficult scenes and asks probing questions, it moves readers to ponder social realities and their own relation to these realities.

Kevin Railey

THE WONDERS OF PHYSICS
An Introduction to the Physical World

Author: Irving Adler (1913-   )
First published: 1966; illustrated
Type of work: Science
Subjects: Education, jobs and work, nature, and science
Recommended ages: 10-15

A longtime high school mathematics teacher and the author of many science books for children, Adler describes the role played by physics in everyday life.

Form and Content

Irving Adler's *The Wonders of Physics: An Introduction to the Physical World* describes the role played by this branch of science in everyday life. Although simple mathematics are found throughout the book, the purpose of this book goes beyond that of a textbook. Rather, the author attempts to stimulate the interest of the reader in their world. Adler introduces the text with a basic discussion of what physics involves. In addition to providing a basic definition of the subject, this introductory chapter begins by addressing questions to events occurring around people that they often take little time to observe. Topics are described using a basic question-and-answer format. For example, the reader is asked about the rising and setting of the sun. In this manner, Adler introduces his readers to such concepts as planetary motion.

The text is subdivided into chapters, each dealing with a specific application of the physical sciences. First is introduced the concept of measurement; the terms commonly used to carry out physical measurements are explained. In a sense, these first chapters merely introduce subjects in order to pique the interest of young readers. From this point on in the book, Adler emphasizes the applications of physics. Each chapter begins with an explanation of the subject; individual chapters deal with such topics as the forms of matter, relativity, and radiation. A brief history is provided for the subject matter; for example, in the chapter addressing relativity, the role played by Albert Einstein in introducing relativity both to fellow scientists and to the general public is discussed. Even though each chapter may involve a diverse set of material, Adler explains the information at a level appropriate for young readers. Following an explanation of the material, the author moves into the area of application, presenting several examples of increasing complexity.

The book was written in the 1960's, and some of the text is arguably dated, particularly with respect to certain examples or applications (satellites, for example, are more complex than the simple radios that the author describes). The basic context of the material remains general enough, however, that it can still be applied to everyday life. Since 1966, human beings have walked on the moon and space probes have been sent out of the solar system, but the underlying physics does not change. It is here that Adler is strongest in his descriptions. Illustrations in the form of cartoons are plentiful and useful in understanding much of the material (although the stick-figure format may be perceived as silly by more sophisticated youths who have access to computers). The book finishes with descriptions of further applications of physics, in areas such as astronomy and nuclear fission or fusion. The sun is often the focus of such applications, used to illustrate aspects of planetary motion, as a source of radiation, and indeed as a prime example of what can happen as a result of the release of energy during certain forms of nuclear reactions. The book concludes with additional questions and answers that would appeal to young readers.

Analysis

Adler recognized that physics can be an all-encompassing subject, with relevance to many different areas. Consequently, he divided the subject matter into individual topics; while topics are related to one another, each chapter can be read and digested on its own merits. Adler begins each chapter with an explanation of the subject matter, its meaning, and its historical context. Rather than presenting the material in a dry textbook fashion, he brings his own sense of wonder to the subject, directing the reader to specific questions and examples.

Terms or concepts are introduced in the language of the young reader as an interested novice rather than as a student of science, and clear applications are included. For example, in his discussion of Sir Isaac Newton's laws of motion, rather than any reference to inertia, a term beyond the scope of the young reader, Adler applies the concept to satellites flying around the Earth. He discusses the fact that orbits are curved because the satellite tends to move in a specific direction, while at the same time being pulled by gravity back toward the ground. The result is a circular motion. In like manner, Adler discusses the wave nature of energy. Rather than a dry definition of the concept, Adler uses the image of a row of dominoes. If energy, in the form of a push, is applied to the first domino, the "pulse" of energy moves in wavelike fashion through the entire row. The energy is not directly observed, but its effects are seen. A wave itself can be observed through flicking a rope, or tossing a pebble into a resting body of water. In each case, movement is observed in the form of a wave. It is the use of such commonplace examples that makes the material clear to the reader.

Another striking example of the use of everyday analogies is found in the chapter dealing with Einstein and relativity. Instead of simply stating motion as being relative, Adler uses the example of a boy sitting on a moving train. Motion in the outside world as observed by someone on the train will be different than by someone on the outside looking at the same scenery. In other words, motion is relative to the frame of reference. In his discussion on the motion of molecules, Adler describes the molecules in a moving body as similar to a series of marching soldiers: Motion is orderly. When heat is applied, however, increasing the energy of the system, the situation becomes increasingly more disorderly; the molecules now behave in a more chaotic manner, like unruly children.

Illustrations are used to support the descriptions that are provided. Although the stick-figured drawings are somewhat cartoonish (and thus dated), such diagrams nevertheless convey in a meaningful manner the point that is being addressed. Adler seemed to have a particular interest in the atom and its nucleus, as many of his discussions deal with this subject. Indeed, a significant proportion of his science books deal with this topic. This focus may reflect the period in which *The Wonders of Physics* was written: the 1960's, when atomic energy was still thought of as being an answer to many of the world's energy problems.

Adler closes his book with additional questions for his readers. Rather than leaving his audience at the conclusion of the subject, he brings further insights to the discussion. It is clear that science is exciting to the writer; the goal of this book, and his other works, is to convey this curiosity to the reader. The frequent use of analogies is intended both to aid in understanding the concepts themselves and to stimulate the imagination of readers in hunting for their own examples.

Critical Context

Irving Adler spent more than twenty years as a teacher of mathematics in the New York City school system. In 1952, he altered his career, becoming a writer of children's books on the subject of science and mathematics. Adler based his writings on his own interests—that is, dealing with subjects about which he wished to know in more detail. He remembered his own interests as a child and teenager, and his work reflected the assumption that these questions are universal and timeless. Never losing his wonder at the world around him, Adler addressed his writings specifically to those individuals who had not yet lost their own curiosity about the world: the young. The goal of his writings was to create a picture for his readers, thereby stimulating their imaginations. His experience as a teacher was an immense help in achieving this goal.

Adler went on to publish more than seventy-five children's books, mainly in areas of science. He has the capacity to present the material in the language of his readers; he never talks down to them but, with the use of clear examples and analogies, is able to bring his points across. *The Wonders of Physics* is typical of such writing. When this book was first published in 1966, it was considered among the best science books directed toward a youthful audience. Adler followed it shortly afterward with books in a similar vein directed at the same audience: *Atoms and Molecules* (1966), *Magnets* (1966), and *Energy* (1970). The successful format used previously was continued in the series. In like manner, Adler has also written for an adult audience, remaining as popular with his older readers as with a more youthful audience.

Richard Adler

THE WORLD ACCORDING TO GARP

Author: John Irving (1942-   )
First published: 1978
Type of work: Novel
Type of plot: Psychological realism and social realism
Time of work: During and after World War II
Locale: The Steering School in New England and Dog's Head Harbor in New Hampshire
Subjects: Coming-of-age, emotions, gender roles, and sexual issues
Recommended ages: 15-18

T. S. Garp, reared by a single mother at the Steering School, embarks on the arduous task of comprehending the world amid the confusing messages about sex, emotions, and gender roles.

Principal characters:

T. S. GARP, the son of the famous feminist Jenny Fields who becomes a writer and struggles to comprehend an irrational world

JENNY FIELDS, a feminist before her time, a highly independent individual who becomes famous with her autobiography *A Sexual Suspect*

HELEN HOLM, the only daughter of Ernie Holm who marries T. S. Garp and becomes an English professor

DUNCAN GARP, the first son of T. S. Garp and Helen, who becomes a painter and illustrates his father's books

WALT GARP, the second son of T. S. Garp and Helen

JENNY GARP, third child and only daughter of T. S. Garp and Helen, who becomes a doctor devoted to cancer research

ROBERTA MULDOON, a transsexual follower and friend of Jenny Fields and the T. S. Garp family; formerly Robert Muldoon a famous tight end for the Philadelphia Eagles

ELLEN JAMES, a rape victim who inspires a group of female followers who call themselves The Ellen Jamesians and who becomes the director of the Fields Foundation

Form and Content

The World According to Garp is the bizarre and detailed story of the life of T. S. Garp, from the moment of his unusual conception to his untimely death. As the novel progresses, Garp's life unfolds as he struggles to comprehend a world governed by chaos and mishap. Each chapter depicts a new stage of Garp's social, emotional, and sexual maturation, which is paralleled in his writing career. On his perilous journey through life, Garp must strive to understand the relevance of random events and the significance of the eccentric people whom he meets along the way. The lengthy story of T. S. Garp's life is often interrupted by "mini-fictions," with each subfiction mirroring a stage in his social and emotional development.

Garp is born into the world with unique disadvantages. He is not only the only son of the first famous feminist, Jenny Fields, but also an illegitimate child who has limited knowledge of his father, a situation that has profound effects on him. In addition, Garp is reared in a single-parent family by a woman who detests men, lust, and sex. In an effort to protect her only son from the pains of the world, Jenny Fields rears Garp in the sheltered and enclosed environment of the infirmary at the Steering School, the all-boys preparatory high school where she works as a nurse.

After his graduation from the Steering School, Garp travels with his mother to Vienna, where he plans to begin a writing career. While his mother writes and completes her famous feminist autobiography, *A Sexual Suspect*, Garp struggles to write and experiments sexually with prostitutes. It is in Vienna where he writes—but does not complete—his first novel, which eventually brings him money and fame.

After the Vienna excursion and many unsuccessful attempts at writing imaginative stories, Garp marries Helen Holm, his childhood sweetheart, and soon has two children. Instead of playing the role of loving and committed husband and father, however, Garp is the overprotective, paranoid, and fearful father who tries to shield his children from the chaotic outside world. As a result, he becomes obsessed with safety in his neighborhood, is unfaithful to his wife, and is plagued with permanent writer's block. While Helen pursues her academic career as an English professor, Garp cooks, cleans, and takes care of the children.

It is at this point in his life when tragedy strikes in the form of a car accident. This graphic scene occurs after Garp and his two children return home early from seeing a motion picture and interrupt his wife administering oral sex to another man. The accident leaves the Garp family dismembered: Garp's jaw is broken and his ego is bruised; his eldest son is mutilated; his younger son is dead; his wife has facial bruises; and the other man is left with one-third of a penis. While recovering at Jenny Field's infirmary, Garp tries to write but is unsuccessful because he cannot separate his personal life from his imagination.

Garp's moment of recognition and true comprehension of the world and his place in it happens at his mother's funeral, the first feminist funeral for women. Garp attends dressed as a woman, and it is on this day that he truly feels the torment with which women must deal in their everyday lives. Utterly disgusted with the way in which women are treated, he vows to live like his mother, selfless and devoted to helping others in need. From this point on, Garp is generous and helps women who are dispossessed and disadvantaged in society.

Garp's metamorphosis includes becoming a loving, committed, faithful, and responsible husband and father. By the end of the novel, he has become a famous and successful writer, and some even call him the first male feminist writer. In the end, the members of the Garp family form a close, intimate bond as they reflect on the positive influence that T. S. Garp has had on each of their lives. The reader is left with a hopeful and upbeat message that although all people must die, their spirits live on in others.

Analysis

The World According to Garp is an intricate and sophisticated novel that focuses on many complex issues, such as transsexuality, gender roles, parenting, murder, death, assassination, illegitimacy, infidelity, marriage, sex, growing up, and writing. Writing in a chronological format, John Irving vividly portrays the life of a man who is born into a society on the verge of change, struggling to integrate the new feminism, nontraditional family structures, and reversed gender roles. In addition, the novel expresses concern for such feminist issues as rape, single motherhood, the aspirations of women for political power, nontraditional family structures, and domestic role reversal.

The World According to Garp is a classic example of a novel of initiation, which focuses on the life and development of a young protagonist making the passage from childhood to adulthood. This genre is especially appealing to young adult readers, who may be encountering similar problems. Young adult literature can serve as an aid and perhaps even a guide for readers as they venture through a difficult and confusing period of transition. Garp, like many young adults, goes through a painful process of maturation during which he develops his own values.

Irving continues the tradition of the young adult novel that leaves its protagonist on a positive and uplifting note. On the surface level, the epilogue emphasizes the cyclical nature of life as it is riddled with accounts of death. Irving sprinkles seeds of optimism, however, as he illustrates the positive influence that Garp has had on his family.

Irving immediately links the bipolar issues of death and sex, a connection that recurs throughout the novel as if to suggest that from sex comes life, the opposite of death. The World According to Garp begins with the unusual story of T. S. Garp's conception: Jenny Fields, in essence, rapes a dying soldier so that she can avoid the traditional role of wife. Soon after Garp's conception, the soldier dies and Garp is destined to be reared by a single mother. The fact that he is born fatherless affects his development as a writer as he struggles to form his own identity apart from being the son of Jenny Fields, the champion feminist.

The tone of the novel is a unique blending of the serious and the almost comically absurd. Amid the violence, the grotesque, and the craziness is an energetic, racy style that is quite appealing.

Critical Context

The World According to Garp is in many ways John Irving's most traditional novel, recounting the life story of a man, his family, his friends, and his world. In a sense, Irving's The World According to Garp is a modern version of Laurence Sterne's The Life and Opinions of Tristram Shandy, Gent. (1759-1767). Like Irving, Sterne combines wit and sentiment to produce an original novel with the ultimate purpose of making readers laugh. Both novels recount sentimental journeys, including serious subjects such as death, misfortune, and sex, but they are humorous as well. The source of humor is inherent in the style of both of the novelists as they defy readers' expectations. Both Irving and Sterne seek to show a view of what life really is like, which is the goal of the realistic novel. Furthermore, both novels show a concern for human relationships and for the difficulty of communication between people. Although they are filled with violence and death, the focus is on the affirmation of life.

Susan Lytle

THE WRIGHT BROTHERS
How They Invented the Airplane

Author: Russell Freedman (1929-   )
First published: 1991; illustrated
Type of work: Biography
Time of work: 1871-1948
Locale: Primarily Dayton, Ohio, and Kitty Hawk, North Carolina
Subjects: Aviators and inventors
Recommended ages: 13-18

Freedman describes how Wilbur and Orville Wright, two self-taught bicycle me-
chanics, achieved the world's first powered, sustained, and controlled airplane flight
in 1903 and documented their invention with photographs.

Principal personages:
   WILBUR WRIGHT (1867-1912), the older brother of the inventing team,
   a visionary who is thorough and methodical but prone to
   absent-mindedness
   ORVILLE WRIGHT (1871-1948), the younger brother, a dapper and
   outgoing man full of practical knowledge

Form and Content

Russell Freedman traces the journey taken by the Wright brothers as they ushered
in modern aviation. *The Wright Brothers: How They Invented the Airplane* examines
the brothers' early lives and their careers as printers, newspaper publishers, bicycle
mechanics, and pioneer aviators. The book begins with an eyewitness account of the
historic flight in Dayton, Ohio, 1904, marking the first time that a plane made a
complete circle during flight. The story then shifts back to a third-person account of
the Wrights' childhood, growing up years, and adulthood.

Most of the chapters deal with the Wright brothers as adults and their contributions
to aviation. Orville and Wilbur's partnership is explored. As Wilbur is quoted, "From
the time we were little children, my brother Orville and myself lived together, played
together, worked together and, in fact, thought together." The brothers shared the
inventing, mechanical, designing, and piloting responsibilities equally. Spurred by
reading newspaper accounts of gliding and flying experiments, Wilbur Wright wrote
to the Smithsonian Institution and asked for information about flight experiments.
Using this information and their mechanical knowledge, the brothers started to draw
plans for a flying machine. They flew successful gliders, then graduated to powered
flight.

The historic 1903 flight at Kitty Hawk, North Carolina, is detailed, as well as the
brothers' vast contributions to aviation. Their invention process is explored. The
brothers experienced many setbacks and frustrations. Unfavorable weather condi-

tions, mechanical failures, and design problems sent them back to the drawing board in order to perfect the airplane. When they did succeed, they continued to improve their plane and to record longer flight times and distances. By 1908, Wilbur and Orville Wright were publicly demonstrating the airplane in Europe and the United States. Both men remained active in the field until their deaths.

Freedman provides an index, information on places to visit, and a list of further reading. The book is illustrated with ninety-four black-and-white photographs taken by the Wright brothers, plus their drawings and plans and family photographs. The airplane has been called the first major invention documented by photography. Wilbur and Orville Wright were very aware of the historical significance of the airplane, and they wished to leave a detailed record of their work. Always partners, the brothers took turns flying and taking photographs, which vividly illustrate the Wright brothers' lifework.

Analysis

Freedman portrays Wilbur and Orville Wright as real people with multidimensional personalities. Each man had strengths, and each had foibles and idiosyncrasies. Wilbur was not concerned with neatness or his dress. He was the visionary of the two, able to see the "big picture" and the entire project. He was quiet and self-assured. Orville was more outgoing, described as having a bubbly personality. He had a reputation as a practical joker and a tease. Mechanical operations fascinated him; he loved taking things apart and putting them back together. Wilbur was the first who dreamed of building an airplane and flying, while Orville's enthusiasm and dedication carried the project. Yet, each man is presented with respectful realism, and they are both shown as regular people who did not seem to be destined for great things. What the author admires about Orville and Wilbur Wright is their ability to make a dream come true through hard work and dedication.

Freedman emphasizes the partnership between the brothers and their hard work. These men were defined by their work; neither married or had outside interests. It was the challenge of manned powered flight that made their lives exciting. They tried their flight theories first on kites and then on gliders, and then they attempted powered flight. The book documents this methodical progression. The Wrights went to Kitty Hawk in 1900 to fly gliders in the first of three trips. Freedman again shows the brothers' meticulous research, long hours, and dedication to achieving manned flight. Conditions were primitive at the Kitty Hawk camp. Photographs reveal a lack of cooking facilities in the first camps. Running water was not available; all water for drinking and bathing had to be hauled to the camp. Staying there meant great hardship and sacrifice, but the Wrights were determined to perform their tests and flights.

The Wright brothers did not stop inventing after they achieved manned flight. Freedman chronicles their dedication while discussing their other contributions to aviation. They were the first to put wheels on an aircraft instead of skids, and Orville Wright invented an automatic pilot system and the split-flap airfoil still in use during World War II.

The use of the Wrights' actual photographs sets this book apart from others about the brothers, providing insight into what the Wright brothers perceived as important. The invention process is carefully recorded. Because it was vital to be accurate about the process, they also photographed mistakes and failures. Thus, a complete history is preserved, not simply the glorious triumphs achieved by the two inventors. Wilbur and Orville Wright fully realized the value of their invention. Even while still experimenting with kites, Orville was quoted as saying that he believed in the future of powered flight to carry mail and passengers. The brothers were careful to protect their invention with patents. Wilbur Wright spent much of the early twentieth century in court fighting lawsuits to protect those patents.

Critical Context

Critics, young adults, middle school readers, and adults praised Russell Freedman's well-researched text illustrated with photographs taken by the subjects themselves. Nominated for the Texas Bluebonnet Award in 1993 and named a Newbery Honor Book for 1992, *The Wright Brothers: How They Invented the Airplane* continued in the tradition of Freedman's Newbery Medal-winning, *Lincoln: A Photobiography* (1987). The concept of text and illustration working together has long been reserved for picture books, but Freedman presents biographies for young adults in which the illustrations are an integral part of the work. The impact of his books is greater because of this marriage of illustration and text.

In *The Wright Brothers*, Freedman presents a real picture of these men. When the brothers built their first experimental kite in 1899, humans in flight seemed no more real than a fairy tale. Ten years later, flight was a reality. The Wright brothers introduced modern flight to the world, yet they were ordinary bicycle mechanics from the Midwest who showed hard work, dedication, and spirit. No attempt is made in the book to make them more heroic; their lives are not fictionalized or reduced to one accomplishment. Freedman takes a balanced approach to his subject, portraying the Wright brothers as two men who had a dream that became an invention that changed the world.

Jane Claes

YEAGER
An Autobiography

Authors: Chuck Yeager (1923-   ) and Leo Janos (1933-   )
First published: 1985; illustrated
Type of work: Autobiography
Time of work: 1923-1985
Locale: Hamlin, West Virginia; Tonopah, Nebraska; war-torn France, Spain, and England; Wright Field in Dayton, Ohio; Muroc Air Base in the Mojave Desert, California; postwar Germany and Russia; Korea; Vietnam; and Pakistan
Subjects: Aviators and military leaders
Recommended ages: 15-18

Chuck Yeager, the first pilot to fly faster than the speed of sound, tells of his West Virginia origins, his World War II exploits, his life as a test pilot, and his continued military service, while his wife, friends, and colleagues add reminiscences that broaden and deepen the reader's understanding of the man and his accomplishments.

Principal personages:
CHUCK YEAGER, the test pilot who was the first to break the sound barrier
GLENNIS YEAGER, his wife
ALBERT HAL YEAGER, his father
SUSIE YEAGER, his mother
CLARENCE E. "BUD" ANDERSON, his friend, a World War II military pilot
ALBERT G. BOYD, the head of Wright Field's flight test division
FRED J. ASCANI, Colonel Boyd's executive officer
JACQUELINE COCHRAN, a colonel in the WASPs, the holder of speed records, and the president of Fédération Aeronautique Internationale
"PANCHO" (FLORENCE LOWE) BARNES, a female flyer and the owner of a bar and motel frequented by test pilots

Form and Content

Chuck Yeager's autobiography is unusual if not unique in the variety of voices employed to describe his life. While most of the basically chronological tale is told by Yeager in the first person, many sections are told in "other voices." While these "other voices" speak of themselves in the first person, they are more biographical (about Yeager) than autobiographical (about the individual authors). While Leo Janos' role as coauthor is obscured (and often ignored) by the designation of "autobiography" and by the various first-person writings, he is most likely responsible for the overall unit of time, tone, and theme that emerges despite the variety of voices.

While the term "chapter" is not used, the thirty-three divisions listed by their individual titles in the table of contents clearly function as chapters. The first, "Always the Unknown," relates a life-threatening flight that occurred the day after Yeager broke the sound barrier. This short chapter is written in the present tense, printed in italics, and out of sync with the chronological order that dominates the rest of the work. It is the second chapter, "Starting from Scratch," that tells of Yeager's birth and upbringing in West Virginia.

The third chapter relates his enlistment in the Army Air Corps, his pilot training, and how he met the woman who would become his wife. Near the end of the chapter is the first subheading of "Other Voices: Glennis Yeager," which offers her first-person account of the incident that he had introduced. In the next chapter, Yeager gives an account of being shot down over occupied France. In the middle of the chapter is a one-paragraph interruption in Glennis' voice. The next chapter begins in the voice of Bud Anderson, who gives his information on the same incident. The chapter then continues as Yeager details his escape through Spain. While such shifts in tense and voice may be disconcerting to some readers, the additional voices widen the scope and increase the authority of both the factual and the emotional material, much the same as televised biographies use personal interviews to supplement other materials.

After Yeager escaped through Spain, he returned to England and obtained permission to fly additional missions. (Escapees did not usually return to the war.) Early in 1945, Yeager completed his war missions, was transferred to Wright Field in Dayton, Ohio, and married Glennis. As assistant maintenance officer, Yeager flew many different kinds of planes. While his lack of education was a drawback, he eventually was trained as a test pilot and in 1947 was chosen to fly the X-1 as it attempted to break the sound barrier. He continued testing planes and, after his achievement was made public, reluctantly combined his flying with public appearances. After test flying a Russian MiG that had been obtained through a defecting North Korean pilot, Yeager became a squadron commander in Europe during the Cold War. He then became the first commanding officer of the Air Force Aerospace Research Pilots School. He continued an active military career, serving in Korea, Pakistan, and Vietnam until he retired in 1975.

Three small sections interspersed in the text provide photographs of Yeager, his wife, his friends, his planes, and important events in his life.

Analysis

While most readers are drawn to read *Yeager* because of a single incident in his life—the breaking of the sound barrier—the greatest strength of the biography is the exciting and unique military career of Chuck Yeager, which began during World War II and continued through the Vietnam War.

Unlike many of the pilots of World War II, Yeager had never even seen a plane "close up" until he was fifteen, when one "bellied into a cornfield on the Mud River" near his home in Hamlin, West Virginia. He joined the Army Air Corps in the summer of 1941 and was trained as an airplane mechanic. Although he became violently ill during his first plane ride, he applied for the "Flying Sergeant" program. He persevered through the airsickness phase, learned the mechanics of flying, excelled in seeing and then shooting air and ground targets, and was recommended to become a fighter pilot. More training ensued, interrupted by a temporary assignment as a test pilot. Yeager was shot down over occupied France after only eight missions.

Yeager's account of his escape from occupied France is as exciting as any fiction, but the present tense of this account and its contrast with the more logical past-tense narratives of the "other voices" weaken the impact of the writing. Whether the present tense was a concession to Yeager's natural speech patterns or an attempt to add a sense of immediacy to the retelling of certain events, readers may find its use distracting.

Yeager often refers to his own lack of education, his fears concerning competition with college graduates, and the frequency with which he outperformed them in the air. His grammar use reflects this past. By 1985, however, the author of this autobiography was no longer the poorly educated, unintelligible teenage pool hustler who joined the service. Anyone who can in one section pen the sentence, "Without realizing it, I was about to take charge of my life and push it in a direction where everything that happened in later years was a logical outcome for a career fighter pilot who had compiled an outstanding combat record," can write other sections in the appropriate tense. While one should not hold the highest rhetorical standards to a popular-culture autobiography, one should not ignore those standards in any serious analysis of the work.

Although Yeager indicates in some passages that he believed that he was in control of his life, many more passages indicate that he attributed much of his success to "luck." In the next-to-last chapter, "A Summing Up," Yeager says, "what really strikes me looking back over all those years is how lucky I was. How lucky, for example, to have been born in 1923 and not 1963, so that I came of age just as aviation itself was entering the modern era." Later he adds, "I've also been lucky to retain my health, stamina, and skills so I can stay current with the latest generation of military airplanes."

Critical Context

The young adult who reads *Yeager* learns about a half century that might seem to be "ancient history," but the events portrayed will continue to have been first-person experiences for many people living several decades past the year 2000. Young readers who are specifically interested in Chuck Yeager or who have a general interest in aviation would enjoy and benefit from reading the entire book. Those who have a limited interest in aviation or who are only interested in World War II, the Korean conflict, Vietnam, or Pakistan might be better served by reading specific selections.

Yeager's reckless pursuit of "fun" in his youth almost destroyed his career more than once. Breaking his ribs the night before he broke the sound barrier was minor compared to some other personally irresponsible incidents that he relates, and although he makes some attempt to justify orders that he and other U.S. pilots were given to kill "innocent civilians" during World War II, he also labels the results as an "atrocity." Yeager's failure to accept responsibility for his own actions, private and public, makes him a questionable role model.

Of the three women portrayed in depth—Glennis Yeager, Jacqueline Cochran, and Pancho Barnes—and the countless prostitutes and the nameless "girls to chase," Glennis is the only one who might be considered an acceptable role model for young women. In fact, many readers may find the attitude toward women to be offensive.

Nevertheless, *Yeager* is an interesting and entertaining book for adults. Whether young adults will also benefit from reading the biography will depend on their level of maturity.

Betty-Lou Waters

THE YEAR OF THE GOPHER

Author: Phyllis Reynolds Naylor (1933-   )
First published: 1987
Type of work: Novel
Type of plot: Psychological realism
Time of work: The late twentieth century
Locale: Minneapolis, Minnesota
Subjects: Coming-of-age, family, friendship, and jobs and work
Recommended ages: 13-18

George Richards disappoints his upper-middle-class parents when he decides to reject their offer of a free college education and instead gets a job to pay rent to his parents in order to achieve economic independence.

>   *Principal characters:*
>   GEORGE RICHARDS, a seventeen-year-old who is trying to decide what to do with his life after graduation from high school
>   OLIVER (OLLIE) RICHARDS, George's younger brother, a slow learner whom George tries to protect from their parents' unrealistically high expectations
>   PATRICIA (TRISH) RICHARDS, George's so-called perfect older sister, an honor student on scholarship at Cornell University who has a nervous stomach
>   JERI RICHARDS, George's younger sister, an excellent student who rebels against her parents by dating older men
>   MOM RICHARDS, their mother, who refuses a promotion because she does not want to leave the classroom to become an administrator yet demands that her children pursue financially lucrative careers
>   DAD (PHILIP) RICHARDS, a wealthy lawyer and Harvard graduate that wants George to follow in his footsteps

Form and Content

The Year of the Gopher is a poignant, realistic, fast-paced novel depicting the high parental expectations of a wealthy family. The locale is Minneapolis, but the story could take place anywhere. This first-person narrative begins with seventeen-year-old George Richards writing sarcastic remarks on Ivy League school applications in order to rebel against his parents and their aspirations for him. Eventually, George goes on an unsuccessful trip visiting these colleges, and his relationship with his father becomes tense.

George nurtures and tries to protect his younger siblings from their parents' expectations. He teaches his brother, Ollie, to train with weights and supports his dream to become a forest technician instead of going to college. Ollie is so upset with his parents' constant nagging that he has a tic. His younger sister, Jeri, rebels against their parents by sneaking out at night to meet older men. When she runs away from her abusive older boyfriend, Gus, George warns him to stay away from her. George's older sister, Trish, a sophomore at Cornell University, comes home to marry a summa cum laude graduate of the college. She appears to be perfect, yet she must watch what she eats and drinks liquid antacid by the quart.

When George's rejection letters start arriving, his parents conclude that George botched the applications. In a heated confrontation, George announces that he will not attend college in the fall. Instead, he will work full-time and pay rent to his parents.

George asks Maureen Kimball, who has been passionately pursuing him, to the prom. Later that evening, George and Maureen have sex, an activity that Maureen initiates. George feels guilty because he does not love Maureen and decides to keep the encounter a secret. As George spends more time with his friends, his parents become anxious about his relationship with David Hahn because David's father is gay. Later, after his friend Psycho gets drunk and almost drowns in the lake, George learns to become responsible with alcohol.

As his friends go off to college, George begins his first job as a gofer at a garden center. He enjoys his job and becomes romantically interested in Anne, an attractive coworker. George quits the job, however, as a result of sexual harassment from his female supervisor. George's next job, as a courier for a messenger service, proves to be a valuable experience. Pedaling his bicycle from assignment to assignment, he has time to think and to resolve some of his conflicts. In particular, George decides to reapply for college in the fall. This decision makes his parents, who have mellowed, happy and they begin to accept him as an adult capable of making up his own mind. George also comes to the conclusion that happiness is more important than money. His successful rebellion paves the way for Ollie and Jeri to pursue their dreams.

Analysis

Gloria Naylor's coming-of-age novel *The Year of the Gopher* connects readers with such universal young adult concerns as self-identity, life goals, sexuality, and relationships with parents. The strength of the story lies in Naylor's accurate depiction of the feelings and emotions of a typical frightened and confused adolescent struggling to find himself and become emotionally and economically independent of his parents.

The major conflict in *The Year of the Gopher* is generational expectations versus individual desires. George's parents love him and truly want what they think is best for him. George sarcastically regrets, however, that he has only one life for his father to live. George's conflict with his parents is a common experience for many young adults, who may be pressured by their parents to chose a financially rewarding career. He is expected to follow in the family footsteps going to an Ivy League school and becoming a lawyer like his Harvard-educated father and grandfather. Furthermore, George is expected to take over the family law firm.

The Year of the Gopher is an insightful novel that has many lessons to teach young readers who are unsure about what they want to do with their lives. George matures and starts to value women for qualities other than sexual ones, having learned that friendships with women are easier than romantic relationships. George also learns that one must be responsible with alcohol because life is precious and easy to lose. He realizes that adults, such as his parents, sometimes make mistakes and that he wants to be free to make his own decisions even though he too will make mistakes.

George spends a considerable amount of time watching his friends and family and discovers that they are not who they seem to be. Trish, an overachiever, is unhappy despite her perfect appearance. His friend Dave, by being promiscuous, is trying to prove that he is not gay like his father. Despite his own parents' disapproval of Dave's father's lifestyle, George realizes that homosexuality is merely another label. In addition, George must deal with his mother's hypocrisy when she plans to turn down a promotion in order to remain in the classroom while she expects her children to go for the big money.

George Richards is reminiscent of Holden Caulfield in J. D. Salinger's classic novel *The Catcher in the Rye* (1951). Like Holden, he struggles with the imperfections of adults and society and tries to come to terms with the world around him. George and Holden are pressured to succeed, and both try to protect their younger siblings from the phoniness and corruption of materialism. Their poignant conclusion is that happiness is more important than wealth.

Critical Context

In more than seventy novels for children, young adults, and adults, Gloria Naylor has displayed her gift for creating thought-provoking stories full of wit and comedy. She is well known for excellent writing in a variety of styles and forms and for realistic dialogue and memorable, complex characters with whom young adults can identify. Most of the subjects of Naylor's novels for young readers are based on incidents in her life. *The Year of the Gopher* is based on Naylor's firsthand observations of how parents pressure their children to achieve material wealth. Her former marriage to a mentally ill man inspired the writing of the young adult novel *The Keeper* (1986). *Shiloh* (1991), her Newbery Medal-winning novel, was written after Naylor found an abused stray dog. Her enormously popular Alice stories, about a motherless girl, come from Naylor's diaries and are indicative of her talent for writing comedy. She uses her gift for humorous invention to motivate her readers and to help them handle anxiety and gain deeper insight into problems. For example, in *The Year of the Gopher*, George is reminded by his father that he must be the best because, out of the four hundred million spermatozoa that raced for the ovum, he is the one who got there first.

Naylor is acclaimed for writing insightful, sensitive, honest stories of young adults confronting problems in contemporary family life. Without sentimentality, her young adult protagonists struggle with such problems as the death of a newborn baby and the questioning of religious beliefs in *A String of Changes* (1982), the divorce of parents in *The Solomon System* (1983), the mental illness of a parent in *The Keeper*, and the death of a parent in *The Dark of the Tunnel* (1985).

Margaret Theresa Sacco

YEAR OF THE UNICORN

Author: Andre Norton (1912-   )
First published: 1965
Type of work: Novel
Type of plot: Fantasy
Time of work: Unspecified
Locale: The lands of the Dales and Arvon on the Witch World
Subjects: Coming-of-age, love and romance, and the supernatural
Recommended ages: 13-18

> *Gillan must discover who and what she is if she is to survive the dangers of the land around her and escape the trap of the Were Riders.*

Principal characters:
> GILLAN, one of thirteen brides intended for the Were Riders, who has powers that she does not understand
> HERREL, a half-blooded Were Rider who wins Gillan as his wife
> HYRON, the leader of the Were Riders, a group of shape-changing warriors
> HALSE, a Were Rider who is jealous of Herrel and who covets Gillan for his own
> KILDAS, one of the thirteen brides

Form and Content

Year of the Unicorn is for the most part a coming-of-age story set in a fantasy world. Gillan, the first-person narrator who is in her late teens, goes on both a physical journey to another land and a mental journey of self-discovery and self-reliance. Along the way, she faces many magical and physical obstacles that must be overcome, including finding her "other" self in a dream land. Andre Norton presents a strong female protagonist who finds love and self-reliance after many hard-fought battles.

Gillan is an orphan in the Dales. She does not fit in and knows that she is different, both in appearance and temperament, from those around her. She faces a bleak future until she takes the place of one of the brides meant for the Were Riders. For helping the Dales in a war, the Were Riders were promised thirteen brides. When the brides meet them, Gillan sees through the illusion that the Were Riders cast and is drawn to a cloak lying to the side of the rest. She thus becomes the bride of Herrel, the owner of the cloak.

Herrel and the rest of the Were Riders discover Gillan's witch powers and fear her, even though she has used those abilities to save them from an evil spell set by their enemies. The Were Riders, without Herrel's knowledge, take Gillan's spirit to a dream land and take part of the spirit to make a copy of her. They then abandon the true Gillan while they ride through a gate into their homeland of Arvon, taking the copy with them. Halse, Herrel's rival, takes control of the Gillan copy.

The true Gillan is confronted by marauders, who threaten her with violence, but she uses her powers to escape and climbs over the mountains into Arvon. By learning to use her powers and her will, she manages to overcome each obstacle that confronts her. She finds herself getting weaker, however, and realizes that she casts no shadow. When she is finally able to let Herrel know what has happened to her, the other Were Riders cast a spell on him and send him to destroy her. Gillan breaks him out of the spell, and they are reunited. Herrel tells her that the two parts of her spirit must be made one again or else she will die. They confront the Were Riders, and Herrel champions Gillan and defeats Halse. During the battle, the connection between the copy and Gillan is severed, and the copy is lost in the dream land, where Gillan and Herrel must go to search for it. Gillan finds herself, figuratively and literally, and then saves Herrel as well. They return from the dream land and leave the Were Riders to seek their own future.

Analysis

Year of the Unicorn contains many themes of importance for young adults. The first of these is the idea of finding one's identity and place in the world. In a related theme, the story deals with what it is like to be an outcast or a misfit in society. Finally, the novel looks at what it means to trust and love another person. Norton explores all these issues in the rich fantasy setting of the Witch World.

Gillan has no idea of who she is or from where she has come. Brought to the Dales on an enemy ship as a child, she has no memory of her previous life. She is taken in by a good family but eventually winds up in the cloisters of the Dames, a religious sect in the Dales where she has few friends. Gillan picks up a few hints that she might come from a land across the sea. She chooses to go with the Were Riders to do something else with her life and to avoid a bleak future in the cloisters. What she finds are further hints about her true identity, but none of much help. She is called a witch, but that epithet tells her little. As with many stories of self-discovery, *Year of the Unicorn* uses the journey or quest motif. Gillan's physical journey leads her into Arvon and partial answers, but it is not until she goes into the dream land literally to find herself that she discovers what her powers truly are and who she is. She realizes that the answers have been inside her all along.

One of the reasons that Gillan wants to find out about herself is because she is a misfit in society. While most of the Dale folk are fair-skinned with light hair, she has black hair and pale skin. Her mentality differs as well; she lives in the cloisters but will not become part of the order. Among the brides, she is also an outcast because she can see through the illusions of the Were Riders. Gillan's status may explain why she is drawn to Herrel's cloak: He is an outcast among the Were Riders. Herrel is only a half blood, and the Were Riders continually tell him that he is less than they are, an inferior in blood and skill. When Gillan and Herrel meet, they help each other to reach their full potential and realize that they are not in the least inferior. Together, they overcome the prejudices of those around them.

Before Gillan can let Herrel help her, however, she must learn to trust him and her heart. After seeing him shape-change, she fears that he is more monster than man. She has never asked for help from anyone and finds it hard to ask for his assistance. Only after she is split in two does Gillan finally overcome her fears. In doing so, she helps him to become the man that he could be. The love that they have for each other makes them stronger as a pair than they were as individuals. Norton shows that it is important to look beneath the masks that people wear to find the true person beneath.

Norton weaves these themes together in her popular setting of the Witch World. It is a place of magic and wonder, of monsters and heroes. As Gillan narrates, the reader sees the magical land of Arvon through her eyes. The reader feels her fear as she encounters That Which Runs the Ridges. The reader sees her amazement at the sparkling waters and blossom-laden trees. The reader senses her disgust as she confronts the spiderlike hounds of the dream world. The reader can also marvel at the mind magic of Gillan, as well as the power of the shape-changing Were Riders. Norton brings all these things to life in this and other Witch World novels.

Critical Context

Year of the Unicorn was Andre Norton's third book set on the Witch World, following *Witch World* (1963) and *Web of the Witch World* (1964). This novel differs from the first two because it is not a direct sequel. Norton explores the same themes, however, of self-discovery and being an outcast in each of these novels and in most of her other works, including the direct sequel to *Year of the Unicorn*, *The Jargood Pard* (1974).

Year of the Unicorn is also important for its strong female protagonist, another characteristic of Norton's books. At the time it was written, science fiction was heavily male-dominated, and few female writers had found a place in the genre. Norton gave female readers, as well as male readers, a place to start and brought many readers and writers into the field. Her influence has been compared to that of Robert Heinlein, and many female authors give her credit. In 1985, Susan Schwartz edited a collection called *Moonsinger's Friends: An Anthology in Honor of Andre Norton* in which she and other authors talked about Norton's influence.

Norton has written more than a hundred books that are read and enjoyed by readers of all ages. She continues to write novels about the Witch World and continues to explore the important themes of self-discovery and finding a place in society.

P. Andrew Miller

YOU CAN'T TAKE IT WITH YOU

Author: George S. Kaufman (1889-1961) and Moss Hart (1904-1961)
First performed: 1936
First published: 1937
Type of work: Drama
Type of plot: Moral tale
Time of work: The mid-1930's
Locale: New York City, "just around the corner from Columbia University"
Subjects: Family and love and romance
Recommended ages: 13-18

Martin Vanderhof, the patriarch of an eccentric New York City family during the Depression, demonstrates that wealth and social standing are not necessarily the keys to happiness.

> *Principal characters:*
> MARTIN VANDERHOF, better known as Grandpa, a man who took a very early retirement from the rat race and has never regretted it
> PENELOPE SYCAMORE, Martin's daughter, currently a writer of unperformed plays
> PAUL SYCAMORE, Penelope's husband, who manufactures fireworks in the basement
> ESSIE CARMICHAEL, the Sycamores' elder daughter, whose life revolves around at-home ballet lessons
> ED CARMICHAEL, Essie's husband, an amateur printer
> ALICE SYCAMORE, the Sycamores' younger, altogether "normal" daughter
> TONY KIRBY, a young man in love with Alice
> MR. and MRS. KIRBY, Tony's wealthy and decidedly upper-crust parents

Form and Content

You Can't Take It with You, winner of the 1938 Pulitzer Prize, is a classic American stage comedy that deftly blends elements of farce, slapstick, whimsical humor, social commentary, and romance, together with a generous dash of good-natured optimism about the human condition. First staged in December, 1936, at a time when the United States was only beginning to recover from the bleakest days of the Great Depression, *You Can't Take It with You* was the third play written by the team of George S. Kaufman and Moss Hart, the most successful collaborators in the history of the American theater.

The play is set in New York City, in the Sycamore household, a zany little kingdom presided over by Grandpa Vanderhof, who thirty-five years before had decided that the world of business could get along quite nicely without him and has "been a happy man ever since." Grandpa's iconoclastic attitudes toward work, money, and happiness have obviously infected the entire household: As the stage directions announce, "This is a house where you do as you like, and no questions asked." In the best tradition of "screwball" comedy, the family is made up almost completely of lovable eccentrics. Mrs. Sycamore, for example, has passed most of her time for eight years writing plays (with titles such as "Sex Takes a Holiday"), not from any deep artistic motives but only because a typewriter was delivered to the house one day by mistake. Mr. Sycamore manufactures a variety of fireworks in the basement with the assistance of Mr. De Pinna, a man who showed up years before to deliver ice and simply decided to stay, and oldest daughter Essie, when she is not making candy that she stores in a skull, takes ballet lessons from a burly Russian emigré named Kolenkhov. The only exception seems to be the Sycamore's younger daughter, Alice, an attractive and "normal" young woman who loves her family dearly in spite of their eccentricities but wonders at times why they "can't be like other people."

The comic antics of the Sycamore household, however, while delightful enough, primarily serve as the background for the play's central action, which involves Alice's romance with Tony Kirby, whose wealthy father owns the Wall Street firm where Alice works. Alice is understandably worried about how Tony's quite proper and conservative parents will respond to her family, and she does her best to arrange a dinner party at her home where everybody will be on their best behavior. The Kirbys show up a day early, however, catching Alice's family in their full comic glory and ensuring exactly the sort of disaster that Alice has dreaded.

One misunderstanding leads to another, and the Kirbys' visit ends with an explosion in the basement and with nearly everyone, including the Kirbys, being carted off to the police station by government agents responding to several seditious circulars unwittingly printed and distributed throughout the city by Essie's husband, Ed. Humiliated, Alice decides on the following day to abandon her marriage plans and leave town, but Grandpa is able, after Tony and his father return, to bring the young lovers back together and to persuade everyone that love and personal contentment are much more likely to produce happiness than wealth and social standing. Even Mr. Kirby becomes a convert to Grandpa's way of thinking, and the play ends with the entire household sitting down to a dinner of cheese blintzes prepared and served by a Russian grand duchess introduced by Kolenkhov.

Analysis

American stage comedies generally aim for laughter rather than enlightenment, and this is particularly true of the best of the Kaufman-Hart comedies of the 1930's. Still, such plays as *Once in a Lifetime* (1930), *You Can't Take It with You*, and *The Man Who Came to Dinner* (1939) do contain some elements of social satire and commentary, although these elements are often muted by the presence of a romantic sentimentalism that insists on a happy ending in which all vestiges of conflict are reconciled. In the case of *You Can't Take It with You*, Kaufman and Hart devised a plot especially dear to the hearts of American audiences: One essentially good-hearted, stubborn individual is pitted against the "system." Grandpa Vanderhof emerges both as a splendid comic character in his own right and as an exemplar of purely American individualism, ingenuity, and plain common sense. By turning his back on the traditional pursuits of wealth, power, and social standing, Grandpa manages to flout—in his wise and gentle way—most of the social conventions that govern the day-to-day lives of men and women.

Comedy nearly always flirts with social anarchy, and most of the great comic characters—from William Shakespeare's Falstaff to the Three Stooges—have generated laughter and delight by gleefully violating those very rules of everyday conduct by which the rest of the world is forced to live. In addition to providing riotous entertainment, the result can be both cathartic and reassuring: Comic chaos subverts the established norms, often revealing the many cracks in the social façade, but in the end the prevailing human values of love and family win out and order is reestablished. This is exactly what happens in *You Can't Take It with You*, although with a novel twist provided by Kaufman and Hart. Instead of introducing a set of comic characters into a seemingly normal situation (as Kaufman did in the three Marx Brothers films for which he wrote screenplays during the 1930's), they arrange for several "normal" characters to visit the topsy-turvy world of the Sycamores, thereby bringing into collision two radically opposed sets of values. Since any audience is likely to respond to the characters inhabiting the Sycamore home with affection and sympathy, the Kirbys, ironically (but not accidentally), come off rather badly, and what the Kirbys represent—money, prestige, the sacrifice of personal happiness for worldly success—is held up to criticism.

Although one may then wonder whether it is therefore possible to see *You Can't Take It with You* as a satiric indictment of the American Dream, this is not really the case. There has never been a healthy and sustained tradition of satire on the American stage, and Kaufman in particular, although famous for his acerbic wit, had severe doubts about the money-making potential of even first-rate theatrical satire. In addition, both Kaufman and Hart had risen to lives of sophisticated opulence in the New York theater world from very modest beginnings—Hart, in fact, from virtual impoverishment—and one never senses that they wish to question too deeply the traditional American ethic of hard work guaranteeing success, even though other Depression-era dramatists were doing exactly that. One can probably better account for the undeniable comic power of *You Can't Take It with You* by focusing on its humorous and upbeat appeal to two very American characteristics: the instinctive American distrust of wealth, power, and the institutions that create and sustain wealth and power (such as Wall Street), and the sympathy that most Americans instinctively feel for the underdog. These factors seem much more likely explanations for the play's effectiveness and continuing popularity.

Critical Context

Over a period of eleven years, from 1930 until 1940, George S. Kaufman and Moss Hart collaborated on eight plays, all of them financially successful, two or three of them among the best comedies ever presented on the Broadway stage. On that basis alone, it is safe to say that they made an enormous contribution to the American theater. More important, plays such as *You Can't Take It with You*, which continues to be staged in revivals across the country, have influenced several generations of dramatists and theatergoers, helping to create and shape a brand of comedy that is enduringly funny—and distinctly American.

Michael Stuprich

YOU COME TOO
Favorite Poems for Young Readers

Author: Robert Frost (1874-1963)
First published: 1959; illustrated
Type of work: Poetry
Subjects: Animals, emotions, friendship, jobs and work, and nature
Recommended ages: 13-18

Consistent with Frost's claim that poems should begin in delight and end in wisdom, this selection includes enjoyable and thought-provoking poems on a variety of themes and in a variety of styles.

Form and Content

The fifty-one poems in Robert Frost's *You Come Too: Favorite Poems for Young Readers* are organized into sections according to subject, each section titled with a line from one of the poems that follow. The first grouping, for example, is titled "I'm going out . . . " (from "The Pasture") and contains poems about walking out of doors. The poems in this section concern the same general subject; however, they represent a variety of specific themes, from simple delight in farm scenes in "The Pasture" to complex considerations of loneliness in "Acquainted with the Night."

The title page for each section includes an original wood engraving illustration by Thomas W. Nason, and fourteen additional Nason engravings appear on the cover and throughout the book. A foreword by Frost's friend Hyde Cox introduces the poems and provides young people with sensible suggestions about reading poems.

You Come Too contains representative selections of Frost's poems. It includes many of the commonly anthologized pieces, such as "The Pasture," "Stopping by Woods on a Snowy Evening," and "The Road Not Taken," as well as less well known poems. Among these are "Good Hours," in which an alienated speaker seems shut out of the warm homes he walks by, and "The Telephone," in which the speaker fancies that he hears a loved one calling him from a flower.

The collection contains lyric poems such as "A Patch of Old Snow," "The Oven Bird," and "The Freedom of the Moon," as well as narrative poems, including the comical "Brown's Decent" and the contemplative "Death of the Hired Man." It includes blank verse as in "Christmas Trees," complicated or experimental rhyme and other sound effects as in "Stopping by Woods on a Snowy Evening," and easy *aabb* rhymes as in "Looking for the Sunset Bird in Winter"—although fewer than one might expect.

A few of the poems seem intended specifically for children and young adults. "The Exposed Nest" is addressed to a young reader, a child who has discovered a full nest of birds on the ground revealed and left vulnerable by a mowing machine. One section takes its title, "I was one of the children told . . . ," from "A Peck of Gold," in which the speaker is a child. Other poems in the section include "The Last Word of a

Bluebird: As Told to a Child" and "A Girl's Garden." Most of the other poems (and perhaps even these) are written to a broad audience of young and old alike by a poet wise in years but young at heart.

Analysis

The title of Frost's earliest collection of poems was *A Boy's Will* (1913), and his poems are included in school readers and considered appropriate reading for children. When *You Come Too* was published, Frost was a great-grandfather, yet he was not a writer of children's verse nor as grandfatherly and benign as he looked.

Although Frost did write many lovely descriptions of nature ("A Hillside Thaw"), some humorous verses ("The Rose Family"), and even a few romantic sonnets ("Never Again Would Birds' Song Be the Same"), he also wrote of "boughten friendships," despair, and death. The same man who wrote, in "The Pasture," "I'm going out to fetch the little calf/ That's standing by the mother. It's so young/ It totters when she licks it with her tongue" also wrote, in "Desert Places," "They cannot scare me with their empty spaces/ Between stars—on stars where no human race is./ I have it in me so much nearer home/ To scare myself with my own desert places." This reality is represented in *You Come Too*, which includes some dark and disturbing poems. "Departmental" describes death in the ant world; "Death of the Hired Man," the last hours of an old farmworker; and "Fire and Ice," the destruction of the world. "Good Hours" and "Acquainted with the Night" communicate loneliness and aliena-tion.

Many other poems in the collection present to readers ideas that seem to ask—as Cox suggests in the foreword—to be invited in while one gets to know them. In "Birches," the reader is prompted to contemplate the tension between the pleasures of earthly life and longings for Heaven. In "The Tuft of Flowers," the reader must puzzle out the meaning of Frost's concluding couplet: " 'Men work together,' I told him from the heart,/ 'Whether they work together or apart.' " In "Two Tramps in Mud Time" is another work idea: "My object in living is to unite/ My avocation and my vocation/ As my two eyes make one in sight."

A common misconception about Frost is that he was primarily a "nature poet"; he was fond of saying that all but three of his poems had human beings in them. In *You Come Too*, nature—whether in the woods or on the farm—almost always reveals a general truth or teaches a human lesson. "A Drumlin Woodchuck" suggests that, like the woodchuck, people are vulnerable and need to look to their defenses. In "A Minor Bird," wishing that the bird would fly away makes the poet realize that "there is something wrong/ In wanting to silence any song." The forces of nature that tumble the New England stone walls in "Mending Wall" suggest that barriers between people are unnatural and unnecessary.

Frost is often quoted as having said that writing poems without rhyme was like playing tennis without a net, the implication being that he was a traditionalist or formalist who had little use for experimentation or innovation. The poems in *You Come Too*, however, suggest otherwise. Four of the selections are written in blank verse (regular rhythm but no rhyme). In "The Telephone" and "After Apple-Picking," Frost experiments with varying line lengths. The long first line of the latter poem—"My long two-pointed ladder's sticking through a tree"—especially followed by the shorter "Toward heaven still," sticks out from the poem like the ladder through the tree. "After Apple-Picking" also experiments with sprung rhythms and sound effects, as does "Stopping by Woods on a Snowy Evening," in which the sound of the snow is whispered in the lines "The only other sound's the sweep/ of easy wind and downy flake."

One of Frost's most significant innovations was his theory of "sentence sounds." In a letter to John Bartlett, Frost wrote: "A sentence is a sound in itself on which other sounds called words may be strung. . . . They are gathered by the ear from the vernacular and brought into books." These sentence sounds—the sounds of New England voices—ring in several of the poems in *You Come Too*. "Some say the world will end in fire" (from "Fire and Ice") sounds like the voice of an old folk philosopher musing in the general store. The best source of sentence sounds in the collection is "Death of the Hired Man," in which Mary, a sympathetic farm wife, says of the hired man: "He don't know why he isn't quite as good/ As anybody. Worthless though he is,/ He won't be made ashamed to please his brother." The lines contain the colloquialisms and natural rhythms of New England speech yet preserve the iambic pentameter of the poem.

The young reader does not have to be conscious of these elements of prosody in order to appreciate and enjoy the poems in *You Come Too*. The genius of Frost's poems is that they appeal to children and young adults quite as much as they do to poets and scholars.

Critical Context

That Robert Frost participated in the selection of the poems commends *You Come Too*, which is still widely available in libraries. The continuing popularity of Frost's poetry among children and young adults is suggested by Henry Holt's publication of two subsequent collections in their Books for Young Readers series: *Birches* (1988) and *Christmas Trees* (1990).

Among more recent collections of Frost's poems, one of the best is *Poetry for Young People: Robert Frost* (1994), edited by Gary D. Schmidt with watercolor illustrations by Henri Sorenson. The poems are organized by seasons, and almost half of them are among those found in *You Come Too*. This collection also includes a biographical-critical essay on Frost and New England life, as well as a few brief helpful notes on the poems. A discussion of books of Frost's poems for young readers would be incomplete without mentioning Susan Jeffers' beautifully illustrated *Stopping by Woods on a Snowy Evening* (1978). Nevertheless, *You Come Too* remains the standard collection of Frost's poems for children and young adults.

Gaymon L. Bennett

Z FOR ZACHARIAH

Author: Robert C. O'Brien (Robert Leslie Conly, 1918-1973)
First published: 1974
Type of work: Novel
Type of plot: Science fiction
Time of work: The near future
Locale: A farm in a valley
Subjects: Coming-of-age, gender roles, health and illness, and war
Recommended ages: 13-18

Ann Burden, a teenager who is the only survivor in her rural community after nuclear war destroys the world, must cope with the arrival of an adult scientist whose values differ radically from her own.

> Principal characters:
> ANN BURDEN, a sixteen-year-old farmer who has successfully
>   maintained a community of one and who now confronts the
>   problems that another person may pose
> JOHN LOOMIS, a former graduate student in his early thirties obsessed
>   with his own survival and that of humankind

Form and Content

Robert C. O'Brien's last novel takes the form of journal entries written by Ann Burden a year after nuclear war has destroyed her family and much—perhaps all—of the outside world. The poisoned environment keeps Ann within her family's valley, which enjoys "its own weather" and so has largely escaped the disaster. The story begins when Ann sees campfire smoke and realizes that a stranger is about to arrive; it ends months later as she abandons her homestead and embarks upon her own journey of discovery. *Z for Zachariah*, then, is at once a Robinson Crusoe story, a rewriting of the Eden myth, and an adventure focusing on generational and gender conflict.

The plot is deceptively simple. Ann, who had intended to become an English teacher, is a humanist who welcomes the idea of companionship. Although she is in some ways a dreamer, imagining marriage and children as one possible outcome of John Loomis' arrival, she also has the strong practical streak that has enabled her to manage by herself, growing her own food and augmenting it with the stocks culled from the local store. Her understanding of humanity's darker side prompts her to conceal herself from Loomis until she can ascertain what sort of person he is. As she watches him, he makes the mistake of swimming in Burden Creek, the one contaminated part of the valley, and contracts radiation sickness. Ann nurses him through his severe illness, gradually learning his history—more from his delirious ramblings than from his conscious statements.

Loomis is potentially both an asset and a threat. On the one hand, he is technologically sophisticated, able to advise Ann on returning her father's tractor to use and to design an electric generator. He owes his own survival to his possession of "the last useful thing anybody ever made," a "safe-suit" that repels radiation; with the safe-suit, Ann realizes, they may venture out into the world to bring back the books her hungry mind craves. On the other hand, he is ruthless: he has killed his laboratory partner in order to keep the suit. While Ann understands that the murder may have been justifiable as self-defense, Loomis' inability to consider anyone's viewpoint but his own leads him to attempt to rape Ann, apparently as the first step in repopulating Earth. Eluding him, she embarks on an insecure existence in the woods, but he refuses to allow a stalemate; he tries to capture her and keep her a prisoner in her family's house. The situation requires Ann to implement a ruthlessness akin to his own, causing the death of her dog (the only living link to her family) because Loomis is using the animal to track her and finally stealing the safe-suit in order to search for another miraculously preserved enclave, a more stable community where there will be children to teach.

Analysis

The novel takes its title from a religious alphabet book that Ann had as a child, which began "A is for Adam" and concluded "Z is for Zachariah"—a progression that led the toddler to deduce that if Adam was the first man, then Zachariah must be the last. This point emphasizes that O'Brien's narrative will be an inverted Creation story, although it is less about the creation of a new world than it is about the hoped-for reclamation and reformation of an old one. O'Brien uses such reversals throughout the story, from Loomis' hypothesis that the valley has been preserved through "some kind of an inversion" to the author's use of the younger character to embody the values of tradition (literature, the pioneer spirit, and religion) and the older character those of inventiveness, change, and iconoclasm, as Loomis scoffs at Ann's churchgoing and burns her copy of *Treasured Short Stories of England and America*. Similarly, O'Brien goes against stereotypes in associating his female character with physical labor in the out-of-doors, while the male character stands for weakness and confinement to domestic spaces. Gender, indeed, is something that Ann has relinquished, as she has learned to enjoy the "male" tasks that she once disliked and to feel comfortable in the male clothing that circumstances have forced upon her, so that Loomis' attempt to coerce her into the female sexual role is doubly a violation.

Yet, Ann is less an inversion of femininity than a new version of it—and, perhaps, of humanity overall. If she is the culture-bearer, preserving through her piano playing and poetry reading the intellectual equivalent of the seed crops that she tends in order to enable future agricultural bounty, she simultaneously symbolizes the rejection of certain mistakes that her culture has made in the past. Loomis' lack of human connection (he seems indifferent to his childhood and never founded a family of his own), his calculating and haunted personality, his obsession with achieving absolute mastery over his surroundings—all hint at the failings that have caused this society to destroy itself. Ann's very different mode of intelligence and competence suggests that when she finds her future home—and the narrative gives readers reason to hope that she will indeed discover a new place to live—she will teach the rising generation another way to live, without abandoning the independence and capacity for hard work that she and Loomis have in common.

The novel is also a coming-of-age narrative in which the protagonist must come to terms with adult sexuality (which she is allowed to reject), with the recognition that romantic dreams may have little to do with reality, and with the necessity of leaving the "garden" of the home in order to enter a difficult and inhospitable world. In this sense, *Z for Zachariah* goes beyond the boundaries of conventional science fiction or pacifist/political didacticism to become a quasi allegory about maturation and the changes that it demands of a peacefulness that might threaten to turn into stagnation. The happy ending here requires that Ann and Loomis switch places instead of returning to the roles that each occupies at the beginning of the story: Loomis needs the fertile and productive isolation of the valley if he is to gain the perception—the knowledge of good and evil—that he lacks, while Ann needs not calm but flux, not a community of one or two but a larger community where she can both learn and teach. That O'Brien offers hope in this rewriting of Genesis even for the snake, as one last hears Loomis calling out to Ann with directions that may lead her to new life, reminds readers that growing up, even under adverse circumstances, is as positive as it is painful. To come of age is necessarily to go forward, even if it means leaving Eden behind.

Critical Context

Although Robert C. O'Brien's three novels for young readers are all suspicious of science and of power imbalances, they are startlingly different in conception. *The Silver Crown* (1968), which is set in the present but looks backward to the Dark Ages, meditates on technology's dangerous and "magical" ability to force even good people to conform to its destructive demands; the more lighthearted *Mrs. Frisby and the Rats of NIMH* (1971) uses talking animals to ask its audience to ponder whether society should properly be parasitic or symbiotic.

Z for Zachariah has the simplest plot of the three works but arguably demands the greatest amount of thought from readers because of its heightened recognition of moral ambiguity—as Ann recognizes, she and Loomis have much in common. *The Silver Crown* derives its excitement from the dramatic struggle between good and evil, suggesting that evil is artificial and eradicable. *Z for Zachariah* is both less melodramatic and less naïve. In its use of archetype and the connection that it makes between plot and underlying message, this novel is allied to such works of science fiction for young adults as Sylvia Louise Engdahl's *Enchantress from the Stars* (1970), another artistically successful narrative that links the maturing process of an individual with that of a culture. Historically, juvenile science fiction has often been condemned as pulp, criticized for using cardboard characters and preferring action to thought. Novels such as O'Brien's are reminders that these complaints are sometimes unjust.

Claudia Nelson

ZLATEH THE GOAT AND OTHER STORIES

Author: Isaac Bashevis Singer (1904-1991)
First published: 1966; illustrated
Type of work: Short fiction
Subjects: Animals, death, family, religion, and the supernatural
Recommended ages: 10-15

> *The stories in this book—comic, tender, and frightening—re-create the rich life of a culture destroyed by the Holocaust.*

Form and Content

The seven stories in this collection recapture a world that no longer exists—that of the pre-World War II, Eastern European Jewish shtetl (village or small town). It is the world that Isaac Bashevis Singer knew as a child, and his stories have their origins in the folklore and legends of the shtetl. Singer wrote them initially in Yiddish, the language of the shtetl, and then translated them into English with his editor, Elizabeth Shub. Award-winning illustrator Maurice Sendak also traces his family roots to the shtetl. Arthur Bell's review of *Zlateh the Goat and Other Stories* notes how Sendak's illustrations resemble early twentieth century photographs of New York City's Lower East Side, many of whose inhabitants immigrated from Eastern Europe.

The book's title story, "Zlateh the Goat," takes place in a shtetl very much like those in which Singer lived as a small boy. A warm winter means bad business for Reuven the furrier, and his young son Aaron is sent to sell the family goat, Zlateh, to a butcher in town. A fierce snowstorm forces them off the path, and they seek shelter in a haystack, which furnishes them warmth and also nourishment. Zlateh eats the hay and feeds Aaron with its milk, and each has a way of comforting the other. On the third night, after the storm has ended, Aaron and Zlateh return home. There is no more talk of selling Zlateh, and, adding to the celebratory mood, the storm has brought colder weather and thus business to Reuven.

"Fool's Paradise" offers wry insights into human nature. A lazy young man named Atzel, who learns that those in Paradise have no need to work, wishes that he were dead. After seemingly getting his wish, he is overjoyed to learn that there has been some mistake and that he must return to Earth. He marries his longtime love in a finale frequent in Singer's work—that is, a wedding feast.

A few rollicking, humorous stories introduce readers to comic characters popular in Jewish folklore: the schlemiel and the townsfolk of Chelm. The schlemiel is a fool who is always getting into trouble. Schlemiels tend to come from Chelm, whose inhabitants appear all the more foolish because they are convinced that they are wise. "The First Shlemiel" is about a fellow who bungles everything, including his suicide, when he is left home to mind the baby while his wife sells vegetables in the marketplace. In "The Snow in Chelm," the Chelmites aspire to wealth from the jewels that they see in the new-fallen snow, while in "The Mixed-Up Feet and the Silly Bridegroom," the Elder of Chelm resolves dilemmas involving Shmelka, his wife Shmelkicha, and their four daughters.

Goblins, demons, and the Devil himself appear in two brief tales that take place during the Hanukkah festival. In "Grandmother's Tale," the Evil One is exposed deceiving children playing dreidl, a Hanukkah game. In "The Devil's Trick," the Hanukkah lights shining through the window guide a lost young boy home; the quick-witted boy saves his parents by catching the Devil's tail in the door and threatening to cut it off unless they, too, are returned.

Analysis

Singer draws on the rich tradition of myths to tell his stories. The most immediate source of his legends and fables is the pietistic literature familiar to Eastern European Jews. Such literature is known in Yiddish as *bubah meises* (roughly translated as "tales my grandmother told me"), serving to transmit lessons and values from generation to generation. As pointed out by Canadian critic J. A. Eisenberg, Singer's fiction derives its emotional charge from the principle that the greater the fall, the more forcefully the intended "ethical concept" comes through. Adding to this effect is the stories' shtetl setting, its intensely religious atmosphere heightening the tension between ideal and practice.

Because such archetypal figures as the Devil play vital roles in shtetl consciousness, Singer is able to blend seamlessly the real and the mythical in his tales. By providing a mythological framework integral to the character's lives, he avoids an artificiality and abstractness that can deaden allegorical writing, especially for young readers.

Contributing to the immediacy of Singer's style, as well as effectively dramatizing inner conflict, devils and demons personify drives that torment the psyche. While some critics might be concerned about the risk that their grotesqueness might traumatize young readers, psychologist Bruno Bettelheim would argue that the more monstrous the opponent, the more effectively are embodied a child's anxieties and the greater the release provided by the opponent's defeat. Bettelheim therefore cautions against adults' misguided efforts to sanitize fairy tales or other folk literature. His theories also help explain the enduring popularity of this literature with children.

In the world of myth, not only are powerful demons vanquished but a helpless creature such as Zlateh can assume heroic proportions as well. Zlateh's simplicity and innocence, which appear to be weaknesses, are revealed as strengths in the light of love and understanding. While Singer, a vegetarian, is clearly protesting the butchering of animals in "Zlateh the Goat," he is also championing the undervalued and overlooked in the world. This story, as well as "The Devil's Trick," show that such individuals have reserves of power that require only the proper key to be unlocked. Stories culminating in the triumph of the insignificant and the underestimated are naturally satisfying to young children.

Laughter is also satisfying to children. Their ability to laugh at a schlemiel distances them from his folly and ill fortune. Traditionally, the schlemiel is plagued by bad luck that is somehow of his own making, as he mistakes his delusions for conditions as they actually are. Children, who are in the process of acquiring their culture's values and standards, can gain a sense of belonging as they, too, understand the joke in a schlemiel tale.

Forging a sense of self in the spheres of family and community is a task that begins in childhood. Celebration of the Hanukkah festival, reinforcing family and community ties, figures prominently in three of the stories: "Zlateh the Goat," "The Devil's Trick," and "Grandmother's Tale." A wedding, symbolizing the union of male and female, the foundation of the family, happily concludes "Fool's Paradise" and "The Mixed-Up Feet and the Silly Bridegroom." A wedding also ritually affirms faith in community tradition.

The characters' anticipation of integrating self and community is made poignant by Singer's dedication of the stories in the collection to "the many children who had no chance to grow up because of stupid wars and cruel persecutions." Singer here is paying tribute to young victims of the Holocaust. The Nazi's Final Solution dealt a blow to shtetl life from which it never recovered. Singer the storyteller evokes the power of memory and imagination to overcome the loss, because for "the writer and his readers all creatures go on living forever."

Critical Context

Zlateh the Goat and Other Stories was Isaac Bashevis Singer's first book for children. He was sixty-two years old and a well-established author when an editor of juvenile fiction at Harper & Row persuaded him that his writing—full of demons and imps—was, as he recalls, "the very stuff that children might love."

Most reviewers agreed. In *Horn Book* magazine, Helen B. Crawshaw described the collection as "a gift of seven stories for all children." In 1967, *Zlateh the Goat and Other Stories* was named a Newbery Honor Book. Singer would publish sixteen additional books for children before his death in 1991.

In the tradition of Hans Christian Andersen, Lewis Carroll, and Kenneth Grahame, respect for children's understanding marks Singer's writing for them. "No matter how young they are," he remarked, "children are deeply concerned with so-called eternal questions." Singer, who would win the Nobel Prize for Literature in 1978, credited children with being "the best readers of genuine literature." That it is "rooted" in folklore "alone makes children's literature so important," he claimed, adding that without folklore, "literature must decline and wither away."

The shtetl's wise men of Chelm, it has been critically noted, resemble Britain's legendary wise men of Gotham. Additionally, the schlemiel is kin to fools encountered in folk literature the world over. "The more a writer is rooted in his environment," Singer has explained, "the more he is understood by all people." In the decades following the publication of *Zlateh the Goat and Other Stories*, more folktales from around the world would appear in books for children in the United States, in response to an increasing interest in multiculturalism.

Amy Allison

BIBLIOGRAPHY

General Works: Critical, Biographical, Historical

Bator, Robert, ed. *Signposts to Criticism of Children's Literature*. Chicago: American Library Association, 1983. A collection of groundbreaking critical essays treating a variety of children's texts.

Beetz, Kirk H., ed. *Beacham's Guide to Literature for Young Adults*. Vols. 6-8. Washington, D.C.: Beacham, 1994. Offers detailed analyses of many major texts for young adults. Includes discussion questions, bibliographies, and biographical information. See also volumes 1 through 5.

Berger, Laura Standley, ed. *Twentieth-Century Children's Writers*. 4th ed. Detroit: St. James Press, 1995. An encyclopedic reference volume of essays on twentieth century writers for children.

_____, ed. *Twentieth-Century Young Adult Writers*. Detroit: St. James Press, 1994. Contains biographical and critical introductions to numerous young adult writers.

Blishen, Edward, ed. *The Thorny Paradise: Writers on Writing for Children*. London: Kestrel Books, 1975. A rich collection of articles by contemporary British children's writers about their work.

Blount, Margaret. *Animal Land: The Creatures of Children's Fiction*. London: Hutchinson, 1974. An exploration of the endowment of human traits to animals in classic children's texts.

Butler, Francelia, and Richard Rotert, eds. *Triumphs of the Spirit in Children's Literature*. Hamden, Conn.: Shoe String, 1986. Twenty-five essays treating "triumphs" of the human spirit as depicted in children's literature.

Cadogan, Mary, and Patricia Craig. *You're a Brick, Angela!: The Girls' Story, 1839-1985*. London: Gollancz, 1986. An excellent historical introduction to children's books with female protagonists.

Cameron, Eleanor. *The Green and Burning Tree: On the Writing and Enjoyment of Children's Books*. Boston: Little, Brown, 1962. A variety of essays by a major critic and writer of contemporary children's literature. Especially good on children's fantasy.

Carpenter, Humphrey. *Secret Gardens: A Study of the Golden Age of Children's Literature*. Boston: Houghton, 1985. A largely biographical examination of classic children's writers such as Lewis Carroll, Kenneth Grahame, and E. Nesbit.

Carpenter, Humphrey, and Mari Prichard. *The Oxford Companion to Children's Literature*. New York: Oxford University Press, 1984. Contains brief encyclopedic entries on children's authors and illustrators, characters from children's books, and other aspects of literature for the young.

Carr, Jo, ed. *Beyond Fact: Nonfiction for Children and Young People*. Chicago: American Library Association, 1982. An anthology of articles on informational books for young readers.

Cech, John, ed. *Dictionary of Literary Biography. American Writers for Children, 1900-1960*. Vol. 22. Detroit: Gale Research, 1983. An excellent collection of essays on American children's writers of the first half of the twentieth century.

Cott, Jonathan. *Pipers at the Gates of Dawn: The Wisdom of Children's Literature*. New York: Random House, 1983. A collection of articles on contemporary children's writers.

Coveny, Peter. *Poor Monkey: The Child in Literature*. London: Rockliff, 1957. An examination of the image of the child in British and American literature.

Crouch, Marcus. *The Nesbit Tradition: The Children's Novel in England 1945-1970*. London: Ernest Benn, 1972. A historical study of modern British children's books, focusing on the influence of E. Nesbit.

Egoff, Sheila, et al. *Only Connect: Readings on Children's Literature*. 3d ed. Toronto: Oxford University Press, 1996. A rich selection of more than forty essays reflecting a variety of critical issues related to children's literature. See also the first and second editions.

Estes, Glenn E., ed. *American Writers for Children Before 1900*. Vol. 22 in *Dictionary of Literary Biography*. Detroit: Gale Research, 1985. Biographical-critical essays on American children's writers, mostly from the nineteenth century.

    _____, ed. *American Writers for Children Since 1960: Fiction*. Vol. 52 in *Dictionary of Literary Biography*. Detroit: Gale Research, 1986. Biographical-critical essays on contemporary American children's fiction writers.

    _____, ed. *American Writers for Children Since 1960: Poets, Illustrators, and Nonfiction Authors*. Vol. 61 in *Dictionary of Literary Biography*. Detroit: Gale Research, 1987. Biographical-critical essays on contemporary American children's poets, illustrators, and writers of nonfiction.

Gallo, Donald R., ed. *Speaking for Ourselves: Autobiographical Sketches by Notable Authors of Books for Young Adults*. Urbana, Ill.: National Council of Teachers of English, 1990. Autobiographical sketches by ninety-two contemporary writers of young adult literature. See also Gallo's *Speaking for Ourselves, Too: More Autobiographical Sketches by Notable Authors of Books for Young Adults* (1993).

Green, Roger Lancelyn. *Tellers of Tales: British Authors of Children's Books from 1800-1964*. Rev. ed. New York: Franklin Watts, 1965. A chronological survey of British children's writers from the Golden Age through the mid-twentieth century. Includes bibliographies and a chronology of influential works for children.

Griswold, Jerry. *Audacious Kids: Coming of Age in America's Classic Children's Books*. New York: Oxford University Press, 1992. A psychoanalytical examination of twelve major novels from the Golden Age of American children's literature.

Hearne, Betsy, and Marilyn Kaye, eds. *Celebrating Children's Books: Essays on Children's Literature in Honor of Zena Sutherland*. New York: Lothrop, Lee, & Shepard, 1981. Essays by a number of contemporary children's writers, including Paula Fox, Virginia Hamilton, and E. L. Konigsburg.

Hopkins, Lee Bennett. *Pause: Autobiographical Reflections of 101 Creators of Children's Books*. New York: HarperCollins, 1995. Autobiographical sketches featuring a variety of children's writers and illustrators, collected from more than thirty years of interviews.

Hunt, Caroline, ed. *British Children's Writers Since 1960*. Volume 161 in *Dictionary of Literary Biography*. Detroit: Gale Research, 1996. Detailed analytical and biographical essays on contemporary British children's writers.

Hunt, Peter, ed. *Children's Literature: The Development of Criticism*. London: Routledge, 1990. A collection of essays reflecting literary criticism of children's literature from the late eighteenth century to the present.

    _____. *Criticism, Theory, and Children's Literature*. Oxford, England: Basil Blackwell, 1991. An examination of the relationship between children's literature and critical theory.

    _____. *An Introduction to Children's Literature*. Oxford, England: Oxford University Press, 1994. A concise history of British children's literature that also addresses the special nature of this field.

Kutzer, M. Daphne, ed. *Writers of Multicultural Fiction for Young Adults: A Bio-critical Sourcebook*. Westport, Conn.: Greenwood Press, 1996. These biographical and critical essays treat writers of multicultural literature for young adults.

Kuznets, Lois. *When Toys Come Alive: Narratives of Animation, Metamorphosis, and Development*. New Haven, Conn.: Yale University Press, 1994. An excellent theoretical look at children's texts about toys and "little people."

Lanes, Selma G. *Down the Rabbit Hole: Adventures and Misadventures in the Realm of Children's Literature*. New York: Atheneum, 1971. A study of a variety of children's texts, especially for younger readers.

Lurie, Allison. *Don't Tell the Grown-Ups: Why Kids Love the Books They Do*. New York: Little, Brown, 1990. An interesting examination of the subversive nature of classic children's texts.

MacCann, Donnarae, and Gloria Woodard, eds. *The Black American in Books for Children: Readings in Racism.* Metuchen, N.J.: Scarecrow, 1972. These essays focus on the treatment of African Americans in children's literature.

McGavren, James, Jr., ed. *Romanticism and Children's Literature in Nineteenth-Century England.* Athens: University of Georgia Press, 1991. A collection of essays on classic British children's texts and their view of the child.

Nilsen, Alleen Pace, and Kenneth L. Donelson. *Literature for Today's Young Adults.* 4th ed. New York: HarperCollins, 1993. A standard introductory textbook on literature for young adults. Features detailed discussion of various genres popular with young adults, as well as a number of specialized bibliographies.

Nodelman, Perry. *The Pleasures of Children's Literature.* New York: Longman, 1992. An introduction to children's literature drawing on contemporary critical theory.

_____, ed. *Touchstones: Reflections on the Best in Children's Literature.* Vol. 1. West Lafayette, Ind.: Children's Literature Association, 1985. Contains essays on works of fiction taken from the association's "Touchstones" list. Includes an introduction and bibliographies.

Rees, David. *The Marble in the Water: Essays on Contemporary Writers of Fiction for Children and Young Adults.* Boston: Horn Book, 1980. A children's author and critic examines the work of a number of other writers, including Judy Blume, Beverly Cleary, Robert Cormier, Paula Fox, E. L. Konigsburg, E. B. White, and Paul Zindel.

Rose, Jacqueline. *The Case of Peter Pan: Or, The Impossibility of Children's Fiction.* London: Macmillan, 1984. Uses James M. Barrie's *Peter Pan* (1904) to illustrate various approaches to interpreting children's literature.

Rudman, Masha Kabakow. *Children's Literature: An Issues Approach.* 3d ed. White Plains, N.Y.: Longman, 1995. A guide to studying and selecting books for children, focusing on their treatment of social issues.

Sale, Roger. *Fairy Tales and After: From Snow White to E. B. White.* Cambridge, Mass.: Harvard University Press, 1978. A scholarly examination of children's fantasy including works by writers such as Lewis Carroll, Kenneth Grahame, Rudyard Kipling, and E. B. White.

Sloan, Glenna Davis. *The Child as Critic.* New York: Teachers College Press, 1975. A critical introduction to children's literature drawing on the theories of Northrop Frye.

Something About the Author: Facts and Pictures About Contemporary Authors and Illustrators of Books for Young People. Detroit: Gale Research, 1971-   . A multivolume reference tool containing biographical and critical entries on a variety of children's authors and illustrators.

Townsend, John Rowe. *A Sense of Story: Essays on Contemporary Writers for Children.* London: Longman, 1971. This collection of essays by a British children's author examines the work of such writers as Meindert De Jong, Eleanor Estes, Paula Fox, Madeleine L'Engle, Scott O'Dell, and Ivan Southall.

_____. *Written for Children.* Rev. ed. London: Penguin Books, 1991. An excellent one-volume treatment of the history of children's literature.

Wintle, Justin, and Emma Fisher. *The Pied Pipers: Interviews with the Influential Creators of Children's Literature.* New York: Two Continents, 1975. Interviews with twenty-four children's writers including Roald Dahl, E. B. White, Scott O'Dell, Madeleine L'Engle, Judy Blume, and Rumer Godden.

Zipes, Jack. *Fairy Tales and the Art of Subversion: The Classical Genre for Children and the Process of Civilization.* New York: Wildman, 1983. A sociological look at the influence of fairy tales on the development of children's literature.

Selection Aids

Adamson, Lynda G. *A Reference Guide to Historical Fiction for Children.* New York: Greenwood Press, 1987. Provides summaries of a variety of works of historical fiction for children grouped by historical periods.

Association for Library Service to Children. *The Newbery and Caldecott Awards: A Guide to the Medal and Honor Books*. Chicago: American Library Association, 1994. An annotated bibliography treating the Newbery and Caldecott winners and honor books, including critical and biographical references.

The Black Experience in Children's Books. New York: New York Public Library, 1994. A constantly revised bibliography of children's books treating African American culture and life.

Booklist, 1969- . Published twenty-two times a year by the American Library Association. A periodical containing reviews of current children's texts.

Bulletin of the Center for Children's Books, 1958- . Published monthly except August by the University of Illinois Press. This periodical reviews around sixty new books for children in each issue.

California State Department of Education. *Recommended Literature: Grades Nine Through Twelve*. Sacramento, Calif.: Author, 1990. This bibliography contains recommended books for young adults and features a variety of genres. An author/title index is included.

Children's Book Review Index. Detroit: Gale Research, 1975- . An index to reviews appearing in more than two hundred periodicals. Published three times a year.

Children's Literature Review: Excerpts from Reviews, Criticism, and Commentary on Books for Children and Young People. Detroit: Gale Research, 1976- . An excellent introductory tool for any scholarly work dealing with children's literature. Each volume treats a variety of authors and includes bibliographical and biographical information, as well as excerpts from related book reviews and critical articles.

Dreyer, Sharon Spredemann. *The Bookfinder: A Guide to Children's Literature About the Needs and Problems of Youth Aged 2-15*. Circle Pines, Minn.: American Guidance Service, 1977. A subject guide to children's books dealing with a variety of special needs and social issues. Published in various editions.

The Horn Book Guide to Children's and Young Adult Books. Boston: Horn Book, 1989- . Published twice a year. This book contains brief reviews of hardcover books for children published during the previous six months. See also *The Horn Book*, a journal of reviews and articles relating to children's literature published six times a year.

Jenkins, Esther C., and Mary C. Austin. *Literature for Children About Asians and Asian Americans: Analysis and Annotated Bibliography, with Additional Readings for Adults*. New York: Greenwood Press, 1987. An annotated bibliography of children's materials about Asians and Asian Americans grouped by country and genre.

Kobrin, Beverly. *Eyeopeners!: How to Choose and Use Children's Books About Real People, Places, and Things*. New York: Penguin Books, 1988. A practical introduction to nonfiction books for children.

National Council of Teachers of English Bibliography Series. A series of frequently updated bibliographies for the young. Titles include *Adventuring with Books: A Booklist for Pre-K-Grade 6* (1993, 10th ed., edited by Julie M. Jensen and Nancy L. Roser); *Books for You: An Annotated Booklist for Senior High Students* (1995, edited by Leila Christenbury); *High Interest-Easy Reading: An Annotated Booklist for Middle and Senior High School* (1996, 7th ed., edited by Patricia Phelan); *Kaleidoscope: A Multicultural Booklist for Grades K-8* (1994, edited by Rudine Sims Bishop); and *Your Reading: An Annotated Booklist for Middle School and Junior High* (1996, edited by Barbara G. Samuels and G. Kylene Beers).

Oppenheim, Joanne, Barbara Brenner, and Betty D. Boegehold. *Choosing Books for Kids: Choosing the Right Book for the Right Child at the Right Time*. New York: Ballantine, 1986. A good overview of children's literature for a general audience. Includes annotated bibliographies classified by age group.

Schon, Isabel. *Contemporary Spanish-Speaking Writers and Illustrators for Children and Young Adults: A Biographical Dictionary*. Translated by Jason Douglas White. Westport, Conn.: Greenwood Press, 1994. Offers biographical and bibliographical information about Spanish-speaking children's writers.

School Library Journal: The Magazine of Children's, Young Adult, and School Librarians,
   1977-   . Published monthly. Reviews current children's and young adult texts.
Subject Guide to Books in Print. New York: R. R. Bowker, 1957-   . Published annually.
   Groups children's texts under a variety of subject headings.

Works by Author

Hans Christian Andersen

Bredsdorff, Elias. *Hans Christian Andersen: The Story of His Life and Work, 1805-1875*. New
   York: Charles Scribner's Sons, 1975.
Godden, Rumer. *Hans Christian Andersen*. New York: Alfred A. Knopf, 1955.
Grønbech, Bo. *Hans Christian Andersen*. Boston: Twayne, 1980.
Haugaard, Erik C. "The Poet Who Lives." *Horn Book* 51 (October, 1975): 443-448.
Stirling, Monica. *The Wild Swan: The Life and Times of Hans Christian Andersen*. New York:
   Harcourt, 1965.

Avi (Avi Wortis)

Avi. "Children's Literature: The American Revolution." *Top of the News* 33 (Winter, 1977):
   149-161.
_____. "Seeing Through the I." *ALAN Review* 20, no. 3 (Spring, 1993): 2-7.
_____. "*The True Confessions of Charlotte Doyle*." *Horn Book* 68 (January/February,
   1992): 24-27.

Natalie Babbitt

Aippersbach, Kim. "*Tuck Everlasting* and the Tree at the Center of the World." *Children's
   Literature in Education* 21, no. 2 (June, 1990): 83-97.
Babbitt, Natalie. "Fantasy and the Classic Hero." In *Innocence and Experience: Essays and
   Conversations on Children's Literature*, edited by Barbara Harrison and Gregory Maguire.
   New York: Lothrop, Lee & Shepard, 1987.
DeLuca, Geraldine. "Extensions of Nature: The Fantasies of Natalie Babbitt." *Lion and the
   Unicorn* 1, no. 2 (Fall, 1977): 47-70.
Levy, Michael M. *Natalie Babbitt*. Boston: Twayne, 1991.
Lynch, Catherine M. "Winnie Foster and Peter Pan: Facing the Dilemma of Growth." *Proceed-
   ings of the Children's Literature Association* 9 (1982): 107-111.

Patricia Beatty

Beatty, Patricia. "Writing the Historical Novel for Young Readers." The Writer (March, 1989):
   17-19.

Judy Blume

Garber, Stephen M. "Judy Blume: New Classicism for Kids." *English Journal* 73 (April, 1984):
   56-59.
Hamilton, Lynne. "Blume's Adolescents: Coming of Age in Limbo." *Signal* 41 (May, 1983):
   88-96.
Maynard, Joyce. "Coming of Age with Judy Blume." *New York Times Magazine* (December 3,
   1978): 80-86, 90, 92, 94.
Saunders, Paula C. "Judy Blume as Herself." *Writer's Digest* 59 (February, 1979): 18-24.
Siegel, R. A. "Are You There God? It's Me, Me, Me!: Judy Blume's Self-Absorbed Narrators."
   Lion and the Unicorn 2 (Fall, 1978): 72-77.
Weldt, Maryann. *Presenting Judy Blume*. Boston: Twayne, 1990.

Ray Bradbury

Bradbury, Ray. "Memories Shape the Voice." In *The Voice of the Narrator in Children's
   Literature*, edited by Charlotte F. Otten and Gary D. Schmidt. New York: Greenwood Press,
   1989.

Dominianni, Robert. "Ray Bradbury's 2026: A Year with Current Value." *English Journal* 73 (November, 1984): 49-51.

Mogen, David. *Ray Bradbury*. Boston: Twayne, 1986.

Toupance, William F. "Laughter and Freedom in Ray Bradbury's *Something Wicked This Way Comes.*" *Children's Literature Association Quarterly* 13, no. 1 (Spring, 1988): 17-21.

_____. *Ray Bradbury*. San Bernardino, Calif.: Borgo, 1989.

Sue Ellen Bridgers

Bridgers, Sue Ellen. "People, Families, and Mothers." *ALAN Review* 9, no. 1 (Fall, 1981): 1, 36.

Hipple, Ted. *Presenting Sue Ellen Bridgers*. Boston: Twayne, 1990.

John Ciardi

Clementi, Vince, ed. *John Ciardi: Measure of the Man*. Fayetteville: University of Arkansas Press, 1987.

Groff, Patrick J. "The Transformation of a Poet: John Ciardi." *Horn Book* 40 (April, 1964): 153-158.

Odland, Norine. "Profile: John Ciardi." *Language Arts* 59 (November/December, 1982): 872-876.

Beverly Cleary

Burns, Paul C., and Ruth Hines. "Beverly Cleary: Wonderful World of Humor." *Elementary English* 44 (November, 1967): 743-747, 752.

Chaston, Joel D. "Toothpaste Squiggles and Slacks for Ella Funt: Work and Play in *Ramona and Her Mother.*" *Oregon English Journal* 17, no. 1 (1995): 34-36.

Cleary, Beverly. "Newbery Medal Acceptance." *Horn Book* 60 (August, 1984): 429-438.

DeLuca, Geraldine. "'Composing a Life': The Diary of Leigh Botts." *Lion and the Unicorn* 14, no. 2 (December, 1990): 58-65.

Mackey, Margaret. "Ramona the Chronotype: The Young Adult Reader and Theories of Social Narrative." *Children's Literature in Education* 22, no. 2 (June, 1991): 97-109.

Pflieger, Pat. *Beverly Cleary*. Boston: Twayne, 1991.

Vera and Bill Cleaver

Cianciolo, Patricia J. "Vera and Bill Cleaver Know Their Whys and Wherefores." *Top of the News* 32 (June, 1976): 338-350.

Townsend, John Rowe. "Vera and Bill Cleaver." *Horn Book* 55 (October, 1979): 505-513.

Elizabeth Coatsworth

Abbott, Barbara. "To Timbuctoo and Back: Elizabeth Coatsworth's Books for Children." *Horn Book* 6 (November, 1930): 283-289.

Coatsworth, Elizabeth. "Upon Writing for Children." *Horn Book* 24 (September, 1948): 389-395.

Crouch, Marcus. "Elizabeth Coatsworth: 1893-1986." *Junior Bookshelf* 51, no. 2 (1987): 68-72.

Kuhn, Doris Young. "Elizabeth Coatsworth: Perceptive Impressionist." *Elementary English* 46 (December, 1969): 991-1007.

Rice, Mabel. "The Poetic Prose of Elizabeth Coatsworth." *Elementary English* 31 (January, 1954): 3-10.

Robert Cormier

Bixler, Phyllis. "*I Am the Cheese* and Reader Response Criticism in the Adolescent Classroom." *Children's Literature Association Quarterly* 17, no. 1 (Spring, 1985): 13-16.

Cormier, Robert. Interview by Geraldine DeLuca and Roni Natov. *Lion and the Unicorn* 2, no. 1 (Fall, 1978): 109-135.

Head, Patricia. "Robert Cormier and the Postmodernist Possibilities of Young Adult Fiction." *Children's Literature Association Quarterly* 21, no. 1 (Spring, 1996): 28-33.

Nodelman, Perry. "Robert Cormier Does a Number." *Children's Literature in Education* 14, no. 2 (Summer, 1983): 94-103.

Susina, January *"The Chocolate War* and 'The Sweet Science.'" *Children's Literature in Education* 22, no. 3 (September, 1991): 169-177.

Velahn, Nancy. "The Bland Face of Evil in the Novels of Robert Cormier." *Lion and the Unicorn* 12, no. 1 (1988): 12-18.

Harold Courlander

Courlander, Harold. Interview by Diane Wolkstein. *School Library Journal* 20 (May, 1974): 19-22.

Roald Dahl

Bosmajian, Hamida. *"Charlie and the Chocolate Factory* and Other Excremental Visions." *Lion and the Unicorn* 9 (1985): 36-49.

Culley, Jonathan. "Roald Dahl—It's About Children and It's for Children—but Is It Suitable?" *Children's Literature in Education* 22 (March, 1991): 59-73.

Dahl, Roald. *Boy: Tales of Childhood*. New York: Farrar, Strauss & Giroux, 1984.

_____. *Going Solo*. New York: Farrar, Strauss & Giroux, 1986.

Treglown, Jeremy. *Roald Dahl: A Biography*. New York: HarperCollins, 1994.

West, Mark I. *Roald Dahl*. New York: Twayne, 1992.

Meindert De Jong

Burgess, Eleanor. "Meindert De Jong, Storyteller." *Elementary English* 32 (May, 1955): 267-276.

Carr, Marion Grudier. "Meindert De Jong and the World's Children." *Top of the News* 27 (June, 1971): 395-402.

Cianciolo, Patricia Jean. "Meindert De Jong." *Elementary English* 45 (October, 1968): 725-730.

De Jong, Meindert. "Newbery Award Acceptance." *Horn Book* 31 (August, 1955): 241-246.

Gard, Roger. "Meindert De Jong's Tower by the Sea." *Use of English* 21, no. 3 (Spring, 1970): 221-223, 227.

Charles Dickens

Ackroyd, Peter. *Dickens*. New York: HarperCollins, 1990.

Hornback, Bert G. *"Noah's Arkitecture": A Study of Dickens's Mythology*. Athens: Ohio University Press, 1972.

House, Humphry. *The Dickens World*. 2d ed. London: Oxford University Press, 1960.

Johnson, Edgar. *Charles Dickens: His Tragedy and Triumph*. New York: Simon & Schuster, 1952.

Lucas, John. *The Melancholy Man: A Study of Dickens's Novels*. London: Methuen, 1970.

Miller, J. Hillis. *Charles Dickens: The World of His Novels*. Cambridge, Mass.: Harvard University Press, 1958.

Stone, Harry. *Dickens and the Invisible World: Fairy Tales, Fantasy, and Novel-Making*. Bloomington: Indiana University Press, 1979.

Elizabeth Enright

Cameron, Eleanor. "The Art of Elizabeth Enright." *Horn Book* 45 (December, 1969): 641-51 and 46 (February, 1970): 26-30.

Hunt, Caroline. "Elizabeth Enright and the Family Story." *Lion and the Unicorn* 14, no. 2 (1990): 16-29.

Smedman, M. Sarah. "Elizabeth Enright, 1909-1968." In *Writers for Children: Critical Studies of Major Authors Since the Seventeenth Century*. New York: Charles Scribner's Sons, 1988.

Eleanor Estes

Estes, Eleanor. "Gathering Honey." *Horn Book* 36 (December, 1960): 487-494.

Rice, Mabel R. "Eleanor Estes: A Study in Versatility." *Elementary English* 45 (May, 1968): 553-557.

Russell, David. "Stability and Change in the Family Saga: Eleanor Estes' Moffat Series." *Children's Literature Association Quarterly* 14, no. 4 (Winter, 1989): 171-174.

Sayers, Frances Clarke. "The Books of Eleanor Estes." *Horn Book* 28 (August, 1952): 257-260.

Smith, Louisa. "Eleanor Estes' *The Moffats*: Through Colored Glass." In *Touchstones: Reflections on the Best in Children's Literature*, edited by Perry Nodelman. Vol. 1. West Lafayette, Ind.: Children's Literature Association, 1985.

Paula Fox

Bach, Alice. "Cracking Open the Geode: The Fiction of Paula Fox." *Horn Book* 53 (October, 1977): 514-521.

Fox, Paula. "Newbery Acceptance." *Horn Book* 50 (July/August, 1974): 345-350.

Heins, Paul. "Paula Fox: Hans Christian Andersen Medal Winner." *Horn Book* 54 (October, 1978): 486-487.

Nodelman, Perry. "Through a Glass, Intimately: The Distant Closeness of Paula Fox's *One-Eyed Cat*." *Children's Literature Association Quarterly* 16, no. 1 (Spring, 1991): 23-27.

Shute, Carolyn. "Stout as Jessie's Shadow in *The Slave Dancer*." *Children's Literature Association Bulletin* 14 (1988): 216-217.

Russell Freedman

Dempsey, Frank J. "Russell Freedman." *Horn Book* 64, no. 1 (1988): 152-156.

Freedman, Russell. "The *Booklist* Interview: Russell Freedman." Interview by Stephanie Zvrin. *Booklist* 88, no. 10 (January 15, 1992): 926-927.

_____. "Newbery Medal Acceptance." *Horn Book* 64, no. 1 (1988): 144-151.

_____. "Why I Voted for Lincoln and Roosevelt." *Horn Book* 68, no. 6 (November/ December, 1992): 688-696.

Rumer Godden

Hines, Ruth, and Paul C. Burns. "Rumer Godden." *Elementary English* 44 (February, 1967): 101-104.

Simpson, Hassell A. *Rumer Godden*. New York: Twayne, 1973.

Kenneth Grahame

Gilead, Sarah. "The Undoing of Idyll in *The Wind in the Willows*." *Children's Literature* 16 (1988): 145-158.

Grahame, Kenneth. *First Whisper of the Wind in the Willows*. New York: J. B. Lippincott, 1944.

Kuznets, Lois. *Kenneth Grahame*. Boston: Twayne, 1987.

Philip, Neil. "*The Wind in the Willows*: The Vitality of a Classic." In *Children and Their Books: A Celebration of the Work of Iona and Peter Opie*. Oxford, England: Clarendon Press, 1989.

Poss, Geraldine D. "An Epic in Arcadia: The Pastoral World of *The Wind in the Willows*." *Children's Literature* 4 (1975): 80-90.

Jacob and Wilhelm Grimm

Bettelheim, Bruno. *The Uses of Enchantment: The Meaning and Importance of Fairy Tales*. New York: Alfred A. Knopf, 1976.

Bottigheimer, Ruth B. *Grimm's Bad Girls and Bold Boys: The Moral and Social Vision of the Tales*. New Haven, Conn.: Yale University Press, 1987.

Kamenetsky, Christa. *The Brothers Grimm and Their Critics: Folktales and Their Quest for Meaning*. Athens: Ohio University Press, 1992.

Mallet, Karl-Heinz. *Fairy Tales and Children: The Psychology of Children Revealed Through Four of Grimms' Fairy Tales*. New York: Schocken, 1984.

Tatar, Maria. *The Hard Facts of the Grimms' Fairy Tales*. Princeton, N.J.: Princeton University Press, 1987.

Zipes, Jack. *The Brothers Grimm: From Enchanted Forests to the Modern World.* New York: Routledge, 1988.

Virginia Hamilton

Apseloff, Marilyn. "Creative Geography in the Ohio Novels of Virginia Hamilton." *Children's Literature Association Quarterly* 8, no. 1 (Spring, 1983): 17-20.

Hamilton, Virginia. "The Mind of the Novel: The Heart of the Book." *Children's Literature Association Quarterly* 8, no. 4 (Winter, 1983): 10-14.

_____. "Newbery Award Acceptance." *Horn Book* 51 (August, 1975): 337-343.

Moss, Anita. "Gothic and Grotesque Effects in Virginia Hamilton's Fiction." *ALAN Review* 19, no. 2 (Winter, 1992): 16-20.

Russell, David L. "Cultural Identity and Individual Triumph in Virginia Hamilton's *M. C. Higgins the Great.*" *Children's Literature in Education* 21, no. 4 (December, 1990): 253-259.

Jim Haskins

Haskins, Jim. "Writing Sports Biographies for Young Readers." *Lion and the Unicorn* 4, no. 1 (Summer, 1980): 32-40.

Nist, Joan. "Master of Nonfiction: James Haskins." *Journal of African Children's and Youth Literature* 3 (1991/1992): 105-108.

Marguerite Henry

Henry, Marguerite. "Newbery Acceptance Paper." *Horn Book* 26 (January, 1950): 9-17.

_____. "A Weft of Truth and Warp of Fiction." *Elementary English* 51 (October, 1974): 921-925.

Wilt, Miriam E. "In Marguerite Henry—the Thread That Runs So True." *Elementary English* 31 (November, 1954): 387-395.

S. E. Hinton

Chaston, Joel D. "S. E. Hinton." In *Twentieth-Century Young Adult Writers*, edited by Laura Standley Berger. Detroit: St. James Press, 1994.

Daly, Jay. *Presenting S. E. Hinton.* Boston: Twayne, 1989.

Hinton, S. E., et al. "Readers Meet Author." *Top of the News* 25 (November, 1968): 27-39 and (January, 1969): 194-202.

Mills, Randall K. "The Novels of S. E. Hinton: Springboard to Personal Growth for Adolescents." *Adolescence* (Fall, 1987): 641.

Langston Hughes

Emanuel, James A. *Langston Hughes.* New York: Twayne, 1967.

Hughes, Langston. *The Big Sea: An Autobiography.* New York: Hill & Wang, 1963.

Meltzer, Milton. *Langston Hughes: A Biography.* New York: Thomas Y. Crowell, 1988.

Rampersad, Arnold. *The Life of Langston Hughes, 1902-1941: I, Too, Sing America.* Oxford, England: Oxford University Press, 1986.

_____. *The Life of Langston Hughes, 1941-1967: I Dream a World.* Oxford, England: Oxford University Press, 1988.

Mollie Hunter

Chaston, Joel D. "Mollie Hunter." In *British Children's Writers Since 1960*, edited by Caroline Hunt. Vol. 161 in *Dictionary of Literary Biography.* Detroit: Gale Research, 1996.

Hickman, Janet. "Profile: The Person Behind the Book—Mollie Hunter." *Language Arts* 56 (March, 1979): 302-306.

Hollindale, Peter. "World Enough and Time: The Work of Mollie Hunter." *Children's Literature in Education* 8, no. 3 (1977): 109-119.

Hunter, Mollie. *Talent Is Not Enough: Mollie Hunter on Writing for Children.* New York: Harper & Row, 1975.

Hadley Irwin

Haws, Rae, and Rosalind Enge. "When One Plus One Equals One: Hadley Irwin." *Children's Literature in Education* 18, no. 4 (Winter, 1987): 195-201.

Randall Jarrell

Flynn, Richard. "Happy Families Are All Invented: Randall Jarrell's Fiction for Children." *Children's Literature* 16 (1988): 109-125.

_____. *Randall Jarrell and the Lost World of Childhood*. Athens: University of Georgia Press, 1990.

Griswold, Jerome. *The Children's Books of Randall Jarrell*. Athens: University of Georgia Press, 1988.

Pritchard, William H. *Randall Jarrell: A Literary Life*. New York: Farrar, Strauss & Giroux, 1990.

Wright, Stuart. *Randall Jarrell: A Descriptive Biography, 1929-1983*. Charlottesville: University Press of Virginia, 1986.

M. E. Kerr

Kerr, M. E. "Her, Her, Her: An Interview with M. E. Kerr." Interview by Gray B. Allison. *Voice of Youth Advocate* 13, no. 6 (February, 1991): 337-342.

_____. *Me, Me, Me, Me, Me: Not a Novel*. New York: Harper & Row, 1983.

Kingsbury, Mary. "The Why of People: The Novels of M. E. Kerr." *Horn Book* (June, 1977): 288-295.

Nilsen, Alleen Pace. *Presenting M. E. Kerr*. Boston: Twayne, 1986.

Piehl, Kathy. "The Business of Religion in M. E. Kerr's Novels." *Voice of Youth Advocate* (February, 1986): 26-29.

Sweeney, Patricia Runk. "Self-Discovery and Rediscovery in the Novels of M. E. Kerr." *Lion and the Unicorn* (Fall, 1978): 37-42.

Rudyard Kipling

Blackburn, William. "Rudyard Kipling, 1865-1936." In *Writers for Children: Critical Studies of Major Authors Since the Seventeenth Century*. New York: Charles Scribner's Sons, 1988.

Bloom, Harold, ed. *Rudyard Kipling*. New York: Chelsea House, 1987.

Green, Roger Lancelyn. *Kipling and the Children*. London: Elek, 1965.

Haines, Helen E. "The Wisdom of Baloo: Kipling and Childhood." *Horn Book* 12 (May/June, 1936): 135-141.

Havholm, Peter. "Kipling and Fantasy." *Children's Literature* 4 (1975): 91-104.

Orel, Harold, ed. *Critical Essays on Rudyard Kipling*. Boston: Twayne, 1989.

Seymor-Smith, Martin. *Rudyard Kipling*. London: Macdonald Queen Anne, 1988.

E. L. Konigsburg

Hanks, Dorrel Thomas, Jr. *E. L. Konigsburg*. New York: Twayne, 1992.

Konigsburg, E. L. "The Double Image: Language as the Perimeter of Culture." *School Library Journal* 16 (February, 1970): 31-34.

_____. "Newbery Acceptance." *Horn Book* 44 (1968): 391-395.

Rees, David. "Your Arcane Novelist—E. L. Konigsburg: An English Viewpoint." *Horn Book* 54 (1978): 79-85.

Kathryn Lasky

Erol, Sibel. "*Beyond the Divide*: Lasky's Feminist Revision of the Westward Journey." *Children's Literature Association Quarterly* 17, no. 1 (Spring, 1992): 5-8.

Lasky, Kathryn. "Shuttling Through Realities: The Warp and the Weft of Fantasy and Nonfiction Writing." *The New Advocate* 6, no. 4 (Fall, 1993): 235-242.

Patricia Lauber

Lauber, Patricia. "What Makes an Appealing and Readable Science Book?" *Lion and the Unicorn* 6 (1982): 5-9.

_____. "A Writer's Responsibility: The World at Large, the Child Within." *Catholic Library World* 62, nos. 4-5 (January-April, 1991): 367-369.

Madeleine L'Engle

Hettinga, Donald R. *Presenting Madeleine L'Engle*. New York: Twayne, 1993.

L'Engle, Madeleine. "The Expanding Universe." *Horn Book* 39 (1963): 351-355.

Patterson, Nancy-Lou. "Angel and Psycho-pomp in Madeleine L'Engle's Wind Trilogy." *Children's Literature in Education* 14, no. 4 (Winter, 1983): 195-203.

Perry, Barbara. "Profile: Madeleine L'Engle, a Real Person." *Language Arts* 54 (October, 1977): 812-816.

Schmidt, Gary D. "See How They Grow: Character Development in Children's Series Books." *Children's Literature in Education* 18 (1987): 34-44.

Schneebaum, Katherine. "Finding a Happy Medium: The Design for Womanhood in *A Wrinkle in Time*." *Lion and the Unicorn* 14, no. 2 (December, 1990): 30-36.

Jack London

Lachtman, Howard. "Criticism of Jack London: A Selected Checklist." *Modern Fiction Studies* 22, no. 1 (1976): 107-125.

Lundquist, James. *Jack London: Adventures, Ideas, and Fiction*. New York: Frederick Ungar, 1987.

Owenby, Ray Wilson. *Jack London: Essays in Criticism*. Santa Barbara, Calif.: Peregrine Smith, 1978.

Sherman, Joan. *Jack London: A Reference Guide*. Boston: Twayne, 1977.

Tavernier-Courbin, Jacqueline, ed. *Critical Essays on Jack London*. Boston: Twayne, 1983.

Ward, Susan. "Jack London as a Children's Writer." *Children's Literature* 5 (1976): 92-103.

Lois Lowry

Chaston, Joel D. *Lois Lowry*. New York: Twayne, 1997.

Kimmel, Eric A. "Anastasia Agonistes: The Tragicomedy of Lois Lowry." *Horn Book* 63 (1987): 181-187.

Lowry, Lois. "Newbery Medal Acceptance." *Horn Book* 66 (1990): 412-421.

_____. "Newbery Medal Acceptance." *Horn Book* 70 (1994): 414-422.

_____. "*Number the Stars*: Lois Lowry's Journey to the Newbery Award." *Reading Teacher* 44, no. 2 (October, 1990): 98-101.

Zaidman, Laura. "Lois Lowry." In *American Writers for Children Since 1960: Fiction*, edited by Glenn E. Estes. Vol. 52 in *Dictionary of Literary Biography*. Detroit: Gale Research, 1986.

David Macaulay

Ammon, Richard. "Profile: David Macaulay." *Language Arts* 59 (April, 1982): 374-378.

Chaston, Joel D. "David Macaulay." In *Twentieth-Century Children's Writers*, edited by Laura Standley Berger. 4th ed. Detroit: St. James Press, 1995.

Hoare, Geoffrey. "The Work of David Macaulay." *Children's Literature in Education* 8, no. 1 (Spring, 1977): 12-20.

Macaulay, David. "Caldecott Medal Acceptance." *Horn Book* 67, no. 4 (July/August, 1991): 410-421.

Stott, Jon C. "Architectural Structures and Social Values in the Non-fiction of David Macaulay." *Children's Literature Association Quarterly* 8, no. 1 (Spring, 1983): 15-17.

Robin McKinley

Altmann, Anna E. "Welding Brass Tits on the Armor: An Examination of the Quest Metaphor in Robin McKinley's *The Hero and the Crown*." *Children's Literature in Education* 23, no. 3 (September, 1992): 143-156.

McKinley, Robin. "Newbery Medal Acceptance." *Horn Book* 61, no. 4 (1985): 395-405.

Meek, Margaret. "Happily Ever After." *The Times Literary Supplement* (November 25, 1983): 1212.

Woolsey, Daniel P. "The Realm of Fairy Story: J. R. R. Tolkien and Robin McKinley's *Beauty*." *Children's Literature in Education* (June, 1991): 129-134.

Patricia MacLachlan

MacLachlan, Patricia, and Charlotte Zolotow. "Dialogue Between Charlotte Zolotow and Patricia MacLachlan." *Horn Book* 65 (November/December, 1989): 736-745.

Trites, Roberta Seelinger. "Claiming the Treasures: Patricia MacLachlan's Organic Postmodernism." *Children's Literature Association Quarterly* 18, no. 1 (Spring, 1993): 23-28.

_____. "Is Flying Extraordinary: Patricia MacLachlan's Use of Aporia." *Children's Literature* 23 (1995): 202-220.

Margaret Mahy

Berkin, Adam. "'I Woke Myself': *The Changeover* as a Modern Adaptation of 'Sleeping Beauty.'" *Children's Literature in Education* 21, no. 4 (December, 1990): 245-251.

Grose, Elliot. "Fairy Tale and Myth in Mahy's *The Changeover* and *The Tricksters*." *Children's Literature Association Quarterly* 16, no. 1 (Spring, 1991): 6-11.

Lawrence-Pietroni, Anna. "*The Tricksters*, *The Changeover*, and the Fluidity of Adolescent Literature." *Children's Literature Association Quarterly* 21, no. 1 (Spring, 1996): 34-39.

Mackey, Margaret. "Many Spaces: Some Limitations of Single Readings." *Children's Literature in Education* 24, no. 3 (September, 1993): 147-163.

Mahy, Margaret. "Joining the Network." *Signal* 54 (1987): 151-160.

Raburn, Josephine. "*The Changeover*: A Fantasy of Opposites." *Children's Literature in Education* 23, no. 1 (March, 1992): 27-38.

Harry Mazer

Reed, Arthea J. S. *Presenting Harry Mazer*. New York: Twayne, 1996.

Norma Fox Mazer

Holtze, Sally Holmes. *Presenting Norma Fox Mazer*. Boston: Twayne, 1987.

Mazer, Norma Fox. "Young Adult Literature: An Inner View." *Voice of Youth Advocate* 21, no. 3 (1989): 147-148.

Milton Meltzer

Meltzer, Milton. Interview by Geraldine DeLuca and Roni Natov. *Lion and the Unicorn* 4, no. 1 (Summer, 1980): 95-107.

_____. *Nonfiction for the Classroom: Milton Meltzer on Writing, History, and Social Responsibility*. New York: Teachers College Press, 1994.

_____. *Starting from Home: A Writer's Beginnings*. New York: Puffin, 1991.

_____. "Who's Neutral?" *Children's Literature in Education* 14 (1974): 24-36.

Weedmon, Judith. "A Step Aside from Self: The Work of Milton Meltzer." *Children's Literature Association Quarterly* 10, no. 1 (Spring, 1985): 41-42.

Eve Merriam

Cox, Susan Taylor. "A Word or Two with Eve Merriam: Talking About Poetry." *The New Advocate* 2, no. 3 (Summer, 1989): 139-149.

Sloan, Glenna. "Profile: Eve Merriam." *Language Arts* 58 (November/December, 1981): 957-964.

Walter Dean Myers

Myers, Walter Dean. "Let Us Celebrate the Children." *Horn Book* 66 (January/February, 1990): 46-47.

Phyllis Reynolds Naylor

Naylor, Phyllis Reynolds. "Becoming a Writer." *Five Owls* (November/December, 1989): 17-22.

_____. Interview by Joyce L. Grahame. *Journal of Youth Services* 6, no. 4 (Summer, 1993): 392-398.

_____. "Newbery Acceptance Speech." *Horn Book* 68, no. 4 (July/August, 1992): 404-411.

_____. "The Writing of *Shiloh*." *The Reading Teacher* 46, no. 1 (September, 1992): 10-12.

E. Nesbit

Bland, Edith Nesbit. *Long Ago When I Was Very Young*. London: Whitling & Wheaton, 1966.

Briggs, Julia. *A Woman of Passion: The Life of E. Nesbit, 1858-1924*. London: Hutchinson University Library, 1987.

Knoepflmacher, U. C. "Of Babylands and Babylons: E. Nesbit and the Reclamation of the Fairy Tale." *Tulsa Studies in Women's Literature* 6, no. 2 (Fall, 1987): 299-325.

Moss, Anita. "E. Nesbit's Romantic Child in Modern Dress." In *Romanticism and Children's Literature in Nineteenth-Century England*, edited by James Holt McGavran, Jr. Athens: University of Georgia Press, 1991.

Streatfield, Noel. *Magic and the Magician: E. Nesbit and Her Children's Books*. London: Ernest Benn, 1958.

Mary Norton

Davenport, Julia. "The Narrative Framework of *The Borrowers*: Mary Norton and Emily Brontë." *Children's Literature in Education* 14, no. 2 (Summer, 1983): 75-79.

Kuznets, Lois. "Mary Norton's *The Borrowers*: Diaspora in Miniature." In *Touchstones: Reflections on the Best in Children's Literature*, edited by Perry Nodelman. Vol. 1. West Lafayette, Ind.: Children's Literature Association, 1985.

Pace, Patty. "The Body-in-Writing: Miniatures in Mary Norton's *Borrowers*." *Text and Performance Quarterly* 11, no. 4 (October, 1991): 279-290.

Rees, David. "Freedom and Imprisonment: The Novels of Mary Norton." *School Library Journal* 36, no. 3 (1988): 83-86.

Stott, Jon C. *Mary Norton*. New York: Twayne, 1994.

Thomas, Margaret. "The Danger of the Difficult Daughter: A Feminist Reading of Mary Norton's *Borrowers*." *Children's Literature in Education* 23, no. 1 (March, 1992): 39-48.

Scott O'Dell

Johnson, Walter H. "A Stepping Stone to Melville." *English Journal* 73 (April, 1984): 69-70.

Maher, Susan Naramore. "Encountering Others: The Meeting of Cultures in Scott O'Dell's *Island of the Blue Dolphins* and *Sing Down the Moon*." *Children's Literature in Education* 23, no. 4 (December, 1992): 215-227.

Nodelman, Perry. "A Second Look: *Sing Down the Moon*." *Horn Book* 60 (February, 1984): 94-98.

O'Dell, Scott. "Acceptance Speech: Hans Christian Andersen Award." *Horn Book* 48 (October, 1972): 441-443.

_____. "Newbery Award Acceptance." *Horn Book* 37 (August, 1961): 311-316.

Stott, Jon C. "Narrative Technique and Meaning in *Island of the Blue Dolphins*." *Elementary English* 52 (April, 1975): 442-446.

Katherine Paterson

Chaston, Joel D. "Flute Solos and Songs That Make You Shatter: Simple Melodies in *Jacob Have I Loved* and *Come Sing, Jimmy Jo*." *Lion and the Unicorn* 16 (1992): 215-222.

_____. "The Other Deaths in *Bridge to Terabithia*." *Children's Literature Association Quarterly* 16 (1992): 238-241.

Huse, Nancy. "Katherine Paterson's Ultimate Realism." *Children's Literature Association Quarterly* 9 (Fall, 1984): 99-101.

Paterson, Katherine. *Gates of Excellence: On Reading and Writing Books for Children*. New York: Elsevier/Nelson, 1981.

_____. *The Spying Heart: More Thoughts on Reading and Writing Books for Children.* New York: E. P. Dutton, 1989.

Schmidt, Gary D. *Katherine Paterson.* New York: Twayne, 1994.

Smedman, M. Sarah. "Out of the Depths to Joy: Spirit/Soul in Juvenile Novels." In *Triumphs of the Spirit in Children's Literature,* edited by Francelia Butler and Richard Rotert. Hamden, Conn.: Shoe String, 1986.

Gary Paulsen

Barron, Ronald. "Gary Paulsen: I Write Because It's All I Can Do." *ALAN Review* 1, no. 2 (Winter, 1993): 5-7.

Salvner, Gary M. *Presenting Gary Paulsen.* New York: Twayne, 1996.

Richard Peck

Gallo, Donald. *Presenting Richard Peck.* Boston: Twayne, 1989.

Hartvigsen, M. Kip, and Christen Brog Hartvigsen. "The Divine Miss Blossom Culp." *ALAN Review* 16, no. 2 (Winter, 1989): 33-35.

Peck, Richard. *Love and Death at the Mall: Teaching and Writing for the Literature Young.* New York: Delacorte Press, 1994.

_____. "Rape and the Teenage Victim." *Top of the News* 34 (Winter, 1978): 173-177.

Sutton, Roger. "A Conversation with Richard Peck." *School Library Journal* 36.6 (1990): 36-40.

Cynthia Rylant

Rylant, Cynthia. "The *Booklist* Interview: Cynthia Rylant." Interview by Ilene Cooper. *Booklist* 89, nos. 19-20 (June, 1993): 1840-1841.

_____. "*Missing May.*" *Horn Book* 69, no. 1 (January/February, 1993): 52-53.

_____. "Newbery Medal Acceptance." *Horn Book* 69, no. 4 (July/August, 1993): 416-419.

Ward, Diane. "Cynthia Rylant." *Horn Book* 69, no. 4 (July/ August, 1993): 420-423.

Carl Sandburg

Callahan, North. *Carl Sandburg: His Life and Works.* University Park: Pennsylvania State University Press, 1987.

Lynn, Joanne L. "Hyacinths and Biscuits in the Village of Liver and Onions: Sandburg's *Rootabaga Stories.*" *Children's Literature* 8 (1980): 118-132.

Niven, Penelope. *Carl Sandburg: A Biography.* New York: Charles Scribner's Sons, 1991.

Perkins, Agnes Regan. "Carl Sandburg, 1878-1967." In *Writers for Children: Critical Studies of Major Authors Since the Seventeenth Century.* New York: Charles Scribner's Sons, 1988.

Kate Seredy

Higgins, James E. "Kate Seredy: Storyteller." *Horn Book* 44 (April, 1968): 162-168.

Kassen, Aileen M. "Kate Seredy: A Person Worth Knowing." *Elementary English* 45 (March, 1968): 303-315.

Markey, Lois R. "Kate Seredy's World." *Elementary English* 29 (December, 1952): 451-457.

Shel Silverstein

Hemphill, James. "Sharing Poetry with Children: Stevenson to Silverstein." *Advocate* 4 (Fall, 1984): 38-45.

Kennedy, X. J. "Rhyme Is a Chime." *The New York Times Book Review* (November 15, 1981): 51, 60.

MacDonald, Ruth K. "The Weirdness of Shel Silverstein." *Studies in American Humor* 5, no. 4 (Winter, 1986/1987): 267-279.

Strandburg, Walter L., and Norma J. Livo. "*The Giving Tree*: Or, There Is a Sucker Born Every Minute." *Children's Literature in Education* 17, no. 1 (Spring, 1986): 17-24.

Isaac Bashevis Singer
Allison, Alida. *Isaac Bashevis Singer: Children's Stories and Memoirs*. New York: Twayne, 1996.
Berkeley, Miriam. "Isaac Bashevis Singer." *Publishers Weekly* 223 (February 18, 1983): 65-66.
Bernheim, Mark A. "The Five Hundred Reasons of Isaac Singer." *Bookbird* 1-2 (1982): 31-36.
Kimmel, Eric. "I. B. Singer's *Alone in the Wild Forest*: A Kabbalistic Parable." *Children's Literature in Education* 18 (Fall, 1975): 147-158.
Singer, Isaac Bashevis. "I See the Child as a Last Refuge." In *Signposts to Criticism of Children's Literature*, edited by Robert Bator. Chicago: American Library Association, 1983.
_____. "The Stories Behind the Stories: An Interview with Isaac Bashevis Singer." Interview by Diane Wolkstein. *Children's Literature in Education* 18 (Fall, 1975): 136-145.

Zilpha Keatley Snyder
Karl, Jean. "Zilpha Keatley Snyder." *Elementary English* 51 (September, 1974): 785-789.
Snyder, Zilpha Keatley. "Alternate Worlds." In *Innocence and Experience: Essays and Conversations on Children's Literature*, edited by Barbara Harrison and Gregory Maguire. New York: Lothrop, Lee & Shepard, 1987.

Ivan Southall
Bayfield, Juliana. "From *Simon Black* to *Ash Road* and Beyond." *Bookbird* 6, no. 4 (1968): 33-35.
Fox, Geoffrey. "Growth and Masquerade: A Theme in the Novels of Ivan Southall." *Children's Literature in Education* 6 (1971): 49-64.
Pausacker, Jenny. "Not Under Glass: The Novels of Ivan Southall." *Meanjin* 51, no. 3 (Spring, 1992): 660-669.
Pirani, Alex. "Writers for Children." *Use of English* 22 (Spring, 1971): 233-237.
Southall, Ivan. "Depth and Direction." *Horn Book* 44 (June, 1968): 343-346.
_____. *A Journey of Discovery: On Writing for Children*. London: Kestrel, 1975.

Elizabeth George Speare
Apseloff, Marilyn Fain. *Elizabeth George Speare*. New York: Twayne, 1992.
Cohen, Phyllis. "A New Look at Old Books: *The Bronze Bow*." *Young Readers' Review* 3 (October, 1966): 12.
Hutton, Muriel. "Writers for Children: Elizabeth George Speare." *School Librarian* 18 (September, 1970): 275-279.
Speare, Elizabeth George. "Newbery Award Acceptance." *Horn Book* 35 (August, 1959): 265-270.
_____. "Report of a Journey: Newbery Award Acceptance." *Horn Book* 38 (August, 1962): 337-341.

William Steig
Bottner, Barbara. "William Steig: The Two Legacies." *Lion and the Unicorn* 2, no. 1 (Spring, 1978): 4-16.
Hearn, Michael Patrick. "Drawing Out William Steig." *Bookbird* 3-4 (1982): 61-65.
Higgins, James. "William Steig: Champion for Romance." *Children's Literature in Education* 9, no. 1 (Spring, 1978): 3-16.
Moss, Anita. "The Spear and the Piccolo: Heroic and Pastoral Dimensions of William Steig's *Dominic* and *Abel's Island*." *Children's Literature* 10 (1982): 124-140.
Steig, William. "The Artist at Work." *Horn Book* 69, no. 2 (March/April, 1993): 170-174.
Wilner, Anne. "'Unlocked by Love': William Steig's Tales of Transformation and Magic." *Children's Literature* 18 (1990): 31-41.

Robert Louis Stevenson
Blake, Kathleen. "The Sea Dreams: *Peter Pan* and *Treasure Island*." *Children's Literature* 6 (1977): 165-181.

Butts, Dennis. *R. L. Stevenson*. New York: Walck, 1966.

Daiches, David. *Robert Louis Stevenson and His World*. London: Thames & Hudson, 1973.

Furnas, Joseph C. *Voyage to Windward: The Life of Robert Louis Stevenson*. New York: Sloane, 1951.

Heins, Paul. "A Centenary Look: *Treasure Island*." *Horn Book* 59 (April, 1983): 197-200.

Stern, Gladys Bronwyn. *Robert Louis Stevenson: The Man Who Wrote "Treasure Island": A Biography*. New York: Macmillan, 1954.

Mark Twain

Cadwell, Guy. *The Man Who Was Mark Twain*. New Haven, Conn.: Yale University Press, 1991.

Fishkin, Shelley Fisher. *Was Huck Finn Black?: Mark Twain and African-American Voices*. New York: Oxford University Press, 1993.

Gerber, John C. *Mark Twain*. Boston: Twayne, 1988.

Hearn, Michael Patrick, ed. *The Annotated Huckleberry Finn*. New York: Clarkson N. Potter, 1981.

Peck, Richard. "A Second Look: 'The Prince and the Pauper.'" *Horn Book* 61, no. 5 (September, 1985): 541-543.

Sloane, David E. *Adventures of Huckleberry Finn: America's Comic Vision*. Boston: Twayne, 1988.

Yoshiko Uchida

Chang, Catherine E. Studier. "Profile: Yoshiko Uchida." *Language Arts* 61 (February, 1984): 189-193.

Jules Verne

Evans, Arthur B. *Jules Verne Rediscovered: Didacticism and the Scientific Novel*. New York: Greenwood Press, 1988.

Gallagher, Edward J. *Jules Verne: A Primary and Secondary Bibliography*. Boston: Twayne, 1980.

Lowndes, Marie Belloc. "Signal Reprints: Jules Verne at Home." *Signal* 10 (January, 1973): 3-13.

Martin, Andrew. *The Mask of the Prophet: The Extraordinary Fictions of Jules Verne*. Oxford, England: Clarendon Press, 1990.

Cynthia Voigt

Dresang, Eliza T. "A Newbery Song for Gifted Readers." *School Library Journal* 30 (November, 1983): 33-37.

Greenway, Betty. "'Every Mother's Dream': Cynthia Voigt's Orphans." *ALAN Review*, 19, no. 1 (Fall, 1991): 15-17.

Henke, James T. "Dicey, Odysseus, and Hansel and Gretel: The Lost Children in Voigt's *Homecoming*." *Children's Literature in Education* 16, no. 1 (Spring, 1985): 45-52.

Jameson, Gloria. "The Triumph of the Spirit in Cynthia Voigt's *Homecoming, Dicey's Song*, and *A Solitary Blue*." In *Triumphs of the Spirit in Children's Literature*, edited by Francelia Butler and Richard Rotert. Hamden, Conn.: Shoe String, 1986.

Reid, Suzanne. *Presenting Cynthia Voigt*. New York: Twayne, 1995.

E. B. White

Agosta, Lucien L. *E. B. White: The Children's Books*. New York: Twayne, 1995.

Elledge, Scott. *E. B. White: A Biography*. New York: W. W. Norton, 1984.

Griffith, John. "*Charlotte's Web*: A Lonely Fantasy of Love." *Children's Literature* 8 (1980): 111-117.

Mason, Bobbie Ann. "Profile: The Elements of E. B. White's Style." *Language Arts* 56 (September, 1979): 692-696.

Neumeyer, Peter F. Introduction and Notes to *The Annotated Charlotte's Web*, by E. B. White. New York: HarperCollins, 1994.

Nodelman, Perry. "Text as Teacher: The Beginning of *Charlotte's Web.*" *Children's Literature* 13 (1985): 109-127.

Rollin, Lucy. "The Reproduction of Mothering in *Charlotte's Web.*" *Children's Literature* 18 (1990): 42-52.

Laurence Yep

Cai, Minshui. "A Balanced View of Acculturation: Comments on Laurence Yep's Three Novels." *Children's Literature in Education* 23, no. 2 (June 1, 1992): 107-118.

Johnson-Feelings, Dianne. *Presenting Laurence.* New York: Twayne, 1995.

Yep, Laurence. "The Green Cord." *Horn Book* 65 (May/June, 1989): 318-322.

_____. "World Building." In *Innocence and Experience: Essays and Conversations on Children's Literature*, edited by Barbara Harrison and Gregory Maguire. New York: Lothrop, Lee & Shepard, 1987.

_____. "Writing *Dragonwings.*" *Reading Teacher* 30 (January, 1977): 359-363.

Jane Yolen

White, David E. "Profile: Jane Yolen." *Language Arts* 60 (May, 1983): 652-660.

Yolen, Jane. "The Route to Story." *New Advocate* 4, no. 3 (Summer, 1991): 143-149.

_____. *Touch Magic: Fantasy, Faerie, and Folklore in the Literature of Childhood.* New York: Philomel, 1981.

_____. "Traveling the Road to Ithaca." In *Innocence and Experience: Essays and Conversations on Children's Literature*, edited by Barbara Harrison and Gregory Maguire. New York: Lothrop, Lee & Shepard, 1987.

Paul Zindel

Clarke, Loretta. "*The Pigman*: A Novel of Adolescence." *English Journal* 61 (November, 1972): 1163-1169, 1175.

Froman, Jack. "Fathers and Mothers, Boys and Girls: Gender Treatment in Paul Zindel's Young Adult Novels." *Journal of Youth Services in Libraries* 2, no. 1 (1988): 71-75.

_____. *Presenting Paul Zindel.* Boston: Twayne, 1988.

Hansen, Kim. "Something Wonderful, Something Beautiful: Adolescent Relationships Through the Eyes of Paul Zindel." *ALAN Review* 18, no. 2 (Winter, 1991): 41-43.

Henke, James T. "Six Characters in Search of the Family: The Novels of Paul Zindel." *Children's Literature* 5 (1976): 130-140.

Hoffman, Stanley. "Winning, Losing, but Above All Taking Risks: A Look at the Novels of Paul Zindel." *Lion and the Unicorn* 2, no. 2 (Fall, 1978): 78-88.

Zindel, Paul. *The Pigman and Me.* New York: HarperCollins, 1991.

Joel D. Chaston

TITLE INDEX

This title index lists articles by set name, volume, and page number using the following codes: Lit = Masterplots II: Juvenile and Young Adult Literature, Supplement; Fic = Masterplots II: Juvenile and Young Adult Fiction; Bio = Masterplots II: Juvenile and Young Adult Biography.

I

AUTHOR INDEX

This author index lists articles by set name, volume, and page number using the following codes: Lit = Masterplots II: Juvenile and Young Adult Literature, Supplement; Fic = Masterplots II: Juvenile and Young Adult Fiction; Bio = Masterplots II: Juvenile and Young Adult Biography.

AUTHOR INDEX

AUTHOR INDEX

AUTHOR INDEX

SILVERSTEIN, SHEL
Light in the Attic, A, *Lit* II-762
Where the Sidewalk Ends, *Lit* III-1320

SIMAK, CLIFFORD D.
City, *Fic* I-248

SIMON, NEIL
Brighton Beach Memoirs, *Lit* I-162

SINGER, ISAAC BASHEVIS
Day of Pleasure, A, *Bio* I-451
Golem, The, *Lit* II-527
When Shlemiel Went to Warsaw and Other
Stories, *Lit* III-1316
Zlateh the Goat and Other Stories,
Lit III-1373

SKINNER, CORNELIA OTIS
Madame Sarah, *Bio* III-1139

SLEATOR, WILLIAM
House of Stairs, *Fic* II-665
Interstellar Pig, *Fic* II-712

SMITH, BETTY
Tree Grows in Brooklyn, A, *Fic* IV-1504

SMITH, HOWARD E.
Daring the Unknown, *Lit* I-289

SMITH, LULA CARSON. *See* McCULLERS,
CARSON

SMITH, URSULA, *and* LINDA PEAVY
Dreams into Deeds, *Bio* II-517

SNEVE, VIRGINIA DRIVING HAWK
When Thunders Spoke, *Fic* IV-1609

SNYDER, ZILPHA KEATLEY
Egypt Game, The, *Lit* I-376
Witches of Worm, The, *Fic* IV-1643

SOBOL, DONALD J.
Encyclopedia Brown series, The, *Lit* I-404

SOLZHENITSYN, ALEKSANDR
One Day in the Life of Ivan Denisovich,
Lit II-935

SOMMERFELT, AIMÉE
Road to Agra, The, *Fic* III-1231

SONE, MONICA
Nisei Daughter, *Bio* III-1320

SORENSEN, VIRGINIA
Miracles on Maple Hill, *Fic* III-962

SOTO, GARY
Baseball in April and Other Stories,
Lit I-96
Fire in My Hands, A, *Lit* I-429
Living up the Street, *Bio* III-1109

SOUTHALL, IVAN
Ash Road, *Lit* I-79
Walk a Mile and Get Nowhere, *Fic* IV-1564

SOUTHWORTH, JOHN VAN DUYN
Monarch and Conspirators, *Bio* III-1237

SOYINKA, WOLE
Aké, *Bio* I-24

SPARK, MURIEL
Prime of Miss Jean Brodie, The,
Fic III-1170

SPEARE, ELIZABETH GEORGE
Bronze Bow, The, *Fic* I-158
Sign of the Beaver, The, *Lit* III-1133
Witch of Blackbird Pond, The, *Fic* IV-1640

SPECHT, ROBERT
Tisha, *Bio* IV-1729

SPENCER, CORNELIA
Sun Yat-sen, *Bio* IV-1641

SPERRY, ARMSTRONG
Call It Courage, *Fic* I-170
John Paul Jones, Fighting Sailor, *Bio* II-973
Voyages of Christopher Columbus, The,
Bio IV-1818

SPINELLI, JERRY
Maniac Magee, *Lit* II-799

SPYRI, JOHANNA
Heidi, *Fic* II-616

STAPLES, SUZANNE FISHER
Shabanu, *Lit* III-1117

STEELE, WILLIAM O.
Wayah of the Real People, *Fic* IV-1585

STEFFENS, LINCOLN
Autobiography of Lincoln Steffens, The,
Bio I-152

STEIG, WILLIAM
Abel's Island, *Lit* I-5
Doctor De Soto, *Lit* I-328

STEIN, GERTRUDE
Autobiography of Alice B. Toklas, The,
Bio I-141

STEINBECK, JOHN
Of Mice and Men, *Lit* II-917
Red Pony, The, *Fic* III-1217

STEPTOE, JOHN
Train Ride, *Fic* IV-1497

STERLING, PHILIP
Sea and Earth, *Bio* IV-1537

STEVENSON, ROBERT LOUIS
Black Arrow, The, *Lit* I-132
Kidnapped, *Fic* II-771
Strange Case of Dr. Jekyll and Mr. Hyde,
The, *Lit* III-1177
Treasure Island, *Fic* IV-1500

STEWART, MARY LOUISA. *See*
MOLESWORTH, MARY LOUISA

STILLMAN, MYRA, *and* BEULAH
TANNENBAUM
Isaac Newton, *Bio* II-923

STODDARD, HOPE
Famous American Women, *Bio* II-591

STOKER, BRAM
Dracula, *Lit* I-355

YEAGER, CHUCK, *and* LEO JANOS
Yeager, *Lit* III-1353
YEP, LAURENCE
Child of the Owl, *Fic* I-227
Dragonwings, *Fic* I-350
Lost Garden, The, *Lit* II-777
Tongues of Jade, *Lit* III-1250
YEVTUSHENKO, YEVGENY
Precocious Autobiography, A, *Bio* III-1436
YOLEN, JANE
Children of the Wolf, *Lit* I-212
Friend, *Bio* II-682
Girl Who Cried Flowers and Other Tales, The,
Lit II-500
YONGE, CHARLOTTE M.
Little Duke, The, *Fic* II-845
YOSHIKAWA, EIJI
Musashi, *Bio* III-1260

YOUD, C. S. *See* CHRISTOPHER, JOHN
YOUNG, BOB, *and* JAN YOUNG
Liberators of Latin America, *Bio* III-1070
YOUNG, MARGARET B.
Black American Leaders, *Bio* I-226

ZINDEL, PAUL
Effect of Gamma Rays on Man-in-the-Moon
Marigolds, The, *Lit* I-369
Pigman, The, *Fic* III-1137
ZINDEL, PAUL, *and* CRESCENT
DRAGONWAGON
To Take a Dare, *Lit* III-1246
ZINSSER, HANS
Rats, Lice, and History, *Lit* III-1049
ZOLOTOW, CHARLOTTE
Early Sorrow, *Lit* I-359

BIOGRAPHICAL INDEX

This biographical index lists articles by set name, volume, and page number using the following codes: Lit = Masterplots II: Juvenile and Young Adult Literature, Supplement; Bio = Masterplots II: Juvenile and Young Adult Biography.

BIOGRAPHICAL INDEX

BIOGRAPHICAL INDEX

BIOGRAPHICAL INDEX

BIOGRAPHICAL INDEX

BIOGRAPHICAL INDEX

BIOGRAPHICAL INDEX

BIOGRAPHICAL INDEX

SUBJECT INDEX

This subject index lists articles by set name, volume, and page number using the following codes: Lit = Masterplots II: Juvenile and Young Adult Literature, Supplement; Fic = Masterplots II: Juvenile and Young Adult Fiction; Bio = Masterplots II: Juvenile and Young Adult Biography.

SUBJECT INDEX

MASTERPLOTS II

SUBJECT INDEX

SUBJECT INDEX

SUBJECT INDEX

GENDER ROLES

SUBJECT INDEX

LXXXIX

SUBJECT INDEX

SUBJECT INDEX

Andrew Jackson (Coit) *Bio* I-102
Anthony Burns (Hamilton) *Bio* I-121
Autobiography of Lincoln Steffens, The
  (Steffens) *Bio* I-152
Barbara Jordan (Jordan *and* Hearon) *Bio* I-172
Ben-Gurion (St. John) *Bio* I-191
Benito Juárez (Wepman) *Bio* I-195
Benjamin Franklin (Meltzer) *Bio* I-207
Bismarck (Taylor) *Bio* I-222
Black American Leaders (Young) *Bio* I-226
Caesars, The (Massie) *Bio* I-281
Chanticleer of Wilderness Road (Le Sueur)
  Bio I-315
Cherokee Chief (Clark) *Bio* I-352
Chou En-Lai (Archer) *Lit* I-226
Citizen of New Salem (Horgan) *Bio* I-369
Cleopatra (Leighton) *Bio* I-385
Cleopatra's Children (Desmond) *Bio* I-389
Commodore Perry in the Land of the Shogun
  (Blumberg) *Lit* I-251
Conqueror and Hero (Krensky) *Bio* I-409
Day Lincoln Was Shot, The (Bishop) *Bio* I-447
Duce, Il (Lyttle) *Bio* II-521
Education of Henry Adams, The (Adams)
  Bio II-533
Eleanor and Franklin (Lash) *Bio* II-545
Elizabeth and Essex (Strachey) *Bio* II-549
Elizabeth the Great (Jenkins) *Bio* II-553
Empress of All Russia (Noble) *Bio* II-564
Eva Perón (Fraser *and* Navarro) *Bio* II-576
Falcon and the Dove, The (Duggan) *Bio* II-583
Famous Mexican Americans (Morey *and* Dunn)
  Bio II-595
Famous Puerto Ricans (Newlon) *Bio* II-599
FDR Story, The (Peare) *Bio* II-619
Felisa Rincón de Gautier (Gruber) *Bio* II-623
First in Their Hearts (Fleming) *Bio* II-635
Franklin Delano Roosevelt (Johnson) *Bio* II-670
George Washington (Cunliffe) *Bio* II-717
George Washington, Leader of the People
  (Judson) *Bio* II-713
Herbert Hoover Story, The (Peare) *Bio* II-830
Heroes and History (Sutcliff) *Bio* II-834
I Mary (Randall) *Bio* II-889
James Edward Oglethorpe (Blackburn)
  Bio II-933
Jawaharlal Nehru (Lengyel) *Bio* II-948
Jennie (Martin) *Bio* II-952
Lady Queen Anne (Hodges) *Bio* III-1013
Leader by Destiny (Eaton) *Bio* III-1044
Life for Israel, A (Dobrin) *Lit* II-755
Life of Winston Churchill, The (Wibberley)
  Bio III-1078
Life Sketches (Hersey) *Bio* III-1081
Lincoln (Freedman) *Bio* III-1089
Madmen of History (Hook) *Bio* III-1143
Make Way for Sam Houston (Fritz) *Bio* III-1153

Mischling, Second Degree (Koehn) *Bio* III-1222
Monarch and Conspirators (Southworth)
  Bio III-1237
Mother Jones (Atkinson) *Bio* III-1241
Naked to Mine Enemies (Ferguson) *Bio* III-1284
Napoleon (Chandler) *Bio* III-1292
Napoleon (Komroff) *Bio* III-1296
Nicholas and Alexandra (Massie) *Bio* III-1316
Odd Destiny (Lomask) *Bio* III-1333
Our Golda (Adler) *Lit* II-947
Penn (Vining) *Bio* III-1407
Peter, the Revolutionary Tsar (Putnam)
  Bio III-1410
Profiles in Courage (Kennedy) *Bio* III-1439
Queen Eleanor, Independent Spirit of the
  Medieval World (Brooks) *Bio* III-1451
Queen Victoria (Strachey) *Bio* III-1455
Ralph Bunche (Haskins) *Bio* III-1467
Ralph J. Bunche (Kugelmass) *Bio* III-1471
Rise and Fall of Adolf Hitler, The (Shirer)
  Bio IV-1497
Roosevelt Family of Sagamore Hill, The
  (Hagedorn) *Bio* IV-1509
Seven Kings of England (Trease) *Bio* IV-1553
Seven Queens of England, The (Trease)
  Bio IV-1557
Some Dissenting Voices (Weinberg *and*
  Weinberg) *Bio* IV-1585
Sun Yat-sen (Spencer) *Bio* IV-1641
Ten Brave Men (Daugherty) *Bio* IV-1664
Ten Famous Lives (Plutarch) *Bio* IV-1668
Ten Tall Texans (Kubiak) *Bio* IV-1672
Thomas Jefferson, Champion of the People
  (Judson) *Bio* IV-1698
Twelve Citizens of the World (Kenworthy)
  Bio IV-1781
Winston Churchill and the Story of Two World
  Wars (Coolidge) *Bio* IV-1911
Woodrow Wilson Story, The (Peare) *Bio* IV-1941
World of Samuel Adams, The (Chidsey)
  Bio IV-1949
Young Man from the Piedmont (Wibberley)
  Bio IV-1967

POLITICS AND LAW
After the First Death (Cormier) *Fic* I-22
Alice's Adventures in Wonderland (Carroll)
  Fic I-28
Animal Farm (Orwell) *Fic* I-41
Bell for Adano, A (Hersey) *Fic* I-106
Beloved (Morrison) *Fic* I-109
Ben and Me (Lawson) *Lit* I-117
Bury My Heart at Wounded Knee (Brown)
  Lit I-177
Campion Towers (Beatty *and* Beatty) *Fic* I-182
Candide (Voltaire) *Fic* I-185
Childhood's End (Clarke) *Fic* I-230
Clockwork Orange, A (Burgess) *Fic* I-251

XCIII

SUBJECT INDEX

SUBJECT INDEX

REVOLUTIONARY LEADERS. *See* MILITARY
AND REVOLUTIONARY LEADERS

RULERS. *See* POLITICIANS AND RULERS

SCIENCE

SCIENCE FICTION

C

SUBJECT INDEX

SUBJECT INDEX

MASTERPLOTS II

SUBJECT INDEX

CIX

MASTERPLOTS II